FRANCE BETWEEN THE WARS

France between the wars is often seen as a time of great political instability: governments changed frequently, supporters of the right and the left clashed bitterly and there was the fear of another world war. This book argues that the period saw another kind of instability, for these were years when the all-male monopoly over political life in the French Republic was being undermined and challenged.

Siân Reynolds looks at political life in inter-war France from the perspective of gender relations. From the implications of new technologies, like aviation or the factory assembly-line, to the politics of social work at the dawn of the welfare state, *France Between the Wars* reveals the significant political roles taken by women. This is important not only for our understanding of France in the period, but also for demonstrating how a history focused on gender can contribute to new kinds of historical analysis.

FRANCE BETWEEN THE WARS

Gender and politics

Siân Reynolds

London and New York

First published 1996
by Routledge
11 New Fetter Lane, London EC4P 4EE

Simultaneously published in the USA and Canada
by Routledge
29 West 35th Street, New York, NY 10001

Routledge is an International Thomson Publishing company

Typeset in Baskerville by Routledge
Printed and bound in Great Britain by
TJ Press (Padstow) Ltd, Padstow, Cornwall

British Library Cataloguing in Publication Data
A catalogue record for this book is available from the British Library

Library of Congress Cataloguing in Publication Data
Reynolds, Siân.
France between the wars: gender and politics/Siân Reynolds.
Includes bibliographical references and index.
1. Women in politics – France.
2. France – Politics and government – 1914–1940.
HQ1236.5.F8R49 1996
320'. 082–dc20   95–52016 CIP

ISBN 0–415–12736–X (hbk)
ISBN 0–415–12737–8 (pbk)

For Mair Williams and Ben Reynolds
who were married on 28 October 1939

CONTENTS

CONCLUSION 222

ACKNOWLEDGEMENTS

In writing this book I have built up many debts over the years. For permission to reproduce in modified form material which appeared first elsewhere, thanks to the Cambridge University Press (in Chapter 5, for material published in M. Alexander and H. Graham (eds), *The French and Spanish Popular Fronts, comparative perspectives*, 1989), the *Journal of the Institute of Romance Studies*, and *French History*. For financial help towards research visits to France, I am very grateful to the British Academy and the Carnegie Trust for the Universities of Scotland, as well as to the Universities of Sussex, Edinburgh and Stirling. Like many historians, I am in the debt of the inestimable Institut Francophone de Paris. For help in shouldering departmental burdens while the writing was being done, heartfelt thanks to all my colleagues in the French Department at Stirling, especially Bill Kidd. Many librarians and archivists have come to my aid: particular thanks to the staff at the Bibliothèque Marguerite Durand in Paris, and the Bibliothèque de Documentation Internationale Contemporaine at Nanterre; to Colette Chambelland and Françoise Blum at the Musée Social, to Jenny Marshman and Bet Inglis at the University of Sussex Library, and to Gordon Willis at Stirling. Parts of the book have been given as research or conference papers in Scotland, England, France and the USA: the comments colleagues, friends and students made were of incalculable help. If the result remains a shade opinionated, they are in no way to blame.

Where to begin to acknowledge intellectual debts and personal kindness? Three people in particular have special thanks. Michelle Perrot, now the *doyenne* of women's history in France, supervised my thesis on labour history, back in the 1970s: she has been a constant source of inspiration since we originally met through our mutual friend, the late Gene Schulkind. Rod Kedward has for many years given excellent advice and warm encouragement in conversations, correspondence and through his own pioneering work on French history. And Claire Duchen has been a true intellectual friend, jogging my elbow throughout the composition years, reading chapters, lending books and making sure I didn't give up. I have also had helpful and stimulating discussions with Laura Frader, Françoise Thébaud, Karen Offen, Michèle Riot-Sarcey and Mariette Sineau, who have all generously read sections and sent me their own work in progress. I have greatly benefited from borrowing the theses of Paul Smith and Christine Bard before publication, with their permission; other people who have kindly let me see material before publication include Hanna Diamond, Anne Cova, Hilary Footitt, Helen Harden Chenut and Linda Clark. Maurice Larkin and David Watson, who are neighbours as well as colleagues, both gave timely help. Among many people who have made my visits to Paris a pleasure, Claude-Hélène Perrot, Paule Braudel, Christophe and Lucy Campos, Jenny Jones and Paul Volsik have been particularly kind and hospitable. Several readers of the proposal made helpful suggestions and one heroic anonymous reader of the original (much longer) manuscript made both encouraging and pertinent comments. Heather McCallum at Routledge put faith in the project from the start and was a tower of strength. Kay Edge copy-edited the manuscript with much patience and Philip Gooch saw it through the press. My husband Peter France is not a historian, but a specialist on rhetoric: anything I could say here about my debt to him would be an example of litotes. Kate, Rose and Siri provided laughs along the way.

ABBREVIATIONS

AN	Archives Nationales
APD	Association pour la Paix par le Droit
APPo	Archives de la Préfecture de Police
ARAC	Association Républicaine des Anciens Combattants
BDIC	Bibliothèque de Documentation Internationale Contemporaine
BHVP	Bibliothèque Historique de la Ville de Paris
BIT/ILO	Bureau International du Travail/International Labour Office
BMD	Bibliothèque Marguerite Durand
CCRP	Caisse de Compensation de la Région Parisienne
CFLN	Comité Français de Libération Nationale
CFTC	Confédération Française des Travailleurs Chrétiens
CGT	Confédération Générale du Travail
CGTU	Confédération Générale du Travail Unitaire
CLAJ	Centre Laïque des Auberges de Jeunesse
CMFCGF	Comité Mondial des Femmes contre la Guerre et le Fascisme
CNFF	Conseil National des Femmes Françaises
CNR	Conseil National de la Résistance
DBMOF	Dictionnaire biographique du mouvement ouvrier français
ENS	Ecole Normale Supérieure
GDFS	Groupe des Femmes Socialistes
GFEL	Groupes Féministes de l'Enseignement Laïque
HBM	Habitations Bon Marché
ICW	International Council of Women
INED	Institut National des Etudes Démographiques
IWSA	International Women's Suffrage Alliance
JAC/F	Jeunesse Agricole Chrétienne/Féminine
JC	Jeunesses Communistes
JEC/F	Jeunesse Etudiante Chrétienne/Féminine
JOC/F	Jeunesse Ouvrière Chrétienne/Féminine
LDH	Ligue des Droits de l'Homme
LFAJ	Ligue Française des Auberges de Jeunesse
LFDF	Ligue Française du Droit des Femmes

LICP	Ligue Internationale des Combattants pour la Paix
LIFPL	Ligue Internationale des Femmes pour la Paix et la Liberté (section française)
LIMEP	Ligue Internationale des Mères et Educatrices pour la Paix
LPF	Ligue Patriotique des Françaises
MRP	Mouvement Républicain Populaire
OPMES	Office de la Protection de la Maternité et de l'Enfance de la Seine
PCF	Parti Communiste Français
RUP	Rassemblement Universel pour la Paix
SAP	Section de l'Aviation Populaire
SDN	Société des Nations [League of Nations]
SFIO	Section Française de l'Internationale Ouvrière [French Socialist party]
UFCS	Union Féminine Civique et Sociale
UFFCGI	Union des Femmes Françaises contre la Guerre Impérialiste
UFSF	Union Française pour le Suffrage des Femmes
UJFF	Union des Jeunes Filles Françaises
UNVF	Union Nationale pour le Vote des Femmes
WILPF	Women's International League of Peace and Freedom [cf. LIFPL]

INTRODUCTION

Writing about inter-war France: the textbook as text

> A history of historiography that takes account of the presence or absence of women is
> still to be written.
>
> (Pomata 1993: 11)

> Textbooks ... can make people disappear, but only temporarily, for the objects from
> the suppressed past – the public records, private papers and oral traditions – survive to
> pique the curiosity of another generation of inquirers.
>
> (Appleby *et al.* 1994: 294–5)

Writing about French history, especially as an outsider, is not an enterprise for the faint-hearted. Pierre Nora, the editor of the series *Lieux de mémoire*, has agreed that history is itself a 'lieu de mémoire' for the French, a site of memory, if not an obsession: 'History has played the same role in France as philosophy has in Germany or the "American way of life" in the United States ... that of cementing together the national community.'[1] A British observer has similarly observed that French history is full of myth and counter-myth, 'not in the sense of fiction, but in the sense of a construction of the past elaborated by a political community for its own ends' (Gildea 1994: 12).

Commemoration, that obsession of the late twentieth century, has helped to expose the fragile nature of what we call history. A clearer illustration of the construction of a national history could hardly be provided than the bicentennial of the French Revolution. In 1989, 'a commemoration that was intended to adorn the Republic instead divided the nation.' So bitter were the disputes about whether the Revolution was 'over' or not, and whether it should be celebrated, deplored or simply regarded as something to be avoided if possible, that questions about the Revolution were deleted from the secondary school examinations that year (Appleby *et al.* 1994: 291; Gildea 1994: 13–17). An even more painful process of commemoration of events closer to the present has been the re-examination of the French experience of Occupation during the Second World War. A series of fiftieth anniversaries in the early 1990s prompted the official recognition of 16 July, the date in summer 1942 of the Rafle du Vél d'Hiv when, on German orders but with the collaboration of the French authorities, several thousand Jewish families living in Paris were rounded up for deportation. This new *lieu de mémoire* could be seen as the result of a process of historical review. Both 1789 and the Occupation are examples of episodes in the French past that have been constructed, taken apart and rewritten more than once, with a view to exploring the national history. However disturbing, both could be seen as yielding positive experiences from the historical point of view, in spite or rather because of their result: a more fragmented picture than earlier versions of these critical and traumatic events. In both cases, though, the task of the writer of textbooks, on which much of national history reposes, was made more difficult. We have come a long way from the time when the 'petit manuel Lavisse', the schoolbook read by millions of French schoolchildren at the turn of the century, could be seen as 'the primary schoolteacher of the nation' telling them what they took to be the literal truth. But we are still in an age when students are anxious to find a 'clear and well-informed guide' to national history.[2]

Some episodes in the past have posed a less obvious challenge, but feminists might argue that their construction by historians is just as fragile and partial. One of the benefits of the fragmentation of the historiography of the Revolution, after all, was that more space opened up for consciousness of the presence or absence of women in revolutionary history. By contrast, the inter-war period, the subject of this book, has not been subjected to the same drastic revision and interpretation as the two previous examples. There may be considerable nuances in the way the story is told, but the narrative outline of 'what happened in France' between 1918 and 1939 will be found in recognizable form in most student textbooks or histories for the general reader. This book sets out to rethink that period from a feminist perspective, not so much to challenge what has so far been written as to query what has not been written, using the new research of recent years to ask different questions and – inevitably – to propose some alternative readings. It aims to apply the perspectives and the findings of what is variously known as women's history, gender history or feminist history to a rather resistant historical 'site of research'. I do not underestimate the difficulty of trying to do this. It was after having taught twentieth-century French history to students, and found it awkward to incorporate the findings of women's history into it, that I began this project. Authors of textbooks, who must try to write concise accounts, have my sympathy. But the prevailing gender-blindness of so much of the historical literature has been a spur to explore how it could be otherwise. It is not a matter of 'putting the record straight': this account, like others, will be partial, in both senses of the word.

The choice of period was not random. The history of inter-war France is a particularly clear example of a broader historical problem: the non-integration of women into political and chronological historical narratives, or to put it another way, the absence of gender as a framing structure of such history. What we have in most political history is a single-sexed narrative that does not speak its name. This is not through some 'conspiracy of historians', although virtually all political history of inter-war France has so far been written by men, but neither is it accidental. As it happens, during these years French women were barred from any formal share in parliamentary or even local politics, since they could neither vote nor stand for election before 1944. As a result, authors of general or political histories of the inter-war years might well plead that they have found it either unnecessary or just too difficult to identify women as participants in the national history. Their exclusion is sometimes stated, but not as a rule analysed. But we should beware of taking this as an adequate explanation: the political history of France after 1945 has not been remarkably gender-conscious either. Part of my purpose is therefore to question a definition of politics that eliminates all mention of those without formal power, or which fails to recognize the gender structures governing a history in which all the significant actors belong to one sex. The logical consequence of that is to do at least two things: to reconsider the conventional political arena to see how gender relates to it; and to open up for enquiry some areas not always perceived as part of the political field. Both approaches will be tried in what follows. Before explaining more fully the outline of the book and the spirit in which it has been approached, let me briefly review first the state of historiography of the inter-war years in France, and then the ways in which a gender-conscious approach might approach rethinking history.

THE TEXTBOOK AS TEXT

To write about inter-war France is to venture on to very fully mapped territory in one sense. Most of the existing works have been produced in France itself. Hardly surprising, perhaps: in most countries, the national history has pride of place. But it is not a matter of indifference where history is written.[3] The prevailing historical narratives will inevitably reflect the structures and – to be blunt – the power relations at the centre of French historical production: the institutions, the personalities, the schools of thought, all reflected in the syllabuses adopted by schools and universities. Our period is perhaps a special case. Twentieth-century France has become a popular topic with students of history because it overlaps with the study of politics, a subject accorded much respect in the French educational system. Hence the large numbers of textbooks (*manuels*) and general histories of a more discursive kind (*synthèses*) devoted to the inter-war period. Both kinds of books have a script which it is hard to depart from. Because the politics, domestic and international, of the inter-war period were dramatic, and because they contain the origins of the Second World War, the need to tell that story tends to dominate any brief study. The writer is obliged to present the reader with a sequence of familiar events that seem to lead with tragic inevitability to September 1939: the Treaty of Versailles, the occupation of the Ruhr, the Briand interlude, the depression and the rise of fascism, the 6 February riot, the Popular Front, Munich. Interwoven with this story is the more jerky narrative of French domestic politics, with its battles between left and right. Sections on the economy or society may introduce some variety and choice of material, but the 'mainstream' history seems to write itself. The textbook writer, it could be argued, really has little choice: deemed to present a synthesis of received wisdom on the subject, he or she must tell a simple tale.

But as Gianna Pomata has written, in an illuminating article, 'the textbook is not a neutral form':

It is a form created with a specific pedagogic intent when history was introduced into the schools. The fundamental message entrusted to the textbook seems that of transmitting a 'universal' and synthetic image of history. How is this universal dimension constructed? By means of the generalizations that do not explicitly deny, but implicitly omit as irrelevant, certain differences in historical experience, such as the difference between men and women. This is the reason why the chronological format is fundamental in this kind of text. The textbook needs a universal and abstract standpoint from which to organize the historical material. The idea of historical time as neutral time [the time of chronology] allows events to be represented through an 'objective' medium, independent from the point of view of the people who experienced them. Thus the illusion of a 'general' and unified vision of history is created. This is also the reason why textbooks are usually obsessed by the need to 'cover' everything (they often pass on this obsession to their readers). I do not know of a history textbook that openly admits any gaps in our knowledge or that presents historical knowledge as an open-ended research process. To do this would be an admission of partiality and fallibility that the textbook cannot afford, because it is a direct contradiction of the image of omniscient universality claimed by this kind of text.

(Pomata 1993: 42)

At one level, this comment prepares us for the potential for despair of the unfortunate textbook writer: the format drives him or her to claim that Olympian detachment which we all know to be an illusion. The assignment is mission impossible. At another level, Pomata's observation points towards something else: the cultural power of the textbook. Reaching a mass audience, directly or indirectly, it shapes popular views of history. In France in particular, with a centralized school-leaving exam, a large student population and competitive entry to the *grandes écoles*, textbooks sell regularly every year to high school and university students. Their authors are under all manner of editorial pressures, partly because they write for a mass market. Series like the 'Cursus' books (Armand Colin) and the new 'Premier Cycle' (PUF), designed for first-year university students, cater for an apparently insatiable demand, inside France and to some extent outside. When television programmes are made about history, the textbook writers are the first to be consulted. These are the books that will in the end have shaped the overall view of a given time in the past, will have been read by the largest number of individuals and will have laid down what counts as historical knowledge. Priorities, rhetoric, great men, famous sayings – here they all are.

But what counts as a textbook? It may seem both sweeping and unfair to class *manuels* and *synthèses* together. Whereas the textbook aimed at, say, high school students has to be fairly schematic and simple, the general history, aimed at more advanced students and their teachers, can afford to add nuance, to include details and exceptions, to discuss rival interpretations and, through its footnotes and

4

references, to send the reader to the particular histories of which it provides a general synthesis. It is invariably more thorough, more far-reaching and more speculative than the textbook. A good example of the general history for our period would be the relevant volumes of the *Nouvelle Histoire de la France Contemporaine*, newly revised and updated.[4]

The problem is that, more often than one might imagine, and in the case of inter-war France in particular, the dividing line between the textbook and the more advanced general history is not quite as clear cut as it might seem. As a rule, both are available in paperback editions, and the most realistic readership for both is the student body, at different stages of expertise. The available books would be more sensibly arranged along a continuum from the simple to the advanced, rather than divided into separate groups. What is more, the writers of the textbooks are sometimes the same individuals as the authors of general histories. And because in France many specialists on the twentieth century are political historians (in the broad sense) there is a certain convergence of their approach. No secret this, it has been openly acknowledged in the introduction to a book of historiographical essays entitled *Pour une histoire politique*:

> [The collection reflects] the concrete existence of a group of historians; they have over the years built up an intellectual familiarity, in a spirit of trust and friendship .... [They vary in approach, but] there is a practical solidarity which has its own topography. It has been constituted on an axis running between the University of Paris-X Nanterre and the rue St Guillaume, home of the Institut d'Etudes politiques .... We all have links with one or other or both of these institutions.
>
> (Rémond 1988: 9)[5]

Anyone working on twentieth-century France will have regularly used books by this group of historians over the years with profit, and their writings will often be cited in what follows. In that sense there is a classic corpus, inspired by a collective ethos. That ethos is, moreover, far from being confined to the approach of 'traditional political history'. Indeed, the essays in that collection set out to 'dispel the prejudices which persist about political history'. It should, the authors argue, no longer be assimilated to *l'histoire événémentielle* [the mere narrative of events], but has been 'revitalized', interacting dynamically with other sectors of history – 'the cultural, economic and social'. Well placed at the centre of a lively research culture in Paris, these historians and their associates are responsible for many of the most stimulating developments in twentieth-century history. Doctoral theses and specialized studies of the period have multiplied in number in recent years, as the inter-war years recede into the past.

Not so very long ago, Theodore Zeldin could argue that it was still too early to try to write seriously about the inter-war years:

> The history of inter-war France remains far less documented than that of Germany in the same period ... the French national archives have only

recently been (partially) opened to historians . . . . It is only gradually that the perspective that regards these years as ones of exceptional chaos and failure will recede and allow the changes that took place in them to be seen in a less negative way, and with some sense of what was permanent and what was superficial.

(Zeldin 1977: 1041)

Archives were opened faster in the 1980s than before, partly because of the expiry or abolition of fifty-year rules: the 1986 commemoration of the Popular Front helped release some documents. Gaps remain in many archival series – politically sensitive papers were often removed or destroyed – so the sources are still patchy. But some outstanding theses have now appeared, with a wealth of detail impossible before. New subjects have been tackled: technology, social movements, religion, welfare, the arts – topics falling outside the political histories penned in the 1950s and 1960s, and more akin to social and cultural history. Some studies show more awareness of gender than others, but taken together they provide a huge resource of secondary material. To mention only three which have been published in France in the last few years, we now have Jean-François Sirinelli's exhaustive study of the students at the Ecole Normale Supérieure between the wars (1988), Pascal Ory's thesis on the cultural policy of the Popular Front (1994) and Christine Bard's survey of feminism between the wars (1995). Far more has now been written about the economy and society of these years, as well as about the politics.

Some of this has found its way into the general narrative histories at the sophisticated end of the textbook spectrum. Yet the priorities of the writer of syntheses do not seem to have changed greatly. The major controversies are still very largely determined by left–right differences, and concentrate on the issues of French foreign and domestic policy, including the rise of fascism, and whether the Popular Front was a 'good' or a 'bad' thing. For all the undeniable 'revitalizing' that has taken place, in one respect little has changed: with one or two notable exceptions, historians of twentieth-century France continue to pay remarkably little attention either to women as actors in history or to gender as a historical concept.

From a feminist perspective, then, even the 'new' political history seems to mean business as usual. What mattered between the wars was done, directed and experienced primarily by men – and a certain category of men at that: politicians. Women are so absent from, so shadowy in the recounting of events that they might as well not have existed. Banished to subordinate clauses, parentheses, paragraphs on showbusiness or fashion, negative implications (such as not bearing enough children), or simply omitted altogether, women will be sought in vain in most versions of the central narrative – which is in turn not explicitly presented as single-gendered.[6] I don't want to construe this as sexism, although some readers may be tempted to do so. It represents to my mind a conceptual difficulty that still surfaces surprisingly often in the form of contradictions in the writings of historians. To take an eminent example, René Rémond, doyen of political historians, is the chief author of a 900-page synthesis of twentieth-century French history, *Notre siècle* (no textbook this). In the conclusion, Rémond remarks interestingly that 'the most important social phenomenon in the last fifty years has probably been the change in the condition of women.' Yet the body of the text hardly refers to women, and the *avis au lecteur* on the book's jacket (normally penned by the author) encapsulates what is instantly recognizable – to the sensitive antennae of a feminist at least – as the 'privileging of the male subject in history':

> A Frenchman born at the start of the century will have experienced two world conflicts, of a length not attained since the Revolutionary and Napoleonic wars, and a series of colonial confrontations. Above all, he will have lived through a disaster to which only the distant memories of the Hundred Years War can be compared: the defeat of 1940 and the traumas that followed. He will have suffered at least two major economic crises, which threw into question acquired benefits he had believed achieved for good. He will have seen four political systems in succession, one of which abolished democracy, and will have witnessed two or three crises of the regime, and five or six shifts of power between left and right, with the enactment of grandiose reform plans. Need one add how much his standard of living and way of life have changed and how all his cultural and emotional landmarks will have been transformed? Our century has indeed been one of change.
>
> (Rémond 1988: 951 and back cover)

To decode this passage from a gendered perspective is to see that Rémond, or his publisher, does not attempt to historicize the sex difference he refers to in his conclusion. The passage is written in the masculine, as if this were an unproblematic identity for all French nationals. The reference to abolishing 'democracy' refers to the Vichy regime of 1940–4: but for women there was no formal democracy before 1940 to be abolished. The reference to 'acquired benefits' conceals considerable differences at different historical moments between men and women (in pay levels, civil rights and unemployment benefits to take some obvious examples). And so on. With the best will in the world, something the author recognizes as important cannot be encompassed in the rhetoric of generality. So while respecting much of the existing work available on inter-war France, I take the view that it remains flawed and incomplete. To rethink the period will mean working *both with and against* some of the classic histories or student textbooks which have structured the cognitive field of study.

If 'mainstream' history has had a tendency to overlook women, women's history until recently had a tendency to overlook the inter-war period. In the great expansion in women's studies in the 1970s, the inter-war years were rather neglected, partly because they were simply too recent, as noted above. Much of the early research on women's history focused on the nineteenth century and/or periods further back in time. Over the last ten years or so, by contrast, women's history has provided more data about the first half of the twentieth century. Here, as elsewhere, more official papers and documents are now available; another incentive has been the new visibility of the substantial collections of private archives assembled by women who lived through these years; oral history is still a possibility. Inside and outside France, there is no shortage of scholars working on the history of women during these years. Some of this work is in the form of 'littérature grise' – unpublished theses and doctorates, articles in journals of specialist interest. But there are also several published books, familiar to anyone working in the field.[7] New ideas have raised new questions. The possibilities for attempting some kind of synthesis have therefore multiplied lately. But what approach is called for?

The First World War has been described as 'one of those classic cases of dissonance between official male-centred history and unofficial female history' (Gilbert 1987: 199). As it happens, these two histories have been confronted in recent years as cultural historians and others have examined the Great War for its complexity, its potential for disruption between the sexes and its legacy of cultural anxiety.[8] What strikes one about the history of the inter-war years, on the other hand, is the near-total disjunction between the particular narratives coming from women's history and the general narratives of 'male-centred history', what has been described here as the textbook. Is this simply an unbridgeable gap?

One strategy adopted by women's historians, rather than attempt a synthesis, is to write completely separate 'textbooks of women's history'. Having surveyed some examples of the genre, Gianna Pomata concluded that while some may succeed better than others, separate versions of history are indeed the answer:

> Nowadays a women's history textbook should not be written either to legitimate women's history as a separate field or to pursue the objective of an integrated and unified notion of historical knowledge. It should be written instead simply to reflect, with unavoidable partiality, that multiple, non-unified vision that is emerging from current research. Most importantly, it seems to me that the temptation of integration and synthesis, the temptation of the 'general' dimension, may be dangerous for women's history. In my opinion, we need to achieve a prior objective, before we insert women in 'general' history. We need, first of all, to question the very distinction between 'particular' and 'general' history. We must investigate how these categories were constructed in the historiographical discourse we have inherited.
>
> (Pomata 1993: 43)

While agreeing to some extent with this, I have chosen not to write a textbook of women's history as such. But neither will this be an attempt to write a 'general history' of France between the wars, 'putting the women back in' as it were. That was its original ambitious aim, but it is indeed optimistic to assume we can achieve some elusive synthesis easily and quickly. As the book has taken shape, it is clear that it consists of a set of challenges rather than answers; that it is more concerned with historiography than it was originally intended to be; that it has been obliged to take issue with other historians on a number of territories; and that it too is a particular rather than a general history. All the same, it is not a history of women in the period, still less a history of feminism. Neither is it a cultural history, if by cultural history we understand an explicit attempt to decode the discourses about men and women embedded in the cultural production of the period. The present book is intended to be in some sense a *political history*, if not a general history. The best formulation I can find at present is that it is a survey, hinting at the possibility of an alternative political history. It deals with subjects that may genuinely interest any student of the period, but tries to write about them in a different language, worked out by the many historians who have grappled with gender as a historical concept.

GENDER AND HISTORY

While the expressions 'women's history', 'history of women' and 'feminist history' were all to be found during the 1970s, the terms 'gender' or 'gender history' gradually gained currency in English-language publications during the 1980s. Spreading with disconcerting speed, the word sometimes seems to have replaced 'sex' (as in 'there are two genders') or to have turned into code for 'women'. It has not gained anything like as much acceptance in France (the word *genre* is seen as confusing) and is sometimes rendered by 'la différence des sexes'.[9]

The distinction between 'sex' and 'gender' which became current in the United States and Britain from the 1970s was a deliberate attempt to introduce a theoretical terminology. Sex referred to biological features, regarded then (more than they would be now, perhaps) as 'given'; gender referred to the sexual differences constructed by society: the cultural and social factors associated with maleness and femaleness, masculinity and femininity. In its most common acceptance, it still carries this cultural meaning. In history, its introduction marked a new stage in the development of women's history, and it is worth insisting that the term – which is now applied to both men and women – would never have emerged at all if it had not been for the revolution in women's history. It was certainly not implicit in the logic of men's history before that revolution.

Gisela Bock has described the concept as having followed two earlier phases of 'restoring women to history' and 'restoring history to women' – that is acknowledging that 'women's history concerns not merely half of humankind but all of it.' Whereas earlier studies had concentrated on making women 'visible' to the historical gaze, or hearing their 'silenced voices' – metaphors reflected in the titles of several books – it had become clear that this led towards rethinking history quite radically, by identifying everyone as a sexed – or gendered – being. Relations between the sexes and the new visibility of men as gendered beings could now become the object of study: it is no coincidence that the use of the term 'gender' and the earliest works on men and masculinity more or less coincided. Gender was, as Bock put it, 'an intellectual construct, a way of perceiving and studying people, an analytic tool that helps us to discover neglected areas of history. It is a conceptual form of sociocultural inquiry that challenges the sex-blindness of traditional historiography.'

Bock's definition, which has also been called the 'social science view of gender', assumes reasonably coherent identities for the category 'men' and the category 'women', while recognizing that there will be variations related to other social factors (such as class, or culture). And it goes further than a simple 'add-on', complementary view, that 'men's history plus women's history equals total history'. Gender history assumes that human activity and relations need conceptualizing, not just describing, and that there is a dynamic, and in part inevitably a power relation between gendered groups: 'gender relations are equally as important as all other human relations and ... gender relations contribute to and affect human relations' (Bock 1989: 11–16).

Such a definition might seem fairly straightforward and perhaps not too controversial. But not everyone has agreed that the shift in emphasis is desirable. Some feminist historians have argued that it is really taking the sting out of analysing women's oppression, which many see as still the 'primary task of women's history'. Judith Bennett suggests that the term 'patriarchy' has fallen from favour, even as 'gender' has come up. The real question, she argues, is 'why and how the oppression of women has endured so long and in so many different historical settings'. Without being completely opposed to gender history, she is concerned that it should not dominate the field (Bennett 1989: 251–72). Stronger reservations have been expressed elsewhere. One reason is that gender is perceived as a recuperable notion leading towards a kind of neutrality in the war between the sexes. If the gender identity of both men and women is equally constructed socially, who is oppressed? Gisela Bock herself argued that rather than a 'gender-neutral' approach, a 'gender-encompassing' one was desirable. By that she meant one that did not leave out the politics of sexual difference.

Not all women's historians were convinced that was possible; many have preferred to remain explicitly historians of *women*, the more urgent task as they see it. Even more controversial is the related debate, particularly in the United States, over what has become known as the 'post-structuralist' view of gender, most closely associated with the historian Joan Wallach Scott. A respected specialist in French history, Scott first published her article 'Gender a category of historical analysis' in 1986, and added to it in her book *Gender and the Politics of History* in 1988, unleashing a debate that is still going on.[10]

While this debate fits into the broader philosophical debates about relativism, it has had a particularly passionate character all its own. Scott was critical of much of women's history, including some of her own earlier work, as showing 'the limits of descriptive approaches that do not address dominant disciplinary concepts – or ... not in forms that can shake their power and perhaps transform them'. What was at issue here was the debate between 'those who assert the transparency of facts and those who insist that all reality is construed or constructed'. Scott's chief concern was with the epistemology of history. Thus her definition of gender went beyond the 'social construction of sex difference' she has described as the social science view. Instead, she described gender as

> knowledge about sexual difference ... such knowledge is not absolute or true but always relative. . . . This does not mean that gender reflects or implements

fixed and natural physical differences between men and women; rather gender is the knowledge that establishes meanings for bodily difference.

(Scott 1988: 3)

Drawing on concepts more familiar in critical theory than history, and on the thought of Michel Foucault in particular, her argument was that post-structuralist theory challenged the assumption that there is a fixed and permanent subject possessing total autonomy. By drawing attention instead to language as a set of retrospective discourses produced at historically specific moments, such a theory could be seen to offer a way of historicizing and deconstructing conventional terms of sexual difference – for instance – by showing how and when they were produced. Scott conceded that in a way the whole feminist project had always been revisionist by rejecting certain binary divisions claimed to be self-evident, but suggested that in so doing, it had perhaps paid too much attention to such all-powerful explanations as patriarchy or the means of production. 'We need to replace the notion that social power is unified, coherent and centralized with something like Foucault's concept of power as dispersed constellations of unequal relationships, discursively con-structed in social fields of force' (Scott 1988: 42). Elsewhere, she challenged one of the pillars of women's history, arguing that we could not assume the authenticity of 'experience' as self-evident: 'experience is at once always already an interpretation and something that needs to be interpreted.' Again a critical reappraisal of women's history was present, implying that over-simple conclusions had been drawn from experience, assumed to reflect the 'real world' (Scott 1991b: 773 ff.).

This brief summary cannot do justice to the scope of Scott's theoretical writing, but enough has been said to show that it could be read as criticism of some previous women's history as over-descriptive, insufficiently theorized, over-reliant on the evidence of an experience that had not been problematized. In an exchange with Scott which contains pointers to the way the debate would go, Linda Gordon argued that the 'post-structuralist' approach failed to identify a hierarchy of oppression; if there are a mass of conflicting power discourses, the felt reality (experience of oppression for example) is obscured. Such an analysis appeared to do away both with an enemy and a resister, leaving no room for human agency. To those who already saw 'gender history' and academic feminism generally as undermining the revolutionary thrust of the women's movement, pushing it to become domesticated and acceptable, the new approach looked like further theoretical underpinning for compromise, putting neither patriarchy nor the class enemy on trial, as women's history once had.[11] The heart of this debate is similar in some ways to the earlier objections to the use of gender: it is about an assumed break with politics. Another dissenter from Scott described her philosophy as a rather 'bleak' one that seemed to leave feminist historians all stranded in the webs of discourse, instead of in some sense striving for change (Downs 1993: 414 ff.).

Scott has argued, against such interpretations, that her approach is inherently political and indeed deeply destabilizing towards 'what has passed for objective neutral and universal history in the past, because that view of history included in its

11

very definition of itself the exclusion of women'. In the preface to her book, perhaps the best introduction to her position, she writes: 'My motive is and was one I share with feminists and it is avowedly political: to point out and change inequalities between men and women', an enterprise which is difficult to carry out 'if one lacks an analysis of how gender hierarchies are constructed, legitimated, challenged and maintained' (Scott 1988: 3).

This debate may continue to be polarized for some time, although not all historians choose irrevocably to line up on one side or another. The particularly strong reaction from some women's historians against the post-structuralist approach has obviously been aroused by its unsettling potential. Not only does it challenge 'old-fashioned certainties', to some of which feminist history has gladly taken the axe itself, but in its assumed premise that all text is discourse it has been seen as undermining the stability of language and of any priorities. The temptation is to feel a certain vertigo at this point. Why bother writing history at all if complete relativism rules?

The recent jointly authored book *Telling the Truth about History* is one attempt to provide a survival guide in an age of what its authors describe as 'noisy conversations' about the possibility of historical truth. Despite being hailed as a rejoinder to 'those who wish to undermine history', this careful set of essays actually concedes a great deal to relativism. Three-quarters of the book contains a persuasive account of the manufactured nature of historical traditions, from the Scientific Revolution through the Enlightenment to national history (of the United States, but it could have been France), before moving to consider the more recent contributions of the twentieth century, including relativist post-structuralism. Its authors argue for compromise – for taking the good insights of post-modernism, while rejecting the 'exaggerated skepticism' it embodies. The label they attach to their compromise is 'practical realism', broadly if not exactly elegantly defined as the belief that because 'something exists as an image of something's being in the mind, [that] does not in the least diminish its external existence or its knowability through the medium of language'. Practical realism, they assert, is what encourages scholars 'to get out of bed in the morning and head for the archives, because they can there uncover evidence, touch lives long passed and "see" patterns in events that otherwise might remain inexplicable' (Appleby *et al.* 1994: 247–51). A more uncompromising relativist offers another version of what motivates the historian to take that trip to the archives: it is commitment to a history that recognizes its own identity as a discourse, enabling 'present-minded people(s) to go to the past, there to delve around and reorganise it to their needs . . . . [S]uch history may well have a radical cogency that can make visible aspects of the past [previously] hidden or secreted . . . overlooked or sidelined, thereby producing fresh insights that can actually make emancipatory, material differences to and within the past' (Jenkins 1991: 68).

Both these remedies contain that old-fashioned cure for accidie, curiosity. We can all recognize the excitement of working with 'authentic' documents – but we do not suspend our critical judgement to do so. We have always known, to put it at its most basic, that ideas only exist if there is someone around to think them, and this knowledge only occasionally keeps us awake at night. Anyone writing from a feminist perspective – which is what I am doing when using the term gender as a key to exploring the past – must surely agree that history is not fixed or stable, and that part of the interest of doing it lies in being aware that whatever we write will be a new narrative, a new reading of our sources. We should be as wary of our own narratives as we are of other people's, let alone of the rather special master-narrative which I have described as 'the textbook'. That need not mean abandoning a certain number of working rules and being as scrupulous as possible about the use of evidence. The past speaks only when we give it voice, but history that obviously distorts or ignores what other people have uncovered in the way of evidence is not doing the job properly.

This book is being written in the 1990s, thanks to many 'noisy conversations' conducted by other historians in whose debt it remains, whether or not it takes issue with them. I owe a special debt to Joan Scott, for the salutary stimulus her work has given me to thinking about gender, though she might find much old-fashioned empiricism in what follows, alongside my simultaneous efforts to unravel narratives. I have long found particularly helpful her formulation of the link between gender history and the need for self-consciousness in the historian:

> History [is] a participant in the production of knowledge about sexual difference. I assume that history's representations of the past help construct gender for the present. Analyzing how that happens requires attention to the assumptions, practices and rhetoric of the discipline, to things either so taken for granted or so outside customary practice that they are not usually a focus for historians' attention. These include the notions that history can faithfully document lived reality, that archives are repositories of facts and that categories like man or woman are transparent. They extend as well to examinations of the rhetorical practices of historians, the construction of historical texts and the politics – that is the power-relationships – constituted by the discipline.
>
> (Scott 1988: 2–3)

My aim in this book, then, is to examine what may have been taken for granted and to see whether things could be presented otherwise. I am indebted to my predecessors for providing my first route maps, but using the term gender as a restructuring concept means suggesting different ways of reading the past: not so much a reinterpretation, more a widening of the angle of vision. For instance, I am not setting out to prove that French men were more, or less, 'oppressive' of women than at other times or in other countries, nor that French women were more, or less, 'feminist', although those interpretations might be placed on some subjects discussed here. My contention is rather that both men and women, with all their varieties of status, age, actions and beliefs, were part of the historical entity 'France' between the wars. That is really the core of the book. Although it may often seem as if there is more material on women, it will be hard to find many sections in it where men are not mentioned at all – and in that respect it will differ both from general (or men's) history and from a specifically women's history. Concretely, in what follows, I have tried to apply theory to practice, along lines articulated among others by Arlette Farge in the early days of gender history:

> ... to establish at long last a history of the tensions between men's and women's roles, and to construct from their conflicts and complementarities some common thread running through all historical narrative. It would certainly not mean devising a closed field of knowledge, on the contrary it would oblige historians to ask a new set of questions, by introducing the notion of gender [*la différence des sexes*], by trying to identify the consecutive and often simultaneous moments when power relations, periods of indifference, struggles for supremacy, dislikes and desires, operating between women and men, wove together not only the entire social and political fabric but also shared between them the cultural system and the corresponding universe of the imagined [*l'imaginaire*].

> (Farge 1984: 33)

Such thoughts have only been thinkable in fairly recent times, and relativist and post-structuralist approaches, among others, have helped to make them so.

ORIGINS AND STRUCTURE OF THIS BOOK

The problem as it originally took shape was rather daunting: how to argue that gender ought to be taken seriously as a structuring concept in history. What was more, having chosen to take inter-war France as a sort of testing ground, it might seem as if my intention was to incriminate French historians and/or other historians of France. That was not exactly the point of departure, although the awkward fact remained that most of what had been written about this period did come from a group of French historians with a certain ethos, as explained above. Perhaps this is the place to say something about my outsider status. It may seem presumptuous to be considering critically the historiography of another country, but it is probably a measure of the fascination that French history exerts over English-speaking historians. Their observations, which have more than once led to critical reappraisal, have on the whole been welcomed in France. It is a pity that comparatively few French historians have returned the compliment and studied Britain and the United States. National histories can surely benefit from being able to 'see oursels as others see us'. In this instance, it might be fair to say that France has proved rather resistant to attempts by feminist historians to change the national agenda, at a time when the English-speaking world has been more open to rethinking.[12] But whether in France or anywhere else, political history has proved a particularly hard nut to crack – for very understandable reasons. So France is the case study, but the question is a much wider one.

Taking a short period of history, but one with a specific character, seemed the most manageable approach. I have already suggested some reasons for choosing the inter-war period. The central shape of the book assumes that it makes sense to

14

talk about such a thing as 'inter-war France'. This might be challenged – after all, one of the contributions of women's history has been to dispute conventional chronologies. Françoise Thébaud has argued that the periodization of 'general history' breaks down when one tries to write the history of women. In particular, she writes, 'the classic date of 1945, which ushered in an age of democracy and economic growth in the West, just does not work, in spite of the granting of the vote to women in several countries' including France (Thébaud 1992: 20). Behind this statement is the view noted earlier that whereas the Vichy period in France is often seen as an interruption to republican democracy, such a break does not exist from a women's perspective. Pre-war, Vichy and post-war governments can also be seen as fitting seamlessly into a continuum of a family policy which encouraged women to have children and not to take paid work.

To challenge the particular periodization of conventional chronology is not the same as denying the importance of chronology in general. I agree that to read twentieth-century history for signs of continuous 'progress' is inappropriate. And 1945 is indeed a problematic year in France – a date regarded as important for women but not for men. It can by contrast be argued that the 1914–18 war affected everyone in the country, men and women, old and young, so it makes sense to look at the years after it as having historical specificity, while resisting the temptation to see them as a block. In that sense, this is a book about 'post-war France'. On the other hand, it seemed best to avoid looking at these years entirely as if they 'led' to the defeat, Occupation and Vichy regime (although there are inevitably forward references, and at times the narrative reaches into the years 1939–45). Finally I wanted to be able to engage with the heart of the problem – the primacy of politics, to look in particular at some aspects of the politics of the age, using gender as an analytic tool. That is why it has deliberately focused on a relatively short but eventful period, as a sort of experimental glasshouse in which to study how things developed in the short to medium term.

The structure of the book is not strictly chronological, although within the sections chronology is important and the reader is also advised to consult the chronology at the end. The principle of selection was to choose topics where 'something happened' during the inter-war years that had not been present before the war. But the chapters also have both an internal and to some extent an external chronology, forming a sequence of linked essays. The Treaty of Versailles, the depression and the Popular Front will all be found here but, to paraphrase Jean-Luc Godard, not necessarily in that order. The book assumes at least some acquaintance with the traditional history to which it provides an alternative.

The first three chapters take subjects where change had perceptibly taken place in French society as a result of the First World War. Chapter 1 on demography considers the preoccupation with the birth rate which followed the mass slaughter of young men, but argues that the history of reproduction need not be separated from political history, and suggests ways of linking the two. Chapter 2, on growing up differently, considers the idea of *mixité*, the coexistence of the sexes, by looking closely both at children's books, secondary and higher education and youth movements, all of which saw changes during the post-war years. Chapter 3 takes aviation as an example of new technology and also of the way in which military priorities shaped life in post-war France. The mystique of flight seemed to associate women, as well as men, with the liberating forms of mobility after 1918, but to what extent?

The following chapters could all be seen as exploring the Popular Front slogan 'Bread, Peace and Liberty', from the perspective of gender. Chapter 4 re-examines the data we can now assemble about the post-war sexual division of labour, at a time when parts of the French economy were changing quite rapidly, because of new technology or relations of production. Chapter 5 examines the impact of the 1930s economic depression on an industrial workforce with newly gendered structures, and continues with an analysis of the strike wave of 1936.

The last four chapters tackle the heartland of politics, from the uncertain 1920s to the confrontational 1930s, with special emphasis on the years of the Popular Front. Chapter 6 considers how the French state and local authorities tackled the public provision of welfare, and the degree to which men in power relied on women to take executive roles in the embryonic social services. It takes as an example the work of the Health Minister of the Popular Front, Henri Sellier, and his women colleagues, including junior minister Suzanne Lacore. In Chapter 7, the infiltration of formal politics by women and the alternative politics of interest groups are analysed in some detail. Chapter 8 considers attitudes to war and peace and the largely unexplored role of women alongside men, whether internationally (at the League of Nations in Geneva) or domestically (in the peace movements throughout France). Finally, in Chapter 9, 'Rights and the republic', the question of political rights is tackled head-on. Whether or not women should be granted the vote was a preoccupation of inter-war politicians, despite their reluctance to take the plunge. This chapter seeks to set this question in context, looking forward to the eventual enfranchisement of women in 1944/5 and suggesting that the inter-war years may have fundamentally destabilized all-male politics.

The study as a whole aims to bring to the history of this period a greater awareness of both the politics of gender and the gender of politics operating at the heart of every theme tackled. It is not a monograph, but a survey. However, in some identifiable ways it is an anti-textbook. It does not claim to be universal and authoritative, but is undoubtedly selective: there is more here about women than about men (one of the side-effects of writing it was to bring home how much is taken for granted about 'men's history' in this period, and how unexplored it is). Its approach is not uniform: some chapters are broad in range and synthesize the research of other historians; others are based on my own research on primary sources and go in for more in the way of 'thick description'. Lastly, it probably raises more questions than it answers. In many ways, this is an agenda for further research, not a work of reference.

But it has an agenda of its own too: to look again at the cognitive map of inter-war France we have inherited, a map that continues to be drawn using criteria that anyone concerned with either women's history or gender analysis will surely find inadequate. The conclusion will draw together the threads of what has gone before and reflect on whether it can change our view of the period.

In a critical study of French historiography, in which she questions Pierre Nora's selection of *lieux de mémoire*, Suzanne Citron refers ironically to *non-lieux de mémoire, trous de mémoire*, or memory lapses, a notion she borrows from Gérard Noiriel's comments on the 'non-remembering' of immigration in French history (Citron 1991: 12–13, 278). The history of gender relations too, though she does not mention it, is one such *trou de mémoire*, or non-remembering, with all that that implies in the way of silencing, forgetting, overlooking – much of it unconscious. Pierre Rosanvallon's remarkable study of universal suffrage in France opens with the arresting reflection that we now take for granted the participation of all adults in politics: 'If women have had the vote in France only for the last half-century, this already seems to us to relate to some very distant history, extraordinarily distant . . . referring to a sort of prehistoric age of modern society, almost incomprehensible today' (Rosanvallon 1992: 11). If this is really true, a shift in mentality must somehow have occurred. In fact, that statement looks like a good example of a *trou de mémoire*. The age being referred to – concretely, the time before 1945 – is hardly remote, but can be recalled by people still alive. It casts a long shadow into the second half of the century, if the readiness of women to enter the political world and the readiness of men to accept them there is anything to go by. It needs to be historicized, not consigned to some penumbral pre-history, as if French women only came into the light when Man granted them the vote.

1

DEMOGRAPHY AND ITS
DISCONTENTS

If France stops producing large families, you can put the grandest clauses in the treaty [of Versailles], confiscate all Germany's cannon, do anything you please and it will be to no purpose: France will be lost, because there will be no more Frenchmen.

(Georges Clemenceau, 11 October 1919)[1]

An unpopulated country cannot be a free country. It lies wide open to every invasion, a prey vulnerable to every appetite. We shall therefore pursue a policy of pronatalism which will enable France to remain what she was in the last century.

(Edouard Daladier, 4 June 1939)[2]

Oh yes, there were many, many abortions (unnamed woman, interviewed about the 1930s).

(Thébaud 1986: 299)

In December 1927, two schoolteachers appeared before magistrates in the French town of Saumur. Henriette Alquier and Marie Guillot were accused of offences under the 1920 law forbidding propaganda for birth control. The 'Alquier affair' as it became known inspired heated outbursts inside and outside parliament, both for and against the accused.

The 1920 law had been passed by the first post-war National Assembly, in reaction to the loss of life during four years of fighting, when almost 1.5 million French soldiers had died and thousands more had been disabled. Anxiety about the French birth rate, already historically low before the war, inspired a current of opinion generally known as pronatalism, that is support for measures to increase the numbers of births. It had supporters in almost all political parties. The same parliament passed another law in 1923, redirecting abortion cases to magistrates' courts instead of to juries, with the aim of obtaining more convictions. Both laws redefined and extended penalties for offences associated with abortion or birth control. They have retrospectively become famous, though there was comparatively little public outcry at the time: what press comment there was sympathized with the pronatalist anxiety of the day.[3]

Henriette Alquier (née Clergue), mother of a small daughter, was twenty-nine, a village schoolteacher from south-west France: she had joined the Groupes Féministes de l'Enseignement Laïque (GFEL), a tiny minority of left-wing feminists within the schoolteachers' union closest to the Communist party, of which she and

18

her husband were also members. The report she prepared for the 1926 Grenoble conference of the GFEL was on 'Motherhood as a social function'. Most of it was an outspoken protest at child poverty, as witnessed by primary schoolteachers, and in particular at the high rate of infant mortality in France, estimated at 100,000 a year. She described the partial solutions offered by legislation or private charity over the years – maternity allowances, free milk, crèches – as inadequate, and proposed that motherhood should become a 'social function', paid for by the collectivity. It was not this proposal which caused trouble, however, but the closing section, calling for more information about sex and contraception. Putting the accent on class, Alquier claimed that bourgeois legislators, 'whose own wives can limit the number of their children in the privacy of their boudoir or adulterous love-nest', had passed strict laws against publicity for birth control, so that 'working-class women who needed information were deprived of it'. Contraception 'hurts nobody', the report continued, 'it does not damage the physiology of man or woman and it is puerile to claim that destroying a spermatozoon or cell is attacking human life. [One day in the future], it will be possible to teach contraceptive techniques openly'.[4]

Read out at the conference in Alquier's absence, the report was published in a special number of the GFEL Bulletin (printed in Saumur). Marie Guillot as editor was responsible for its contents. Not many people would have read it, had it not been referred to in May 1927 in a parliamentary question to the Minister of Education, put by a right-wing *député* Georges Pernot, an energetic pronatalist, and supporter of the 1920 law.

By 1927, parliament was no longer as preoccupied with the birth rate as it had been in 1920. The 1924 elections had produced a majority further to the left, but the first coalition government, based on the Cartel des gauches and led by the radical Edouard Herriot, fell in 1925. By 1927, the Cartel was in ruins and Herriot was Minister of Education in a government led by Raymond Poincaré, the centre-right politician who had stabilized both the plunging franc and public opinion. Holding on to the Education Ministry, and thus to the state school system, was one of the concessions the Radical party had obtained after the Cartel's collapse. As premier, Herriot had proposed several anticlerical measures, including strictures against religious congregations, which had provoked such sharp reactions that he had backed down. Now Catholic organizations and pronatalists alike called for action to be taken by the Minister of Education against Mme Alquier, a state-salaried 'corrupter of the young'. Birth control was still a sensitive topic. It would seem no accident that dissidence over this issue should come from state primary schoolteachers, viewed by the church as the foot-soldiers of anticlericalism.

Even a Radical party leader was not disposed to defend in public any kind of 'neo-Malthusianism', as the birth control movement was known in France, and Herriot had himself voted for the 1920 law. Pressed to take action against one of the ministry's employees, he described Alquier's report as 'provocative, a slap in the face of authority and inciting to immorality'. He promised that legal steps would be taken and that should the author be acquitted by the courts, he would press for sanctions within the educational system, via the ministry.[5]

Surprised by this reaction from a man of the anticlerical left, the teachers' union hastened to Alquier's defence. Her socialist lawyer argued that his client was being victimized. She had given no details of contraceptive methods (the real target of the law), merely expressing the wish that they could be openly revealed, whereas the authors of several works of fiction had been more explicit. The campaign attracted support not only from the extreme left but from the republican and non-communist Ligue des Droits de l'Homme, as well as from freemasons and trade unionists. After a string of witnesses testifying to the 'irreproachable' characters of the two accused, Alquier and Guillot were acquitted by the Saumur magistrates. Alquier returned to her village, where she carried on teaching and for a while became treasurer of the local branch of the Communist party.

Starting with this incident is one way of approaching a subject at once unavoidable and daunting. In inter-war France the apparently private world of family and reproduction stood in the forefront of public debate. By no means neglected, the subject has on the contrary been written about a great deal. The very comprehensiveness with which it has been covered has been an effective way of roping off a demographic history in which women are present, if only in a reproductive role, from a political history peopled exclusively by men. This chapter will draw on what exists already, rather than repeat it. There is no need for another account of France's demographic history, or of the measures taken by governments in response to that history. Nor will it explore the cultural aspects of the question, illuminatingly discussed by Mary Louise Roberts, who suggests that the preoccupation with the birth rate after the Great War was a sign of the need to 'purge moral and gender anxieties as well as military and economic ones' (Roberts 1994: 214).

The approach here will take the form of exploring the gender issues at the heart of the population question in a political context, relating them both to the politics of the day and to the way they are treated in historical accounts. What may strike us now is how both contemporaries and historians seem to be preoccupied with a single aspect of population change, namely conception – or contraception. Such selectivity has influenced the way this particular 'field of gender' has come to be viewed, a point that will become clearer if we review the existing historical narratives through which 'the population question' in France has been approached. Broadly speaking, they fall into two groups: the first having its origins in demography, the second inspired by libertarian or feminist politics. (Right/left distinctions, while not irrelevant, are not always the most useful ones in this context.) These approaches provide a useful, indeed an inevitable starting point, but they have structured the field in a rather limiting way. The second step will therefore be to indicate some of the gaps in the story.

THE DEMOGRAPHIC LAMENT AND ITS CHALLENGERS

Almost all general histories of the inter-war years approach the population question through the optic of 'the demographic lament' voiced by the pronatalists. The lament can be simply summarized: the French were/are having too few children and the government ought to do something about it. In this perspective, the inter-war years were and still are seen as an age of acute crisis. As the words of Clemenceau and Daladier suggest, the 'demographic lament' had already appeared in the nineteenth century in response to the comparative population figures in France and in other European countries.[6] The French population had stopped expanding as fast as that of its neighbours well before 1900. In its early days, the lament was inspired by fear of military defeat. The Franco-Prussian War could still be remembered by middle-aged adults in 1914, and the catastrophic losses during the Great War understandably lent the anxiety new strength. France might have emerged on the winning side, but rarely had victory been so dearly bought, and the next generation was gravely depleted. By the later 1930s deaths were exceeding births in France so when, during the Second World War, Marshal Pétain famously blamed a shortage of 'children, weapons and allies' for the crushing defeat of the French army in 1940, many will have believed him, although retrospectively military historians have not confirmed his claim.

The scientific version of the demographic lament was produced by the French school of demography (a word coined in France). From the nineteenth century to the present, demographers have argued that energetic government measures to encourage more births were/are desirable. Commitment to this idea is recognized to run high in the institutions of French population studies, in particular the Institut National des Etudes Démographiques (INED).[7] Demographers, as the intellectual interpreters of the raw material of statistics, the census returns, have provided most of the data used by historians. If, as in France, a strong focus is placed on the birth rate, that delimits the subject in such a way as to marginalize other topics. The demographic agenda has helped structure general political histories of France, in a way unmatched elsewhere. So while today playing down its military significance, historians and textbook writers still give plenty of space to the birth rate, usually including it as a structural feature. It has become common-place to suggest that a sagging demographic profile was associated with France's general stagnation before 1939. The low birth rate, which persisted despite the best efforts of the pronatalists, is seen as an index of immobility, lack of vigour and vision ('un pays de vieux'), and anxiety about change – by contrast with the post-1945 years, opportunely characterized by a baby-boom and eventually by economic take-off. This powerful and by no means implausible account links population size both explicitly and implicitly with progress and economic development.[8]

In this perspective, the historian could read the Alquier affair as symptomatic of the climate of opinion. The scandal caused by her report could be explained by demographic anxiety, and the decision to prosecute seen as evidence of the watchfulness of a pronatalist movement confident that its views were shared. Pernot had no doubt been alerted to raise the matter in the Assembly by the energetic Alliance Nationale pour l'Accroissement de la Population Française, the chief pronatalist political movement.[9] It could also be read as a sign that no

21

government could afford to ignore pronatalist protests once they had been aroused. After all, elections were due in 1928.

But while staying within a demographical perspective, Henriette Alquier's summons and acquittal could equally well be inserted into a variation on the story, this time stressing the *lack of impact* of punitive policies, such as the 1920 law, on the birth rate figures – with the suggestion that her views might secretly have been shared by many French people. If the case was dismissed, the magistrates must have thought the charges excessive. And the pro-Alquier campaign showed that enough people were sufficiently moved by the cause to express their dissent in public. In other words, the affair drew attention to the *ineffectiveness* of the 1920 law.

Effectiveness became an integral part of the demographic debate. Already, in 1920, the pronatalist *député* Professor Pinard had remarked more in sorrow than in anger that repressive measures would do nothing to alter the birth rate (Guerrand *et al.* 1990: 70). Another pronatalist described the measures as 'a sword-thrust in water'. The logic of effectiveness has been a potent shaper of historical narrative. The routine rhetoric describing the inter-war period as a time of high anxiety but low results informs the reader that it was '*not until* such and such a measure was passed that the population question was being seriously tackled'. Prominent in the logic of effectiveness is the economic argument. Both contemporaries and historians have argued that whereas repression only led to people evading the law, financial encouragement to have children might have produced more results. (In the end, the French state tried both.) Alquier herself had called for state subsidies for motherhood, an approach that might be supported from both left and right. Pronatalists of the right favoured family subsidies across the board, making families with children, whatever their circumstances, better off than those without. Those on the left wanted redistribution in favour of working-class or low income families. Historians, by entering into the effectiveness debate and suggesting that (repressive) measures aimed at raising the birth rate were ineffective, while more vigorous economic ones might have succeeded, appear to accept the premises of the demographic lament, while avoiding what is sometimes seen as the reactionary discourse of pronatalism.[10]

If they wish to avoid the latter it is for two reasons: first because pronatalism has come to be associated with the despised Vichy regime of 1940–4, of which it was an integral policy, and second because of the growth of a more recent libertarian tradition in history, strongly opposed to the demographic lament. By and large, the history of birth control or of 'Malthusianism' has been written by those who approve of it. In this school of history, it is the demographers and pronatalists who are described as irresponsible and backward-looking: French demographers 'have allowed themselves to forget the objectivity required by a scientific work and to succumb to partisan passion' (Ronsin 1980: 227–9). From a libertarian perspective, the inter-war years are viewed, with the Vichy years, as a time of harsh repression. 'Pro-birth control' narrators argue that the spread of contraception has been a force for progress, improving the quality of life of both children and parents. They chronicle the efforts of pioneers of family planning and the opposition they encountered from pronatalism – depicted as the enemy, whether inspired by church or state. Singled out for particular condemnation are the 1920 and 1923 measures outlawing contraception and abortion ('les lois scélérates'). Family allowances, while not openly criticized, are seen as partly vitiated by their incentive force (since they have always rewarded larger families disproportionately). Progress in this context is interpreted as the modern, rational and scientific control of family size: small families would represent a forward-looking rather than a stagnant or backward-looking society. In the progressive agenda, gender is not ignored, but is considered in a campaigning mood rather than analysed, since the 'pro-Malthusian' literature largely dates from the atmosphere of sexual liberation after May 1968, in a France where non-therapeutic abortion was only legalized for the first time in 1974, and where contraception had long been subject to legal restrictions. This literature tends to characterize the inter-war period in adversarial terms, so that the *famille nombreuse* of the pronatalist's dream is read straightforwardly (perhaps a little simple-mindedly), as a site of women's suffering and oppression. In this perspective, Alquier is an anti-authoritarian heroine in a sort of golden legend of progressive pioneers.

As one would expect, she also figures fairly prominently in feminist history. In the first wave of women's history, after 1968, a tale of emancipation was being told, including praise of the unsung heroines of the birth control movement (cf. Bouchardeau 1977). Such narratives take for granted opposition to pronatalism: what interests them is faster or slower progress towards emancipation for women. As historical writings, they reflect the period of their composition, when a generation reacting violently against the ideology of motherhood was campaigning for legal abortion and contraception. The rhetoric takes on a resistance flavour: 'Unmoved by the family propaganda then at its height, women ran their . . . private lives according only to their own aspirations' (Sohn 1992: 95). Although the actual reasons for demographic trends may have been 'complex and not reducible to women's assumed desire, or lack of it, to have children' (Roberts 1994: 123), Alquier can clearly be viewed as a brave resister to the oppression of women, especially working-class women.[11]

These examples certainly don't exhaust the possibilities for tackling the population question, but they indicate some of the main approaches, rooted in demographic history on one hand, and emancipation history on the other. Both logics are perfectly defensible in their own terms, but seem to me unduly limiting.

In the early days of women's history, great hopes were placed in demography as a counterweight to traditional political history, in which no women figured. But, before long, enthusiasts were disconcerted to find

that [even] a pioneering sector like historical demography, should say so little about women, considering them simply as a variable of reproduction; that it takes an interest only in couples, rather than isolates who were probably in the majority, especially among women; and that when it reconstitutes

families, it retains only masculine patronymics, adopting a patrilinear vision
of history.

(Perrot 1984: 9)

The demographic perspective, highlighting the birth rate, had no sooner reintro-
duced women to the historical record than it apparently reduced them from whole
human beings to temporarily fertile bearers of children. Of no period does this
seem to be more true than of the inter-war years.

Perhaps as a result, in general histories of this period, the subject of reproduction
is usually treated as a preliminary structural feature, or located within a discussion
of the economy, rather than given any political dimension. Demography is one of
the few sections of a general historical narrative where sexual difference is always
remarked upon, but it is treated as a fixed 'apolitical' background to a more
chronologically presented, all-male, political history. The 'repressive' laws of 1920
and 1923 are regularly cited in demographic contexts, but not in a political account
of that legislature, and only rarely do they figure in a political chronology.

This segregation is unfortunate and by no means inevitable, for population
policy cannot be separated from politics. As Joan Scott has said of family policies in
general,

> political decisions were represented as protections of natural social relation-
> ships among family members, especially mothers and children. This kind of
> representation depicted social policy as *outside politics* – when in fact vast social
> and political reorganizations were being attempted or implemented.

(Scott 1987: 27)

Similarly, Susan Pedersen has pointed out that certain French employer strategies
in the 1920s and 1930s 'have largely escaped the detection and scrutiny of
historians because they operated through the legally autonomous, ostensibly
benevolent and *apolitical* family allowance funds' (Pedersen 1993b: 288). Defining
what is and what is not political has been one of the major ways of obscuring gender
in the past.

That said, the early campaigning history by feminists and libertarians, while
usefully challenging what it saw as a prevailing pronatalist consensus with political
dimensions, also has blind spots. Its logic is bound by conflict and an oppression/
resistance model, inclining it to give exaggerated importance to prescriptive
material, such as the literature of pronatalism, or the persecution of pioneers, like
Alquier, whose views are more commonplace today. Just as there seems to be little
room to discuss the structures of patriarchy in an account preoccupied with the
effectiveness of measures to promote the birth rate, so there is little room to discuss
the politics of parenthood in a history driven by praise for those who avoided it. This
is not a matter of deliberate omission so much as of priorities. Narrative logics
inevitably lead historians to stress some kinds of data and to ignore or underplay
others. But there is no reason not to explore the gaps and contradictions in what we

have inherited, asking slightly different questions and borrowing the lamp of new research where it exists.

GAPS IN THE STORY

To investigate all the gaps in this complex story would take a book not a chapter. What follows is a brief survey of half a dozen topics linking gender to politics, which seem to have attracted scant attention. The last topic, organized childcare, is treated at a little more length, for reasons to appear.

Let us first consider the *relation between population and electorate*. The most striking statistic every student of these years encounters is the loss of close to 1.5 million Frenchmen, in the prime of their lives, in the 1914 war. Its consequences for the gender balance of the French population are rarely ignored. Everyone knows that there were many more women than men of this age group living in France during the 1920s. But the imbalance is normally approached either within the context of childbearing or in one about ageing. The childbearing consequences are obvious: many of the women widowed during the war had no, or no further children, while some younger women of the wartime generation never married at all. But the second most usual place to find references to gender imbalance in a demographic narrative is in an age pyramid. The logic of the inter-war age pyramid leads one to scan it for its negative demographic factors: namely the absence of young men. France was becoming a country of the old, or as some writers prefer to say, 'of old women', a rhetoric with its own value judgements.[12]

Less remarked upon is a negative political factor: the demographic structure of the electorate. Since the greatest losses were of men in their twenties and thirties during the war, the imbalance between the sexes was reflected in this generation within the French electorate throughout the inter-war years. This could be analysed in a different, political perspective, particularly when seen in conjunction with the growing numbers of of immigrants in the 1920s. Recent research has drawn much more attention to the immigrant groups than demographers traditionally did. Immigrants to France in the 1920s – chiefly Italians, Belgians, Poles and some North Africans – came in response to the call for reconstruction workers. They were mostly male, young and unmarried. Especially during the 1920s, a 'compensatory' male population came to be concentrated in certain areas, made up of men broadly in the age groups of those who had been killed in the war. But the newcomers had no citizenship or voting rights unless, as some later did, they took out naturalization papers. (In the 1930s, in the wake of the depression, many immigrants returned to their country of origin while others had become integrated into French society, so that statistically they became less visible.)[13]

In the 1920s, then, and rather less so in the 1930s, the French republic's electorate, by being confined to French males over twenty-one, excluded the majority of adults resident on French soil, i.e. those who were either not male or not French. The resident population over twenty-one had for a while a very different profile from that of the electorate: it was much younger for one thing. What was more, serving soldiers, 'sous les drapeaux' were not allowed to vote either. For fear of politics in the barracks, especially after the Dreyfus affair, the army was 'la grande muette'. This further removed from the electorate in any given year thousands of young French conscripts who reached their twenty-first birthday while serving, as well as the 28,000 or so regular officers, plus varying numbers of enlisted men. It could be argued that one of the aspects of the 'ageing population' was its ageing electorate, since it excluded so many of the young of both sexes. Statistics for the population after 1918 are not usually presented this way, although contemporaries were aware of the surplus of women: opponents of women's suffrage regularly pointed out that there were more women than men in France, and feared 'rule by petticoat'. But that is a statistic irrelevant either to a narrative about the birth rate (which views women as reproductive machines) or to one about political history (which does not mention immigrants or women at all, on the grounds that they were simply non-voters, a quite different emphasis). The point to be made here is not a counter-factual hypothesis about what might have happened if the French electorate had been larger, rather it is a point first about legitimacy (what exactly do we mean by 'France' or 'the republic' in this period?) and second about population structure. Demographic studies of the period are so concerned with births and deaths that they pay little attention to the composition and profile of the surviving population in the years after the war. All electorates have demographic characteristics, and relate in certain ways to the overall population. It is perhaps ironic that what has been described by political scientists as 'the golden age' of the 'republican model', producing a 'sort of social ecosystem' (Sirinelli *et al.* 1993: 94), should have occurred at the time when the electorate represented a smaller, older and more male proportion of the adult population of France than at any time from 1870 to the present – literally more *patriarchal* than any electorate of the last hundred years.[14]

To turn now to *participants in the population debate*, a distinction which has not been referred to so far is that between pronatalism and the 'mouvement familial' or pro-family lobby. Both these movements have been reassessed in recent times from different perspectives, and I am saying nothing new in distinguishing between them, though there is a tendency in the post-1968 literature to describe them as equally oppressive towards women. That there were considerable differences between them emerges from Robert Talmy's account of the *mouvement familial*, the standard but strongly sympathetic work on the subject. The family movement favoured family values and in particular lobbied for special treatment for large and legitimate families. While approving of a higher birth rate, it stressed the need for rewards for those who had 'done their duty' rather than incentives for those who had not. Most politicians of the early 1920s, sometimes viewed as united in their eagerness to promote both the numerical birth rate and family values, were by Talmy's reckoning 'timid and inadequate' in their approach, failing to choose between 'a policy of natality or one of the family'. Where the family movement wanted legislation banning divorce and pornography (two things it regarded as equally pernicious), parliament, site of 'a profound individualism inherited from the eighteenth century', remained unmoved. It disregarded the wishes of the family movement that benefits should go to legitimate children only (Talmy 1962, vol. 1: 118–19, 243–5, 248–9, etc.). The historian of the Alliance Nationale puts it more strongly, claiming that most parliamentarians of the 1920s were more bothered about 'the exchange rate than the birth rate . . . the falling franc rather than the falling number of children' (Tomlinson 1986: 147–9, 139). While both pronatalists and familialists found it hard to retain the average politician's attention, the pronatalists were more successful in promoting their agenda.

From a post-1968 point of view, the family movement, with its roots in Catholic values, was no doubt more 'reactionary' than the republican pronatalists described by Tomlinson. But from the point of view of women's history, it is in the family movement that women actors are to be found, rather than in a pronatalist movement confined largely to male scientific and political circles. In both movements, leaders and opinion makers were overwhelmingly male. But there is a distinction to be made between the two. 'Quantitative' pronatalism in the shape of the Alliance Nationale, according to its historian, did not invite any particular comment from women: it simply never seriously asked itself why women might be reluctant to have many children (Tomlinson 1986: 165). By contrast, certain women were more present and vociferous in the family movement. The allowance for 'mothers who stayed at home' was campaigned for ardently from 1927 by one women's association, the social Catholic Union Féminine Civique et Sociale, led by Andrée Butillard. The UFCS made much of the findings of its enquiries into working women's lives, particularly one survey indicating that married women worked in factories only because they needed the money and would prefer not to. In the 1930s, the Ligue de la Mère au Foyer, created by the UFCS, agitated to have the question of an allowance for stay-at-home mothers put on the parliamentary agenda. Eventually enshrined in the Code de la Famille, this particular benefit, modified as an allowance payable to single-income households, accounted for the highest total of payments under family legislation during the Second World War. The campaign for it obviously bolstered traditional views of women as mothers and it certainly doesn't fit any progressive model of 'feminism'. But as between the quantitative and qualitative approaches to demography, if one can put it that way, we find some articulate and strong-minded women prominent in the latter. They placed a positive value on motherhood and wanted its conditions to be improved, rather than engaging in militaro-numerical arguments. Whether or not they can be called feminists (a matter of dispute), they were playing a non-negligible role. By stressing the care of children already born, they were in a way the counterparts to the social hygienists and gynaecologists, men for the most part, who sought to reduce infant mortality. These women may, as Susan Pedersen suggests, have been caught up in a process they did not ultimately control, but they cannot be described as being 'outside' politics.[15]

A third area of enquiry informed by gender politics is that of *family allowances*. Most demographically centred accounts look favourably on the spread of family allowances, but say little about the differential impact of the system on men and women. The history of allowances in France starts with bonus pay schemes for male workers with children offered by Catholic textile employers in the years before and during the First World War; it continues with the law of 1932 obliging more employers to bring their workforce into the schemes, and culminates, pre-war, in the Code de la Famille of 1938–9. Family allowances (to this day financed out of employers' contributions) remain an element of French state policy to encourage the births of more children, and the tariff is still incremental, that is weighted to third and later children. There is by now a large body of specialized literature.[16] But since, outside such works, the subject is usually approached within the logic of effectiveness in encouraging the birth rate, some aspects of it are less obvious.

A major aspect of family allowance policy, recognized by French trade unionists at the time, and highlighted in Pedersen's recent study, is that those responsible for introducing it did not *necessarily* have demographic expansion or family welfare as their main motive. While such concerns may have motivated some early pioneers, the plans to expand the system were to protect employers who did make the extra payment to workers with children from competition from those who did not, hence the collaboration of large employers to set up common *caisses* or funds. Furthermore, by redistributing the wage bill in favour of workers with children, it displaced the need for higher wages across the board, the preferred option of the trade unions. The French employer-led initiative can also be seen as strategically designed to reduce worker radicalism in certain cases, by tying payments to loyalty to the firm, or to regular attendance. Welcomed by pronatalists in high places, the system became too entrenched to be reversed, especially since the trade union movement was weak during the critical years in the later 1920s and early 1930s.

The system was a strange mixture of patriarchy and delegation of power to women, a paradox that emerges clearly if one asks who received the money of the family allowance. In Britain, it was a 'core feminist demand' that the money should be paid to the mother, rather along the lines that Henriette Alquier had advocated, as compensation for the social function of motherhood, and to provide mothers with some independent resources. In France, on the other hand, there was powerful pressure to insist that the *père de famille* should control this money. When in 1921 a proposal was made to pay the state bonuses for large families (a different scheme from the family allowance) directly to the mother, as the person most likely to be caring for the children, it was withdrawn in the face of opposition to this insult to the paterfamilias. However, as Pedersen points out, 'industrialists felt no such deference to their male employees' regarding family allowances. For fear that fathers might not direct the money to children but spend it elsewhere, such as at the café, the Parisian fund always sent the postal orders to mothers, and persuaded the government that it should continue to do so after 1932. The same was true of several other funds, for pragmatic rather than ideological reasons; it had nothing to do with women's rights or rewarding motherhood (Pedersen 1993b: 129–30, 270–80, 402 ff.).

Feminists could be found on either side in this debate, either arguing for the

28

allowance to be paid in recognition of motherhood, or on the contrary saying that it was likely to tie women into their domestic roles ever more firmly. Interestingly enough, the UFCS, being 'reluctant to question the legitimacy of family hierarchy', did not before 1939 press for payment to be made to mothers. Either way, women's voices were not always heeded in a debate that was hijacked by other interests. Its most relevant aspect for us is the way a formally patriarchal system depended for its operation on those who were not its supposed agents. In most families (unless headed by a working widow) the allowance resulted from a relation between the children's father and his employer, that is, it was based on the concept of the *père de famille*. Yet clear instructions were given by most fund administrators to pay the benefit directly to a woman. The married woman, who was not allowed to be civilly responsible until 1938, and who was an un-person in the entitlement procedures, was regarded as the more 'responsible' parent, when it suited the authorities to do so. A communication network was being created and would be extended by the intervention of social workers – themselves all women – specifically singling out women as the agents of transmission for new forms of social benefits (or some might say social control), for which the inter-war period was the testing time. As Pedersen remarks,

> To put money in the hands of any individual – mother, father or social worker – is to make a decision about personal, as well as collective rights. It offers officials a chance to favour some family members against others and to alter, perhaps decisively, the distribution within the family itself.
>
> (Pedersen 1993a: 261)

This can be viewed as a pragmatic decision in the interests of children, or as an attempt to divide and rule within the working-class family, hoping that wives would dissuade their husbands from jeopardizing the allowance through militancy or by changing jobs. Either way, the French state (or its agent in the form of the family allowance funds) depended on a large number of female non-citizens to take on responsibility for a system devised without their formal participation. Arguments about the effectiveness of the scheme have obscured the extent to which public policy used gender as a criterion for distribution.[17]

More difficult to situate historically is the impact of *legislation on abortion and contraception*. Recent research has lifted the taboo on trying to explore this area, where sources are inadequate and unreliable and where recourse to conjecture is inevitable.[18] Since birth rates remained low, despite the legislation, it seems logical to conclude that the laws were indeed 'ineffective'. My proposal here would be that the inter-war years should be contextualized in relation to the historical record as a whole. Between the wars, it is true, both pronatalists and pro-family movements deplored the high rate of abortion and campaigned for even sterner penalties. Between the wars, it is true, certain kinds of contraceptives were banned and sex education was not available. But, in any case, contraception was a matter of luck rather than judgement. The law was a comparatively small obstacle compared to the inbuilt problems of avoiding pregnancy, before modern contraceptives.

To limit [the number of births] there were only very simple methods: withdrawal, soap, male condoms. The Ogino method was much debated at the time. In fact what people mostly said was that there was less risk during a woman's period. Yes, there were many, many abortions.

(Thébaud 1986: 299)

Common sense suggests that this remained true right down to the 1960s and beyond in France. Opponents to pronatalism have given the 1920/1923 legislation a particularly high historical profile as oppressive and barbaric. It bears the brunt of post-1968 disapproval of anti-abortion and anti-contraception measures. But it is not always made clear that the 1920 and 1923 legislation is *still* in force in France: the more liberal laws on abortion and contraception brought in in the 1970s did not repeal these laws, they merely replaced sections of them. Post-war politicians had not raised the issue. Vasectomy is still technically illegal in France. The 1919 'Chambre bleu horizon' has been blamed more on this count than the Daladier government, backed by the more left-wing assembly elected at the time of the Popular Front. Yet Daladier's Code de la Famille of 1938–9 imposed even stiffer penalties for abortion, a practice regarded as out of control by the late 1930s.

The rhetoric of anti-natalism tends to my mind to put a misleading emphasis on the 1920s repression, while minimizing something that *was* distinctive about these years: namely much more sexual anxiety than the years before or since. The risk of falling pregnant was literally an everyday matter until about the 1960s, but during the inter-war years many French couples, mostly in the urban middling classes, did have smaller families on average than before 1914 or after 1945. The reality concealed behind ironic comments about 'ineffectiveness' must have been one of considerable worry. The risk of unwanted pregnancy was averted every month, uncomfortably but voluntarily by most men in the form of withdrawal; and when that did not work, it was averted more painfully and dangerously by many women. The evidence is circumstantial and sometimes transmuted into fiction, but it is hard to escape the conclusion that anxiety about unwanted conception was a structure of everyday life, not an exceptional event.[19] The rate of anxiety may not have been quite so high before 1914 (birth rates were not so low; urbanization was less advanced) or after 1945 (birth rates were high, children were apparently more desired). A new anguish about unwanted births surfaced again in the early 1960s – only now within a very different generation of French people who, instead of holding their peace, called for a change in the law. Many analyses of post-1960s change assume that freedom from pregnancy has been a major factor in the leap in women's employment and changed attitudes. But freedom from prolonged child-bearing had been reached statistically at least two generations earlier. Was that earlier relative freedom from childbearing, already there for the inter-war genera-tion of women, bought at a high price of constant anxiety that prevented them using such freedom in other ways? In order to build this elusive material into a narrative about gender relations, we need to de-connect it from repressive rules which were not unique to these years. The banning of abortion, in particular, or as one might now put it, the non-medicalization of abortion, had existed long before 1914 and was to last until 1974.

Finally, we come to the heart of the subject, the children who were born during these years, the *desired objects of public policy.* Childbirth, along with conception, the central traumatic enactment of the birth rate, is unaccountably missing not only from the demographic literature, but from the emancipation narratives too. Françoise Thébaud's was the first detailed study of childbirth in inter-war France and it remains oddly isolated and under-used, since it does not quite fit anyone's agenda. Demographers have always tended to reduce childbirth to statistical formulae. Even a recent comprehensive survey like the *Histoire de la population française* (Dupâquier 1988) still has little to say on the subject. There are separate chapters on fertility rates and population policy, but public welfare is referred to only briefly in a chapter on medicine, while developments in the conditions of childbirth are not detailed at all. The point is well made by one contributor, Martine Segalen. Referring briefly to the reduction of the number of deaths in childbirth and the fall in perinatal mortality during the twentieth century as a whole, she writes:

> Such medical advances are comparable to the revolution of moving from candle light to electricity, but for some mysterious reason (in a country as obsessed with the birth rate as France) they have passed comparatively unnoticed, or are pushed into the background, behind the noisy claims made [in recent years] for 'painless' childbirth for instance.
>
> (Segalen in Dupâquier 1988: 508)

Thébaud's book devoted to the medicalization of childbirth points out that this led to regimentation as well as progress, but pays particular attention to the 'hygienists', the doctors, paediatricians and social reformers whose concern was to preserve life once the child was born, rather than to encourage more births. Her narrative aims to be 'both a contribution to the history of women and to the history of medicine in its battle against infant deaths'. As a result, she sheds more light on the subject of childbearing as a reality than either the demographers or their challengers. But her work and that of other specialists on the structures of childbirth has still to be fully absorbed either into recent demographic history or into the history of women's emancipation, let alone into the textbooks.

What strikes us today about the inter-war period as compared to the years before 1914, for all the emphasis on pronatalism, is the relative absence of *national* policies focused on childbirth, or of formal legislation about the monitoring of child welfare. It is not just that it is mis-remembered: it was difficult to get it on to the statute book. In 1920, the indefatigable activist Senator Paul Strauss had proposed a co-ordinated system of monitoring child welfare, the *carnet de santé.* The proposal shuttled to and fro between the two chambers of parliament for fourteen years before being rejected eventually, because funds could not be found. Catherine Rollet's very detailed thesis on Third Republic policy on small children, which describes this proposal, reveals clearly how much more was done in this area before

31

1914 than after. There was certainly concern in welfare and medical quarters over child health after 1918, as will be seen in a later chapter, but with the brief exception of the Popular Front government, action was often left to local administration and private initiatives. *Size of family* seems to be the only subject in this area with a real parliamentary profile, and therefore perhaps the only subject to have a regular place in the history books.[20]

If at this point we think back to Henriette Alquier's report, it is hard not to connect the selective response of the authorities in 1927 with the selective historical picture that has come to dominate the topic. The authorities did not react to her criticism of child poverty, nor to the stark infant mortality statistics, but they responded smartly to her mention of birth control. If, in turn, this is all that the historian reacts to in the Alquier affair, she is allowing the single-mindedness of both pronatalists and birth control supporters to push other questions off the historical agenda.

So I have chosen to end by shifting the focus to a different section of Henriette Alquier's report, namely the inadequate number of crèches. Care of young children is a question to which neither the demographic nor the libertarian approach pays much attention. But it enables us to signpost what will be a thread running throughout this book: the discrepancy between the political issues given a high profile by the male-dominated parliament and those that were struggling to be born, so to speak. Both national and local authorities, whether with reluctance or alacrity, were starting to recognize that social security, public health, welfare and other kinds of social intervention were going to be part of twentieth-century government. The inter-war period in France was a time of piecemeal and some-times incomplete initiatives, but in almost all cases they affected French people of both sexes, and increasingly they drew women into the mechanisms of provision because of gendered assumptions about women's sphere of action. We have already noted that this was one, usually neglected, aspect of family allowances. The crèche, although created much earlier, saw a shift in attitudes towards it during these years which can be related to political change.

THE CRÈCHE AS POLITICAL ISSUE

A French invention, the first crèche in the world was opened in Paris in the 1840s by J.-B. F. Marbeau, a local official and representative of social Catholicism, motivated by charity.[21] It was destined for babies whose mothers, 'poor, honest and hard-working, are obliged to work outside the home'. Originally, no fees were charged and the staff were either voluntary or paid from mainly private funds. In the Paris region, the number of crèches grew steadily from 7 in 1846 to 45 in 1880 and 73 in 1892. By the eve of the First World War, in 1913, there were 115.

The motivation for the first crèches was humanitarian concern with the high infant mortality rates caused both by poverty and by farming children out to wet-nurses, a common practice in nineteenth-century French cities.[22] These were early days for public intervention into childcare, preceding the Pasteur revolution. In practice, the early crèches themselves had high mortality figures, but in time they could claim to have a better record than the wet-nurse. They were not universally welcomed or used. Most private crèches refused to take illegitimate children and few were originally provided in areas where many working-class parents lived. Mothers are reported to have considered them unhealthy, unkind and possibly given to using pernicious narcotics to keep the babies quiet (Fuchs 1988: 306).

Supporters of the crèches argued that 'however inadequate they might be' they were better than the alternative. Senator Strauss, a leading figure in the campaign for maternity leave, and other welfare measures for mothers, gave his blessing to the crèche at a lecture in 1901:

> crèches and residential nurseries [*pouponnières*] are ... protective and life-saving institutions ... there was a time when the crèche was misunderstood, but now we can see that it enables working mothers to have their children cared for and fed.[23]

All the same, he stressed, it was a 'second-best', a *pis-aller*, a view shared by both philanthropists and pronatalists who viewed it as a lesser evil, not unlike the Gouttes de Lait ('drops of milk') charity, which provided germ-free milk in hygienic conditions for babies who could not be breastfed.

Greater reticence about the early crèches was expressed on the left and in progressive circles. The main reason was their association with private charity, and in most cases with the church. Crèche attendants were sometimes members of religious orders, sometimes *dames de bonnes oeuvres*. Republican town councils (all-male at this date) withdrew subsidies from some of the early crèches in northern France on these grounds; factory crèches, inaugurated in some northern textile mills, were seen as bosses' crèches. The preferred model on the left was the municipal crèche, but until 1914 these had no official standing: local councils provided subsidies but rarely took reponsibility for existing crèches, almost always private foundations. Feminists were not particularly enthusiastic about the crèche at this time either.[24]

The factory crèche attained new visibility during the First World War, with the drive to recruit women into munitions from late 1915 onwards. As large-scale recruitment of women into factories took place, the emphasis shifted significantly. First the workplace crèche on the mill-town pattern (rather than the local crèche) became more frequent; second, greater stress was laid on the *nursing mother* rather than on the working mother in general. The Comité du Travail Féminin, created in April 1916 and presided over by Strauss, pressed for both crèches and nursing facilities, but only the latter reached the statute book with the law of 5 August 1917. This specified that all establishments employing over 100 women should provide a *salle d'allaitement* (nursing room) and that nursing mothers should have extra breaks morning and afternoon to feed their infants. Nursing rooms were cheaper since the law called only for 'decent shelter' and trained staff were not required to supervise the 'sleeping' babies. Sometimes the nursing room was simply the concierge's lodge. Of the large firms covered by the law, while 75 per cent had a nursing room by spring 1918, only 20 per cent had a crèche. There were spectacular exceptions, for example at the Citroën works where a nearby school was converted to give 200 crèche places. But many places remained unfilled: women disliked taking a baby on long journeys to work, and the draconian hygienic rules in force may also have been a deterrent: mothers told inspectors that they felt more free with informal child-minders. The garment-makers' union, whose members were mostly women, expressed a clear preference for the municipal crèche over the workplace crèche, and for weekly residential nurseries staffed and controlled by workers' representatives.[25]

In other words, much of the pressure in favour of wartime childcare still came not from mothers but from official bodies concerned with the health and hygiene of the newborn, with the laudable aim of reducing infant mortality (which was still 100 per thousand in 1914). The facilities provided, with the best of intentions, were designed to combine hygiene with the requirements of arms production, rather than the priorities of working mothers. The wartime nurseries were a solution, imposed from above, for a problem still being interpreted as the need to medicalize and regulate working-class motherhood, while meeting wartime production needs.

When the munitions factories laid off women workers after the war, nurseries closed too. But as the 1921 census shows, many married women were still in industrial employment. The 1920s saw expansion of existing workplace crèches and the creation of some municipal nurseries depending on the politics of the council. Unlike in Britain, it seems that the efforts of concerned groups before the war to promote the crèche as a better solution than the wet-nurse had succeeded in legitimizing the crèche in a way that has never happened in Britain. Precisely because the crèche had been promoted as *beneficial for children rather than convenient for mothers*, it could readily be included within municipal socialism's welfare policies, without necessarily shocking pronatalist opinion. In fact what seems to have happened between the wars is that while pronatalists grew increasingly hostile to the crèche, calling instead for mothers to stay at home with young children, the 'welfare left' came to look on it with more favour than before.

Statistics on crèche attendance between the wars are fragmentary. But the reports of factory inspectors during the 1920s indicate that some nursing rooms and crèches were opened: women in state employment in particular, such as the tobacco factories, benefited from stricter observance of the law. In 1930, almost every Paris postal district had a crèche for the children of women postal workers. In the private sector, in textile mills and sugar refineries, crèches and nursing rooms were being created, in some cases after requests from the workforce. Facilities could vary greatly in the number of places, the age of the children and the quality of care provided. Some workplace crèches were short-lived. Nevertheless, while never widespread, the factory crèche was a definite reality between the wars, benefiting from the wartime legislation and to some extent blurring the difference between the crèche and the nursing room.[26]

The same period saw the rise of the municipal crèche. Socialist town councils elected in 1919 launched some ambitious municipal projects such as school complexes with a crèche attached. Henri Sellier, mayor of Suresnes, just outside Paris, had a programme that included 'protecting early infancy by developing *crèches-garderies*, strictly supervised medically and run by well qualified staff'. But socialist town councillors did not take the same view of the crèche as the pronatalists. For the left, the crèche was part of an overall effort to improve the health of the working class, rather than raise the birth rate. Tuberculosis was still a major illness in working-class districts and as much stress was laid by socialists on child health clinics, open-air schools or holiday camps as on the crèche, rarely singled out as a priority.

Much the same would be true of the communists when in 1935 they made their political breakthrough, winning control of a number of municipal councils, many in the Paris region. The attitude of the official left, whether communist or socialist, can be seen as a reformulation of that of the philanthropists before 1914. Crèche provision was primarily part of a crusade for healthier working-class children. It was certainly not an attack on the family (indeed the Communist party quite energetically promoted family values in the mid-1930s as part of its campaign of 'the outstretched hand').[27] Still less was it a move towards the liberation of women. If the crèche was at this time becoming identified as a 'progressive' cause, it was in the context of rescuing social services from charitable, often religious bodies, which were pilloried in the left-wing press for inefficiency and dogmatism. That there was little mention, even on the left, of the crèche as a means of freeing mothers to go to work is hardly surprising. But one might perhaps have expected to hear such arguments from women's or feminist organizations.

As hinted above, 'feminism' in France in this period could vary from the radical to the very sedate. Most feminists were rather guarded in their public pronouncements on collective services, and those who went on record for radical solutions to childrearing were generally isolated figures. Madeleine Pelletier, a socialist feminist doctor, had called in her book *La Désintégration de la famille* for collective services of all kinds. 'Society should be run so that the child can be born and thrive without the woman having to sacrifice any of the full development of her individuality' (Bouchardeau 1977: 198). But the official conference of socialist women, held in 1933 to discuss women's work during the depression, was more cautious, simply passing a resolution calling for 'more crèches and residential nurseries, and all public establishments designed to protect the children of the workers'. This embodies the welfare view of the crèche rather than a call for freeing mothers for work.[28]

What was new was that women's groups closer to the political right were for the first time beginning to come out more strongly *against* the crèche. The UFCS, which we have already met, also held a conference in 1933 on working mothers in industry. In line with the UFCS's family-first approach, feeling was overwhelmingly opposed to the crèche. In 1925 Senator Strauss was still arguing that 'the crèches have not in the least lost their usefulness as a second-best to assist mothers who cannot devote themselves entirely, wholeheartedly and exclusively to the upbringing of their babies.'[29] But at the UFCS conference, Mlle Lalieux's general report said: 'However many crèches and nursing rooms are created, their advantages will never compensate for the harmful effects of journeys in all weathers and at all hours, the sudden transition from the warmth of the nursery to the cold of the street, the jolting of trains and buses . . . . If a mother is in the habit of leaving a child with a minder, or in a crèche, she is unlikely to have more children.'[30] A spate of books and articles arguing for the 'return of the mother to the home' came from both men and women associated with the UFCS in the late 1920s and early 1930s, swelling the flood of pronatalist literature that attacked working mothers. There seems to have been little or no reaction from other women's groups in defence of the crèche, though they did defend married women's (as distinct from mothers') right to work, increasingly under attack during the depression.

From the evidence available, it seems that during the inter-war years the crèche stopped being seen by social Catholics and philanthropists as a necessary weapon in the crusade to protect infants – while this had never been the chief concern of the pronatalists. It is significant that the Code de la Famille made no mention at all of the crèche. Some pronatalists began to attack the crèche as a pernicious encouragement to mothers to work. On the left, by contrast, the crèche was beginning to find favour (if not without reservations) as part of the programme to improve the health and welfare of the working class. It had become an institution, if not as yet a very widespread one: in 1940 there were about 360 crèches in France, with a total of 12,000 places (Davidson 1964). The children in the crèche were mostly from urban families of modest means, and at this stage it was very far from being firmly established as a feminist demand.

CONCLUSION

By considering the beginning of Henriette Alquier's report, as well as the end, we can begin to contextualize both the demographic lament and the objections of its opponents. The increase or decrease in the birth rate between the wars was only one aspect of the population question, admittedly an important one. But it has been singled out for special attention since it relates very closely to the preoccupations of various writers since the last war. Whether reminding people of the perpetual threat of depopulation (still a force in French government policy) or celebrating the move to more liberal laws on sexuality, these writers have helped to shape the historical dimensions of the population question in ways that cut it loose from the political context of its own time. But the population question was not somehow free-standing: it was one of the clearest ways in which ordinary French people of both sexes were jointly implicated in political decisions. It was related for instance to the labour relations policies of French employers; in other respects to the clerical question and the parliamentary balance of power; and lastly to the politics of welfare provision which were gradually being devised both by the state and local authorities. On all these points, political interests sometimes clashed. We have already noted that the Alquier case came at an awkward moment in the 1924–8 Assembly's life.

In terms of participants in the debate, the apparent monopoly of male politicians in this area can be seen as less than complete. We may not have much direct access to the opinions of the women who were the budget-holders when family allowances were paid out, or to those who used and staffed the crèches. But it cannot be said that women's voices went unheard. Any investigation of the crèche, as indeed of any kind of welfare during this period, quickly shows that large numbers of women, whether for or against the crèche, expressed views on it: they might be factory inspectors such as Gabrielle Letellier, teachers like Henriette Alquier, activists like Mlle Lalieux or Madeleine Pelletier, or women workers communicating with the authorities through their trade union or the inspectorate. The entire staff in every crèche was of course composed of women. Henriette Alquier herself, like all these women, had no voting rights at the time of her trial: she was literally not a French citizen. Yet she stood at the centre of a political row in which she played an active part. True, she was hardly a 'typical French woman', since she had pronounced radical views, not widely shared. But neither was she in an obscure or marginalized social position. As a trained primary schoolteacher, she was one of thousands of educated working women in France benefiting from equal pay (achieved in 1920), blocked by no marriage bar (as she would have been in Britain), and playing a full role in the state educational machine on which the Third Republic was so explicitly dependent. In no sense was she outside politics. Her case draws attention to the contradiction between formal enfranchisement (being a citizen with a vote), and the possibility of making a political impact.

Citizenship and the birth rate might be linked by some kinds of rhetoric. After the 1919 Assembly vote in favour of women's suffrage, feminists had hoped that French women would become citizens, a hope dashed by the Senate in 1922. In the interval, the feminist Dr Clotilde Mulon, medical officer to a munitions factory during the war prepared a report (1920) of a 'co-ordinated plan of action for the medical, hygienic, moral and financial protection of motherhood among working women', a copy of which also reached the Conseil Supérieur de la Natalité. In it she strikingly connected repopulation, citizenship and child welfare:

> I am myself aware how illogical it is to campaign for an increase in the number of *citizens*, when we cannot house those who are alive or prevent them dying from tuberculosis, nor even to avoid the most avoidable ills. I should not allow myself to preach repopulation if I did not hope that the time was close when our *democracy* will become aware of its duties towards the family. [My italics][31]

In other words, a woman doctor, well-connected to those in power, was assuming that 'the time was close' when women would vote and when citizenship and child welfare would be more explicitly connected.

2

FROM KINDERGARTEN TO YOUTH HOSTEL

Growing up between the wars

In Breughel's painting *Children's Games*, the canvas is filled with images of children playing. Some games are played only by boys, some only by girls; a few are mixed. It offers a tempting image for approaching the gendered history of children (or indeed adults). If one were to paint out all the girls, one would be left with a set of all-boy games (football, politics) which would keep their coherence and assume greater importance within the overall picture. Where the girls had figured, on the other hand, there would be a set of gaps, hidden games (skipping, convents) about which nothing would be known. Some games played by both sexes would have become hard to understand (hide-and-seek, the family). Not only that, but we would have lost all sense of balance between the children. And the same would be true the other way round, if we had lost the boys.

It is in reaction to the historical 'painting out of the girls' that so much effort on the part of women's history has gone into painting them back in. The sexes require equal attention if the painting is to make sense. But giving equal attention is not quite enough: the dynamics of the picture have also to be worked out. Breughel's playground is really a dictionary of games, a set of structures, harmoniously portrayed. Real playgrounds are the site of power and conflict as much as of co-operation and harmony: some children are excluded, some games are off limits. If both sexes are present, the power games will have a gendered aspect.

The previous chapter looked at the way childbirth has been selectively remembered and written about, with political overtones. The subject of this chapter is the separation or mixing of the sexes in their youth in inter-war France. French has a term, 'la mixité' which is missing in English. Literally 'mixedness', it can be defined as 'the coexistence of two sexes in a shared social space'. Only recently has this term attracted serious attention. Long a contentious issue in French education, co-education was achieved during the 1970s, whereupon interest in it waned and it was comparatively little examined. Did 'mixité' imply an alignment on the male norm? Or the coexistence of separate 'others'? Is a genuine 'mix' in any sense possible?[1] Historians have found themselves rather constrained in discussing it. In the history of secondary education, for instance, they have usually found it convenient to talk about boys and girls separately, rather than to attempt any synchronic comparisons. There are good reasons for doing so. Most aspects of the educational system were devised with boys in mind, before provision was made for girls. The chronology is different and the institutions were separate – in the secondary sector, girls had distinct syllabuses, examinations and diplomas from about the 1880s to the 1920s.

The question to be addressed here is a little different: was the inter-war period one in which relations between the sexes in childhood and youth changed significantly? Could children and young people now begin to think of themselves as the 'younger generation', in ways that altered their relation to the other sex? Further, can we explore through this subject the 'undergrowth of politics', the factors which might alter relations between the sexes in the political culture, the subject of later chapters?

To approach the history of childhood or youth is to walk out on to quicksands.[2] Our sources are invariably at some remove: memories of childhood from adults who have left it far behind; prescriptive literature on how to bring up children; histories of education based on official texts; random collections of diaries, letters, family papers; schoolbooks, novels and children's literature. Furthermore, the subject is inherently unstable. Childrearing habits did not change quickly or evenly in the past. Between the wars, some French children were being brought up as their own parents had been before 1914. The children's reader *Le Tour de la France par deux enfants*, written in 1877, was still being used in French primary schools in the 1930s, at a time when its young readers were also discovering Mickey Mouse.[3]

For all the continuities, the inter-war period differed in several respects from the *belle époque*. But how? Antoine Prost argues that this was not a 'generation of rebels', that the weight of the Great War lay heavily on its shoulders, and that the major divisions between young people remained those of class. Gérard Cholvy, on the other hand, has argued that 'the post-war adolescent was less docile than his (her) predecessors. Family discipline was slacker' (Prost 1987a; Cholvy *et al.* 1986, vol. 2: 385). It is hard to agree or disagree with generalizations as broad as this, but one can examine their implications for the gender divide. From a sheaf of possible subjects, this chapter concentrates on three topics: the literary horizons of the young child when more children's books and comics were being published than ever before; changes in French secondary schooling; and the birth of the youth movements, from scouts and guides to the young communist leagues, something which touched the lives of many French adolescents in the 1920s and 1930s. These topics are not marginal or neglected, but they are not usually discussed simultaneously, nor approached from the viewpoint of *mixité*.

MIXITÉ AND LITERACY AMONG THE VERY YOUNG

Learning to read took place for most children in a single-sex environment, at primary school. Compulsory schooling started at the age of six, when boys and girls were sent to separate schools. Some, especially in towns and from poorer families, might have attended the mixed *école maternelle*, literally mother-school, known elsewhere as nursery school or kindergarten.[4] But nursery schools were seen as a branch of welfare at this time rather than of education, and were staffed entirely by women. No men set foot in the nursery school, except when the governors visited or when there was an inspection – on which occasion they represented the authority of the outside (masculine) world, entering an extension of the (feminine) home. Not much reading went on there, though François Cavanna, the child of an Italian bricklayer and a French charwoman, claims to have learnt to read at the 'nursery school on the boulevard Galliéni' in Nogent-sur-Marne in the late 1920s from some 'very old picture-books, their pages torn, full of ogres and toads and bears and devils.... The colours ran over the edges of the drawings, especially the blood – and there was plenty of blood.... I know now that they were albums of Epinal prints, dating from the time of Napoleon III' (Cavanna 1978: 181–2).

The decision to separate the sexes at the age of six originated with the church, and was perpetuated by the Republic. François Jacquet-Francillon has written illuminatingly about the church's belief that mixing the sexes would lead to precocious sexuality (in Baudoux *et al.* 1992: 18–40). The proposals to expand schooling for girls after the 1830s caused problems for small villages without enough resources for two schools. In the nineteenth century, what seem to us extravagant measures were adopted to keep the sexes apart in the classroom – a wooden partition between the boys and girls, staggered school hours, or even exchanges between villages. By the early twentieth century, such devices had mostly been abandoned, but the general rule was for single-sex primary schools, except in very small villages. Although the syllabus was broadly the same, the girls in the primary sector were still supposed to be learning sewing, cooking and childcare long after the requirement for boys to do 'military training' had lapsed. Several studies have commented on the different syllabuses and textbooks for girls and boys, indicating that a thoroughly domestic ideology was directed at the girls in state primary education.[5] On the other hand, we still know comparatively little about what happened in practice, or whether schooling was really very different in mixed or single-sex schools. There are plenty of references in memoirs to segregation, fewer to the actual relations.[6]

But in one respect at least, boys and girls were faced with a different context from that of previous generations: what they could read. Whatever their social class, children of the inter-war years were more exposed than any previous generation to a wealth of reading matter deliberately aimed at them, whether school textbook or children's comic (*illustré*). Did this bring the sexes together or pull them apart? This section samples the imperfect evidence on the 'uses of literacy' out of school.

The *école Jules Ferry* did not make France literate at a stroke. In the towns, literacy had already broadly been achieved before 1900, though in rural districts there were still some elderly people baffled by the written word. But by 1914, several generations of schoolchildren had been through the elementary school syllabus from the age of six to twelve or thirteen. Reading matter for children and young people was a growth area in publishing. Alongside studies of schoolbooks (often from a gendered perspective) there is now more research on children's literature. Such work tells us above all what was produced. The main issues it discusses are those of censorship (by teachers and parents); class (content of stories); quality (how well produced and long lasting books were); and national culture (to what extent there is a French children's book tradition). References are sometimes made to boys' or girls' preferences; and many books were explicitly identified as for one or other sex. But there is little systematic study of 'reading by gender'.[7] It is not an easy field to survey. For children's reactions to books, the historian is usually confined to non-contemporary evidence, the memories of adults recalling (and reconstructing) their childhood days.[8] Some French children growing up between the wars later became famous and often-quoted witnesses – articulate and engaging ones perhaps, though hardly typical of their generation. Their testimony is valuable but has to be handled with care.

What these ex-children often report is first, that in the early years of the century the classics were still their staple fare, but second, that they were starting to be tempted by the alluring new comic papers. In one of the rare contemporary records of children's views, the 'readers' journal' of the Paris children's library L'Heure Joyeuse, virtually all the books singled out as 'our favourites' are translations of English-language classics.[9] Jules Verne and the Comtesse de Ségur were still the favourite French authors for the well read (Renonciat 1991: 26). Such authors might be thought difficult going for children less privileged than that omnivorous reader, the infant Sartre: 'I began my life as I shall no doubt end it: surrounded by books. In my grandfather's study they were everywhere' (Sartre 1964: 29). But picture books and illustrated magazines for children had already started to appear before the Great War, to gladden the hearts of the 'génération de 1904', as Pascal Ory calls it (Sartre was born in 1905). The most famous – or the best remembered – of these early children's comics were L'Epatant (b. 1908), Cri-Cri (b. 1911) and La Semaine de Suzette (b. 1905), destined to see a host of competitors between the wars. They seem to have been intended for sex-segregated readerships to some extent, although one cannot be sure that brothers and sisters did not read each other's weekly magazines.[10] If their autobiographies can be trusted (a big if), both the young Sartre and the young Cavanna, fifteen years his junior and from a very different background, shared a taste for comics. Here is Sartre on his 'vraies lectures' – indulged in alongside his precocious forays as 'a miniature adult with adult reading habits'. Fearing brain fever for her son, who read nothing but the classics,

> during one of our walks, Anne-Marie [Madame Sartre] stopped as if by chance at the kiosk which still stands on the corner of the Boulevard Saint-Michel and the Rue Soufflot: marvellous pictures greeted my eye, their bright colours fascinated me. I clamoured for them and had my way. I was captivated. I wanted to buy them every week after that: Cri-Cri, L'Epatant, Les Vacances, Les Trois Boy-Scouts by Jean de la Hire, and Le Tour du Monde en Aéroplane by Arnould Galopin, which came out in instalments on Thursdays.
> (Sartre 1964: 57–8)

Cavanna, by contrast, had to read his comics in secret. He had by now

41

discovered the classics in the schoolroom, but at home was reduced to reading the labels on the Camembert. Eventually he persuaded his mother to buy him *Le Petit Illustré*, which he swapped with a schoolfriend for *L'Epatant*. 'When you got caught with that in your satchel at school, even if you weren't reading it, that was that: confiscated.' Worse still, the priest prescribed only safe comics: 'I knew about these – the sort of stuff that the children read in the houses where my mother went to clean. Goody-goody and boring' (Cavanna 1978: 257–9).

In both sets of reminiscences the adventure comic for boys seems to have been part of a personally constructed masculine identity, something that set one apart from girls. The three disreputable Pieds Nickelés, rogues who figured regularly in *L'Epatant*, were famous for the extravagance and vulgarity of their language, for instance – unsuitable for girls' eyes. They could either reinforce or replace real-life adventures. The lonely young Sartre had to imagine that the other boys in the Luxembourg Gardens invited him to be the swashbuckling Pardaillan in their adventure games. His adventures were male fantasies. Possibly the same is even true of his claims about his 'vraies lectures' – as a rule forbidden to children of his milieu.

If boys would not be seen dead reading *La Semaine de Suzette*, the converse was not always true. As in later years, it seems likely that more girls (educated middle-class girls, at least) read boys' books (and occasionally magazines) than the other way round. Simone de Beauvoir, another voracious reader, started with the classic children's books:

> Lying flat on my stomach on the crimson carpet, I would read Mme de Ségur, Zénaide Fleuriot, fairy tales by Perrault, Grimm, Mme d'Aulnoy, or Father Schmidt, illustrated Topfer and Bécassine albums, the adventures of the Fenouillard family or Trooper Camember, [Hector Malot's] *Sans famille*, Jules Verne, Paul d'Ivoi, André Laurie and the Larousse 'Livres roses' series, which contained stories from all round the world; during the war, I read tales of heroism.
>
> (Beauvoir 1980: 70)[11]

Despite the censorship imposed on her (she seems to have been one of the most policed girls in France, obliged to read books that had sections pinned together by her mother), the reading she lists here and elsewhere in her memoirs could be described as fairly 'unisex'. Annie Kriegel, almost twenty years younger, came from a more modest background but still one carefully controlled by her mother, who was 'deeply opposed to our reading comics' – with the exception of Bécassine. Interestingly, her remembered list of books has several points of contact with Beauvoir's:

> the comtesse de Ségur, Jules Verne (oh! *Les Enfants du Capitaine Grant*, *L'Ile mystérieuse*), Paul d'Ivoi, Alexandre Dumas – not forgetting *Uncle Tom's Cabin* or Hector Malot's *Sans Famille*, which I read over and over until my copy, drenched with my tears and clutched to my heart, just fell to pieces . . . [then

a whole series of French and international classics] ... books from La
Bibliothèque Rose and the Hachette Série Verte.

(Kriegel 1991: 31)

Kriegel herself comments that her list coincides closely with one made by the
Russian scientist Andrei Sakharov, and suggests that there was a shared culture
among the (well-read) European young before 1939, with Jules Verne as its
cornerstone. Kriegel, who is not over-sympathetic to feminist readings, does not
make the equally interesting point that, in that milieu, it was shared by both
sexes.[12]

While comics might be frowned on by parents, adventure books were not.
Beauvoir, like Kriegel, mentions very few illustrated magazines (and those are the
permitted Catholic ones: *Le Noël, l'Etoile noëliste*) though she does refer to 'pulp
fiction', which she devoured during the less supervised holidays with her cousins.
But she regularly read 'boys' adventure books' by writers like Fenimore Cooper
(Beauvoir 1980: 117 ff. and 119 ff.). In general, it seems that boys chose reading
matter that confirmed or extended their masculinity, whereas girls could without
sanction read 'classics' and adventure stories which clashed with their femininity,
alongside other books and magazines that encouraged it. Beauvoir and Kriegel do
not tell us what the average French schoolgirl read, but they give us the outer limits
so to speak – what was possible for the educated girl. For the young, as well as for
their elders, the Great War may have exerted a contradictory pull on the sexes. Boys
were encouraged to assert themselves as masculine; girls, especially the growing
numbers of educated girls, had a chance to distance themselves from femininity by
aligning their reading with a masculine norm such as the adventure story. Yet at the
same time, as Beauvoir's conscientious admission about 'pulp fiction' reveals, they
might increasingly be drawn, especially in adolescence, towards a 'female'
literature, a graded sequence leading to the romantic novel, which their elders
read in large numbers. The recollections of a number of members of the working-
class Christian girls' fellowship, the JOCF, suggested that while they did not recall
reading much at all, teenage girls in this milieu were more likely to quote *Nous Deux*,
Histoires vraies and *photo-romans* than anything else (Aubert 1991: 112–13).

There were some shared reading experiences for children of both sexes, notably
the great 'animal revolution', taken up later by Walt Disney. Books about animals
were a major development in the period. Previously translations of Beatrix Potter
and Rudyard Kipling had been published in France, and Benjamin Rabier's books
were known to a minority, but in 1931 two highly popular French phenomena
arrived on the children's bookshelves: Jean de Brunhoff's first book about Babar the
elephant, and the first two in the series 'Les Albums du Père Castor', cheap books
for modest purses. A series entitled 'Le Roman des Bêtes' told the life stories of
animals and birds, with beautiful pictures. Nursery schools immediately began to
stock them, and by 1939 there were eighty titles in the collection. Publishers aimed
at children of both sexes. Stock's Collection Maia, starting in the the mid-1920s,
'was for all modern young readers, girls and boys', though the animals usually had a

clear male or female identity and traditional social role – the uxorious Babar and Céleste, for instance.[13]

Another shared reading area, which bowled over boys and girls in equal numbers, was the great innovation of the 1930s, the American strip cartoon, with its flagship *Le Journal de Mickey* (first number 21 October 1934). As Cavanna tells it with brio, the old-style French picture-stories looked out of date at once to his ten-year-old self:

> At the first assault, our favourite old-fashioned little comics were sent head over heels. Les Pieds Nickelés, Bibi Fricotin, l'Espiègle Lili, with their tiny pictures and great chunks of close-printed text underneath, that nobody read (except me!), just couldn't stand up to these giant-size pages covered with pictures, pictures, nothing but pictures, nice square ones, with colours that really hit you in the eye, in sequences like in the films, and with the words cut down to the bare minimum, dialogue in balloons coming straight out of the characters' mouths... and the sound-track! Splat! Thud! Squelch! Yuk! Grrr! Bang, bang! Vroom! Yikes! Eeek!
>
> (Cavanna 1978: 260–1)

Pascal Ory points out that American influence had already arrived before 1934, and that the speech bubble had been used by the inventors of Zig et Puce and Tintin (Ory in Chartier *et al.* 1986: 495–503). All the same, the phenomenal success of the Paul Winckler titles, *Robinson* (1936–44) and *Hop-Là* (1937–40) as well as *Mickey*, brought about 'a revolution in children's publishing'. The scholarly literature on the *Journal de Mickey* is largely concerned with the problem of national culture and Americanization, a subject raised in the 1930s and one with a long future ahead of it: French publishers panicked, not without reason, since the American-inspired craze swept though the country's children. Michel Pierre points out that Catholics and communists joined forces to condemn it, but argues that it may have been ' a useful defence against the torches of Nuremberg'. For our purposes its interest is that, although possibly appreciated more by boys than by girls, the all-out marketing of Disney and other strip cartoons meant that both boys and girls were target readers. This was a shared youth culture, more so than the sex-divided comics of earlier years. 'Youth clubs and political movements might thunder against them, but for the first time a youth culture distinct from that of grown-ups was being created – and under American influence' (Pierre 1990: 118 and 125).

Is there really enough evidence that the world of books and comics tempered the relentless segregation of the sexes that was most children's experience at school? Shared reading is not a frequently recorded activity, though some support for this suggestion can be gleaned from the fragile records of L'Heure Joyeuse library. This unique children's lending library in Paris provides some rare contemporary evidence of children's reactions to their reading matter. True, the children were well-read Parisians, probably from homes with an interest in education. Only a few numbers of the sporadically produced 'readers' journal' survive. But from them the impression of something new and different certainly emerges. The library, with its kindly if high-minded female librarians, its flowers, bright colours and pictures, was a haven from the austerity of school. Within two years it had 1,749 enrolments. Whether it was really mixed socially is hard to say (the journal claimed that it was), but it certainly mixed the sexes, contrary to the Paris schools: 'The most open comradeship reigns,' wrote a youthful editorialist. 'Sitting at the same table, girls and boys learn to know and appreciate each other.' It was at least a mixed location. On the other hand, the editorial committee, though mixed, was mostly male and the bulk of the articles are signed by boys. The subject of the articles too (stamps, crystal sets, how to make fireworks) incline more towards the conventional pursuits of boys than to those of girls. Here, too, while 'mixité' was possible as never before, the prevailing tone was set by boys.[14]

These records date from the 1930s, by which time there was more of a visible 'youth culture' than just after 1918. But the period as a whole was one when pre-war norms were under attack. It could be argued that these twenty years, during which more children were reading material produced specially for them, saw several contradictory trends: a reinforcement of male fantasies, encouraged by cartoon characters like the Pieds Nickelés and Tintin; a counterpart in the production of specialized girls' magazines and romantic fiction for women; yet at the same time the first move towards a new youth culture, where age was coming to matter as well as whether one was male or female – both boys and girls read Bécassine and Tintin; and the possibility, greater than in the past, for the growing number of intellectually ambitious girls to read books or comic strips originally written for boys, adopting 'the male gaze'.

So if children's reading was a combination of an open field and fenced terrains, the fences were more likely to be jumped by girls than boys. What this briefest of surveys suggests is that when girls and boys read different things, these were segregated on gender lines, stressing 'difference'. Wherever girls and boys read the same things, the alignment model seems the most appropriate: girls aligned themselves with something considered 'central', such as Jules Verne, but actually written with boys in mind. Male culture, sometimes accounted 'universal', was accorded higher value than culture specifically identified as female. To cross the gender divide, to read Jack London or Fenimore Cooper, for instance, was 'promotion' for a girl. For a boy to read even such classics as *Little Women* would have been the opposite. Something was certainly happening to create a culture of the young. New reading habits were appearing; but young readers were not identical in exercising their choice: girls were moving on to new territory more often than boys.

SECONDARY EDUCATION AND INTELLECTUAL APPRENTICESHIP: UNMIXED DELIGHT?

Talk of secondary education in France before the Second World War, and one is likely to be talking about children from a privileged background. Most children stayed in the primary sector, never reaching secondary education at all. In inter-war

France, the two sectors were quite separate; transfers, although possible, were not regular. The 'free and compulsory' schooling introduced by the Ferry laws was for children of both sexes between six and thirteen. For further vocational education, they might move on to the higher elementary school. At eleven, if academically ambitious, they might transfer to the state *lycée*, but secondary education was fee-paying until 1930 and remained the preserve of the well-off until after the Second World War. Scholarships enabled a few talented children of modest means to enter *lycées*, but most *lycée* pupils had never been in the primary sector at all, having attendeded the fee-paying 'petites classes' of the *lycée* to the age of eleven. A fair-sized minority of children, girls more than boys, remained in the 'private', mainly Catholic schools, both primary and secondary. In these respects, the inter-war period saw the beginnings of change but no sweeping transformation.[15]

The class distinction between the two types of state education, and the series of projected reforms addressing it, have preoccupied students of the French educational system. Progress towards the ideal of the *école unique* or all-in school, in the sense of socially and academically inclusive, has provided the backbone of histories of French schooling. Division by sex has had a rather uneasy relationship with this narrative. The history of progress towards co-education has not attracted the same attention, and the history of girls' education tends to be seen as a distraction from the story. One academic study simply remarks that the *lyceés* were all-male until 1880; that 'for the first twenty-five years of operation [the girls' *lycées* were] really little more than higher primary schools.... Only after the First World War did boys' and girls' secondary education become *the same*.... For the purposes of this study, no distinction seems necessary between boys' and girls' *lycées*' (Talbott 1969: 10–11). That study devotes many pages to the Bérard measures of 1923–4, but without mentioning that one of the decisions (an event much trumpeted in the history of girls' education) opened the way to identical syllabuses in boys' and girls' *lycées*. On the other hand, James McMillan, duly noting this event, remarks rightly that Bérard was not exactly a feminist: his main concern was to keep the classics at the centre of the syllabus and to ensure 'the formation of an educated elite, now broadened to include bourgeois girls as well as boys' (McMillan 1992: 82). The literature occasionally hints that the extension of something to bourgeois girls is not quite as good an extension as if it had been to working-class boys. Girls' education is as a rule studied separately, and historians gratefully refer to Françoise Mayeur's comprehensive thesis on girls' secondary education as covering the question.[16]

The literature reflects both the concern with social class which has long prevailed in the field, and also the convenience of studying girls on separate terms. By default, boys become the norm, with girls as a sort of variant or appendix. A truly gendered account might attempt to compare a series of age cohorts through their school careers, to see how relations between the sexes changed over time: but this presents near-insuperable methodological obstacles. A more usual approach is to describe the boys' model and to say that girls lagged behind it for about twenty or thirty years before becoming 'just the same as for boys'. Antoine Prost, in a section on girls' secondary schooling, remarks that by 1930, after a series of decrees about syllabus, timetable, the *agrégation* and the *concours général*, 'nothing, from now on, except a few hours of needlework distinguished girls' from boys' education' (Prost 1967: 264). A few hours of needlework, a lifetime of ideological assumptions. After nine years of this apparent parity, there were still only 64,000 girls in secondary schools in 1939, as compared to 140,000 boys.[17]

Why concentrate on the secondary school elite? First because more visible and therefore measurable change happened here than elsewhere in the system; second, because one is comparing boys and girls of like social background, so gender is not compared one way or the other with class; third, it is more manageable. Relations between boys and girls in the non-elite primary sector would be an excellent subject for research, but it will require a rethinking and reordering of much of the existing literature so far. Textbooks and syllabuses have been studied, but less is known on the more inaccessible subject of day to day life, on sex balance in schools and so on. So I have chosen to compare the chances of the academically ambitious boy or girl in that central core of the secondary sector, the *lycée*, looking for evidence of change in the opportunities open to the two sexes.

The chief function of French secondary education in the nineteenth century, whether public or private, was to prepare boys of good family for careers as army officers, civil servants or in the liberal professions. Most private schools for boys were religious foundations from the first, while the public school system was centred on the Napoleonic *lycée*, founded in 1802. For girls from similar families, there were at first no state *lycées* at all; they might be educated at home or at private, mostly convent schools. Even among boys, only a tiny minority frequented the fee-paying *lycées*, and fewer still completed their secondary education, to judge by the number of those who passed the *baccalauréat*, the school-leaving exam and passport (as it still is) to higher education or the professions – only about 6,500 in all of France as late as 1890, though it expanded fast after that. The boys' *lycée* was a spartan, part-boarding establishment as a rule, and the syllabus still concentrated on rhetoric and the classical humanities. Science played a reduced part in the curriculum and consisted in large degree of mathematics. Arts students, until the reforms of 1902 which made a Latin–modern languages option available, had to study Greek.[18]

When the Camille Sée law of 12 December 1880 instituted state *lycées* for girls, it was on a quite separate footing. The point of the legislation was not to encourage girls to think of careers, but to challenge the monopoly of the church over their education. Still, the logic of providing schooling for girls led to increased career prospects for women – if only as teachers in girls' schools. Girl pupils, like boys, were assumed from the start to come from the well-off middle class. In view of competition from the church, which insisted on segregation, separate girls' *lycées*, with all-female staff, were thought desirable. A training college was founded, the Ecole Normale Supérieure at Sèvres (1881) and special *agrégations féminines* (competitive teaching diplomas) were designed, to produce a new corps of women *lycée* teachers.

The entire structure of the girls' *lycée* syllabus was different from that of the boys,

47

being more 'modern' and literary in character and including domestic training, moral education and accomplishments. The new girls' *lycées* did not lead to the *baccalauréat*, but only to a special school-leaving certificate, the *diplôme*, of no value for higher education or a career. The timetable was lighter and the structure of the syllabus encouraged pupils to graduate after three years. 'The whole set of arrangements (length of schooling, timetable, content and spirit of the syllabus) put secondary schooling for girls at a respectful distance from the classic boys' secondary education, and effectively prevented them preparing for the *baccalauréat*', although they were not formally barred from sitting it as private individuals (Lelièvre 1991: 117).[19]

After a slow start, since many middle-class families were still sending their daughters to church schools, the number of girls attending state *lycées* took off after the 1890s. From 4,337 in 1885 it had reached 13,000 by 1900, 29,000 by 1910 and 44,000 in 1920. On the eve of the First World War 30,000 girls and 69,000 boys were at *lycées* (Zeldin 1977: 272; McMillan 1992: 82).

The reason for assuming that boys and girls in *lycées* were on an equal footing after the 1920s was the famous decree of 1924, when the syllabus, while reintroducing compulsory Greek for the *bac*, became 'identical' in both kinds of *lycée*. As hinted earlier, this incident is not quite as straightforward as it might seem. What the decree actually said was that preparation for the *bac* was now an *option* for girls' *lycées*; and that *for those taking the option*, the boys' syllabus would be 'applied in its entirety'. At the same time, 'domestic science, needlework and music are a compulsory part of the timetable in establishments for girls' (Lelièvre 1991: 128–30). Still, it marked a change in principle. Why 1924? Although she does not articulate the data quite as presented below, Françoise Mayeur's thesis provides the essential information for teasing out the gender implications of the move. From her account, it appears that what became an irresistible movement towards identical syllabuses had three chief causes.

First, the nature of the boys' curriculum. The arts *bac*, gateway to the highest honours, depended largely on linguistic skills – those needed to learn the classical and modern languages. The future Prime Minister Edouard Daladier failed the entrance exam to the ENS in the rue d'Ulm in 1904 because his Greek was inadequate (Réau 1993: 21). There was no obvious reason why the mastery of ancient languages could not be achieved by girls (who already studied modern languages), if teachers could be found. Any relaxation of the rules – as in 1902, when the option 'latin + langues [modernes]' was allowed in the *bac* – enabled girls to move in quite easily: all they had to do was learn Latin. Their comparative success proved that it was possible to bring them up to the boys' level in Latin without superhuman effort: 'two years of well-taught Latin enabled them to sit the exam with success.' It also tells us that the standard of classical studies in boys' *lycées* may not have been as high as their mystique implied. It might have been different if science and technology had held more prestige, as they do today. Girls' schools might not have been able to adapt so fast.

Second, the competition from the private sector. Girls in private education, whether traditional Catholic schools or the prestigious avant-garde Collège Sévigné, were by now being taught the syllabus for the *bac* in significant numbers. Parents of schoolgirls after the Great War were anxious to provide their daughters with a worthwhile qualification, for economic reasons. Only the *bac* permitted one to attend university. The private schools had a start in this area, since the state had painted itself into a corner. In its desire for a separate (non-church) girls' secondary sector, it had prohibited all except the state *lycées* from presenting candidates for the now-despised girls' *diplôme*. What had been meant as an advantage had become a problem. To keep their pupils, the *lycées* needed to be seen to be working for the *bac*.

Third, the 1914 war had brought other changes, ending social and economic complacency, and obliging a generation of young women to seek careers rather than marriage, and breaking some taboos. Recruitment of women teachers during wartime had helped bring down barriers. Young women teachers were appointed to boys' *lycées*, and a common syllabus had become more imaginable. Several Grandes Ecoles also opened their doors to women candidates.[20]

Mayeur's account makes it clear that while all the above pressures were at work, at no time was the identical syllabus for both sexes the central issue, although it had been discussed for years. It eventually came about not by legislation, but by mere decree (on 25 March 1924), and the minister responsible was indeed chiefly concerned with restoring Greek and Latin to their former prestige, lost in 1902. Girls' education was tacked on to the main debate. None the less, Bérard had made an earlier speech in 1922 conceding the universality of the principle:

> Girls' secondary schooling no longer corresponds to real-life demands. Girls can no longer be satisfied with the diploma ... the anomaly of two exams has lasted too long. Order, logic and symmetry must be brought to bear on our secondary education system.

> (Mayeur 1977: 424)

Not for the first time, girls' education was dealt with in a way that satisfied a taste for tidiness, without much anticipation of the consequences. Those responsible had assumed that only a tiny minority of girls would want to take advantage of the possibility. This was probably the key to its getting through. They underestimated not only the desire for the *bac*, with all its consequences, but also the intellectual ability of girls to pursue a syllabus which had remained very largely arts-based. In practice, teaching Greek as proposed would have been difficult for girls' schools. But as luck (or the regular practice of the Third Republic) would have it, Bérard's successor immediately reversed this part of the decree and reinstated the *bac moderne* (Latin plus languages). Now girls as well as boys could progress from the *bac* (usually moderne) to university degree (*licence*), to the *agrégation* (*masculine*: but open to both sexes). That girls seized their chance is proved by the immediate upward curve of figures both for passes in the *bac* and for entry to university. The girls' diploma now faded away quite fast, since it led nowhere. Most girls entering higher education chose, however, to study non-science subjects, a pattern that would endure.[21]

What will strike today's readers about all this is that the norm was the boys' syllabus, assumed to be the best model and simply made available to girls' schools. The quarrel over ancient and modern (with its class overtones) has obscured the fact that the boys' syllabus of the 1920s did not have some timeless superiority. The prestige accorded to classical studies has not survived to the present, when mathematics and science have become the measure of intellectual ambition. At the time, though, many heads of girls' schools felt that something of value in itself – the modern studies programme and even domestic education – was being abandoned by girls for the sake of prestige. Realignment on the male norm was the only thinkable way according to the men in the ministry. Furthermore, 1924 is a false date for assuming equality – as is even Prost's wiser choice of 1930, after more adjustments to the syllabus. In any given year between 1919 and 1939, twice as many boys as girls would be getting a full secondary education. Although the *bac* had become more desirable, it was far from taken by all girls in the secondary sector; and the 'few hours of needlework' – not negligible in a school week – were always there to remind academic girls of the difference between their supposed destiny and that of the boys (as it did in much more visible form in the higher primary schools). Catching up was not as simple as one might suppose. And for those girls who wanted to take their education further, equality with boys was not easily achieved (as would be illustrated by the very different history in the late 1920s and 1930s of the two Ecoles Normales Supérieures, one in the rue d'Ulm, the other at Sèvres).[22]

One remembered incident hints at the ambiguity that mixing at school held for this generation. In the opening months of the Second World War, Annie Kriegel's family, like many other Parisians with children of school age, stayed on in the resort where they had spent their summer holidays, Cayeux on the Normandy coast. The local *lycée* had to accommodate them:

> The classes were mixed of course. It had not even been contemplated that the rigorous segregation that was the rule in all French *lycées* at the time could be maintained in this improvised school. The daring change passed unnoticed and did not give rise to any change in the way we spoke or behaved. We had always played mixed games on the beach and the school at Cayeux seemed to be part of our games rather than part of our Parisian school life.
>
> (Kriegel 1991: 115)

Was mixing time out from real life, or was it the intrusion of real life into the school?

YOUTH MOVEMENTS: TO MIX OR NOT TO MIX?

'The inter-war period was a key time for the creation and development of youth movements' (Coutrot 1985: 110). The final section of this chapter concentrates on a more overtly political topic. The commitment to join a youth group was a move towards autonomy. More than at any time before or since, young French people in their teens and early twenties, from every background, joined organized youth groups between the wars. The subject is one of the fastest-growing areas of research in French social history for this period. As with every other kind of association in

France at this time, ideological and religious divisions make for a perplexing variety of names and dates. Few attempts have been made so far at overall synthesis or typology.[23] Aline Coutrot's model based on political science methodology therefore makes a good starting point for the present purpose, particularly since it makes allowances for questions of *mixité* and *non-mixité*. Her model is more generally applicable, as she recognizes, to the religious-based movements (in the broad sense) than to the youth branches of political parties which also emerged at the time.

Coutrot suggests that many French youth movements of this period can be explained by the impact of war. With parents sometimes absent, always preoccupied, older children had to take on family responsibilities earlier than usual, but were also allowed more freedom – girls in particular – than in the past. Some of the adults who helped create movements had been wartime organizers. Second, the impetus often came from 'outside', from other countries such as Britain (for scouts), Germany and Eastern Europe (the youth hostel movement) or Belgium (the JOC and related groups), in some cases in co-operation with the Catholic and other churches. France was a follower, not a leader. Oddly enough, no new youth movement movement originated in the *laïc* (anticlerical) republican tradition which was so powerful a force in the teaching profession. Many French youth movements had religious connections, if they were not directly church-inspired. In some ways this explains why their historiography has been rather chequered.

Whether strongly religious or not, Coutrot argues, they had recognizably similar ideologies and inspiration: a clear sense of their aims, coupled with a certain rejection of the past and a desire among the young to express themselves freely without reference to their elders. They also prized adventurousness, often linked to a stress on outdoor activity. All of them – even if claiming, as the scout and guide movement did, to be apolitical – had political agendas of a kind, in that they took a view on the issues of the time. Most were collectively identified by some outward sign: uniforms, badges, processions, songs. And all of them aspired to self-education and autonomy in organization, which might cause problems with adult 'helpers'. Whereas the traditional *patronage* (roughly the equivalent of a parish youth club) had been a way in which the church controlled the young, most new youth movements wanted to run things their own way. All these elements were new when they emerged on a large scale in the 1920s and 1930s in France. As Jeanne Aubert, the founder of the JOCF (Jeunesse Ouvrière Chrétienne Féminine), put it:

> The particular atmosphere of the JOCF was quite different from that of the youth clubs . . . . The JOCF was a movement set up by young working girls for young working girls and with them, whereas the youth clubs had their 'leaders' who were often not in the first flush of youth and who were really only standing in for the parish priest.
>
> (Quoted in Coutrot 1985: 119)

Even an apparently traditionally inspired movement like the boy scouts/girl guides had what Coutrot describes as a revolutionary pedagogy of 'savoir-faire' (can-do). On the other hand, with few exceptions inter-war youth movements were *not* mixed, but had quite separate groups for boys/young men and girls/young women. As a rule, the formation of the boys' branch came first, with a girls' association emerging a few years later.

We might pause briefly on this point: the need for a girls' branch was new in itself. The organizers of the JOC movement apparently felt it would be incomplete without the girls' branches. That the sexes were separately organized, rather than merged, can be viewed either as traditional fear of immorality, or as creating a separate space for girls to create their own structures: the two are not incompatible. But separation did not mean equality. The acronyms for the two movements are symbolic. All the JOC-inspired movements put an F for 'Féminine' on the end to denote a girls' movement. None of them saw fit to add an M for 'Masculine' to the boys' movement. The latter had independent legitimacy, not only as the first but as the core organization. The girls were the 'others' – not necessarily subordinate, but not the centre of the movement.[24]

That is how it might strike us now, but the very creation of female groups was widely perceived as audacious at first. Whereas many youths or young men might have or expect some form of collective experience, such as military service, families were not so used to seeing their daughters engage in collective activity outside the home before 1914. One point often made by contemporaries is that anxious parents only allowed daughters out on the understanding that it was to an all-female meeting. In what follows, the question of segregation and mixing will be kept in mind. One should remember that it was fairly novel for *any* young people, boys and young men included, to be calling for autonomy from their elders. Adults looked askance at this surge of enthusiasm from the young. It should also be borne in mind that French youth movements never touched more than a minority of young people. It was, however, a vociferous and visible minority. I have chosen four of the most visible for brief case studies: the scout and guide movements; the JOC and JOCF; the young communist groups; and the youth hostel associations. The first two fit Coutrot's model quite well, the latter two significantly deviate from it.

Scouts and Guides

It is easy to see the scouting and guiding movement, now almost a hundred years old, as embodying a traditional ethos, one that has survived several changes in style. Perhaps the remarkable thing about it is that it has outlived the other movements discussed here. But in the early days, it was literally and figuratively a path-breaker.[25]

In its French form, it meets many of Coutrot's criteria and may have been her model. Originating outside France, it was dedicated to a clear and simple ideology with religious underpinnings, attaching great importance to the outdoor life: exercise, exploring, camping. The uniform and corporate identity were an essential part of its appeal. It was and remains segregated: although scouts and guides might meet for ceremonies or joint ventures, their organization was rigorously separate. Guiding appeared a few years after scouting. One hesitates to describe it as a *contestataire* movement, but self-reliance and character-building were among its aims. While the movement relied on adults as leaders, the patrol system could be seen as a sort of devolved leadership.

The main point that would strike outside observers of the French scout/guide movement was its denominational character, resulting in various separate associations instead of a single one, as in Britain. There were Protestant scouts (the first), non-denominational scouts and a separate Jewish movement, but the Catholic movement, known as the Scouts de France, quickly overtook the other groups in numbers. It articulated its philosophy clearly: 'conservative in every sense of the word: the Scout recognizes God, religion, fatherland, society, the family, and his teachers.' Scouting never had the resonance in France it did in Britain. Various reasons are suggested: religious divisions; familiarity with the countryside in rural areas; the opposition of the communist or left-republican traditions in the towns; and one of the usual suspects, French individualism (Cholvy *et al.* 1986: 377–80).

The French girl guide associations followed similar lines, with the Protestants again leading the way: in 1917, Antoinette Butte was sent by a pastor to try to set up a company in Montmartre. 'We more or less made up the rules as we went along.' Once the Catholic movement, Guides de France, was formed in 1923, it became the majority group, though never reaching very large numbers. Here, too, the avowed aims of the movement were not particularly progressive, particularly in the emphasis on homemaking: 'If the scout is made for the outdoor life, the guide is meant for the home' (Cholvy *et al.* 1986: 383).

Still, guides of various denominations went camping, and did have a commitment outside the home. Most witnesses agreed with Antoinette Butte that 'while scouting was not a challenge to society, it brought some freedom, especially to girls'. 'What was the background in which we had been saturated? The god-fearing Victorian era, a rigid and hypocritical bourgeoisie whose undeniable virtues were becoming burdensome'. Odd as it might seem, guiding seemed a threat to some authorities. In Montpellier, one guide still remembered 'with terror' how the mother superior of the convent threatened to expel girls who went on a guide camp (Cholvy *et al.* 1986: 381, 383).

Scouting and guiding are at one end of the traditional/progressive spectrum reflected in miniature in our chosen examples. With their high moral tone and traditional values, they were not alarmingly modern. The difference they made is above all that they came first, and that they reached children very young, with the French equivalents of Brownies and Wolf-cubs. By the 1930s, although not a mass movement, they were a familiar part of the social landscape. Those who wanted to join other youth movements probably benefited from their existence. Most other groups had a later starting date and an older clientele, their youngest members being in their middle teens and their oldest often well into their twenties. Scouts and guides were reassuringly single-sex, reinforcing schooltime segregation. On the other hand, according to witnesses, they made thinkable for the first time activities such as girls going camping at weekends, an unprecedented situation for most parents to handle.

The Jeunesse Ouvrière Catholique (JOC) and JOC Féminine (JOCF): an ideal-type youth movement?

Most writers on youth movements in recent years have paid particular attention to the series of Catholic youth movements of which the JOC was the first and the most active. (The 'Ouvrière' in the JOC's title was replaced by 'Agricole', 'Etudiante' and 'Indépendante' in the JAC, JEC and JIC and their own 'Féminine' parallels the JACF, JECF, JICF.) The renewal of interest in these movements has been unblocked partly by the decline of the more militant forms of *laïcité*, partly by the decline of communism, partly by the revival in the history of denominational movements, especially in a social context, and partly no doubt by the rise of women's studies. Their history is still not entirely neutral ground.[26]

One sees why there is some ambiguity about their role as forces for 'progress' or 'reaction'. Antoine Prost appears to be thinking of JOC-type movements when he describes them as broadly 'integrating' youth into society rather than providing a challenge. The Communist party branded them as 'class collaborators', especially the factory-based Jocistes, who were rivals for the allegiance of young workers. On the other hand, the Catholic hierarchy at times found their development worryingly revolutionary, especially during the Popular Front. Mgr Calvet, visiting a *cercle d'études* in 1936, while impressed by the 'générosité et franchise' of the Jocistes, was concerned that they took no orders from their chaplain: 'They seem to be in charge of themselves!' He also feared that the 'social' might push out the 'religious' element (Christophe 1986: 100).

Clearly both were present. The ambiguity arises from the contrast between the structures and origins of a movement associated with the Catholic church, and its revolutionary style. There was also a potential contradiction between its socially progressive ideology and its morally traditional views, particularly concerning gender. Thus Prost picks out as an example of 'integrative' behaviour, the fact that the Jocistes wanted to 'moralize the Saturday-night dance', by keeping the lights on all the time. Michel Launay, by contrast, argues that the Jocistes were often fighting genuine abuses, which today would be called sexual harassment:

> In many factories, the Jocistes campaigned against mixed cloakrooms and argued that girls should have a space for themselves. On the pretext that in our own time such preoccupations might look out of date [historical] analyses of the occupational environment in the 1930s pass rather quickly over the absence of morality that reigned in many factories. Cases of 'initiation ceremonies' consisting of young girls being more or less handed over to the foreman by their [female] workmates were not isolated. Obscene remarks and gestures, pornographic illustrations were part of everyday life for many [male] apprentices. It was young girls in their first job who were the particular targets of those responsible for this harmful atmosphere.
>
> (Launay in Pierrard *et al.* 1984: 43)

There are echoes here of recent debates. What was more, Jocistes went on to be active in other movements hard to classify by the standard left–right categories of French politics, because of the religious divide: the resistance, the MRP, the worker-priest movement, the CFDT.

The history of the movement explains some of these contradictions. The first JOC group for boys/young men in France was set up in Clichy in 1925, inspired by the Belgian organization created by Abbé Cardijn. The movement received the wary blessing of the hierarchy. One aim of the JOC was to bring the young from 'godless' working-class milieux into contact with the church. From the start, it was seen as an avant-garde movement, likely to clash with structures already in place, such as the *patronages* and the networks of groups and charities run directly by the church. As it spread to other French cities, it met hostility. In Saint-Etienne for instance,

> for many Catholics, whether clergy or lay people, the newly-created JOC was a threat. It was accused of . . . introducing the class struggle into the church. It was criticized for favouring contacts between Christians and unbelievers and by so doing encouraging the young to 'mix with the wrong kind of people'.[27]

The JOC had an energetic style and set of practices centred on the workplace, not the church. The basic JOC unit was the *cercle d'études* or study group which carried out surveys into the lives of young workers, held Bible-readings centred on the teaching of Christ the carpenter, and saw it as its mission to 'make the shop floor Christian before trying to convert people in the shop floor to Christianity'. Its motto 'Observe, consider, act' was an invitation to critical thought and intervention. Membership was a commitment, symbolized by wearing a badge.

When the first branches for girls were set up in 1928, it was on the same lines, and seemed even more of an innovation. An important part of its appeal seems to have been that it took seriously young working girls accustomed to being on the receiving end of orders. Instead of telling them what to do, it convinced them of their own worth. Most of them had no privacy at home, and no status at work, according to a collection of memories of Jocistes from the early days. One recruit described how her reluctance had been overcome:

> The priest . . . took the trouble to see me on my own. He got me to talk about the factory, my work, my problems. It was certainly the first time a priest had taken any interest in my work and listened to me.
>
> (Aubert 1991: 217)

To learn pride in being a worker, to be told that one's soul was as precious as a bishop's – a formula that recurs in the first-hand accounts – was experienced as a revelation. Jeanne Aubert remembers Cardijn saying to the first congress at Paris: 'You are neither slaves nor machines, you are not the wretched of the earth, or the prisoners of hunger [a quotation from the Internationale] – you are the sons and daughters of God!'; and 'The soul of a young working girl is worth more than all the gold in the world!' This, she says, led them to lose their previous fatalism. As with the boys/men, courage was needed to wear a badge at work and own up to membership, but the movement gave its members a great deal of moral support. Girls in particular had to face opposition from their parents over such matters as going out to evening meetings: 'My family asked me to give it up, thinking it was "not proper" to be coming home so late.... But I stood my ground. After that ... they never said any more about it.' 'They were also afraid that we were overdoing it by going to JOCF because our health wasn't too good.' Weekend commitments meant not being there to help with housework on Saturday afternoons (Aubert 199: 42, 212).

If it represented a greater break with tradition, the JOCF could also be seen as an apprenticeship of a kind for taking more public responsibility than such young women would previously have contemplated. Aubert firmly believed that having a separate organization for girls was beneficial:

> With hindsight, I must say that creating and maintaining an association for young working girls, with its own methods of work, propaganda, surveys and services, was not only something quite original within the French labour movement but also had the great advantage of training our girls, getting them to take on responsibilities, which we would never have been able to do if the JOC had been a mixed movement.
>
> (Quoted in Cholvy *et al.* 1991: 72)

There is no overall study of the destinies of the Jocistes to tell us what became of them, but Jean Nizey has surveyed the Maitron dictionary entries on the Jociste militants, male and female, between the wars. The sample, although only covering twenty-one women and eighty-four men, contains some pointers. The JOC/F, it is suggested, from the itineraries of these known individuals, was 'a breeding ground of militants for various areas of associative life', whether in trade unions, party politics, the family movement or social intervention. By definition, to be in the Maitron dictionary implied some participation in the labour movement. But the detailed results suggested to Nizey the effectiveness in particular of 'the JOCF, which really "launched" these girls from a working-class, often Catholic background and turned them into women capable of taking on social responsibilities'. This slightly patronizing remark should not distract from the self-evident truth that the JOCF movement provided an apprenticeship in industrial and social affairs, the more remarkable given the marginal presence of women in the labour movement at the time.[28]

All the literature on the JOC-type movements suggests that the cement of the association was solidarity of the young with each other, and a sense of real contact. In working-class families, much of life was taken up with the struggle for survival, and Jeanne Aubert suggests that the youth movement filled an emotional need:

> the most striking thing in our lives as young workers and Jocistes was the friendship that held us together in the JOC. It would be false and unfair to suggest that working-class families of those days did not love their children. But in the terribly harsh conditions of the time, parents did not know how to

show their love for their children, though they did their best to bring them up properly and honestly. One youngster, when his local JOC branch gave him a party on his twentieth birthday, confessed that birthdays were never celebrated in his family. The friendship we found in the JOCF was not merely a kind of solidarity, it was a real deep friendship. We loved each other like sisters.

(Quoted in Cholvy *et al.* 1991: 74)

The JOC and JOCF were associations of a completely new type, which marked several generations of young people after 1926. Ex-members, whether they later joined the Communist party or the young farmers' clubs, invariably acted as a ferment. In no sense could the JOC be called politically neutral, yet it avoided commitment to political parties: in the late 1930s, it was opposed to Marxism, opposed to the Popular Front, but in favour of the strikers of 1936, in favour of the redesign of industrial society. It was part of the political undergrowth in France. Whereas parliamentary politics was a male monopoly, in the JOCF girls and women were encouraged to take an active part at every level. Their association was parallel with the male equivalent. It is true that in many ways, beginning with the chaplains, men exercised an asymmetrical controlling presence over the JOCF. Nevertheless the spirit of the association was transmitted, without losing any of its energy, to a generation of girls whose mothers, they reported, looked on bemused.

The communist youth movement: party politics

The young communists' association fits less easily into Aline Coutrot's typology. Both in its early and late stages, it reflected the concerns of the adult party leadership rather than the autonomy of the young members. Second, it was at first a mixed organization (though girls were always a small minority) and only in 1936–9 did it set up separate branches for boys and girls. Its history, starting in the pre-war Jeunesses socialistes, has been traced by Jacques Varin. Although 'girls did not often become activists in political organizations', a number of young women held office within it. The young communists were drawn into the party's tumultuous career of the 1920s, and demanded 100 per cent commitment from all members – recruiting, discussing politics, opposing the Catholic JOC ('an openly class-collaborationist outfit'). The Jeunesses communistes movement at first had little in the way of organized activities beyond political discussions, and was indeed reprimanded by Maurice Thorez in the 1930s for playing politics, for 'pretentious jargon' and for 'avant-gardisme' (Varin 1975: 201; cf. also 128, 186; Ory 1994: 78–80, 768–80).

In late 1935, consistently with the party's wish to specialize its appeal to different milieux, it was decided to set up a separate organization for girls, the Union des Jeunes Filles de France. The decision was taken partly to cope with the new influx of members during the Popular Front age: the JC had been trailing along with a claimed 4,000 members in 1934, a figure that had supposedly jumped to 30,000 by the end of 1935. One reason was the need to retain those girls who had joined but might quickly forsake the party, because they were 'not used to politics'. By the end of 1936, the UJFF claimed 10,000 members (Varin 1975: 76, 201, 213, 235). Four leading young women in the party were involved as organizers (Danielle Casanova, Jeannette Vermeersch, Marie-Claude Vaillant-Couturier and Claudine Chomat) and a strategic attitude seems to have been taken from the start, for fear of competition from the single-sex JOC/JOCF, which appealed to the same young workers the party hoped to attract: 'Let me be frank: a mixed movement would have made it hard to recruit members. Parents and girls themselves were opposed to this kind of organization' (Varin 1975: 238; Rousseau 1983: 13 ff.). This was not a line of thinking to the taste of everyone. Colette Jobard, from the mixed JC, resented the change:

> We had a little band of girls in the local groups who were very emancipated, they went round with red scarves, a bit tomboyish in appearance, but that wasn't at all the usual thing for girls at the time. These comrades reacted badly to the segregation policy and some of them left the movement.
>
> (Varin 1975: 239)

Both Varin and Renée Rousseau note the distance separating the 'more advanced girls' who saw segregation as a step backwards, and the 'socialist fathers' who would rather their daughters went to single-sex communist youth groups than to the still-mixed Jeunesses socialistes. The educational and leisure activites of the UJFF emphasized 'difference' and femininity more than equality. In any case, it had a short life in its first incarnation, being dissolved along with other groups associated with the Communist party in the autumn of 1939.

Here, then, was a movement which initially reflected the party's view that people were divided by class not by sex. Just as the adult party was punctilious about not discriminating against women, so it was with the original youth movement, open to girls and boys on the same terms. But in practice, while they took pains to look non-sexist, both the Communist party and the JC were male-dominated. The 1935 decision was a strategic one, no doubt inspired by the different style of the JOC. While recognizing the problem about a new generation of girl recruits the party, by inventing the UJFF, opted for a rather traditional solution – only an apparent paradox, given the party structures of the time. To analyse it like this need not imply anything about the autonomy of individuals: both young communists and young Jocistes might be individually more or less adventurous or conformist.

The youth hostels movement: mixed and proud of it

The youth hostelling movement which blossomed in the 1930s, and in particular under the Popular Front government of 1936, takes us even further from the Coutrot model, towards something less clear-cut and more pragmatic. Once more, the religious question cannot be overlooked. The first *auberge de jeunesse* was opened, on the German model, by Marc Sangnier, founder of the pre-war *Le Sillon*, in 1930. He went on to found the LFAJ (Ligue Française des Auberges de Jeunesse), an interdenominational grouping with Catholics, Protestants and Jews on the committee. A non-religious association, the CLAJ (Centre Laïque des Auberges de Jeunesse) was created soon afterwards, and the two coexisted rather antagonistically for the rest of the 1930s.[29]

The real moment of the youth hostels came in 1936, with encouragement from Léo Lagrange, the young minister whom Blum had appointed to oversee sports and leisure activites. In 1933, the CLAJ was running 45 hostels and recorded 6,000 overnight stays. In 1935, the figures were 90 and 10,000; in 1936, they shot up to 229 and 26,800 (almost 6,000 over the Christmas holidays, showing how popular winter sports were becoming).[30] The two weeks' paid holidays and the forty-hour week, resulting from government measures after the strike wave, freed more young people than ever before to take advantage of the hostels in the countryside. The mountains were particularly popular as mountaineering, skiing and hiking caught on.

In France, despite a certain mythology, youth hostels were not a natural development, but had to be encouraged. Whereas in Germany they had arisen in response to a need, because young people were already in the habit of taking long hikes, in France the hostels came first and the hiking, cycling, etc. had to be coaxed into existence. The core of the movement before 1936 consisted of young teachers, students and *lycéens*, perhaps because they had already had dealings with *colonies de vacances* (holiday camps for schoolchildren), another fast-expanding phenomenon. Even after 1936, despite a deliberate attempt to attract young workers, intellectuals remained pillars of the movement, no doubt giving it its avant-garde character, and taste for cultural activities such as poetry and experimental theatre. Of the total of 364 hostellers recorded in the rather special Provençal hostel of Regain and another in the Vosges between 1937 and 1939, 138 were teachers, 73 students, 45 office workers, 41 in small business and only 31 manual workers (Kergoat 1986: 314; Ory 1994: 184).

The youth hostel associations all encouraged young people to discover nature – and their own nature. They encouraged social mixing, and *tutoiement*, as opposed to the snobbish habits of the bourgeois at play. The hostel was to be 'a veritable miniature Republic of the Young' uniting 'young intellectuals, workers and peasants – sentiments summed up in the *ajiste* song 'Allons au-devant de la vie'.[31] One major difference between the youth hostel movement and the other youth movements was that it was mixed-sex – although dormitories were supposed to be segregated, there were no separate associations or hostels for men and women, at least in the secular wing of the movement. This was one aspect of the movement which was most noticed by photographers and country-dwellers alike – that young people of both sexes, as likely as not wearing shorts (a recent development even for men and thought rather risqué for women), had taken to the outdoor life and were staying overnight under the same roof. Lucette Heller-Goldenberg argues that this was *mixité* of a new and special kind (though perhaps not unlike the pre-1936 young communist league) in that young people 'call each other "tu", to put a stop to the false relations between a conniving young girl looking for a husband and a young man in search of a victim'. She quotes an *ex-ajiste* saying that whereas elsewhere relations between the sexes were governed by the seduction game, 'the youth hostels, though mixed, were not a hunting ground.' Jacques Kergoat, however, suggests that older officials became seriously worried about 'moral laxity' and that the LFAJ in particular began insisting on separate hostels for boys and girls in younger age-groups.[32]

Mixing the sexes was thus potentially confrontational, as was the desire of youth hostellers to shake off the tutelage of their elders. In October 1935, ten young hostellers of both sexes founded the first Users' Club in Paris. As these hostellers' clubs multiplied, the movement escaped from the control of the adults who ran the hostels, to become more like a self-motivated series of youth groups. Lagrange encouraged this move towards autonomy, which expressed itself in the desire for more permanent links and activities outside holiday time, but it was not appreciated by those in charge of the CLAJ, who at first refused the clubs representation on the committees.

Lucette Heller-Goldenberg concludes that overall the youth hostels movement was a genuinely forward-looking and 'indubitably' contributed to the transformation of the French cultural landscape, foreshadowing among other things the contestation of 1968 and the ecologist movement, while providing a model of *mixité* more comradely and free and easy than any yet seen. That does not seem an unreasonable judgement, although it must always be borne in mind that *ajisme* was an avant-garde movement, closely associated with the Popular Front and to some extent politically identified with it too. By comparison with the other groups, *ajistes* were somewhat older, and their whole movement was devoted to having a good time. But *mixité* here was a central question in the creation of a model of society, a function it did not have elsewhere.

It is sometimes suggested that while the *années folles* of the 1920s were marked by avant-garde activities by young and not-so-young adults, the 1930s, marked by depression, saw less freedom from constraint – with the explosion of the Front Populaire as just that, a short 'sunny spell' in Léon Blum's words. If one thinks not of adults but of successive generations of schoolchildren and young people, and in particular of girls, one can glimpse some progressive loosening of conventions. It was far from general, indeed it was very patchy. And we have noted that the Communist party felt it had to bow to the logic of single-sex activities, even at a late date. Nevertheless, in many milieux, and *increasingly*, girls were able to do things out of the question before the war, not as a sudden development, but as a result of structures built up over time and becoming more familiar. Successive generations of young people could think of themselves as 'les jeunes', not as much as in the 1960s perhaps, but much more than in the 1910s.

Second, there was no exclusion of girls from any of these movements, even if their participation varied in intensity and autonomy. In some cases, such as the JOCF, girls came to have an unprecedented confidence in themselves, by the account of survivors. It is harder to say with certainty how girls fared in mixed groups. But whether single-sex or mixed, youth movements were one way in which girls were being socialized, including politically socialized, alongside boys. Where boys had been encouraged to think of life as starting outside the family, it was a comparatively new experience for girls.

CONCLUSION: WAS CHANGE THE EXCEPTION OR THE RULE?

Can our three examples take us any nearer answering the questions posed at the start of the chapter? In some ways, these examples – singled out precisely because they seemed promising of change – were the exceptional ones, where change was particularly perceptible during these years, in a context where much had otherwise remained the same.

In terms of the *environment of the growing child*, the influence of the early years in reinforcing sexual identity is today taken very seriously. To single out reading as having a preponderant role might therefore seem excessive, when in most households boys and girls were treated very differently: the language, tone of voice, expectations of behaviour, the games, the toys were (and largely remain) distinct. Maurice Crubellier suggests that books were themselves more associated with boys, whereas toys and especially the whole 'doll culture' made up the world of girls: 'the loneliness of a [middle-class] boy's childhood was fortified by knowledge from books, that of a girl by social ritual' (Crubellier 1979: 71). But entry to the world of books, coming later for most girls than for boys, took the young reader of either sex into an imaginary universe. It is customary to see reading as a private activity, but the recollections of the witnesses quoted here speak of reading as taking the reader *out* of the home, the school, the study, into what was surely a kind of *public* domain. Annie Kriegel's point about a shared culture of the well-read young European, centred on Jules Verne, takes a special resonance for us if we stress the aspect of it she chooses not to mention – that it was open to girls like herself, and not only to her brothers. In this respect, while the inter-war years saw little dramatic change, they were nevertheless years in which it would become commonplace for young people to read something more than the obligatory school textbook, whether a novel, a children's comic, an illustrated magazine or the newspaper. For girls, whose pre-war horizons had been more limited, the change was inevitably greater.

When it comes to *schooling*, to pick out the academic secondary school is also to choose a privileged area. It was where the greatest progress towards equality between boys and girls was made – but by the smallest groups. The context of the inter-war years was, as in the nineteenth century, and as it was to be until at least the 1960s, rigid segregation of boys and girls for educational purposes. They might follow the same or similar syllabuses most of the time, but they did so out of sight of one another. The message of segregated schooling was that the public arena had different expectations from the individual depending on her or his sex. Changes such as the 1924 ruling on the secondary syllabus look more significant in retrospect, within a narrative about progress towards women's equality, than they seemed at the time to the few girls able to take advantage of them. The same could probably be said of such other reforms as the phasing out of fees for secondary school (1930) and the raising of the school-leaving age to fourteen (1936), both of which affected girls proportionately more than boys. Crubellier says that 'separate education for girls was swept away in a generation' at this time, but he also recognizes that in vocational post-primary education, which potentially affected far more girls, large gaps remained (Crubellier 1979: 293 ff.). Training for an occupation was essentially for boys, with girls admitted only to a very narrow range of 'domestic' trades. Following the Astier law of 1920 regulating apprentice-ships, the number of boys following such courses took off between the wars, and was diversified,while that of girls rose only slightly until the late 1930s. Things have not changed very greatly even in the 1990s, when vocational training still remains the most segregated by sex of the whole system despite the formal presence of *mixité* (cf. Baudelot and Establet 1992). One jaundiced survey of women's progress towards professional equality in twentieth-century France argues that whenever one barrier was overcome, the masculine career path to rewards and prestige changed route: thus science replaced the classics as the gateway to success (Lagrave 1992).

All true, but as Alice says, even the smallest of hills can never be a valley. The intellectual ambitions of girls were at last beginning to be catered for. Enrolments of women students in French universities jumped from 7,297 in 1920–1 to 20,188 in 1930–1, 21 per cent of the whole (Crubellier 1979: 292). In retrospect, this was the heyday of the now-vanished girls' *lycée*, with its seriousness of purpose, strict discipline, dedicated teachers and puritanical ethic which we now see was available for only about forty more years after 1930. Its obvious rigidity is easy to mock from beyond the 1960s, but here was another area where the horizons of the possible altered for girls, while not changing to any great degree for boys. Boys whose own environment remained stable might react to change in various ways – as often as not by increased contempt for 'bluestockings' as evidenced by Sirinelli's account of the rue d'Ulm. The gap between possibilities for girls and boys might not be closing very fast, but the movement was all one way: the girls were the ones who made the move.

As for *youth organizations*, one's impression of change is even greater and over a much broader social range. Again the freedom this represented for girls was proportionately greater and certainly more visible, contributing to a public awareness of change. I have deliberately avoided until now discussion of the 'garçonne' or 'modern girl', that cultural construct of the 1920s. Victor Marguer-itte's controversial novel of that name has recently been reanalysed by Mary Louise Roberts. It was published in 1922, and as she remarks, makes less sense as a reflection of some supposed reality among young French women of the decade than as a paradoxical reflection of the anxiety of the returning soldier and the cultural crisis over gender in French society (Roberts 1994, chap. 2). Like *Lolita* some generations later, the novel (in ways its author did not necessarily foresee) provided a stereotypical image with which various kinds of trangressive behaviour by girls or young women could be aligned. The book was so widely read that many adolescents of the late 1920s and 1930s will have caught sight of it. Monique Lerbier's sophisticated forms of handling despair were not available to the factory girl in northern France. But for the latter, other forms of rebellion, such as joining a youth movement with values different from those at home could equally cause moral upheaval:

> It was my grandfather who made the most trouble for me. He lived with us and was an out-and-out anticlerical. What battles at home! He refused to say anything to the chaplains if they came to the house, accusing them of filling my head with propaganda; he was quite shocked by my going around on a bike and especially if I took a lift in the chaplain's car.
>
> (Aubert 1991: 43)

One could no doubt find examples of a young communist girl at odds with her family: and there, too, the greatest objection might equally be to her bike-riding. Those who joined the movements, if only a minority, were asserting a culture different from that of their parents. There is plenty of printed evidence that adults felt youth was changing. However, the popularity of youth movements was not a figment of their elders' imagination but a conscious choice on the part of the young.

Let me end with a coda on a young woman whose name came to be almost as culturally resonant in the 1930s as the term *la garçonne* in the 1920s – indeed, the word was applied to her by witnesses at her trial for parricide. From a modest background (her father was an engine-driver), Violette Nozière was eighteen when in August 1933 her parents were found unconscious in their flat, as a result of poison. Her mother recovered, her father died. Violette was found guilty and sentenced to death in 1934. The sentence was commuted and she was eventually pardoned. After the war, her original conviction was quashed when an appeal was allowed on the grounds of the defence made at the original trial, that her father had sexually molested her. Press comment before and during the original trial had, however, centred on the wayward and promiscuous life allegedly led by the defendant, roaming the Latin quarter and paying the bills for her law-student lover. A former schoolfriend testified that Violette, who had attended the Lycée Voltaire and the Lycée Fenelon, was 'a good student, always top of the class', who had spoken of becoming a teacher of mathematics. Her own defence lawyer criticized the family for encouraging her to succeed at school: 'instead of this vain education, I would have preferred her to have received some elementary moral guidance.' Her mother gave a particularly telling interview, in which she alleged her daughter's greed for money as the motive, so that she could '*vivre sa vie*, comme elles disent toutes', 'live her own life, as all the girls say these days'.[33]

Vivre sa vie was the catchphrase of the era. Violette Nozière had been born in 1915; she was only seven years old when *La Garçonne* was published; in 1930, the abolition of secondary school fees came in time to relieve her parents of some of her educational costs; and in the early 1930s, when the depression had already struck, she was still apparently trying to live out a version of *les années folles*. Why did the case spark such interest? The first six months of 1933 had seen any number of sensational murders by both men and women (including those by the Papin sisters). It was not so much the fact that a woman was on trial, nor even that the charge was the rare one of parricide. A critical factor was surely that the case centred on a young woman educated above the normal level for her class, who was living a life loosely modelled on that of the *garçonne*, and who apparently showed little contrition when confronted with her crime. If Violette Nozière's 'independent' behaviour had been a genuine exception, she would have been seen as less of a threat to patriarchy. But a self-willed young woman was no longer out of the ordinary and, for that reason, she was particularly disturbing as a sign of her times.

As to how much 'freedom' of any kind in youth relates to politics, the link is far from obvious. As Roberts points out of fashion, 'to look emancipated was not to be emancipated'. She argues that the political impact of the new fashions in the 1920s was chiefly to 'scandalize and infuriate' (Roberts 1994: 85). But we can see something stronger than that at work in the youth movements which girls of quite similar education or background to Violette Nozière sometimes defied their families to join.

3

'A SLIP OF A GIRL CAN FLY IT'
The false promises of aviation

You roll down the runway... and then you fly away, the clouds are your garden.
Thérèse Gauthier (Madeleine Renaud) in Jean Grémillon's film *Le Ciel est à Vous*
(released in 1944, but based on a real-life event of 1938).[1]

Adventures in the air are the supreme epic [*chanson de geste*] of our time.
(Joseph Kessel, 1933, quoted in Wohl 1988: 47)

As a metaphor for liberation, flying was as suggestive in the late 1930s as in the
pioneer days before the First World War. Between the wars, aviation stopped being
an eccentric activity, not unlike a sport, and began to be the fastest way to travel,
part of the industrial, military and commercial future. Flying was still exotic: most
leading politicians had not set foot in a plane. The heroes and heroines of solo flight,
from Lindbergh to Saint-Exupéry, from Earhart to Adrienne Bolland, were rarely
out of the headlines. Flying had a special appeal in France: Kessel's *L'Equipage* was
the literary event of 1923; Saint-Exupéry's *Vol de nuit* (1931) sold over a million
copies. In 1935, the communist daily *Humanité* ran a series of articles entitled 'Les
perceurs du ciel', to appeal to both boys and girls. For, unlike the *chansons de geste*,
flying seemed to be something at which young people of both sexes distinguished
themselves.[2] Although women fliers were always a tiny minority, they were paid
disproportionate attention, showing that – after all – it could be done. Women
pilots were role models for schoolgirls, symbols of success in a modern technological
world. If I have chosen to write about aviation here, it is because it shows
particularly clearly both the opportunities and limitations of the age for a post-
war generation of women. Aviation had political and military dimensions which
histories so far available do not explore.

One could apply to France, with hardly any alteration, Joseph Corn's remarks
about aviation history in the United States:

Although there has been a great deal of attention paid to the history of the
airplane... the largest portion of this literature has been written by aviation
buffs, who have given us detailed accounts of particular types of aircraft, such
as the seaplane or airliner.... [Such studies] are invaluable. Yet not
surprisingly, their authors, writing from within the tradition of aviation
enthusiasm, have not documented or analyzed the feelings, attitudes and

65

behavior which characterize the phenomenon. Nor have any academic historians of aeronautics explored this dimension of the airplane's impact on our culture.

(Corn 1983: vii–viii)

In the French case, what is not military, industrial or technical[3] comes under the heading of anecdotal and romantic. The exploits of the pre-1939 years have been plentifully chronicled, usually with more enthusiasm than accuracy, often providing a good read. But the structures of aviation, unlike the designs of aircraft, remain underexplored. The everyday life of aerial folk has largely to be deduced from incidental data. As for the politics of flying – who had access to the planes – this too lies submerged and unquestioned under a welter of information. When gender is mentioned in this context – and it is, surprisingly frequently – it is generally with a positive message: yes, it was demonstrably possible, if a little unusual, for women to make a career in the air on the same terms as men.[4]

That this kind of statement is a half-truth will be the argument of this chapter. There is no real equivalent in France of Corn's 'gender-encompassing' history of aviation in the USA. Only since the war had respectable young women been able to travel about unchaperoned, yet in no time, it seemed, the new woman, or 'garçonne' was not only driving a car but flying an aircraft.[5] As early as 1919, a young French woman flew in a ridiculously underpowered plane across the Andes, only the second human being to do so: surely things would never be the same again. But the technology of the twentieth century has been neither socially nor historically neutral.

PIONEERS AND DAREDEVILS

Flying in France has a long history. By the outbreak of the First World War, it was beyond the pioneer phase. Already, in 1909, when Louis Blériot became the first pilot to fly the English Channel, he had his own plane-making firm and flying school, and his was one of seventeen French firms exhibiting at airshows. Airfields appealed to a varied clientele: sportsmen, mechanics and artisans recruited for plane-making, enthusiasts male and female. But lessons were expensive for amateurs. Pilots' licences were introduced in 1908, and by 1914, 1,754 had been granted in France, a mere seven of them to women. It may seem tiny, but this was a higher proportion than at any time thereafter. The first licensed woman pilot in France was Elise Deroche in 1910.[6]

The First World War both launched aviation and made it more demonstrably a male activity. After slow beginnings, the potential of the aeroplane not only for reconnaissance, photography and supply but also for bombing and fighting led to remarkably rapid developments in speed, distance and carrying capacity. By 1918, France had produced a total of 51,040 aircraft and 92,594 engines. Wartime recruitment hugely increased the numbers of male pilots: the 12,000 Frenchmen who held licences in the 1920s were war veterans, while the number of women was barely out of single figures (Petit 1981: 37–44; Chadeau 1988: 21). The war not only introduced a generation of young men to aviation, it made them competent professionals, in short order and at the state's expense. All airmen underwent military training, under the instruction of other men. It cost them nothing – except of course that it was undertaken in the dangerous conditions of wartime, and might cost them their lives. But survivors had many hours' flying experience in all weathers and in several types of plane. They were mechanically better prepared than the pioneers, either being mechanics themselves, or having been obliged in emergencies to do running repairs – although throughout the period star pilots continued to rely on their 'trusty mechanics' for expert servicing of their aircraft. It had been an excellent free apprenticeship with experience thrown in.[7]

During the 1914 war, French women were not allowed to fly in any military or even paramilitary capacity. A proposal for back-up planes with women crews, made in 1914 by Marthe Richard (a qualified pilot destined for a colourful life), was rejected by the French high command, on the grounds that the Hague Convention had not recognized women as combatants, so they would not be treated as such by the enemy if captured. Her proposal was for 'a corps of women aviators who will evacuate officers [sic] and carry messages and supplies to the front'. Similar ideas had occurred to another pioneer, Marie Marvingt, who had devised the earliest plans for an ambulance plane in 1910. Although ambulance planes were eventually used in the war, women crews were not. At the time when men were taking part in the massive expansion of aviation, determined by military requirements, women were left out of the reckoning.[8]

But from 1918 French aviation entered an area of turbulence. Aircraft manufacture slumped. Where in 1918 there had been 190,000 workers in the aircaft industry, by 1919 their numbers had fallen to 3,700 (Chadeau 1987: 147 ff.; 153). The end of hostilities released from service several thousand airmen and mechanics who sometimes found it difficult to make a smooth re-entry into civilian life. France did not at first set up a peacetime air force: there were some airborne units, but the Armée de l'Air was not formally constituted until 1933. A few pilots did stay on, attached to the armed forces, but there was no indication of how military chiefs would deploy their aerial resources. Ex-servicemen with mechanical skills opened garages and converted their expertise into servicing automobiles. A few left the force to go it alone in the 'barnstorming' which flourished for a few years in the 1920s. Army surplus planes could be bought cheaply, and the daredevil airshow or the fantastic exploit was one way in which those whose taste for excitement had been whetted by war could reproduce the thrills of flying and make a living. Oddly enough, although disadvantaged in respect of training, women aviators could and did join in this rather anarchic form of activity. Adrienne Bolland, for example, the woman who flew the Andes in her little Renault Caudron G3 in 1919, became famous as a daredevil flier in the 1920s.[9]

Her exceptional career should not divert attention from the material difficulties facing would-be women pilots. Whereas men had mostly qualified during the war, the only way women of the post-war generation could learn to fly was by taking private lessons – usually from ex-air force pilots. They had to pay for lessons, and found it hard to chalk up enough hours in the air for their licences. Access to light planes was not automatic for anyone after the war. But men whose job it was to fly in the air force or on commercial flights, or who had a mechanical background, might have the use of planes, or even the possibility of buying light planes as a hobby. A few hours flying time could usually be wangled. Women were worse placed. They needed private means or had to beg, borrow or save up. The biographies of almost all women pilots tell of early hardship as they saved up to buy even the cheapest and most basic planes – second-hand Gipsy Moths as a rule. Throughout the period, this obstacle – obtaining an airworthy plane – remained the most important, and was only overcome with great determination or luck. Madeleine Charnaux and Maryse Bastié worked respectively as a sculptor and in a shoe factory to earn their living. Bastié was notoriously hard up all her life. Maryse Hilsz paid for her lessons by parachute jumping. Hélène Boucher, whose well-to-do family refused to finance her flying, had to borrow money and was in debt for the rest of her short life.[10] A French flying magazine in 1937 carried the following not untypical advertisement: 'Girl, [jeune fille] pilot, 25, shorthand and typing, good English, offers office work in exchange for flying hours.'[11]

In the early post-war days, the light planes used for stunts and records were often simple affairs made of wood and canvas. Determined individuals could gain access to them, sometimes persuading a manufacturer to provide the plane by proving their skill. Adrienne Bolland had to demonstrate to René Caudron her ability to loop the loop before he gave her the plane in which she crossed the Andes. Maryse Bastié flew under the swingbridge at Bordeaux in 1926 to attract the manufacturers' attention (it still took her two years). Hélène Boucher performed some spectacular aerobatics to persuade Renault to take her on as a test pilot in the early 1930s.

The manufacturer might, as in Bolland's case, derive great benefit from such stunts – though if a woman crashed a plane, it was bad publicity. But there was another aspect of publicity that might have offered women some advantage. In America, where the bulk of manufacturing was directed towards civil transport, efforts were made to acclimatize the public to flying. The publicity given to women aviators was sometimes a deliberate strategy. This could be called the 'duck soup factor'. Louise Thaden put it this way: 'Nothing impresses the safety of aviation on the public quite so much as to see a woman flying an airplane . . . [if a woman can handle it] the public thinks it must be duck soup for men' (Corn 1983: 75).[12]

The approach did not develop in France to any great extent. The natural place to apply it would have been in civil aviation. Plane manufacturers were faced with the problem of converting wartime machines into civilian transports. Innovations initially concentrated on safety and comfort (development of retractable under-carriage; pressurized cabins); intercontinental travel (refuelling, night flying). French companies sponsored 'raids' or long-distance flights essentially in order to see whether viable passenger links could be established – usually to French colonies. Former air aces (Nungesser, Costes) became famous for their expeditions and assaults on speed or altitude records. Between 1919 and 1924, the French held eleven of the fifteen world speed records. In uneasy tension with these spectacular exploits, there was some attempt to interest the public in flying as a safe and reliable means of transport, not simply a sport of reckless daredevils: Michelin (manfacturer of aeroplane tyres) set up the Comité français de propagande aéronautique in 1921 to give the French nation 'l'esprit aviateur' (Petit 1977: 198–9).

But there were at least three reasons why the 'duck soup' factor never really developed in France. The first was that women pilots were banned either formally or informally from all *organized* forms of civil aviation. The second was the overwhelming importance of the military in determining how French aviation developed. And the third was that the popular perception of flying was still deeply marked by the high risks attached: while criticism was sometimes voiced in the press about the high rate of pilot casualties, at the same time there was something of a cult of the sacrificed hero. The literature on flying cultivated the dangerous myth of Icarus: 'duck soup' was exactly what French writer-aviators did *not* want flying to be.

Formal prohibition took the form of the battle over licences. In 1925, the permanent committee of the International Commission on Aviation resolved that women were not to be granted licences to fly passengers on public transport planes (although several women, including Adrienne Bolland in France already held such licences). The French representative, the conservative politician P. E. Flandin, Air Minister at the time, supported the women's claim, but strong opposition from other countries (notably Britain) prevailed. Flandin backed Bolland in her challenge to the ruling, and it was eventually amended to allow the formal granting of licences). But in practice virtually all commercial airlines maintained the ban on women pilots for passenger flights (in France and elsewhere).[13]

Formal banning was only part of the obstacle. Almost as potent was the masculine team ethos, partly inherited from the war, which prevailed in organized air transport. Commercial passenger services developed only gradually, as progress was made in pioneering the routes. The first regular overseas links were not passenger lines at all but airmail services: hence the rise of the famous Compagnie Aéropostale, delivering mail to French territories in Africa and pioneering the South American route. Created by the Lignes Aériennes Latécoère, based in Toulouse, its operations were directed by the formidable Didier Daurat. Most of the pilots were ex-wartime airmen, or had done post-war national service in the air. Among them were celebrities such as Jean Mermoz and Antoine de Saint-Exupéry, whose writings chronicled in only slightly fictional form the atmosphere of this team of adventurers – so used to forced landings in the desert that at first the line always sent two planes at a time to make sure of spare parts, and later recruited 'Moorish interpreters' to help negotiate if the local population was hostile. Aéropostale in its pioneer days depended on a form of comradeship and solidarity based on army experience. Daurat, himself a war veteran, aimed above all to create team spirit and loyalty, and he asked a lot from his staff: 'Outside flying missions, staff are expected to be on the airfield every day, so as to absorb company spirit.' Describing the outfit as a 'melting pot of hearts and social classes', he later wrote that he fought a ruthless battle against 'elements of disruption' – such as the pilots' wives. 'When the latter came to complain about low wages or over-long absences from home' they got short shrift: 'my rôle was to listen to engines not to moaners . . . . My objective was a quite different one . . . the primacy of the Line' (Petit 1977: 188 ff.). As subsequent events showed, the Aéropostale adventure was one in which serious risks were taken with pilots' lives, and the unsound army surplus planes they were originally obliged to fly were far from dependable; 120 crew members are said to have met their deaths in the early days. (Later planes developed by Latécoère were technically much better.) It is no surprise that even the most intrepid woman flier was not to be found in the team. It was not the danger as such – after all, Maryse Bastié in the 1930s was to establish a solo record on the same route to South America as that on which Aéropostale veteran Mermoz had perished the year before. Rather, it was the all-male ethos, which reflected in the airspace over North Africa that of the French legions fighting in the desert below.[14]

There were other airmail and pioneer passenger lines too in the 1920s: Les Lignes Farman, Les Messageries Aériennes, Les Grands Express Aériens – all with somewhat similar collective identities, which would have made it hard to accommodate women. Paradoxically, however, in spite of a very far from woman-friendly culture in aviation, these 'heroic' early days when the activity was still more like a sport enabled the few women individual enthusiasts to appear as not so very different from men, facing many of the same problems and risks, in planes that were not technically much less advanced. In the 1920s, the industry itself was still hesitant, and French military chiefs were reluctant to envisage major development of an air force branch of the army. Civil aviation, still in its infancy, was less in the public eye than the series of individual 'solo' records or 'firsts' which were an almost everyday occurrence in the late 1920s, as new areas of the globe were opened up and as new models pushed back the limits of speed, altitude and endurance for every class of aircraft. If Lindbergh faced a rapturous reception in May 1927, when he landed in Paris after the first solo Atlantic flight 'by instruments', so too did the Frenchmen Costes and Bellonte find a warm reception in New York when they made the first North Atlantic flight by *anyone* from east to west in 1930. A small but significant number of women took part in the raids and expeditions, sometimes as 'the first woman to . . .', sometimes taking on all-comers: Adrienne Bolland received huge publicity for her Andes feat. In 1930, Maryse Bastié took the world endurance record (thirty-eight hours non-stop in the cockpit). In other words, this was still (just) the age of the 'lone flier', when technical advances were piecemeal and chance, luck or courage played a part in every flight. Even so, women's records were often not classified in the same league as men's, either because of the different capacities of the plane, or the assumed capacity of the flier. By 1930, men did not really need to compete for endurance records any more – they had moved on to greater things – whereas Bastié, who was small and slight in build, had to convince a manufacturer that she was physically capable of handling a plane (Bart 1981). But the gulf between men and women widened even further in the 1930s, as military considerations took over.

Experts on French aviation between the wars have dwelt at length on the problems and shortcomings of military procurement and its role in stimulating (or not) the French aircraft industry. General Christienne has pointed out the hostility of the other service chiefs to the creation of the air force for years after 1918, and Emmanuel Chadeau has analysed the effect this had on plane-makers.[15] Without going over the detailed arguments, it can be said that most writers, whatever their perspective, seem to agree that the years 1919–33 were indeed a time of comparative eclipse for France as an aeronautical nation, as it lost its early lead. Lindbergh's feat, despite his warm reception, was perceived as something of a humiliation for France. It should be borne in mind that many French historical accounts are coloured by the urge to explain the small part played by the French air force in 1940, and most of them locate the reasons in the early years after the Great War.

> The war was not lost in 1940 but in 1920. At this time, the outstanding role that aviation had played in the First World War was almost completely overlooked by the French High Command.
>
> (Christienne 1979: 401)

Chadeau, chronicling the ups and downs of the industry, tells a parallel tale of mismanagement, competition and not a little corruption during these years, when instead of a true 'industrial mobilization strategy', a phrase much heard later on, there was a decade or so of institutionalized chaos. Plane-makers depended on state subsidies, but state policy was still erratic. The individual successes – the prototype models designed by gifted individuals and piloted by oddballs and misfits – were what the public saw, reflected in raids and records. In this context, both men and (a few) women could shine: whether the oddball was male or female made little difference. The press was in fact particularly fond of portraying aviatrixes, creating that ambiguous character the liberated woman. But the underlying industrial reality behind the apparent progress was a lack of coherence. From the point of view of gender, the introduction of greater coherence to the industry in the 1930s would indirectly mean the elimination of the individual freelance in favour of more institutionalized structures of aviation – and these were overwhelmingly and intentionally male.[16]

The change got under way in the 1930s. State military procurement had always been the most serious outlet for French plane-makers, even when such procurement had remained obstinately low throughout the 1920s. But in 1933 the air force, after a series of piecemeal decisions, finally received new organizational structures. Despite continuing conflict between service branches and the comparative indifference of the high command to air power as an element in strategic planning, large numbers of aircraft were ordered from the industry in 1934, in an atmosphere of some panic about Germany's potential for rearmament after Hitler's coming to power. Since new prototypes could not be developed at such short notice, these were necessarily 'old' models and by the time they came off the production line, in 1936–7, they were already outdated technologically. However, it has been argued that on 7 March 1936, when German troops entered the Rhineland, 'the [French] air force was probably superior to the Luftwaffe' (Christienne *et al.* 1981: 29). The French air force was notoriously not called upon on that occasion. To keep up with events, new orders had to be placed. A key role was played by the Air Ministry under several administrations, including the 1936 Popular Front.

As Air Minister in 1933, the radical politician Pierre Cot had already presided over the rationalization of the commercial sector under the title Air-France. Recalled to his post by Léon Blum in the Popular Front government of 1936, Cot had three chief priorities: to nationalize the military side of the aeronautical industry and restructure it (in line with the nationalization of the arms industry which was government policy); to restructure the air force; and finally to create a *pépinière* (seedbed) of young fliers and technicians to take over from the veterans of the First World War.[17] From the point of view of this chapter, it is the third of these, recruitment, that most concerns us, and the chief area to be examined is the extent to which a military logic took over in aviation from this time on, because of the international situation. The focus of attention is therefore that phenomenon unique to France, the creation by the Popular Front government of *l'aviation populaire*.

L'AVIATION POPULAIRE[18]

Blum's government had a programme of social reform, which included paying more attention to young people of underprivileged background. But it came to power at a time of great international tension and with the proclaimed desire to oppose fascism. *L'aviation populaire* (best translated as 'flying for all') reflected this contradiction. It was inspired by two quite separate and in the end incompatible agendas. The first was to combat the exclusive nature of private flying clubs and make flying accessible to all. As such it fitted into the logic of the Popular Front's stress on sport, youth, health and leisure for a working class viewed as deprived of these things. Until then, private flying had been very limited: even in 1930, there were only about thirty privately owned planes in France. With the introduction of state subsidies designed to encourage private ownership, the figures went up but only to a few hundred: 480 sold in 1930–2 (Petit 1977: 177). Flying clubs extended the chance of individual flying, by purchasing light planes for the use of their members. But aero clubs still had a very exclusive image, and rates were beyond the pockets of most people. (Just as it has been observed that the young militants of the extreme right in France had the advantage over their left-wing opponents of owning cars, so too it was no accident that the authoritarian Croix de feu movement had its own aero clubs, and even arranged fly-pasts during its paramilitary parades.) At the same time, it was a period when ordinary people with a taste for novelty might receive their *baptême de l'air* ('get their wings') as passengers, either on a scheduled flight or on a joy ride at weekends. Aviation had become more visible in everyday life and enthusiasm for it was tapped by the Popular Front initiative. 'I know the moment has come to call broad sectors of society into aviation,' as Pierre Cot put it in his launching speech (Ory 1990: 1,466).[19]

No less important, however, was the military logic which provided the second agenda. The French air force was still largely staffed by the First World War veterans, who by 1936 were approaching forty, a rather advanced age for an aviator; 313 of the 672 captains on active service had served in the war. The technicians too were ageing: to fly and service the new generation of planes, some renewal was essential (Christienne *et al.* 1981: 43 ff.). What was more, Germany, which for years had been prevented from raising an official air force, had successfully brought many young men into a flying culture through its programme of gliding for all. Gliding, *le vol à voile*, historically rather neglected, was actually the key to resourcing both the foundations of the Luftwaffe and France's *aviation populaire*. Gliders were cheap and could be made up in kit form in aero-clubs (as indeed could light one- and two-seater planes). Already there was a 'popular' (i.e. close to the Communist party) gliding association in France called *L'Aile Tendue*.[20]

The structures of *l'aviation populaire* were threefold, although it operated on a shoestring: the seven million francs allotted via the budget in the autumn of 1936 were insufficient to provide a true training programme and material (Ory 1990: 1,466–70; Vincent 1993: 13 ff.). The first phase was aimed at schoolchildren up to the age of fourteen, and depended on the co-operation of state schoolteachers: children would learn something about aerodynamics and construct model aeroplanes. An exam would be the gateway to stage two, for fourteen to seventeen year olds, when gliding would be part of the programme. Those who qualified further could move on to powered flight, at age eighteen, subject to parental consent. Each flying club was to have an *aviation populaire* section (SAP) with light planes, technical support and insurance subsidized by the ministry. A *conseil* within each section would include one ministry representative, one member of the teaching profession and one representative of the trade union movement. Members of sections would pay a minimal subscription towards learning costs and flying hours: ten francs a month maximum.[21]

From the official description it appeared that both sexes were eligible to join, and girls certainly took part in stages one and two, making models and in some cases progressing to gliding. There was evidently some hesitation about admitting girls to stage three, since it had to be officially announced in 1937 that they could indeed join SAPs 'on the same conditions as boys'. In practice, they were never very numerous, partly because the 18–21 age group had to obtain parental permission to take flying instruction, something less readily granted to daughters than to sons. In one flying journal, which ran a column called 'Ce que pensent les jeunes', twenty-two *témoignages* were printed, of which six came from girls. One of them, Suzette Allègre, explained that she was passionate about flying, but her father had refused permission.[22]

Only a minority of girls might seriously have expected to move on to stage three in any case, but once the whole programme began shifting towards the military agenda, it effectively stopped them going any further. Pierre Cot himself – writing after the event, it is true, and wishing to justify himself militarily in the eyes of posterity – claimed that his priority had been to create a seedbed of youngsters [*de jeunes gens* = young men] having gone through a basic training programme in flying, which would allow the military to select the most promising... these arrangements will provide the air force with the new blood it needs.

(Cot 1939: 142)

Even at the time, according to Pascal Ory, 'as far as the extreme right was concerned, *l'aviation populaire* was simply a vast infiltration plan designed to create an air force made up of popular [read pro-communist] elements' (Ory 1990: 1,471). Stéphane Vincent's research led him to think that 'the air force had always seen *l'aviation populaire* as a vast operation to recruit military pilots' (Vincent 1993: 53). There was obviously some tension from the start between the two aims of the programme.

Although the results, in terms of qualified pilots emerging from the ranks of the young enthusiasts, were not negligible, they failed in the short term to lead to large-scale recruitments into the air force. It was probably this as much as anything which prompted the effective militarization of the critical third phase of the programme in 1938, which did not officially happen until Cot left the ministry. Under his successor, Guy Lachambre, the priority now was 'no longer the development of flying as a sport, as the first documents suggested, but the training of air force pilots'. The regulations were tightened: all would-be fliers in stage three had to have 20/20 vision and undergo a strict medical test. To make it more attractive to potential air force recruits, those who had completed their *certificat de préparation prémilitaire* could be directed preferentially towards the air force when they did their military service, as technicians, navigators and radio operators, as well as fliers. By the end of 1938, of the 5,000 who enrolled for stage three, 3,574 obtained a *certificat de préparation prémilitaire*. In 1939 the status of the programme was formally changed by a decree signed by President Lebrun:

The air force will temporarily take over the military training of young men intending to serve in the air force. For this purpose, it will have access to all the resources presently available to *l'aviation populaire*.

(Vincent 1993: 182)

The gliding and model-making sections of the programme were quietly dropped.[23]

All this necessarily concerned young men between the ages of eighteen and twenty-one. Initially the project was intended to be wider in scope. Over-twenty-ones of modest means who wished to learn to fly had joined 'popular' flying clubs, i.e. attached to the Communist party, and had been able to benefit from some resources of *l'aviation populaire*. Both men and women over twenty-one had joined, although women were always a minority. In one such club, Les Aiglons d'Ivry, whose records were traced by Vincent, only four of the hundred or so members were women: an eighteen-year-old schoolgirl, a nineteen-year-old clerk, a twenty-nine-year-old nurse and a thirty-two-year-old accountant, who was on the committee, no doubt for her budgeting skills. Most of the male members were

74

workers in the metal trades, often skilled technicians. Some popular flying clubs explicitly stated that they admitted both sexes. Even so, many of the women members did more gliding and parachuting than piloting.[24]

It was really the militarization of the programme rather than the explicit exclusion of women that thwarted any hopes they might have had of the 'flying for all' initiative. Older men also suffered from the change in emphasis. And it is hardly surprising that military considerations should have prevailed in the late 1930s. The Spanish Civil War had been the first serious indication to the public of what the bombing of cities might mean (there had been some aerial bombing in the Great War, but its impact was relatively slight). The Spanish experience also revealed chasteningly to the French that the few planes they had delivered to the Republicans before the self-imposed embargo were hopelessly outclassed. The debate over war in the air came to dominate the fear of the approaching conflict. The Luftwaffe had been created in 1935. Displays of aerial force became *de rigueur* at military parades during the last years of peace: with massive fly-pasts and parachute drops or staged bombardments. The French air force had actually performed its first fly-past at the 14 July celebrations of 1935, which were also marked by the demonstration of solidarity for the Popular Front (Petit 1977: 133). Since at this period the armed forces in France were entirely single-sex, aviation too, while becoming more accessible than ever before to young men, became less accessible to women. Once more, military logic closed doors that had been opening.

MEN AND WOMEN IN THE AIR

It is evident that there was a serious mismatch between the contemporary public's perception that flying was for both sexes and the actual imbalance of gender in aviation. The faces of a number of French airwomen might have been familiar to newpaper readers and cinema newsreel audiences, but in the history books, they figure only marginally, since historians look primarily at the larger scale developments in aviation and the overall picture – from which women were structurally excluded. Why is there such a contrast? There is no very great mystery about it. But the detail helps us to see why flying was read a little too easily as a symbol of women's emancipation.

In the first place, the numbers of women qualified to fly were simply always very small, whereas there was a huge jump in the numbers of qualified men after the Great War, compared to pioneer days (and again, of course, after the Second World War). In 1926, in all of France, there were about 12,000 men with current licences (few of them actually flying, admittedly) and only 10 women. By way of comparison, in 1932, by which time there were about 40 French women aviators, there were already about 550 women out of the 18,000 qualified pilots in America – still a small minority, but a much larger percentage. Worldwide at this time, about 2,000 women held licences. Even in 1939, after the impact of *l'aviation populaire*, there were only 150 licensed women aviators in France – a rise from 1926 but not a very large one. So we are talking about very small numbers indeed. On the other hand, of the forty or so active airwomen of the early 1930s, most would be known by name to the French public, their photographs regularly displayed in the press and on the screen, their exploits lengthily descibed, their flying costumes analysed and commented on. They fulfilled something of the same function as women film stars of the same time.[25]

Stars and lone fliers operate as individuals. We have already noted the 'brotherhood' operating within Aéropostale, for instance, and flying fraternities existed wherever large-scale activity was concentrated. What had happened was that women had been left behind in the pioneer stage of aviation, where it was 'merely' an individual sport, before it became a group activity. Banned from the army and from commercial transport, women were forced into the 'artisanal' occupations in aviation, necessarily on a small scale: demonstrating planes for firms; giving flying lessons or jaunts for tourists; delivering planes. And even these kinds of employment were hard to come by. Women were almost forced into spectacular solo work, under sponsorship or more often with haphazard finances; some operated successfully within a husband and wife team.

Hence their presence in record-bagging, particularly in the 1930s. By this time, the raid and record had become little more than a hobby for men, one to be taken on in their spare time or for the glory of the firm or the squadron. In the words of the *Boys' Book of Flying*, 'when there is nothing left for anyone to be first to do, when all the first times have been accomplished, what then is the flying man or woman to do to achieve fame – except break the records already set up?' (Boff 1937: 192). The records that really mattered – speed for example – depended on having access to the most modern aircraft: all-metal planes of the latest design and capacity. These were almost without exception available only to men. Women, on the other hand, went on competing for records most of which certainly called for endurance, courage and determination, but which were no longer of major technical interest. Consequently their only competitors were other women (and this competition was accordingly fierce and sometimes bitter, for the media attention was out of all proportion to the record itself). There is a distinction between carrying off an all-comers' record and being 'the first woman' to do something, although both might receive equal press attention. Thus in 1934 a French woman carried off the 'feminine altitude record for a light two-seater plane with a passenger', while the the claim to have made the 'longest solo flight in a straight line by a woman' was the object of cut-throat competition between several French pilots in the late 1930s. Andrée Dupeyron, whose story was the basis of *Le Ciel est à Vous*, wrested it from Elisabeth Lion in 1938, but went missing in the Arabian desert in the attempt. The nation held its breath until she was found. This kind of record might make headlines, but it was quite marginal to the progress of aviation.

Occasionally French women accomplished all-time feats, such as Maryse Bastié's record time for a solo crossing of the notorious South Atlantic, in 1936, shortly after the national hero Jean Mermoz had perished on the same route (Bart 1981: 63). But on the whole, women's records tended to be for less spectacular flights, thus reinforcing a segregation which was making women's aviation like other 'women's sports'. The dialogue in *Le Ciel est à Vous* is revealing:

Pierre: With a plane like this, we can't aim for anything serious, you do see that? . . .

Thérèse: Of course I know our plane can't go in for any of the men's records. But . . . have you thought about the . . . women's records?[26]

In other words, women were still flying old crates. They were at the stage Aéropostale's pioneers had reached in the early 1920s. Wherever technological advance was to be found, they were absent. Hélène Boucher is an exception here: she had revealed a talent for speed flying, but was probably the victim of her own inexperience with high-powered planes, crashing the Rafale she was test-flying in practice in 1934. Her death further inhibited the employment of women to fly advanced machines.[27]

A French air force commander interviewed in a woman's newspaper in 1939 deplored this waste of talent. Instead of bagging prizes 'flying familiar old planes', he forthrightly suggested they should be learning all the things they did not know how to do – flying by instruments, night flying, how to land fast planes, radio – a significant list. 'It is only in the context of the new aviation that we can conceive of a role for them.'[28] The pilot Madeleine Charnaux said much the same in a lecture the same year, pointing out that record-hunting was turning women pilots into self-centred individualists with a queen bee mentality. Other press articles echoed the refrain, even more pessimistically:

Commercial airline pilots? Out of the question. Test pilots? Ditto. These are occupations requiring long apprenticeship and anyway, they are reserved for men. The air force admires [women] but can't use them. Flying instructors? Can you imagine Toscanini giving children music lessons? The great [male] pilots all have paid jobs, and for them records and feats are just hobbies.[29]

The writer of this article went on to quote the cases of several well-known male pilots, and suggested that women might be recruited to 'a propaganda division in *l'aviation populaire*' – but even this modest suggestion seems to have fallen on deaf ears.

L'aviation populaire must have been a great disappointment to women. The rhetoric about flying for all was essentially a class rhetoric addressed to working-class boys: 'What we particularly need is the working class,' as the Air Minister put it (Cot 1939: 244). Despite pressure from some of the famous women pilots such as Bastié, then at the height of her celebrity, Cot personally expressed himself with great caution on the subject of women fliers: France would have to 'wait for the aeroplane to be thought of as a normal means of transport before we can judge on any serious scale the equal merits of men and women as fliers'. No sign of the duck soup factor here: interestingly, Cot's view from the left contrasts with the attitude of the conservative Flandin in the 1920s, when the context was admittedly more civil than military. The only initiative in women's aviation remotely comparable to what was on offer for men was *l'aviation sanitaire* – a privately organized flying ambulance service, associated with the Red Cross, which recruited and trained women nurses: the idea was that they would serve and if necessary be parachuted into areas of need from planes flown by women pilots. It is not clear whether the *piloting* was ever done by women, although there were certainly parachute-trained nurses.

Most women pilots remained loners, then, strange glamorous figures whose relationship with the rest of the world was conducted through the media. As a result they actually reinforced images of femininity more than they challenged them. It is true that photos of women in flying suits make them look active and emancipated, by contrast with those who were conventionally dressed. But women aviators were under considerable media pressure to look good. There are a surprising number of references to appearance in the anecdotal and biographical accounts. Adrienne Bolland wore smart silk pyjamas under her flying suit for the Andes flight in anticipation of the reception and once admitted she crash-landed 'because my mascara got in my eyes'. This had a serious side to it: glamour was thought to be essential if they were to get financial backing. 'If a woman was neither rich nor pretty she would never be able to fly the Atlantic: it took research and popularity to find the backers.' The only way women could obtain planes was to keep themselves constantly in the limelight, as Charnaux learnt when she went to Morocco for six months, because there were more daylight hours for flying there: she was scolded on her return by her advisers who said that was no way to get backers (Lauwick 1958: 174). The individualistic, film-star treatment of women's appearance has some parallels in male flying too. One has only to think of the number of films (Renoir's *La Règle du Jeu* comes to mind) in which male aviators are regarded as public figures – sometimes, it is true, with feet of clay. On the other hand, it is hard to overlook the collective male-bonding which was deliberately fostered in the perceived identity of airmen. Vincent reproduces photographs of the parades at the great *Fête de l'aviation populaire* during the 1937 Paris Exhibition: the members of the more middle-class Fédération des Aéroclubs de France are in paramilitary uniforms with flags, whereas the 'Front populaire' Fédération Populaire des Sections d'Aviation are bare-chested, in shorts, holding olive branches – either way a stark contrast with the representations of women fliers (Vincent 1993: 86).[30]

The contrast carries over into the moral connotations of the 'flying mystique' as it appears in both contemporary and retrospective writing. The French title of Saint-Exupéry's popular book *Terre des Hommes* (translated into English as *Wind, Sand and Stars*) is no doubt significant. But even in the 1990s a strongly gendered rhetoric still creeps into the mystique of the air. The pioneers went into the sky, 'violant l'espace aérien encore vierge' ('raping the still virgin airs'); they formed 'une race nouvelle', which would lead to 'the improvement of the human race'. Aviation, once it had become a popular aerial sport, would 'transform all these youngsters into men, without exception; and it would transform the men into heroes' writes a young historian without irony (Vincent 1993: 70). The flying mystique, he goes on, included 'a sense of sacrifice, team spirit, disinterest, duty and faith' – qualities asked of men at various times, by political or military authorities, but more rarely required, collectively at least, from women. There are times when the rhetoric of the Popular Front can come close to that of Vichy.

The media treatment of the disappearance over the Atlantic in 1935 of Jean Mermoz (a man of the extreme right) was consistent with the mystique: it was seen as 'the supreme sacrifice', for French aviation, of devotion and commitment. By contrast, *Paris-Match* in 1939 ran a strongly worded article entitled 'Petites Filles' ('Little girls') devoted to deaths of women aviators: those of Amelia Earhart, who had disappeared over the Pacific in 1937, Hélène Boucher, Lena Bernstein (whose death may have been suicide in despair at failing to get finance) and Edmée Jarland (a gliding champion killed in March 1939, in an accident for which she was not responsible). The article, which caused a certain stir, ended by saying that 'these little girls died because they had chosen a calling which was not a woman's calling'. There was no praise here for their pioneer efforts or sacrifices; rather, the article echoes others which criticized women for sacrificing the interests of their actual or even *future* children by taking risks. Mixed views came even from *Marie-Claire*, the 'modern' women's magazine of the late 1930s, which carried enthusiastic articles about women's exploits, in particular Andrée Dupeyron's long-distance trips – but then warned its readers off flying as a career. When Dupeyron went missing on her Middle East adventure, she came in for immediate press criticism as a mother with young children who had left them and risked her life. These ambiguities are faithfully echoed in Grémillon's film, which opens and closes with a party of orphans being shepherded by a priest, to remind the viewer that Thérèse's children might end up motherless.

Mixed signals too come over the degree to which aviation introduced women to modern technology. It should have signalled a promising relation between women and a form of technology hitherto unknown to either sex – and up to a point it did. But there was a curious parallel with women's industrial employment. Technological advance had made it possible, as papers often put it, for a 'slip of a girl' to fly a plane (or drive a car): it required no great technical prowess or strength. Similarly (cf. Chapter 4) technology had reached the point where semi-skilled women and girls could operate machines in industry that carried out tasks formerly done by a skilled male worker. But in both cases, women did not truly control the technology they were handling. Women aviators, with some exceptions, were by their own account able to perform only the simplest repairs to their aircraft, and relied even more than men did on their 'trusty mechanics' (a pattern faithfully reproduced in *Le Ciel est à Vous*: both the real-life Lucienne Ivry, who plays herself in the film, and Thérèse, depend on Pierre to fix their aircraft). They had little technical training. Similarly, the woman factory hand depended on the male fitter who maintained and serviced the machine. The technology of the period opened some doors to women but shut others in their faces.

The extent to which aviation could be linked with broader notions of emancipation, such as feminism, and in France the suffrage issue, is not easy to determine either. Joseph Corn in his book on American aviation has some interesting remarks about women aviators who put their feminism on the back burner, with the exception of Earhart (Corn 1983: 86 ff.). In France, feminism was a diffuse movement (see Chapters 7 to 9). But of the official feminist groups, many were dominated by women of the older generation, whereas women aviators were mostly young in the late 1920s and 1930s. Few examples of feminist statements survive. The one documented incident is perhaps revealing of the constraints upon aviatrixes, rather than of their feminism. In 1934, when the flamboyant suffrage campaigner Louise Weiss launched her Femme Nouvelle movement, seeking to revitalize the battle for the vote, she arranged a number of demonstrations, sometimes with celebrities in attendance. One of them was a grand meeting in Bordeaux (not too far from the aeronautical heartland of Toulouse) at which the three most famous women pilots of the time, Bolland, Bastié and Boucher, all appeared. The local flying clubs turned out and local press reaction was favourable. But shortly afterwards, if we are to believe Weiss's memoirs,

> The planemakers had let my air heroines know that if they defended their rights, they would run the risk of losing precious support. And of course they depended on these manufacturers. They let me know that they could no longer help me.
>
> (Weiss 1974: 43)

CONCLUSION

What is interesting about aviation in the inter-war period is that it is historically specific. Never again in peacetime would so much public attention in many countries be focused on *named* aviators. And never again would women be so visible in this area. Any notions of linear 'progress' towards equality are therefore hard to sustain. In the years after 1945, women's presence in aviation was above all as stewardesses – the role model of the schoolgirls of the 1950s and 1960s. Not until the 1970s, if then, did integration into the structures of flying itself, now massively developed worldwide, become a serious option for women.

This backward move does not seem to have been noticeably affected by the role of women in the Second World War. In some countries, women aviators were used, though only in a fairly limited capacity and always in non-combatant roles: the Luftwaffe had its *Helferinnen* who were employed to deliver machines, tow balloons and targets, etc.; there were up to 100,000 of them and their role was essential. In the US, the WASPS, Women Air Service Pilots, did similar tasks, releasing men for combat roles; and in Britain there were the ATAs (Air Transport Auxiliaries). In France, by contrast, women were scarcely used at all in the armed forces (Christienne 1981: 228–9). True, the French were only involved in conventional combat for under a year at the start of the war and about a year at the end; and several of the women aviators meantime did take part in resistance activities. The record is not entirely blank. In 1939, five known women aviators were requisitioned to help transport planes. Further attempts to provide them with some status during the phoney war did not come to anything, but at least one, Claire Roman, was apparently used to move fighter planes to safety during the invasion in 1940. More positively, when Charles Tillon of the Communist party was Air Minister in 1944–5, he initiated a small-scale unit originally consisting of thirteen experienced women fliers (mostly by now rather over age for military service). The experiment was a victim of the crisis in February 1946 when all military credits were cut (Beauregard 1992: 280 ff. and 335 ff.). But there is no discernible difference between France and any other country in the later employment of women in aviation. With one striking exception, Jacqueline Auriol, French women did not learn to fly the new generation of jet planes and it is only very recently indeed, generally after legislation or changes in regulations made under pressure from the women's movement of the 1970s that women in France or anywhere else have been able to qualify as commercial airline or military pilots.[31]

This is not a story about women's unwillingness or incapacity for flying (although few took it up), nor is it one of consistent and deliberate discrimination and exclusion (although some certainly occurred). It is about the politics of aviation, essentially governed by military factors, the military ethos and the international situation throughout the period – despite the rise of civil aviation. War was a major obstacle to women's control of the new technology of the air, largely because in France, as on the whole elsewhere, women were not permitted to be combatants. Discriminatory practice was embedded into the military establishment and given added impetus by such initiatives as *l'aviation populaire* which were hailed at the time as extending the chance of flying to all, yet excluded a generation of girls who would have been more ready than any previous generation to take up the challenge. This is not to suggest that 'women's rights in aviation' were more important than military imperatives at the time: all I would suggest is that they were not incompatible with them. For example, to enter the military logic of the time, the diagnosis of virtually all observers of the French air force in 1940 was that one of its problems was a shortage of young, trained pilots familiar with the new planes provided both within France and from abroad. One particular source of recruits was never drawn on, although there is evidence that young women would have come forward. Women's non-combatant status is not a fixed ahistorical reality – in various times and places, women have been, are and will be combatants. But not in France at this time. The ideological blocking of gender relations at this point is not usually cited as one of the causes of France's defeat in 1940 – though many other 'social' attitudes have been; and it would be exaggerating hugely to put it this way. But the argument can at least be put that the partial but real emancipation of the woman aviator was effectively suppressed by social and military structures that could not comprehend it, and that this strategy had some resource implications for the later conflict.

The star billing of France's women aviators was in some respects rather like the star billing of those other exceptional figures, the three women ministers in Léon Blum's 1936 government (see Chapter 7). In both cases, exceptions which did not seriously threaten the structures either of politics or of aviation could be tolerated. The structures survived: French women continued to be prevented from voting until 1945, and women fliers continued to be banned from where most French aviation was going on. And yet, as so often when one looks at this period, the ultimate blocking of access to women cannot entirely conceal the fact that relations between the sexes had moved into a new kind of relationship. The assumption that men would dominate the new world of the air could not be sustained any more than that they would monopolize automobiles. Jean Grémillon insisted that in his film, flying was only a metaphor for surpassing oneself. His character Thérèse, he wrote, 'was just a rather limited and selfish petite-bourgeoise', but the story 'purifies her and makes her great . . . . Aviation was just a pretext in this film for transfiguring the reality of a given milieu [an ordinary everyday one: the small-town garage in provincial France] into a superior reality'. Despite the original misogyny of an aeronautical writer like Kessel, who may well have inspired Grémillon and his script-writers to use flying as a metaphor for transcendence of self; despite the deliberate reminder of Thérèse's children in the shots of the orphans, the popularity of *Le Ciel est à Vous* showed that audiences could accept without any trouble the notion of that kind of transcendence being accomplished by a woman.

4

WHAT DID PEOPLE DO ALL DAY?

The sexual division of labour in France between the wars

To distinguish the labour force [or 'working population': in French *la population active*] from within the total population means considering as 'inactive' all those who are not included as active. This may seem logical as regards small children or old people, but is less logical in the case of women taking care of a household. However, *out of respect for tradition and concern for simplicity*, we shall continue to use this definition of active and inactive, while bearing in mind the fact that it is only a convention, and devoting some time to a description of the total and the inactive population.

(Marchand and Thélot 1991: 67, my italics)

To approach official statistics from a gendered perspective is to run straight into questions of definition. The purpose of this chapter is to suggest ways in which we might query the map of the sexual division of labour in France in the inter-war period as it is usually drawn, and the definitions and sources – notably the census – on which it is based.[1] The relevance of apparently neutral statistical records to the politics of gender will be explored after examining the way such data usually reaches us.

Let us take a straightforward description of the employment of women after the First World War:

While the war did indeed mark a high point in women's work [*le travail féminin*], it marked the peak of a long-term upward trend in this respect, and the point at which the trend was to be reversed for some considerable time. For about half a century after 1918, women's economic activity [*l'activité féminine*] was in overall decline in France. On the other hand, the Great War was a more permanent factor in shifting the site of women's work, accentuating certain trends already under way (such as the decline of outworking, *le travail à domicile*), but above all the trend towards white-collar work and the so-called tertiary sector.

(Robert 1989: 451–2)[2]

The language used to convey this kind of analysis calls for some comment. What is meant by the key terms 'work', 'activity' or indeed 'women' in this connection? The terms 'work' or 'labour' (both translatable as *le travail*) are elastic ones in both French and English, and are not synonymous either with employment (*l'emploi*) or

83

economic activity. What is really being referred to in the quotation is 'activity as measured by the census'. 'Work' on the other hand covers a variety of activities which the census classifies according to context, rather than to content. To quote a recent writer, consider the 'observable task of looking after a baby':

> By describing it in these words, one gives the impression that the task is part of the domestic economy: in other words, that it is unpaid work carried out within the household. However this same activity expressed as child-minding becomes a form of employment: it is paid and recognized by the State. When expressed as baby-sitting, the nature of the activity changes again, implying either some kind of undeclared paid work or a reciprocal arrangement of exchange of services between friends [or relatives, etc.].
>
> (Windebank 1991: 3)

The recording process, however scientifically organized, can never be neutral but reflects certain choices. Of the three ways of 'looking after a baby' described above, only the second would be recognized by the census as 'activity'.

All our statistical information about 'who did what' in the recent past is based on the returns of the census, or population count. During the first half of the twentieth century, a census was held every five years in France, except in wartime: 1901, 1906, 1911, 1921, 1926, 1931, 1936, 1946. The basic data consists of the forms which were filled in by, or on behalf of, every individual resident in a household [*ménage*] on census day.[3] Economic activity is a key concept for classifying the data. For instance, because such a high proportion of nineteenth-century French households were agricultural holdings, the census officials needed a concept of economic activity that included this kind of self-employment. So all adults in such homes, men and women, were liable to be registered as 'active' and the convention was also applied to small shops or businesses throughout our period. In all other households, however, a wife who did not declare an outside form of paid work was routinely listed by the census as dependent family and 'non-active'. This convention has remained constant to this day as a defining factor for the important notion of the 'active population'. Both between the wars and since, the non-active population has been taken to consist of all children below school-leaving age; all people in full-time education; all people who have retired; and those persons who declare themselves to be 'without occupation, *sans profession*' – the category used for women referred to in everyday parlance as 'housewives'. (The registered unemployed were recorded as active, even if they had no work on census day.) So far, so obvious perhaps. The reader will see the drift of these preliminary remarks. To classify such women as 'inactive' was neither an accident nor a foregone conclusion. Domestic labour, if carried out within the household and not for payment, was neither measured by the census nor incorporated into national economic statistics. The omission is not fixed and universal, but the result of decisions by the relevant authorities. The 1881 census in England and Wales was the first to exclude domestic labour from the categories of work (Lewis 1984: 175). There is now a very large literature about the hidden domestic economy, with no clear consensus as to what to do about it.[4]

It follows that the first step in rethinking the sexual division of labour in the past must be to query this initial distinction between active and inactive, since in practice large numbers of women have been classified as inactive. In most material available to the historian, the employment or economic activity of 'men' (married or single, fathers of children or not) is taken for granted as a given, not a matter of choice, and in no need of explanation. Nor has men's participation in the domestic economy yet been seriously explored historically. Women, on the other hand, have been viewed as only episodically 'active', while it is their contribution to the domestic economy that has been taken for granted. Even the term 'women' is not transparent. Both in inter-war sources and today, there seems to be constant slippage of the term 'women' to mean 'married women' or even 'married women with children'. In practice, few writers have contested the choice made by the single woman or widow to take employment (before the 1960s, a majority of wage-earning women in France were single), nor that of the married woman to work alongside her husband in smallholding or shop. But 'le travail féminin' is often a coded expression for married women's outside employment, presented as a choice.

The historian cannot take a position of absolute neutrality any more than the census official. But I will try to avoid the debate about choice and necessity, or the positive and negative evaluation of waged work for women. My aim will be to re-examine the results arrived at by the usual measuring process. The first section uses the concept of the informal economy in order to make a guess about what the census does not tell us about the sexual division of labour; the other two sections seek to interpret some of the data the census does provide about gender balance: first white-collar employment and 'educated careers', where there was *quantitative* change after the Great War; then industrial employment, where the changes were *qualitative*, as new technology influenced the situations of men and women workers. The overall aim is not to suggest that 'the figures are wrong', but that the history of the period can be thought and written in different terms.

INACTIVITY AND THE INFORMAL ECONOMY

The concept of the informal economy has been developed in recent years, largely in response to post-1945 economic development (Windebank 1991: 3 ff.). In societies where formal tax and social security systems render most people's income visible and accountable, attention has concentrated on the 'black' economy: one in which goods and services are exchanged for cash or payment in kind, which escapes being recorded. The notion of the informal economy has coincided with the different, but related debate referred to earlier, about the economic value of domestic labour, defined as the everyday maintenance of the existing, future or retired labour force. There is no reason why the concept of the informal economy cannot be applied retrospectively to past societies – since it is obvious that pre-industrial societies had flourishing informal economies. Inter-war France, although changing fast, still retained many of the features of a pre-industrial economy which allowed informality to thrive.

Jan Windebank distinguishes three main types of 'work' which would come under this general heading: first, voluntary unpaid work; second, working for real payment which is not recorded (the 'black economy' proper); and lastly, domestic (or neighbourly) labour, for which no formal payment is given or received. In what follows, all three will be referred to, in relation to what the census described as the 'inactive population' of France between the wars.

Let us take as an example the census of 1931. The total population of France in 1931 was 41,228,000 (figures from Marchand and Thélot 1991: 176–7). The census defined 20,397,000 people as 'actifs', 20,831,000 as 'inactifs'. Of the inactive, 14.3 million were female (3.5 million of them girls under ten) and 6.5 million male (3.5 million of them boys under ten). There is a considerable difference between men and women: while 86.9 per cent of men over thirteen were active, only 43.4 per cent of women were. Taken by age-group, while the figures for men reach a peak of activity between twenty-five and twenty-nine, remain high until the age of fifty-five and decline thereafter, the figures for women fluctuate differently.

'Active' population 1931 by sex and age-group

Age	15–24	25–39	40–54	55–59	60–64	65+
Men	94.0%	97.3%	95.3%	86.7%	75.7%	48.1%
Women	60.9%	41.5%	40.9%	42.4%	37.5%	19.5%

A majority of women were recorded as active below the age of twenty-four, but then there is a sharp drop to only about 40 per cent, for the middle years, falling off more abruptly again after the age of sixty-five. Although French women by no means all gave up work on marriage, the major feature of these figures is the high number of women over twenty-five 'without occupation'.[5]

How can the informal economy help account for the 'inactive' women? First, was there such a thing as literal inactivity, a category of leisured people outside the reach of any definition of 'work'? Some women in the wealthiest classes apparently had a great deal of free time – were more truly 'inactive' than others, even allowing for household responsibility. Bonnie Smith calls the wives of northern mill-owners just that: 'ladies of the leisure class', but her careful analysis of their everyday lives enables us to make up our own minds as to whether they were really 'at leisure' or not (Smith 1981). There is no equivalent scholarly study of the 'femme bourgeoise' of the inter-war period. Instead a certain stereotype has gained currency and attracted particular dislike – perhaps because the *bourgeoise* conspicuously symbolized the luxury money could buy. Common sense tells us that the vitriolic depiction of *la femme bourgeoise* in writers as far apart politically as Drieu La Rochelle and Nizan cannot be accepted at face value, any more than *la Garçonne* can stand for all twenty-year-old Frenchwomen in 1922, but it persists disconcertingly, even in history books. In the bourgeoisie, one recent history of the 1920s suggests,

> while the husband took care of his business, the wife lived in semi-idleness,
> vaguely supervising the children, who were actually cared for by servants,

sewing, reading, visiting or entertaining her women friends, spending the entire summer in the family's country house or renting a seaside villa with the children.

(Becker and Berstein 1990: 363–4)

Retrospective dislike of the wealthy (and 'bourgeois' can cover a wide range of circumstances) hardly justifies such loaded language. If the informal economy is to have any purchase on the *bourgeoise*, the obvious category is voluntary work. Certain women of this particular generation have left traces in the historical record: they were engaged – perhaps more than any previous cohort – in philanthropic or quasi-political activities. Several age-groups had been propelled out of their sheltered lives by war work. Suzanne Lehmann Lefrance, from a well-to-do family, helped her mother in a wartime hospital as a teenager, trained in childcare afterwards and helped set up a crèche. Having married a prosperous businessman, 'I went on working [voluntarily]: the crèche did not take all my time. We had to raise funds, hold charity sales . . . I held clinics for newborns in the day-nurseries. We taught unmarried mothers how to care for their babies' (Germain *et al.* 1982: 147–9). This was a rich woman talking, and one with plenty of household staff, but her commitment to the crèche was real enough, and there were many such *oeuvres* in these transitional years, as welfare slowly moved from private to public administration. Literally thousands of middle-class women undertook unpaid charity or committee work (cf. Chapter 6).

Their importance should not of course be exaggerated. There is really no way of measuring this kind of activity, and those who devoted anything like a full-time week to it were a minority. But the point at issue is comparability with similar activities. A professional male politician – a *député* or a full-time political party official – would figure in the census as fully active. His wife or sister, who might spend up to the equivalent of a working week organizing a pressure group, or doing good works, would count as inactive, since she earned no income. Her means of support, whether inherited or provided by her husband, were not the census's concern. Fund-raising tea-parties would certainly not count as 'work'; and maybe it is stretching the term to its limits to suggest otherwise. But a male municipal councillor, a winegrower in the south say, might spend several daylight hours of his week talking informally with other men in the café, oiling the wheels of local politics – the famous *sociabilité*. The frontier between these kinds of activity is hazy at close quarters.

What of the numerically large percentage of inactive women in more modest households? Some of these might better be described as 'partially active' by the census's own criteria, since they derived undeclared payment for services rendered, in the 'black economy'. It has long been argued that the census unavoidably failed to record casual work properly. A study of outworking (*le travail à domicile*), perhaps the most obvious example, estimated that while in 1936 there were possibly as many as a million outworkers, mostly women, the census recorded only a quarter of a million, and about the same for 'irregular wage-earners', a comparable group.

Incontrovertibly, many outworkers did not declare all their sources of income to the authorities. Some might combine it with another trade, such as small farmer [or partner in same] and only declared one activity. . . . On the other hand, married women, or daughters living with their parents and working at home usually declare that they have no occupation.

(Paulin 1938, quoted in Salais 1986: 96)

Another source of incomplete declarations, mainly concerning women, was domestic labour, if it fell short of full-time domestic service: working as a charwoman or taking in washing or sewing. The actual tasks performed would be identical in nature to those done by a servant or full-time housewife. The question arises here of reliability of self-definition. Perhaps because it looked like the housework they did for themselves, such women and their families were reluctant to consider this as 'real work'. A ribbon-maker in Saint-Etienne (who herself went out to work) was asked: 'Did your mother work after she was married?' 'No, never. She stayed at home, but she did mending for other people. *She was never without some work in her hands*' (Sohn 1992: 96). Outworking might look very like housework. A respondent in one survey, asked the same question about his mother, replied, 'No, she looked after the household' – but went on to say that she made aprons and lingerie braid on her Singer sewing machine; the work brought in 'a little extra, not much'.[6] With full-time domestic servants becoming scarce, the part-time charwoman took their place. François Cavanna's mother, married with one child, went out cleaning during the depression. So common was this part-time, irregular, often undeclared work that the rules for claiming unemployment pay specifically singled out charwomen, who could not claim benefit unless able to prove that they could 'live off their work', estimated as a minimum of twenty-four hours a week. As today, it is wishful thinking to imagine that such work would be recorded, since the chances are that it was deliberately concealed. We may simply note it as another anomaly within the supposed inactivity of women. Some were wrongly so described, by the terms of the census itself, though their number is impossible to calculate.

Lastly, there is the third and largest category of informality: domestic labour or housework. The largest group of 'femmes inactives' were those caring for the daily requirements of husbands and/or children and other dependants. Here the census criteria themselves come into question. Is to omit housework to note 'only half an equation', to persist in the historical discourse that has rendered domestic labour invisible whoever does it? (Oakley 1981: 162).

Jan Windebank has described two of the principal schools of recent thought on the subject of domestic labour as radical and feminist respectively. They are not necessarily incompatible. Put briefly, radical, usually Marxist-inspired theories argue that capitalism needs unpaid domestic labour to rear and maintain the labour force at least cost. In times of need, such as wartime, those doing it can be drawn into waged work as an industrial reserve army. The feminist version argues that capitalism has benefited from pre-existent patriarchy to impose its structures, since domestic work is almost entirely left to women. The leading representative of the latter theory in France, the materialist feminist Christine Delphy, takes the argument to its logical extreme, analysing processes like cooking alongside farming, as adding to the exchange or consumption value of commodities, and arguing that the decision not to count domestic work as part of the economy is the result of patriarchal ideology (Delphy 1984: passim). This debate, and in particular Delphy's analogy between domestic work and family farming, can be applied retrospectively. We might say, to demonstrate how fragile these categories are, that there was *in this period* a potential continuum between the work done by an 'inactive housewife' and that of a partner in a family farm, since

(a) in most households, housework was physically harder, more time-consuming, and required more acquired skills than it does today;
(b) there were more partnerships in family production units in French society than today;
(c) there was considerable overlap between the tasks accomplished by partners in (b) and those of a 'survival/maintenance' kind carried out in all homes, as in (a).

While the theoretical question is not specifically French, the social composition of inter-war France means that this continuum is particularly applicable there. Its advantage is that it allows for nuances, rather than the clear-cut divisions of the census. If we were to draw up an all-woman continuum, on a scale of least-to-most hours of activity, it could start at one end with the lady of leisure with few responsibilities – say the adult daughter of a wealthy family – then run through various kinds of *maîtresse de maison* including the housewife in households of modest means. At the busy end would be those on the 'double shift': the woman partner within the family enterprise who had little or no leisure, and the married woman industrial worker, doing housework on top of a full day's paid work.[7] At one end of the scale the workload was light, at the other it was heavy. The range is so great that it might seem impossible to compare their situations, and the census, by simply disregarding them, did not even try. What these women shared, however, was the knowledge that with few exceptions they, and not the men in the family, were responsible for household tasks and the domestic economy.

Of the hard labour in the majority of French households at the time there are many memories, although France has less survey material than Britain.[8] A description of a regular Monday wash in a modest household in Paris shows that laundry could take all day:

My mother and grandmother went every week to wash the linen in the local *lavoir* [washhouse] . . . . On the ground floor there were sinks to pour in the washing agent and you could buy bucketfuls of hot water. . . . The atmosphere was full of steam and noise, washing paddles and tongues going all the time! When it was well rinsed and wrung out, by hand of course, you had to take it upstairs where there was a row of skylights and compartments with clothes-lines. I helped my grandmother to hang up the laundry and we came back to fetch it next day when it was dry. This was generally the household task for Monday and took up most of the day. While they were at the *lavoir*, the housewives couldn't do the cooking, so they put a stew on to simmer while they were away.

(*Mémoire* 1993: 84)

Making, mending and ironing clothes took a lot of time. 'Mother could do simple dressmaking with her Singer sewing machine, of which she was very proud.' Most clothes were still home made, and mending was all done at home: 'You turned everything – it was an obsession. Shirt collars were turned and extra ones made from one of the shirt tails' (ibid.: 34–5). Many homes lacked running water and electricity for most of this period. Shopping, cooking, washing, cleaning, caring for children was a full-time job, according to eye-witness accounts of life in modest households. Some things, it is true, had changed. Most people no longer baked bread at home, but bought it at the baker's, and this saved time. But the cultural practice of providing two substantial home-cooked meals a day was a regular constraint (Sohn 1992: 101; cf. Martin 1987).

Without labouring the point, then, housework in this period could be constant toil, requiring skills that could not be acquired overnight: neither sons nor daughters were born with innate knowledge of turning shirt collars or cooking nourishing stews. Domestic management required an apprenticeship. Historically this was the time when the 'professionalization' of housework began to be talked about, as domestic servants vanished for good. Much has rightly been written about the changed conditions starting to appear now: the first Salon des Arts Ménagers, the early labour-saving devices, the move towards convenience foods like tinned vegetables. But time spent and division of labour remained obstinately the same. Historians of housework have pointed out that with every new invention, higher standards of time and cleanliness were expected. And until the Second World War, expensive labour-saving devices, such as that genuine liberator the washing machine, were in short supply. Here again, the real changes came only some years after the war. Today even a low-income household can survive somehow, by buying convenience foods and using launderettes, without it being necessary for one individual to spend all day on the housework. Between the wars, this was less possible. Men's participation in housework changed remarkably little, with very few exceptions, nor has it apparently changed very much down to the present day. And the 'profession' of housewife remained a figment of Paulette Bernège's imagination rather than a census category.[9]

Whereas the census deals in cut and dried categories, the idea of a continuum allows us to compare the day of a full-time housewife (not counted) with that of the farmer's wife (rather 'generously' recorded as a full-time worker in agriculture). Alfred Sauvy argued that the census *overestimated* the number of women and of older people of both sexes doing farm work, when it recorded all members of a peasant household as 100 per cent active (Sauvy 1984, vol. 2, chap. 2). If one were to scrutinize her day, he claims, a farmer's wife would not be engaged on agricultural work all day long. The point is well taken. Here for instance is a contemporary observer's description of a typical day in the life of a well-off 'farmer's wife' in central France, on a hot August day in about 1935. (It obviously compounds various possible cases: the writer's chief concern was that such women had little time for church.)

> Up at four, even if the children made it hard to sleep . . . . The men's breakfast must be prepared, the fire lit, the cows milked or the milk put in the creamer. Often the farmer's wife herself supervises and prepares breakfast for the farmhands, who may be numerous. At about six o'clock, the chicks and poultry are fed, the house cleaned, the beds made, even those of the hands. Time is getting on, time to think about the midday meal, fetching vegetables from the garden, drawing water from the well, not to mention watering the calves and giving them their feed, seeing to the pigs, whose rations have to be weighed and carefully distributed. After the midday meal, everything starts again, with the dishes. Some days of the week there is the washing and ironing; mending can be done while guarding the animals in the pasture. A snack for the workers, then it is time to start preparing dinner. The garden must be watered; and when everyone else is in bed there may be urgent repair jobs . . . the child's overall, the husband's shirt. The accounts are almost always her task. At the end of all this, after clearing things away, she is the last to bed. And for her, Sunday is not a day of rest.
>
> (Trouillard-Riolle 1935)

To quote this is not to insist on the hard life of the farmer's wife – well known even today. The point is that this timetable, recognized as full time by the census, is no more than an extended version of the timetable of many urban housewives in France at the time, with meals to make and children to care for. One could turn Sauvy's remark upside down and say that it is not so much the recognition of the farmer's wife as the *non-recognition* of the housewife that is the anomaly. The *fermière* was simply at the 'busy' end of our continuum, whether her activity was related to outside earnings (calves and pigs); to the self-sufficiency of the household (farmyard fowls and garden); or to maintaining family life (preparing food, mending, doing the laundry, like other women). The same would be true of small shops or cafés where both spouses worked. To stop at any particular point on the continuum is open to being described as arbitrary.

At the end of this limited excursion into re-categorization, if we were to add up the forms of voluntary, 'black' and domestic work not captured by the census, the informal economy might account for many waking hours of women listed as 'inactive'. This is not an argument about industriousness or income. It was always easier to take time off for a cigarette and a cup of coffee from housework than from the factory bench. The lady of good works had a far easier and more pleasant life than most men or women of lower income (and so did her husband). And there were positive sides to even the least pleasant jobs: some women factory workers claimed they went to work for the company and fun (Fourcaut 1982: 168–70). The point is that by its terminology the census eliminates many adult women from the status of full participants in the economy, classifying them with the very old and very young as 'unproductive', whereas men's relation to domestic work is normally passed over in silence, their full-time non-domestic activity seen as an absolute. At every level, they were more likely to be recorded as engaged full time in economic activity: uncomplicated full units in the economic – and therefore political – phenomenon 'France'.

What difference does it make to our perception of the inter-war period to point this out? For one thing, the image of the continuum helps to nuance and historicize the informal economy in an age when the housewife, the irregular homeworker and the dabbler in good works made up a greater part of the overall population than they do in France today. Their tasks are now handled by paid workers in social services, restaurants and dry cleaners. Domestic labour has not remained unchanged in France throughout the century: the grandmothers of present-day twenty year olds lived in a quite different domestic economy.

The broader function of questioning the category of 'active', however, is to unsettle the overall classification on which our entire picture of inter-war France, as well as of most other western societies, has been based. The informal economy helps to visualize over the long term a different map of male and female work from that of the census. We require this conceptual framework before we can seriously consider short- and medium-term change, such as differential working patterns during the depression or the impact of rural exodus.

It also helps to understand what is uncounted, invisible and negative in the cumulative portrait of women in France between the wars that we have inherited, something that lies concealed behind such generalities as 'a decline in women's activity'. As Joan Scott points out, if we accept past statistics without decoding them, that perpetuates 'a certain vision of the economy and of statistical science as an essentially objective enterprise' (Scott 1988: 137). It was no small part of the argument about enfranchising women that public and private were separate spheres. By providing 'objective' evidence about the economy couched in terms of 'active' and 'inactive' persons (echoing perhaps the terms 'active' and 'passive' citizens during the Revolution) the increasingly scientific measurements of the economy in the form of the census reinforced the notion that women were less than citizens in the economic sense.

THE FORMAL ECONOMY I: CHANGING GENDER BALANCE IN WHITE-COLLAR AND PROFESSIONAL OCCUPATIONS

For most people who lived through these years, women did not seem to be playing less part in the economy than ever before – on the contrary, it seemed to them that 'women were everywhere'. This apparent change in the gender balance is our next topic.

It was most visible in white-collar employment.[10] For much of the nineteenth

92

century, men had had a near-monopoly in clerical and administrative work. But the major change in the white-collar occupations, by the turn of the century, was gradual feminization. The shift took place within an overall transformation of both the service sector of the economy and white-collar work in the other sectors. Today the tertiary/white-collar sector employs about 14 million people in France, broadly half of them men, half women (Marchand and Thélot 1991: 170–5).

A historical study of the Post Office suggests reasons for the change, which could be applied with very little alteration to other white-collar work. They include new work patterns, some prompted by new technology (such as the telephone or typewriter); difficulties in recruiting qualified men; the availability of better-educated girl school-leavers; and lastly cultural assumptions that women would be less likely to join trade unions or seek promotion, might have shorter working careers and would be content with lower wages (Pézerat et al. 1984: 122; cf. Bachrach 1987).

The Post Office, with its women switchboard operators and postal clerks, offers an ideal-type model for the process – the word 'féminiser' first appeared in France in this context. It was a sign of things to come. Whereas the 1906 census showed one female office worker for every three industrial workers, by 1931 it was one office worker to two industrial workers (Rebérioux 1988: 67). This process had begun in a quiet way earlier. The copy clerk (*expéditionnaire*), a man who wrote out, in careful long hand, all the minutes and memoranda of the government office or company ledgers, needed only a primary school certificate to be taken on. The arrival of the typewriter in the late 1880s changed all that. The 'dame dactylographe' appeared well before the 1914 war: the first typists were young women with higher school-leaving certificates, often would-be primary school teachers unable to find jobs. As the link between women and typewriters became established, a second wave of typists, less qualified in educational terms, was drawn in by the increased demand from offices (Thuillier 1988: 27; Zerner 1987: 16). By 1914, nine out of twelve government ministries had a female typing pool. So the replacement of mobilized men by women typists and clerks during the war was not in itself an innovation, but reflected perceptions of women as particularly suited to office work (Thuillier 1988: 33). After the war, many women kept their jobs. In any case, with the return of full employment for men in the 1920s, and the expansion of the entire tertiary sector, there were now increased opportunities for both sexes. Men appear to have been more readily appointed to higher grades, with women concentrated among low-grade clerks or typists. 'The triumph of the female office worker' therefore seems a slightly two-edged concept: the new generations of women who came in at the bottom of the hierarchy generally stayed there.

In the nineteenth century, administrative jobs in the French civil service had been sought after by parents for their sons for the security they offered; they were obtained partly by patronage and family connections. The move to a more meritocratic scheme of entry meant entrance exams, from which women might have benefited. But a deliberate brake on the number of women was maintained by quotas, and by opening the entrance exams to them selectively, so limiting the impact of meritocracy. As a result, the existing hierarchy was very little disturbed. In the old days, the *expéditionnaire* could expect to be promoted to *commis d'ordre*, a more responsible administrative post and the equivalent of the later term *rédacteur* or minute drafter. For several years before 1914, women were excluded from the new exam on the grounds that they had not completed their military responsibilities – national service. After the war, the exams were opened to women who duly started to be appointed to more senior jobs, although they remained very much the minority the further one went up the hierarchy. Of the 124 *rédacteurs* in the War Ministry in 1928, 96 were men; of the 68 in Pensions, 57 were men; of the 32 in Trade and Industry, 25 were men; of the 44 in Agriculture, 33 were men (Thuillier 1988: 50).[11]

In private companies modern industrial methods, such as Taylorism, called for more central administration and expanded office staff, but a gendered hierarchy quickly established itself here too. In the larger companies there began to appear the cadre, or executive, practically always a man. The presence of women office workers commuting at rush hours created the impression that they were massively entering what had been the all-male world of paper-pushing. Films routinely depicted women as secretaries and office workers. But rather than ushering in a brave new world, Sylvie Zerner argues that this was the beginning of white-collar proletarianization: 'the recruitment to office work was not the point of departure for a rise in society [for women], on the contrary it was its terminus' (Zerner 1987: 513 and 1985: 16). A study of young women doing secretarial courses at the Pigier institute after 1918 concluded that most of them had left school at twelve or thirteen with the *certificat d'études primaires* only, and were mostly of modest origin, living in the working-class suburbs of Paris. Although the pay was low and prospects of advancement limited, office jobs carried more status than the alternatives: factory work or domestic service (Sornaga 1984: 84 ff.). This helps to contextualize suggestions that early generations of women found office work congenial on the whole (Thuillier 1988: 52, 59–60). What looked like a low-grade option to men seemed positively advantageous for a woman. 'Whether at the bottom of the career ladder in a given sector (the Post Office, trade) or in administration, the female office worker was as far removed from the directors of the firm as she thought she was from the manual workers. Whereas men *began* their careers as low-paid white-collar workers, women had no career to move on to' (Zerner 1987: 16).

For all that, when one looks at the history of white-collar professions, 'gender balance' might seem a meaningful term. From having been heavily weighted towards men, the numerical balance was shifting gradually towards equilibrium between the sexes in this period. After 1945, it was to tip even further towards women. The evidence suggests, however, that the concept of 'balance' is not quite the right word. What was emerging was more like a *gender pyramid*, with most women in lower-status jobs, and men on the whole in senior posts. When one turns to occupations already high in status, such as the liberal professions, it is doubtful whether it makes sense to talk about a gender balance at all. In the inter-war years, women were so rare in their ranks as to appear exceptional. A homeopathic dose – just enough to be able to claim equality of opportunity – is more like it.

Yet the fact that the professions were no longer absolutely single sex has been very positively evaluated, at the time and since, as an index of female emancipation. Take the report presented to a conference in Paris in July 1934 by the factory inspectress Gabrielle Letellier (Letellier 1934: 57–61). It started on a positive note: although 'all professions are not yet open to women', those from which they are banned 'are few and their number is falling every year'. She admitted, however, that while there were by now several hundred women barristers, much of the legal profession remained single sex by statute: men alone could aspire to be judges and magistrates in most courts, solicitors, attorneys, clerks to the court or recorders. She did not mention – perhaps it seemed too obvious – that the entire armed forces and the Catholic church hierarchy were all-male, and that salaried political posts such as members of parliament were also closed to women, since they had no political rights. In fact, a clause about 'being in possession of one's political rights' was still commonly found in the rules of admission to senior posts in the civil and diplomatic service, as well as in certain professions, indicating how closely citizenship was linked to professional employment.

Let us look briefly at just three of the professional areas mentioned by Letellier which appeared to be open to women, and where some degree of *mixité* was popularly thought of as having been achieved: diplomacy, medicine and the cultural/intellectual professions. In all of these, well-established career paths existed for young men, through the educational system: *lycée* and *baccalauréat*, followed by a professional entrance exam or further training. Most of the successful men were from well-to-do backgrounds, following family tradition: literature is full of young men obliged to choose a safe career (like the law), but yearning for a more adventurous life. For women, by contrast, the career *was* the exciting alternative.

In the case of diplomacy, because of the single highly publicized success of Suzanne Borel, many people assumed that the foreign service was now open to both sexes. Feted with flowers at the time as the 'first woman to pass the foreign office exam', mentioned in dispatches in the great war of the sexes, Borel herself, although no feminist, has described in forthright terms the obstacles placed in her way: 'Few women are better placed than I to appreciate the cunning, often combined with treachery and persistence, employed by men to place obstacles in the path of those unfortunate women who stray from the beaten track' (Bidault 1972: 20). Because no woman could carry out consular duties abroad, on account of having no political rights, Borel had to accept a home posting, while other graduates went on to diplomatic careers. Soon after her entry, in 1931, hostile forces in the Quai d'Orsay closed the loophole that had allowed her to sit the exam, so no other woman followed in her footsteps. In her memoirs, she recounts her struggle to achieve even minimal career advancement. Not until 1945, and the full recognition of women as citizens, was she eligible for a foreign posting (Bidault 1972: 42).[12]

This example is an extreme case, but it indicates the 'disturbance quotient' of well-qualified women. Other professional areas seemed more promising. Letellier's proudest note was struck in relation to medicine. Medical training in France had been opened to women back in 1875: it was the country to which women came from all over Europe 'and we have over 600 women doctors, surgeons, radiologists, gynecologists and other specialists, not to mention dentists and pharmacists' (Letellier 1934: 58). Six hundred might seem a respectable figure, but at the previous census in 1931 there were a total of 25,410 doctors practising in France, so about 25,000 of them were men (Zeldin 1973: 37). If the six hundred were important to women, they were insignificant within the medical profession, a light brigade indeed. The academic hurdle might be jumped, but it was difficult to find a private practice, acquired either through inheritance or invitation. The career path to hospital medicine also bristled with formal obstacles: 'externships' were easier to find than 'internships' and the latter were long jealously guarded by closing them to women. A disproportionate number of women doctors were obliged to seek posts in the expanding public health sector between the wars: in local clinics, or working for the Assistance Publique. They needed strength of purpose to persevere in the profession, whereas male medical students, following a family tradition, might be no more vocation-driven than Charles Bovary.

Madeleine Pelletier (1874–1939), socialist, feminist and maverick, who had to struggle to earn a living as a doctor, wrote in the early 1900s

> women, who have been admitted to medical schools for thirty years are only just beginning to get patients. For many years, poor women doctors in order to earn a living had to undertake chores that male doctors consider beneath them: with equal qualifications, they had to work as midwives, or masseuses in the richer districts, and doctors let them do injections and dressings.
>
> (Largillière 1981: 69)

By taking up public health appointments, a trend that has continued to the present, they were entering neither prestigious specialist work nor profitable private practice, and could be located within the pyramid of medical professions only slightly above the low-status jobs of nurse and midwife. Midwifery was a clear example of 'a profession in crisis', its social role increasingly being taken over by the health visitor, social worker and nurse – all exclusively female occupations, which men were *not* queuing up to join (Dubesset *et al.* 1993, chap. 10). The gender balance in medicine was not greatly altered by the trickle of qualified women doctors: a homeopathic dose within the profession, it was enough to prove there was no discrimination, not enough to threaten anyone.[13]

Mlle Letellier referred finally to the intellectual and artistic professions: here, she said, there was no field in which there were not distinguished women: architecture, painting, sculpture, music, the theatre, literature of every genre (Letellier 1934: 58–9). If this were really true, the problem for the historian is to bring out the evidence: histories of art, architecture, music, theatre, cinema, appear to record very few women creators. The few women's names that survive are mostly those of performers: actresses, singers, film stars, dancers. One might have expected much from new media like radio and cinema, since there were no established channels of recruitment. But in a recent essay on the beginnings of Radio-Paris in the 1920s, one of the rare pieces of research on radio, there are hardly any references to women (Duval 1990). Was this imbalance because women were indeed very rarely found as radio voices, or because more trace was found of the men in the records? That hypothesis could certainly be advanced of the cinema, where women were often professionally involved in production, as script-writers, continuity secretaries and editors. Almost all the best-known French directors of the 1930s had women editors: but their work, essentially self-effacing, has also been effaced in histories of the cinema. Editing – the organization of the shots and sequences which give the film its order, pace and rhythm – really became a separate profession only with the coming of sound at the end of the 1920s. Many women were handlers of film in the 1920s as manufacturing or process workers, and the first generation of editors had often been process workers. As the *métier* evolved, they were well placed to enter a trade which did not at first require any formal apprenticeship. Taking over the new technology, they became more technically accomplished than anyone else of their generation. Recruitment through unofficial links, independently of trade union or hierarchies, probably helped women to dodge the usual obstacles. Most directors formed a working relationship with their editors, men or women, but it is remarkable how many of the best-known directors (Renoir, Gance, Duvivier, Pagnol, Allégret, for instance) worked for many films with the same women editor (Marguerite Renoir, Marguerite Beaugé, Marthe Poncin, Suzanne de Troeyes, Yvonne Beaugé-Martin). This is not a hidden history so much as one not so far accorded much attention in French cinema history, where the auteur, the creative director, has tended to attract most attention.[14]

Similarly, men overwhelmingly dominate the intellectual field, whether one turns to histories of literature or to the recently prospected field of study, the intellectual generation. For obvious reasons, not least the late development of secondary education for girls, women professors were unlikely to figure prominently in any pre-war university calendars. There were in fact five of them in 1934, something Letellier regarded as quite an achievement – but the number of women in university posts overall was statistically insignificant. These may seem obvious points, but little has yet been done to chart the process by which an all-male intelligentsia still prevailed in an age of change. It has been pointed out that Christophe Charle's pioneering study of the emergence of the intellectual at the end of the nineteenth century, although including a number of previously unrecognized men, still underestimates women: in the period 1880–1900, 778 women were actively publishing, of whom he mentions none (Saint-Martin 1990: 52–6; Moi 1994: 11). The same might be said of the recent studies of intellectuals in the inter-war years, where an emphasis on the institutional seedbed, such as the rue d'Ulm, concentrates attention on a particular group of men and on a narrow definition. It may be that our recording equipment could be improved. Women were certainly nothing like as prominent as men in intellectual circles or in quantity of creative production; but the recording of what they did achieve is still very patchy.

97

This survey cannot be concluded without some mention of women school-teachers. If they have not been singled out here for detailed comment, it is partly because the great changes in this profession preceded the First World War, and partly because they turn up elsewhere in this book. But the largest single group of professionally trained women throughout the inter-war years were the primary and secondary schoolteachers all over France. Teachers were the organic intellectuals of the Third Republic, yet the majority of primary school classes and a fair number of secondary classes were taught by women, non-citizens. They had equal pay with men, suffered from no marriage bar, as they would have done at times in Britain or Germany, and often formed the backbone of local feminist or pacifist organizations to be met in later chapters. This was one area .where women could regard themselves as much on the same footing as men.[15]

In the other professions noted here, different patterns can be detected. On one hand, stirrings of change were real. The educational system would in the long run amend gatekeeping processes, such as entrance exams, to remove overt discrimi-nation. But strong counter-pressures made themselves felt whenever women seriously threatened to oust men from desirable jobs, whether in the law, the diplomatic service or specialist medicine. This was an age of tension and transition: bans and quotas could be reimposed quite legally without provoking protest, and selective discrimination could be maintained while a few keen women were allowed to find some way through (the homeopathic dose). Second, as in office work, women might pass the first hurdle, but find themselves blocked in the least profitable or status-carrying levels of the profession. Third, in the less formal cultural field, sex was not an automatic barrier: a struggling young sculptor had the same chance of success, whether male or female; a new medium such as radio or cinema placed no ban on women entrants. Here the problem may be one of historical detection. Male dominance may have been turned into apparent hegemony by the recording process.

If there was change in this period, it was partly thanks to the women's movement, helped by male sympathizers. But for women who did succeed in this transitional period, and were inevitably seen as exceptional, there was a temptation to assume that their own perseverance and merit, rather than change in public perception of the need for more gender balance, let alone feminism, had done the trick. Pelletier criticized her fellow-women doctors for failing to show solidarity with the feminist cause (Largillière 1981: 69). Suzanne Borel had no time for feminism at all: 'independence can be won, but it is primarily a personal matter.To reach it takes courage, determination, but above all reasonableness and patience: noisy processions behind grotesque banners are not only ridiculous, they are ineffective' (Bidault 1972: 219).

The feminist movement itself, by contrast, claimed credit for success. I would draw a less positive picture than Mlle Letellier did. What can be conceded is that *mixité* in occupations formerly male monopolies did become thinkable, if not always easily accepted. This was an age of hesitant change, with several about-turns on formal discrimination. Predictably, the least resistance was encountered over jobs carrying comparatively low rewards and status. But serious critical mass was being accumulated where it was most visible within society. Even if not as many women were lawyers, doctors or civil servants as people thought, there were enough of them to bring into the open some of the contradictions about women's political and civil rights.

THE FORMAL ECONOMY II: INDUSTRY AND CHANGE

Let us finally turn to a much-studied subject: the industrial division of labour between the sexes. Thanks to the thriving school of French labour history, especially active from the 1960s, with a wealth of studies of particular trades and industries, and of working-class culture as a whole, industry is the most fully researched branch of the French economy. Until the emergence of the recent wave of women's history, there were comparatively few studies of women in industry or in the labour movement for the inter-war period, but that is now changing.[16]

During the Great War, in France, as in other combatant countries, women replaced men in manual occupations, notably munitions manufacture. This provides at once a new departure and a 'high point' of women's industrial employment, depending on how one looks at it. In this section, rather than begin by engaging in the more general debate about whether war work was a force for emancipation or not, I would like to concentrate on industry itself. The percentage of women recorded as working in industry declined overall in the inter-war period, according to the census, as did the proportion of women in the industrial workforce, but not dramatically: women made up about one-third of the workers in industry. We have already noted that there may have been under-recording by the census, but this section is less concerned with numbers than with the qualitative changes within French industry as they affected the sexual division of labour. It will concentrate on two or three questions, with the aim of identifying how things shifted in the inter-war period, and starts with the particular structure of the wartime arms industry.

The reason why the *munitionnette* has a special claim on the historian's attention is not that she represented a 'typical' woman war worker. Women were not in a majority in the munitions factories, nor was it the only form of women's war work. Many women were employed in textiles for the war effort (uniforms and supplies) as well as replacing men in whole range of occupations (cf. Thébaud 1984: chaps 6 and 7). But the *munitionnette* as potential heroine or villain, helping the war effort or, as some male workers and war veterans later argued, manufacturing weapons of doom at cut-rate wages, has a peculiar visibility and symbolic status.

A further reason, however, is that she could be seen the instrument of a new division of labour. The munitions factories can in retrospect be seen as the site of a new industrial pattern. Many of them were converted automobile factories; thus Citroën was by the end of the war employing 11,700 workers to make mass-produced shells (Schweitzer 1982: 55), and Renault, Panhard and Berliet were all heavily engaged in munitions manufacture. The workforce consisted of mobilized male workers, civilian male workers dispensed from military service, drafted workers from French colonies and prisoners of war, as well as women. The percentage of women overall varied from 50 per cent in Citroën by 1918, to 32 per cent at Renault and only 10 per cent at Blériot. Marc Ferro suggests that of the 1.5 million armaments workers about 350,000 were women, roughly a quarter (Noiriel 1986: 155; Thébaud 1984: 172; cf. McMillan 1981: 132).

Detailed studies show, however, that women were used for certain *kinds* of process: they were 'set to work as quickly as possible and only after the most elementary training'. Their work largely consisted of repetitive tasks: shell production for example had been broken down into a series of simple processes. Most supervision and maintenance of the machines and tools was carried out by men. The system of work pioneered in France in the munitions factories had been devised in the United States, in order to render mass production more efficient. It is generally known in France as Taylorism, after its inventor, but is also known as *la rationalisation* or Fordism, and sometimes as *OST, l'organisation scientifique du travail*. The basic principles of OST were: the standardization of equipment used in production; the breakdown of the production process into a series of consecutive operations; the devising of a series of production norms, obtained by time and motion studies; and the application of these norms. In its eventual full-blown form, it meant introducing bonuses for improving on norms, and penalties or docked pay if they were not met. This was the Bedaud system of payment by results (performance-related pay, as it would be called today). It depended on a workforce of 'semi-skilled' or 'specialized' workers, trained on the job rather than serving apprenticeships.[17]

To have introduced such a system outside the emergency atmosphere of wartime would have met considerably more resistance than it did from the workers. In any case, it was suited only to large-scale production, while much of French industry remained small in scale before 1914. The temporary wartime workers, male or female, having no previous experience, were guinea pigs for the system, whose implications were not at first evident. Once the emergency was over, there was no immediate application for OST. When the war ended, armaments factories naturally ran down production at once. Even if there had been no particular targeting of women workers, the majority of temporary semi-skilled munitions workers could have expected to lose their jobs. Many women were brusquely laid off with very little severance pay, and accompanying homilies about returning to their homes. Not only 'the munitions barons' but male fellow-workers and returning soldiers thoroughly approved of their going. Regarded with distrust for being willing to accept lower pay than men, women were also blamed for profiting from the war. Jean-Louis Robert has unearthed some extremely bitter reflections from male trade unionists towards the end of the war: 'You women whose son, husband, father or brother may have been killed, and you did not protest, on the contrary, you sang on the factory floor, well you can dance now that the capitalists have no further use for you' (Robert 1989: 517). He plausibly argues that this is one site of the famous 'rendezvous manqué' – the missed connection between women and the male-dominated labour movement . It was certainly not the beginning of a beautiful friendship. Women had been hired as lower-paid labour, in a context that set them against men, and this was to be one of the features of the inter-war period, if not immediately, then in the medium term. In the short term, they were leaving metal-working, though within ten years they would be back.

Not all women lost their factory jobs. There are some counter-examples of women being taken on again by industry, presumably because of a temporary post-war labour shortage: thus in 1919 Citroën, which was reconverting to automobile production, hired 3,000 workers in four months: only 10 per cent of them were women, but this was still a movement against the trend, and represented higher than average female recruitment in the Paris area (Schweitzer 1982: 57). For the time being, however, in automobile manufacture, skilled male workers were those most in demand: the assembly process was still dependent on craft and knowhow. Women remained a minority. The heavy losses of young men in the war meant that the male survivors of that generation were well placed to find promoted posts as foremen or specialists (cf. Noiriel 1986: 125–6). A young trained male workforce was being built up in the 'new industrial geography' coming into being in the 1920s, while older men were valued for their skill. So a temporary lull in the move towards OST occurred, as the French economy was reorganized. But the wartime employment of women was there as a recent model to be used selectively as industry gradually expanded and modernized.

The most pressing task was physical reconstruction of the war zones, the 'devastated areas'. In the building trade, the loss of young French men was most acutely felt, and here there was no question of women taking their place. Counting the injured and unfit, Noiriel estimates about 3.3 million men had been lost. To some extent a renewed rural exodus contributed some replacements, but most of all the French state encouraged the massive immigration of the 1920s, 'one of the chief sources of the boom in French industry in this period' (Noiriel 1986: 135). From the point of view that concerns us, at least two-thirds of the immigrants were male, mostly young. Figures from the foreign ministry indicate that, in 1927, registered incomers totalled 657,839 men and 304,754 women (quoted Milza 1986: 20). The latter were mostly wives of the men rather than seekers of work themselves, but many of the men were bachelors.

The immigrants were at first employed in all-male sectors: mining, metal extraction and processing, building and other heavy industry: '100 per cent of the Lorraine iron-mine face-workers were Italians.' The coalmasters of the Nord recruited labour directly from Poland, especially young men from farms (Magraw 1990: 64–6). As the situation developed, a hierarchy of French skilled and supervisory staff and foreign unskilled or semi-skilled labour was established in some heavy industries.

It was only in the late 1920s, with the post-Poincaré boom, that serious efforts were made to modernize the more advanced sectors of French industry, in a context of general industrial expansion: '[Although] France had only five of the world's 201 fully-'Taylorized' plants, partial Taylorization occurred in car-plants, locomotive repair shops, petro-chemicals, electricals and military arsenals' (Magraw 1990: 65). Further rationalization took place in textiles, a sector now declining from the dominant place it had held throughout the previous century. As textile manufacture shrank as a percentage of French industry, metals caught up with it: by 1930 both were employing about 25 per cent of the total industrial workforce. Steelworking, automobiles and electrical construction all expanded, as did mining and the building trade, but from an already larger base. A series of 'forteresses ouvrières' changed the industrial landscape around Paris, Lyon and Marseille: 'the huge factory and the working-class suburb came together to give birth to a workers' universe very different from that of the preceding years.' Citroën at Javel was employing 31,000 workers in 1929; Renault at Boulogne-Billancourt 20,000 in 1930. The automobile industry was of course a sector likely to introduce scientific working practices and to employ both women and immigrants: '17 languages were spoken on the shop floor' at Renault (Magraw 1990: 66; overview in Noiriel 1986: 121–5).

The expansion of heavy industry and building required a young male workforce, not necessarily all skilled. The decline of the overall percentage of women in industry does not therefore require ideologically orientated explanations, such as unwillingness to employ women or pronatalist propaganda, although they may provide a context. It was more that the industrial sectors which had previously employed most women were stagnant or declining. In the case of textiles, which traditionally employed many women, and still accounted for one-third of all *ouvrières*, this was an industry still large but prey to stagnation, while all around flourished. Textiles had partly modernized before the war and did not greatly change in this period, with the exception of hosiery. Second, what was known as 'le travail des étoffes', work with fabrics, which had been an important industrial category in 1921, was actually in rapid decline: this included dressmaking, garment industry and laundering. Many of the 'isolées' or independent women workers in the census's 'industrial' trades had been in such occupations; their activity was partly displaced into the domestic and black economy (Zerner 1987: 17–19).

What did change in this period was that a percentage of women moved out of these sectors and into industrial employment in the new, more modern branches of the economy, in many cases those that were introducing forms of OST. Their numbers were not enormous, they were geographically concentrated and they did not greatly perturb the overall statistics, but they were taking up jobs not previously handled by women in peacetime. This has been recognized for some time and was noted by both Guilbert (1966) and McMillan (1981). Sylvie Zerner's thesis (1985) was the first piece of major research to investigate in considerable statistical detail the deployment of women into these sectors and to demonstrate their association with semi-skilled process working. The new sectors included light metal components work, inside or outside automobile factories; electrical assembly; chemicals, leather-working and rubber goods; and food products. The move into light metalworking was a cultural transfer – made possible by the war – breaking with the old tradition of having women work on 'soft' commodities, men on 'hard' ones. Even so, there were still some cultural factors operating to reintroduce segregation: in the food industry, for example, women were in dairy and sugar products, men handled meat.[18] Many of the women taking these jobs were younger emigrants from the countryside, like the 1910 generation studied by Catherine Rhein (1977).

First-hand accounts of such working are rare, but we have an extraordinarily detailed day-to-day description of women's work as process workers in metal components, in the shape of Simone Weil's *Journal d'usine*.[19] Weil worked for several months in 1934–5, first at Alsthom, then at a small factory, finally in Renault. Her journal and the letters contemporary with it show that she was well aware that she was doing 'women's work'. Regrettably, as she saw it, she was almost always working alongside other women, and the tasks she carried out were those routinely assigned to women, never men. The men she saw were either skilled experts who came to fix the machine or they were performing heavy tasks. Much of the time, she operated a single machine, turning out small components of which she had to learn the unfamiliar names, the classic end-products of the women's production line.

When the machines on which she worked went wrong she was powerless to fix them, being dependent on the male fitter's arrival (any lost time lowering the wages of the woman operator). 'In the afternoon, the machine suddenly carries a piece away and I can't get it out . . . . Biol scolds me as if it were my fault' (Weil 1951: 83). Describing the alienation engendered by such work, she wrote: 'The worker does not know what the function of these components is: either 1) the way they are combined with others or 2) the sequence of operations that are carried out on them, or 3) what the whole thing is for, when it is complete . . . . Their [i.e. women's] contact with the machines seems to consist of recognizing the traps in store on each one, and the risk any machine may carry of damaging the components.' At best, 'they can see when something is wrong on a machine with which they are familiar' (ibid.: 151–2). 'I have never seen a woman touch a machine except to operate it' (ibid.: 22). Like all women, Weil was paid at piece-rates. Much of the *Journal* is taken up with complex calculations of how much she earned – not much, since her inexperience and clumsiness often resulted in pathetically low pay. Placed in a different category from men by the tasks they did, by their powerlessness over the machines and by their piece-rate pay, women were, noted the *Journal*, regarded by *all* men as inferior: 'separation of the sexes, scorn of the men for the women'. 'An old woman worker finds it quite normal that a fitter aged 25 tells her what to do' (ibid.: 16).

A similar contemporary first-hand description of routine work carried out by women, in this case the packing department of the Galeries Lafayette, was set down by another intellectual, Berty Albrecht (Fourcaut 1982: 221–48). Recent studies of particular industries have also confirmed the very prevalent pattern of having women handle a series of fragmented work-processes, usually at individual work-stations, rather than an assembly-line, in this phase of industrial transformation. A detailed study of Britain in the 1930s shows a similar, if more advanced situation

(Glucksmann 1990). Zerner argues that, in many cases, these women had been given wholly inappropriate training as girls, in dressmaking, and might previously have worked as outworkers. In the sewing trades, speed *was* skill, a notion easily transferred to piecework, where rapidity in turning out metal components as fast as possible could be both a source of pride and a means of maximizing the pay-packet (Zerner 1987: 123). That it ran counter to the predominantly craft-based ethos of male industrial workers and the labour movement, driving a further wedge between men and women, was obvious. As a low-paid workforce, on piece-rates, women posed a certain threat to male wages. But because the sexes were so segregated in the critical period of its introduction, when employment was still high, the threat was not always clearly perceived. The labour movement was at a low ebb in the late 1920s, *a fortiori* during the depression, and there was no particular move at first by the men either to oust, or on the other hand to try to unionize, the women workers, although they might be resented. Men and women were not in competition for promotion. They might be married to one another but, as workers, they lived on different planes, whether in different factories or under the same roof. Sylvie Zerner's conclusion is that 'for once, woman was indeed the future of man. To see in the hiring of women only the recruitment of cheap labour, in order to bring down the wages of the "real" working class was to fail to see the changes which would affect the working class's technological, social and cultural composition; it was to fail to see the upheaval which would soon affect the entire class' (Zerner 1987: 25).

It would be wrong to see Taylorism as affecting only women, even in the early years. A number of men in the new industries found themselves objectively in the same situation as women – though fewer than would be the case after the Second World War (cf. Navel 1945: 57–8). But this was still the experience of a minority of men, whereas it was becoming a structural feature of women's industrial employment. While for men it might look like a step down, it could be seen as promotion for women. Young women had been heard during the war to say that they preferred factory work to sewing at home – it was less tiring (Sullerot 1984: 422). Here is one reason why there was such incomprehension between women workers and the union movement, in the years before the social explosions of 1936. Everything separated the conditions of work of most women from those of most men: the pay system, the task, the type of skill, the relation to technology, the possibility of advancement, the alternatives open to them.

It is these industrial structures that resulted in a working class segregated by gender. At a time when it was being perceived that women – mostly, but by no means all, young unmarried women – were employed in a whole range of new industries, their life-chances in no way paralleled those of young men of their own generation. Apprenticeship, the gateway to a pride in working-class identity, was virtually closed to them; the label of skill was not attached, either by themselves, their employers or their male colleagues, to the work they were doing. The study of gender, like that of immigration, prompts us to revise monolithic or stereotypical representations of the French working class in this period, to consider, for example, to what extent the work of the low-paid woman lathe operator, and the domestic labour of the working-class wife underwrote a collective identification of the working class which seemed to exclude both of them from its symbolic order, whether craft pride or collective solidarity.

Gérard Noiriel in his study of the French working class comments on the powerful image of the 1936-vintage *ouvrier* in the form of a cloth-capped Jean Gabin. He quotes first Georges Sadoul:

> Jean Gabin imposed the image for the first time of the guy in the cloth-cap: brave, tender, quick to anger, a bit rough, but good at heart – an image which was to bring him international fame, because it corresponded to a very significant French type at the time

and then Benigno Caceres: 'Jean Gabin did not just act the part of a worker, he *was* a worker, similar to those millions of others who had gone on strike in May and June 1936. The workers felt represented for the first time on the screen: in himself, Gabin personified the working class' (Noiriel 1986: 193–4). For Noiriel, this is empty romanticism, centred on the legend of the 'métallo de chez Renault', revered by intellectuals and deliberately fostered by the Communist party and the labour movement in general. Noiriel's criticism is particularly fuelled by his awareness of the immigrant worker. He counters the Gabin myth with a quotation from an Armenian immigrant in Belleville: 'How could a foreign worker with crinkly black hair and dark skin identify with Gabin?' he asks. Noiriel might also have added (it doesn't seem to have occurred to him) that Gabin was not a very helpful role model for women either. As we have seen, the 'métallo de chez Renault' could be a woman. And, as we shall see, the industries where strikes were most numerous in 1936 were those that employed women process workers or service staff.

CONCLUSION

This chapter set out not to challenge the detail of official statistics but to suggest ways of re-reading the data that reach us, with awareness that this reading is never done once and for all. Neither the census nor any other set of sources can restore the past 'as it really was'. But they can be drawn on in different ways. The approach deliberately chosen here is to suggest that destabilizing the usual classifications prompts one to think of the sexual politics of economic measurement making up the apparently neutral 'economic infrastructure' on which conclusions about other aspects of society can securely be based. Choices were made not only by the census authorities of their day, but by the employers and workers, and they are still made by historians.

First, the decision not to count domestic work (and other elements of the informal economy) as 'activity' is not inevitable or neutral. Admittedly, it is convenient, and trying to quantify housework would be a statistician's nightmare.

But the price paid for convenience may be distortion. Take this description of 'French society in 1931', from a recent standard work:

> [French society] was divided into three groups, almost equal in numerical terms: 14 million peasants (*paysans*), four-fifths of them owners or farmers; 13 million workers (*ouvriers*) of various status; and 12 million persons living off the tertiary sector (7 million of the latter being self-employed, owner-employers, shopkeepers, or rural or urban artisans, and 5 million of them wage-earners, white-collar workers, executives, civil servants) . . . [given the percentages of self-employed to wage-earning] over one Frenchman in two (*un Français sur deux*) was his own boss.
>
> (Becker and Berstein 1990: 345)

The total figures quoted show that this is not an analysis of the active but of the *total* population of France (c. 40 million, about half of whom were classified as active). But in the way they are presented, each man, woman and child on French soil on census day has been transmuted into an adult French male, classified by his occupation. The total figures include immigrants of both sexes and all ages; children of both sexes; and adult French women. Age, sex and nationality are reduced to a formula – 'the Frenchman', the economic equivalent of the 'individual' of liberal political theory. The 13 million so-called *ouvriers*, for example, refers to all individuals in households where the head of household has filled in *ouvrier* on the census form. Of those people some would be children; some would be women carrying out entirely domestic tasks; or combining them with some kind of outworking; or perhaps doing a double shift. Others in the household would be unmarried sons and daughters going out to work; some would be retired men and women; and a percentage of such households would not be 'French' at all, in that the adults might not have French citizenship. This description tells us something about the sectors of the French economy, but as a portrait of 'society' its terminology is quite simply peculiar. We have become so used to this kind of conventional peculiarity that we hardly notice it. General textbooks have to use broad brush strokes. But there is now no shortage of rethinking – whether on immigration or on the sexual division of labour – which ought long ago to have rendered this description of 'France' unthinkable in its simplification.

It is no accident that the three groups of human being subsumed into 'les Français' without being named – children, immigrants and women – were all in this period without any political rights. This was not an eternal classification, either for the individual (children could grow up, foreigners could take out naturalization papers and, if they were men, receive voting rights), or for the French state (the age of majority could be lowered, as it was in 1974; women could achieve political rights, as they did in 1944; votes for certain foreign residents are now allowed). But it is significant that economic definitions, used many years later, coincide with political definitions at the time.

Of the three groups, it is that of adult women that most concerns this study.

When conventional terminology defines women as economically inactive, it is both concealing the importance of domestic labour and other unpaid work within the economy and ranking those people who carried it out as un-persons. Within such a perspective, while partnership in a small farm or firm might be viewed as a continuation of domestic labour, under the guidance of the *chef de famille*, and therefore assimilable, women's employment outside the household would commonly be perceived as an alternative to – and basically a deviation from – a norm only recently constructed and given value: the full-time housewife. The norm for men – from which deviation might also be looked at askance – would be to be engaged full time on non-domestic labour of some kind.

Rendering problematic our definition of the overall picture helps to contextualize separate parts of it. In the case of white-collar work and the professions, for instance, women were perceived by men as intruders. The extent of women's work was exaggerated by public opinion, mostly male as voiced in the press. As one of the earliest statistical studies by a woman remarked: 'When people say that since the war there are women "everywhere", they usually add that not only is this well-known and talked about, but that it is visible and that "to claim the contrary is to fly in the face of the evidence"' (Dauriac 1933, quoted in Zerner 1985: 86). Women had, of course, always been 'everywhere', in the sense of being present in all classes of society and on every village street in France; what is meant is that they were visible in places where they had not been seen before – almost by definition, places from which they had been formally excluded by political decision or the politics of conventional manners. The historian can read this in several ways: one can agree with Mlle Letellier that women were 'making progress', penetrating new occupations and professions; or with Rose-Marie Lagrave who argues that such progress was quite illusory, since it takes no account of the fact that men were on the move too, concentrating in the higher reaches of the same sectors to which women had painfully gained access (Lagrave 1992: 459–62).

If we refer back to the original intention to historicize the division of labour, the evidence seems to suggest that just as girls were changing faster than boys during this period, whether in their approach to the written word, education or joining organizations, so too women were changing faster than men at this stage in French history, while men's reactions were just beginning to be perceptible. In the early stages of change men were well ahead of women in the competition for jobs, and had several mechanisms of gatekeeping at their disposal. Significantly, the mechanism used to protect any positions of serious power was the clause about having to have political rights to be fully eligible for them. Again, the boundaries of the political and economic coincided.

The traditional gate mechanism in the working class was apprenticeship. In the gradual shift towards mechanization, traditional apprenticeships were starting their slide towards irrelevance, but they were still well entrenched in this period. All the male skilled workers of the inter-war years would have served apprenticeships in which not only the skills of the trade but the rhetoric and sociability of the worker and of the labour movement were learnt by the adolescent boy. By countenancing the segregation of both women and immigrants in lower-paid jobs in the changing situation of the 1920s, the French working-class leaders set the discursive tone for identifying the class as a whole with the male, usually skilled worker, a character ably impersonated by Jean Gabin. As we shall see in the next chapter, those other symbolic working-class characters, the unemployed and the striker, were also defined as male, something which was surprisingly at variance with historical reality.

5

FROM THE DEPRESSION TO THE STRIKES

Ouvriers and *ouvrières*

My husband laid porcelain tiles.... In 1936 there were times when he had no work.... Life was hard, so I went back to work. Afternoons, I used to iron for private employers. In the mornings from 9 to 12, I minded her children for a nurse at Lariboisière Hospital.

(Madeleine C., quoted Del Re 1994: 176)

June 1936: the industrial proletariat enters history.

(Noiriel 1986: 184)

Having looked at the structures of employment (or non-employment) in inter-war France, we have a context for the upheavals that hit the industrial sector of the French economy during the 1930s. They were not unrelated to political history. If the 1920s had seen some change and expansion, the 1930s were a time of drama and uncertainty. Unemployment haunted the beginning, strikes and unrest marked the end of the decade. Economic crisis was the unlikely background for an extraordinary explosion of workers' militancy in the summer of 1936. While far from predominant in French society, the industrial working class and the labour movement were at the centre of these events. Their history has been scrutinized most for what it tells us about class relations, with only passing reference to gender. Women, like immigrants, may receive sympathetic coverage as a special category, but in overall surveys of these years both 'the working class' and 'the labour movement' appear by default to be largely male and French. The labour movement was after all overwhelmingly male in membership up to 1936, and men were still in the majority, even after the wave of new recruits. But 'the industrial proletariat' was by no means single sex. As for the broader term 'working class', it will be used here to mean all members of working-class households, not just those who clocked in at the factory gate. The aim of this chapter will be to disentangle the separate threads of men's and women's history when they differ, rather than assume that a unified history of the working class can be derived from records which largely refer to men.

GENDER AND THE DEPRESSION

Inherited memories of the 1930s depression, especially in the USA, Germany and Britain, carry several messages about gender. Unemployment is remembered as something suffered most acutely by men in their prime, for whom the dole queue and labour exchange were painful and humiliating. Women, children and old people, we imagine, experienced such things only by ricochet.

The dole-queue image itself is more muted in France, since most historians accept that the depression had a less severe impact there than elsewhere. In his book *The Politics of Depression*, Julian Jackson comments as follows:

> The relative lack of severity of the depression in France is reflected in the comparatively small part it plays in collective memory. The Hunger March of 1933 does not have the same historical resonance as the Jarrow March.... The literature of the 1930s is most notable for the heroics of a Malraux or the misanthropy of a Céline. France does not have its *Grapes of Wrath*, its *Love on the Dole*, its *Road to Wigan Pier*. Simone Weil's *La Condition ouvrière* was about the conditions of work, not about the lack of it. In June 1936, one of the main workers' demands was for *congés payés*, for less work not more.
>
> (Jackson 1985: 221)

It can readily be agreed that the depression has been obscured in French collective memory. Jackson rightly points out that France was less severely and visibly hit by depression than Germany, Britain or the United States. The conventional explanation is that with a more agricultural, less industrialized, less export-led economy, France was more self-sufficient, less vulnerable to world recession. The crisis was longer-lasting, perhaps, but less dramatic. This view has been nuanced by some economists, who argue that the impact of the depression in France was more serious and more internally generated (through underconsumption and overproduction) than was previously thought (Marseille 1980; Scot 1988). Where all agree is that somehow it is under-remembered in France.[1]

France's economic specificity may be one reason for this shadowy memory: fewer people were badly affected. Other suggested reasons include the primacy of politics during the 1930s, or the strong overlay of the even more traumatic memories of wartime. Under-remembered today perhaps, the depression nevertheless leaves traces in the collective memory. One place to look for these might be the cinema and photography of the age, rather than its fiction. Evocatively mentioned in many histories of the 1930s, classic French films possibly occupy the same place as Walter Greenwood's *Love on the Dole* in conveying a certain imagery of which gender is an integral ingredient. If the worker was often portrayed in the French cinema by Jean Gabin, so too was the unemployed worker: Gabin appeared in a series of films of the 1930s not only as an engine driver and a proletarian airman, but also as unemployed, a thief, and as a deserter from the army. Both work and unemployment are shown in these films to be male preoccupations. Female characters are irrelevant to the experience of unemployment when this drives the plot. In a famous example, Duvivier's *La Belle Equipe* (1936) starring Gabin, a group of out-of-work men in a lodging-house win the lottery and set up a co-operative *guinguette* out of town, but their comradeship is disrupted by women, uncomprehending outsiders. French people were not flocking to see these films during the depression, any more than British readers were buying *The Road to Wigan Pier.* But they too have contributed to a historical view of unemployment as a man's burden; the role of women was to offer support and sympathy.[2]

Photojournalism, a new phenomenon in the 1930s, also contributed a fund of images, many of them focusing on the masculine humiliation of the dole queue. They will be familiar from anthologies, or can be rediscovered in the files of illustrated magazines such as *Vu, Regards, L'Illustration.* Men, as producers, were unmanned by losing their jobs. Women are only rarely represented as out of work: they are more usually portrayed as thwarted consumers and resourceful home-makers, anxious to economize, making do and mending, or taking in washing to help out.

At the same time, oddly enough, it is part of the historical narrative about the depression that 'women were the first to lose their jobs'. 'The ... victims were women, whose "natural" place was at home,' as one modern historian puts it, and he is far from alone (Borne and Dubief 1989: 36; cf. Noiriel 1986: 172–3; Kergoat 1986: 12). In Germany and Britain, though not in France, married women were formally barred from some kinds of employment. In all three countries, politicians and the press urged that women should be laid off where there was competition for jobs. Yet, at the same time, women do not figure as 'the unemployed', standing in dole queues or holding hunger marches. It is as if 'women' were neither entirely employed nor unemployed. 'The home', to which it was urged they should be 'returned', seems to operate as a sort of historical black hole, removing the need for comment. While this is a difficult area to explore, we now know enough at least to query the rapid despatch of the undifferentiated mass of 'women' into statistical limbo.[3]

The first question one might ask is: who kept jobs and who lost them, once the crisis started to bite? At the time of the Wall Street crash in October 1929, the French industrial economy was on an upward path. The main post-war problem had been shortage of manpower, especially for heavy industry: unemployment was a rare experience for a man in the 1920s. It was otherwise for women: the majority of women who left (or were asked to leave) the wartime factories had been made redundant, though they were not necessarily registered as unemployed. The female industrial workforce declined from its 1921 peak, but without creating a category of 'unemployed women'. By the end of the 1920s, as noted earlier, women were being hired in new industries where there had been few jobs before 1914: electrical goods, light metal-working and so on – rather than textiles or domestic service. But they entered the workforce at an inauspicious time.

The impact of the stock market crash on France was delayed, and varied by sector. The non-industrial economy was affected in ways stopping technically short of unemployment. Farmers saw their incomes drop, small family businesses struggled or went bankrupt. Many men and women in such households remained 'economically active', despite much hardship. Indeed, the rate of the rural exodus, especially from the family farm, slowed down during the 1930s, as people realized there were fewer jobs to go to in town. Such families suffered a damaging fall in their living standards, but did not contribute to the unemployment statistics. Some wage-earners, such as civil servants and teachers, among whom women were now more numerous, at first actually benefited from a steady or rising real income, as prices fell: later some of their benefits and allowances were cut by discriminatory government decrees, but their jobs were maintained.

It was in industry that the crisis brought most unemployment, but its impact was uneven. Those who lost jobs most rapidly and dramatically in the early days were, according to official figures, those working in heavy industry: iron, steel, coal, the building trade; closely followed by luxury trades such as leather, wood and fashion, before the crisis moved on, even in France, to affect most of the industrial and commercial sector. In the Moselle valley, fourteen of the fifty blast furnaces closed between January 1930 and July 1931. Immigrants in such industries were singled out from the start: 'The first to go were unmarried foreign workers, then married foreign workers, then unmarried French workers, then married French workers' – all men of course (Kergoat 1986: 11; cf. Noiriel 1986 and 1988).

In 1932, the French government introduced quotas for immigrants in some industries and offered foreigners financial aid to return home. Repatriation was enforced in cases of long-term unemployment. By definition, this affected male workers most, since there were fewer immigrant female workers. But by 1932 some immigrants had married Frenchwomen and had children. Such was the Cavanna family. Luigi Cavanna, a bricklayer, was laid off like others in the trade. His French wife, having failed to take steps to preserve her nationality on marriage, was appalled, as her son recalls it, to find that she was expected to 'return' to a poor village in Italy:

> Papa came home with a green card. Come back in two months. Two months and two weeks later: a one-way ticket to Bettola, province of Piacenza, Italy. Maman, thunderstruck. 'Me too?' 'You too, Madame, of course.' 'But I'm French.' 'You are Italian by marriage, Madame. Did you make a special request to keep your nationality? No? Well in that case, you are Italian, no question.' 'And the little one?' 'The child can stay in France, he has the right to choose until he comes of age.' 'But what would he do without us?' 'That's your business, Madame. Next please.'
>
> (Cavanna 1984: 251)[4]

Immigrant workers showed up on the employment figures of the 1920s but not the unemployment figures of the 1930s, unless, like Luigi, they now applied for French nationality. Sending home foreigners was one way of lessening the impact on French society, by hitting the most vulnerable element of the male workforce.

A second strategy, employed almost immediately, according to Jacques Marseille, although it does not show in the official figures before January 1931, was short-time working. A sectional study carried out in the hosiery sector of textiles indicates that, by December 1934, 84 per cent of the workforce was on short time and had been so for some time. This affected both men and women, but it hit semi-skilled workers more than skilled and trusted workers, whom employers tried harder to keep, waiting for an upturn. Since women were more likely to be among the former, particularly in textiles, they were liable to see hours and pay cut. Despite the hardship, both unions and workers welcomed this decision if it averted job losses: it became entrenched for several years.[5]

Most historians assume that a third major strategy to deal with the industrial depression was to target women workers. There is little doubt that this happened, but it is harder than one might suppose to find reliable figures. Above all, the explanatory category 'women' breaks down. Alisa Del Re has pointed out how overall figures as between 'men' and 'women' contain many contradictions, showing sometimes that women were harder hit than men, sometimes the reverse, depending on the origin of the statistics. We know that of the 1,623 jobs lost in the Post Office, 1,400 were those of women (Del Re 1994: 195). But which 'women'? Some firms sacked married women, many 'let older women go'. When the luxury millinery trade of Paris collapsed, hundreds of women workers lost their jobs overnight – but these women were not being sacked in preference to men.

Gabrielle Letellier, author of a survey of the crisis, speaking in 1934, pointed out that since so many women had been recruited for low wages during the 1920s, one would expect economic logic to have kept them on in preference to men when times were hard (Letellier 1934). But to her surprise, she found that this was not automatic, at least at first. If workers had to go, women were often singled out. If a woman was older, married (or both) and above all if she was doing a job that could be done by a man, then the chances were she would be asked to leave, if such was the employer's preference. A man, especially if he was married, and had been apprenticed to a modern trade, might be kept on as part of the firm's core workforce.

But, she pointed out, countervailing pressures were at work. Married or not, women might keep their jobs if they were in industries where so-called 'feminine skills' like dexterity were required: telephones, food handling, garments; or if they were doing the semi-skilled jobs which men never did, in the new industries; or sometimes if they were young and mobile and could be hired on a short-term basis at very low rates. In the drilling and small component workshops of metal firms, where a combination of machines and low-paid women operators had turned out to be cost-effective, women were kept on. In practice, the segregation of the industrial workforce, reinforced in the 1920s, meant that the sexes were not as interchangeable as people supposed. Ideology and pragmatism might clash.[6]

Since detailed data are hard to extract from the overall figures, case studies can be illuminating. Catherine Omnès has studied the employment records of the telephone manufacturing company CFT Thomson-Houston. As elsewhere, the workforce was segregated by activity: outside and installation work was done by men, assembly work by young women (one-quarter of them under twenty and 80 per cent under thirty). During the crisis, there was no short-time working, but some workers of both sexes were laid off completely, leaving a mixed core workforce. As orders fluctuated, the management first laid off workers, then sent them telegrams inviting them back on a short-term basis. About a hundred experienced women, in their mid to late twenties, were kept on continuously, while the total pool of women employees stood at about 2,000 between 1931 and 1939. Many worked for a month or two at a time. Reference records showed that they found jobs easily with similar firms in the Paris region. So the telephone industry operated as a single labour market, moving people about: no one was out of work for too long, yet records of any one firm show a series of lay-offs. Women owed their relative good fortune in this modern industry to traditional stereotyping which gave them a specific role in the work process. Readable in detail, this pattern of employment left few traces in the overall figures (Omnès 1991).

Simone Weil's description of metal-working in *La Condition ouvrière* confirms the view that women were episodically taken on or laid off. For several months in 1934–5, at the height of the depression, she worked in all-women workshops, where workers were hired and fired at short notice. She lost her own job after a few months, but was twice hired elsewhere. One man working in the same firm, and named in her diary, recalled on being interviewed many years later that the firm took on 'many women workers who were not very good at the job. If they couldn't keep up, they were sacked.'[7] A 1933 report supports this impression: those sacked from sewing or textile trades could try metal-working, because women were regularly being hired (and fired) there. But it was not popular, since the work was so arduous and low-paid – hence no doubt the high turnover rate, which in turn led to absence from the statistics.[8]

Some firms were taking women on as fast as others laid them off, then, but not all women were on an equal footing. One factor which sometimes outweighed all others was not, as one might suppose, being a mother of children, but being married. This was apparently internalized by workers themselves, who felt that a two-income household had an unfair advantage. Simone Weil reported that married women were frowned on by the others. One of Françoise Cribier's interviewees was a filing clerk at Michelin. Aged twenty-three and married, she left on maternity leave in 1930, but 'there was this war widow, who had been laid off, and when I came back for my job, she complained. It was fair enough, because my husband was in work. So I was laid off instead. After that I found some work, I went out cleaning.' This woman accepted the argument that she had less right to her job than a widow, so she moved into the unofficial economy. Her child was not a consideration one way or the other.[9]

Youthfulness might be a factor. The telephone company studied by Omnès ignored a directive that married women should be laid off first, and kept on the workers in whom it had most confidence, married or not. But it did exclude older women, presumably because their hand–eye co-ordination was assumed to be less. 'Those over thirty needn't bother waiting,' one witness remembered being told (Omnès 1991: 53). Youth might be a euphemism for attractiveness. Simone Weil was looking for work for several weeks in the spring of 1935. She disliked make-up and usually resisted a conventionally feminine appearance. But in despair, having noticed that the hiring foreman at Renault 'had an eye for pretty girls', she asked a friend to help her put on lipstick and powder, donned a beret – and was hired at once (Petrément 1976: 240).

Whereas the other two strategies, laying off immigrant workers and short-time working, are relatively easy to prove, even in the absence of detailed statistics, this third strategy is not so easily identified. People felt that it was happening, or ought to be happening. And overall, according to the census, the absolute number of women in employment fell by at least 300,000 between 1931 and 1936 (Rebérioux 1988: 74). But for one thing women fell through the statistical net so easily, by changing jobs or working unofficially, that their re-employment went unrecorded. For another, the economy – in particular the industrial economy, most affected by the crisis – had certain structures based on sexual segregation. Women could not always be replaced by men. The telephone company ignored the criterion of marriage, but did apply the criterion of youth.

These patterns were not evident to contemporaries, who assumed simple interchangeability. As part of a press campaign urging 'women to go back to their homes', Charles Richet wrote in *Le Matin* in November 1931 urging that women be released from jobs to free them for men. He was far from alone. French feminist associations reacted by defending the right of women to work.[10] The resulting debate prompted Marguerite Thibert to demonstrate in the *International Labour Review* of 1933 that the rhetoric accusing 'women' of being job-snatchers was misplaced. She argued that once one had subtracted the women who were the sole source of income for themselves or dependents (being either widowed or unmarried) and the women doing jobs which could not (or would not) be performed by men, relatively few jobs held by married or otherwise supported women *could* have been taken over by men, even assuming mobility and the right qualifications. Her argument referred to the segregation which had become so marked a feature of the industrial (and clerical) landscape.[11] But more people read Richet than read Thibert, and there was a general feeling that 'something ought to be done'.

Paradoxically, however, there was every incentive for married women in low-income homes to find work, temporarily or in the 'black economy', because of the rules on unemployment benefit. It was when the skilled, French, male worker, that is the worker most secure in his job, began to suffer from serious unemployment that the mechanisms of unemployment benefit became all-important for the French working class. Before the depression, labour shortage had been the main problem in France: it took time to adjust to the new situation. Male unemployment peaked first in 1932, then again, following France's 'second' crisis, in 1935–6 (with an all-male electorate, this was reflected in the elections). Once the safety valves provided by the three strategies noted above failed to protect the 'core' workers, unemployment payments and relief had to be instituted on a large-scale footing. Not surprisingly, the official identity of the *chômeur secouru* (benefit claimant) was one in which gender mattered.

It was not easy to become a claimant. The unemployed worker had to be either a head of household or a single independent person – bachelor, spinster, widow or widower. Such categories applied to men and women alike: a widow could be head of household, an unmarried woman living alone could claim as an independent person. But a married woman living with her husband could not claim, even if he was ill, incapacitated or indeed unemployed, *a fortiori* if he was in work. She could be awarded only the dependent's allowance, since husbands were assumed to maintain their wives. (Such provisions could cause particular hardship when short-time working was introduced). Cohabitees and young people of either sex living at home with their parents were also ruled out from claiming, but adult brothers and sisters living under the same roof could each claim in their own right. In other words, these categories were not biological (ruling out women by sex) but social, determined by the assumptions of the *Code Civil*, notably as these related to marriage. The net effect of the exclusions was to prevent many women, who might previously have been working, from either registering as unemployed or claiming benefit, if they lost their jobs: young women under twenty-one, and married women of any age.[12]

What was more, the claimant had to be involuntarily out of work, 'for want of employment' and having 'lost his or her job': in other words, one had to present documentary evidence of having been employed, such as a certificate from the employer, normally attesting to at least six months' employment. Women were not the only ones affected: Frenchmen returning from abroad were caught unawares by this regulation too (Navel 1947: 232). But it was particularly difficult for outworkers, *travailleuses à domicile*. Such work tended to be seasonal: when the work fell off, it was risky to go through the official procedure: 'to register as unemployed in the off season, you had to ask your employer for a certificate of redundancy which, in the absence of any employment contract, meant a risk of not being taken on again when the season picked up.' In Calais, a rare committee of unemployed women had as one of its key demands the automatic registration for benefit of *travailleuses à domicile*.[13]

Some of these rules affected men and women alike. But the gender implications of the benefit provisions continued beyond the identity of the claimant. A family was subject to an overall means test of 37 Fr 50 a day. If the head of household was out of work, no one else could claim the full benefit, only the accompanying allowances, themselves determined by a gendered hierarchy: in Paris in 1936, the daily benefit for the male head of household was 11 Fr; the allowance for his spouse was 5 Fr 50 and for each child another 5 Fr 50 – that is, an adult woman's subsistence was reckoned at the same rate as a child's. Some regulations were actually devised to counter particular claims made by women: a woman whose only source of income was as a charwoman (a common fallback at the time), had to prove that she had been making enough money at the job to live (quantified as at least twenty-four hours a week) before she could claim benefit.[14]

As a direct result of all this, there was a powerful incentive for married women to seek employment – the very group about whom disapproval was most loudly expressed. The Letellier survey reported that

> the wife of an unemployed man who had previously stayed home now looked
> for a job. Our survey brought out the remarkable fact that 33 per cent of wives
> of the unemployed were working, whereas for the active population as a

whole, the percentage of working-class women at work was only 17 per cent in 1931.

(Letellier *et al.* 1938, vol. 2: 33)

Many such women ended up in unregistered employment at home or in catering (casual work in hotels etc.). Full-time domestic service went into further sharp decline, but by the same token charwomen were still sought after. Cavanna's mother regularly cleaned for a number of households, taking on extra work when her husband was laid off. Many women textile workers, laid off in the the northern departments by structural decline as well as the crisis, registered themselves as *femmes de ménage* because they could claim no other skill. Despite all the difficulties of registering, women's recorded unemployment went on rising well after 1936 and more now began to meet the criteria for benefit registration – i.e. young, unmarried and previously employed women were by the end of the 1930s finding it hard to get jobs, whereas male unemployment had peaked by 1936 and was declining (Sullerot 1984: 429).

Some general but not self-evident conclusions about the depression in France might now be suggested. Clearly, experience of the depression had different rhythms for working men and working women. In the early stages of the crisis, a man might lose his job if he was an immigrant, a worker in heavy industry such as coal or steel, or a general unskilled labourer (categories which could overlap). But the majority of Frenchmen in work kept their jobs, possibly with some short-time working, until 1932. From then on, lay-offs might affect skilled men who had never been out of work before. Either way, this could come as a shock, a major interruption to the working life, and would be felt and remembered as such. There was a distinct break between work and non-work. To become a *chômeur*, one had to enter a new bureaucratic world, and one's identity and pattern of life would be drastically altered. Several of the men interviewed by Françoise Cribier bitterly recalled being sacked.[15] On the other hand, as it had had a beginning, the crisis came to an end. Most men were able to find work again on a fairly stable basis in the years running up to 1939. The depression therefore had a historical reality for them, which could quite easily be dated and identified with the experience of the dole queue, short or long term. For most women it was different, less clear-cut.

Catherine Rhein conducted a series of in-depth interviews with women in the Cribier sample who had been young during the crisis. Her conclusions were interesting:

The 1930s crisis was not raised spontaneously by these women .... Women of this generation had been working for about ten years [before the depression]. Their activity had essentially been characterized by great mobility, both regarding the choice as to whether to work at all, and between different occupations and sectors. They had been domestic servants or salesgirls, waitresses, factory workers, in dressmaking or the food industry. They were already familiar with seasonal lay-offs, economic fluctuations, being hired and fired at short notice. Despite the rising tide of unemployment among women, reaching its peak in the late 1930s, the crisis did not take them by surprise. It did not mean an abrupt change in their working hours, because they had always had a precarious status.[16]

This oral evidence came from women who mostly did not have children or were just starting a family. We have no surviving material from older women, who might have experienced the depression as a more traumatic episode in their lives – that is, who might have lived it more like men. It has been observed that as a rule men's unemployment (up to the present day) tends to follow the fluctuations of the whole economy, whereas women are either plunged into long-term structural unemployment, as in textiles, or else take a precarious succession of temporary jobs (Salais *et al.* 1986: 130). The historical record for the 1930s is incomplete, but the evidence is that this was just what happened.

The historical view of the depression is, however, strongly coloured by the perception of 'mainstream' male workers, and by the external signs of disturbance to normal patterns (men on street corners during daylight hours). We are less historically alert to the fluctuating responses found among women: the pressure on married women to seek work; the succession of jobs that a well-placed young assembly worker might be obliged to take, giving her short-term insecurity; the willingness of textile workers to turn charwomen, or of former corset-makers and milliners to take jobs as temporary lathe operators. This diversity is too untidy for statistical pinpointing. The differential timescale of men's and women's employment is also obscured by historical emphasis on 1936 and the Popular Front. The measures enacted in 1936 did little to alleviate women's unemployment, and indeed indirectly provoked more unemployment among older female workers. Women's unemployment continued to rise almost until the end of the decade.[17]

So it could be argued that women, already a semi-hidden part of the industrial workforce of the late 1920s – for reasons touched on in the last chapter – became both the invisible reserve army *and* the hidden unemployed of the 1930s. Their crisis was less recorded, less official and full-time than that of men. It had different rhythms and consequences. Some women worked less during the crisis than before or after – but many actually worked more. The foregoing analysis will help explain why – when the strike wave exploded on the social scene in June 1936 – so many of the strikers were women, and why, here too, we need to re-examine the historical record.

MEN, WOMEN AND INDUSTRIAL ACTION: ANATOMY OF A STRIKE WAVE

For much of the inter-war period, industrial militancy among French workers was at a low ebb. 'The 1920s were a time when the French labour movement was seriously weakened' (Noiriel 1986: 170). The failure of the 1919–20 strike movement with its revolutionary overtones had spelled out what Michelle Perrot has described as 'the end of the Belle Epoque for industrial strikes' (quoted in Noiriel

1986: 156). The trade union movement soon afterwards witnessed a split parallel to that between the Socialist and Communist parties, with the formation of the pro-communist CGTU as a rival to the CGT. Union membership began a slide, from the 1.6 million the CGT could claim in 1920 to fewer than 600,000 by the late 1920s, while the CGTU had at most 350,000 and the Catholic CFTC about 100,000 at the same time. Noiriel has argued that economic and structural change, rather more than political division, may account for the quiescence of labour in this period. Some of the old spirit survived in traditional strongholds such as textile towns, and among skilled workers, but it was harder to find in new industrial suburbs and modern automobile plants. To the extent that the latter represented the more dynamic sectors of the economy and therefore the future, he writes, the labour movement was behind the times. Its symbolism and traditions were not the property of a newly uprooted labour force containing many youngsters from rural backgrounds, immigrants and women, categories of worker without previous industrial experience (Noiriel 1986: 157 ff.).[18]

In the case of women, they had never been well represented in the trade unions: before 1914, they accounted for about 10 per cent of the overall membership, a figure that rose briefly to 15 per cent during the war, but fell back thereafter, standing at about 8 per cent by 1936. The reasons are not particularly hard to seek; indeed it would be surprising if the figures had been any higher, and they have been clearly summarized by Madeleine Rebérioux (1988). Historically, the labour movement had, for reasons that seemed self-evident in its own eyes, been opposed to women working wherever they constituted a threat either to men's wages or to their employment. Even before such practices as Taylorism caught on, women were being recruited by some employers in a conscious effort to deskill the labour force. Much union effort had been directed to keeping them out, using arguments such as the appropriateness of women's domestic role and the need for a family wage for men. Where women were no threat, on the other hand, they were tolerated, but no great effort was made to attract them into the unions. After the First World War, the growing segregation of the sexes in the new industrial landscape, with women assigned to unskilled or semi-skilled work, and men monopolizing most skilled jobs, was reflected in the gulf between a union move-ment still broadly guided, as in its early days, by the interests of skilled workers, and a mass of workers who were not members of the unions at all, having no acquaintance with labour traditions. One could add to this the irregular, or interrupted nature of many women's careers as wage-earners, the low pay they received, which did not encourage spending on union subscriptions, and the double shift some had to shoulder, which reduced time or energy for union matters.

The culture, vocabulary, working practices and pride in status which so clearly marked the early CGT, and later the CGTU as well, were not on the face of it easily accessible to women workers; and when they did join, they rarely played prominent roles. After the war, the unions made more effort to recruit women, but even when women were the majority of workers, as in tobacco or garment production, union officials were mostly men. Women's interests were not entirely ignored during these years, but nor were they very strongly addressed by the unions. As historians have pointed out, there were perceptible differences in the approaches of the CGT and the CGTU, with the latter having what might be termed a non-sexist approach, based on calls for equal treatment, the former being more inclined to see women as a special category, requiring protective measures such as maternity leave which fitted within a broadly pronatalist perspective – and also made women less attractive as employees. But if one were to look at the workers in French industry as a whole, only a small proportion of *ouvrières* was to be found in the majority union movement at all.

There was a special case, in the form of the CFTC, the Catholic trade union movement. All-women unions, chiefly for textile and clerical workers, had been formed in the early years of the century and had grouped themselves under its aegis. They maintained their single-sex organization until 1936, a feature which has been analysed from differing perspectives: on one hand, women in these associations acquired experience of running their own affairs; on the other, they were broadly subordinate to a male hierarchy. Just as the CFTC avoided the language of class struggle, the women's unions avoided the language of feminism. As before, one is still talking of very small numbers. That is not to deny the presence of a significant minority of quite energetic individuals in both kinds of movement.[19]

The economic crisis was hardly propitious for any revival of workers' demands, although there had been some strikes during the early 1930s, mostly without success. Workers who were still in jobs had more or less protected their standards of living in real terms: the sections of the workforce most affected by the crisis were suffering either from unemployment or from short-term working, both of which discouraged strike activity. There is no record of union protests against the preferential dismissal of the thousands of women and immigrants who did lose their jobs. However, by the time of the Popular Front, French industry contained a mixture of skilled and experienced workers, from whose ranks the first strikes of 1936 would come, and a larger heterogeneous mass of workers on low wages or piece-rates, non-unionized and without recognized skills. The second category would be of critical importance during the events of 1936.

Those events started in the political arena with the general election called for April–May, against a background of both international and domestic tension. In the run-up to the election, the Rassemblement Populaire – later known as the Popular Front – had gained strength. Originally a broad left alliance against the potential fascist threat from the paramilitary leagues inside France, the Popular Front had become the basis of an electoral pact between the parties of the centre-left and left, from the radicals to the communists.

This was the last single-sex election to be held in France.[20] In fact, the iconography of the period shows that women were not absent from the many political gatherings and street politics of this feverish time. But the most significant aspect of the election from our point of view was that women's wages became an electoral issue. Not that this was explicit: the condemnation of 'starvation wages' by communist and socialist politicians was voiced in more general terms, attacking previous governments for allowing 'the working class' to bear the brunt of the depression. But every time a *salaire de misère* is quoted, it turns out to be a woman's full-time wage (it could hardly be otherwise given women's rates of pay). In this all-male election, male orators were often talking about women's place in the work-force without saying so, perhaps without clearly realizing it themselves. Only after the strikes did women's voices begin to be more clearly heard complaining of low wages, and this was new. Jules Moch recalled the shock of seeing a woman delegate turn to her boss during the collective bargaining in June for the grocery food chains, such as Félix Potin, and say:

> Look Monsieur, this is what I earn. You seem to trust me, because I am a saleswoman at peak hours and a cashier the rest of the time. With what I earn, I can't even buy myself a pair of stockings a month after paying for my keep. When I need a winter coat, will I have to turn prostitute?
>
> (Léon Blum 1967: 98)

Although no landslide, the election results gave a clear victory to the left. The strike movement, which took everyone by surprise, was partly fuelled by impatience with the legalistic delays in handing over to the new government of which the working class had high hopes. The first strikes broke out in the interval between the election results (late April) and the formation of Léon Blum's administration (on 4 June). Starting among skilled workers in provincial aircraft factories in the second week of May, they spread to the Paris area and then throughout France, reaching a peak in early June just after the Matignon agreements, and gradually declining thereafter. The strikes occurred overwhelmingly in the manufacturing sector and in large-scale commerce such as department stores. Civil servants, transport workers, teachers, postal workers did not strike. By and large, as Antoine Prost has remarked, it was the least unionized branches of the economy which struck, the most unionized which stayed at work (Prost 1967: 73).[21] Factories near Paris, particularly in light engineering, electrical goods, automobile production and food processing were prominent in the movement as, later, were the large city-centre stores like the Galeries Lafayette. All these sectors had women in their workforce, though numbers could fluctuate: of the 'métallos de Paris' for instance, 14 per cent were women in 1931 but by the time of the depression that figure was reaching 20 per cent; in electrical appliances, women were 16 per cent of the workforce (it had been higher before the depression); in food processing, 30 per cent of the workforce was always female.[22]

Thus significant numbers of the women workers recruited to just these industries found themselves caught up in the strikes. For many, it was the first time they had taken part in such an action. Contemporary press reports and later histories have referred to the 'naivety' of certain strikers, without relating it to sex, arguing either that it proves the spontaneity of the movement, or on the contrary that it rendered it vulnerable to manipulation. It would be hard in any case to relate participation to sex difference, since there are no systematic figures of any kind about the sex distribution of the strikers.[23] But the surviving evidence can still be explored for what it tells us about sexual difference.

Since most historical accounts suggest that women played a mainly supportive or passive role during the strikes, bringing food to the factory gate for husband or son, or engaging in womanly pursuits like knitting to while away the time in an occupied factory, let us start with this image. Take knitting: this productive activity occurs at the join between the official and unofficial economy. Simply dismissing it as a sexual stereotype underestimates its importance. Why do knitting and similar work hold such a prominent place in first person accounts? ('I have never knitted so much in my life' – Mme B in the Galeries Lafayette.) A male reporter from *Le Populaire*, commenting on a department store where women were in the majority among the staff, wrote: 'We can go round the shop.... It is a real beehive of needlework and knitting. They will have their woollies for the whole of next winter' (Couteaux 1975: 100 and 66). This picture could be repeated a hundred times over. Whereas these hours of enforced leisure were lived by most men as just that – to be spent playing cards, smoking and, in moderation, drinking, for many women, leisure was less attainable – idle hands might be seen as guilty hands. In an age when many clothes were still made and mended at home, every spare moment – in the metro, in lunch breaks – was spent knitting or sewing. In view of what has already been said about domestic labour, this is not particularly surprising – it was simply a continuation of long-established patterns. But the 'explosion of joy' of 1936 has been described as the discovery of the luxury of leisure at the workplace. For women it was only partly true.

Women are also depicted as running a support system for strikers: keeping the canteen running, bringing meals in for the men. It is true that for many women, factory occupations literally led to them preparing more food than usual. But good housekeeping in some cases extended to plant maintenance. Machinery in occupied factories had to be maintained against risk of deterioration; decisions had to be taken about perishable goods. Strike committees were anxious to appear mature and responsible. The evidence is naturally patchy; in so far as it points to a sex divide, men were more likely to be told off to maintain machines, women to protect perishable goods. Thus in a fur workshop, 'the women workers are treating the skins to prevent them being spoilt.'[24] In food manufacture, there were serious risks of damage, not always avoided. The leader of the food federation of the CGT later recalled, however, that 'women did extra work to put the foodstuffs being processed at the time in a safe place. The women were more concerned about this than the men: it was because they really know the value of food' (Birgi 1969: 64). Sometimes maintenance was a new experience for women: when, in a Gennevilliers cotton mill, 'the women workers cleaned the machines', it was the first time they had been allowed to touch them.[25]

It would be wrong to assume that sexual stereotyping automatically governed women's actions. A point that emerges consistently from all archives, newspapers or memories is that a distinction should be drawn between the action of women in all-female factories and those in mixed enterprises. Where women made up the entire workforce, they had to organize their own affairs, draw up their list of grievances and form delegations to see the management. In one all-female canvas workshop, 'the women with children went home at night. The others slept in the factory, some on the tables, some on the floor, rolled in blankets.' Where the workforce was mixed, even if women were in the majority, the organization was invariably handled by men (with or without women representatives) and many of the women were simply sent home (or allowed home, as some put it). Thus in two TSF (wireless component) factories, the all-women labour force occupied the first, while in the second, which was mixed, women went home.[26] In a Corbeil shoe factory, employing hundreds of women workers, 'only the men, about 120, remained on the site'.[27] Marcelle Vallon, who worked at the Magasins Réunis, an enterprise with a majority of women, commented that the movement was organized by men and in the delegations, 'the people you met were all men'. They thought women 'couldn't put two ideas together', she comments (Birgi 1969: 63). In the photo in *Humanité* of 21 June, of the Galeries Lafayette delegation to the employers, there are twenty men and five women, an approximate inversion of the actual sex balance of the workforce. Here, as in so many other contexts, it appears that wherever women were obliged to handle their own affairs they did so, apparently satisfactorily. But in mixed situations, even where women were more numerous, men took control and women accepted it. To say this is not necessarily to imply lack of solidarity between the sexes – there were recorded cases where the men stood out for women's pay claims, when they could have settled earlier – simply that both sexes appear to have accepted that if men were present, they ought to take charge.

One of the main reasons why women were sent home from mixed workplaces was to avoid accusations of immorality, to which strike committees were particularly sensitive. Monique Couteaux, in her research on department stores, perceptively observes that the right-wing press tended to stress sexual difference in its reports, presenting women either as unwilling victims of the decision to strike or as sexual objects, while the left-wing and in particular the communist press sought to smooth over sexual differences, praising women for acting 'just like men', 'as firm in their resolve as the male workers', 'worthy of their companions' and so on. Thus *Gringoire*, the right-wing paper, printed articles hinting at 'orgies' behind the factory gates; *Figaro* quoted a striker's wife who had seen 'photos of the men leaning out of the window sills with women workers'; *Le Petit Bleu* quoted another wife as saying, 'those women are going to use the strikes to take away our husbands. Oh there'll be some ructions on the home front when all this is over' (Couteaux 1975: 73; cf. ibid.: 73–7). *Humanité*, by contrast, reported on 17 June that the 'strike pickets' in one department store 'stay all night and the other employees and *all the women*, go home, to return next morning at 9 a.m.' (my italics). It would probably be unrealistic to be entirely dismissive of the fears: crises and emergencies encourage transgression of all sorts and the atmosphere of collective euphoria no doubt heightened erotic feelings. But it was women rather than men who were perceived (by male journalists or worried wives) as the centre of disturbance.

This was partly because women were relative newcomers to such public events.

For many women strikers, numbers of whom were young, the extraordinary 1936 strike wave was their first experience of a truly collective action. Any previous industrial experience had been more of a kind to isolate and drive them apart than to unite them. The novelty of striking was perhaps best illustrated by a category of women workers who fascinated the press: the employees of the large department stores, particularly the shop assistants. The poignant contrast between the compulsory elegant dress and make-up of these mainly young women and their long hours and starvation wages apparently shocked the stores' customers. Such fragile beings did not correspond to the standard image of a 'striking worker'. The communist paper *Humanité* described as if it would come as a surprise to its readers an overheard conversation between 'two young and pretty salesgirls from the Galeries Lafayette', who spoke of 'the bosses being choked' at 'seeing that the workers could hold out on them'.[28] It was of such women that Henriette Nizan was thinking when she wrote, after the strikes: 'Will they now return so easily to their narrow selfish way of life? Will they abandon the warmth of community? I don't think so .... They have experienced the joy to be had by living in an atmosphere of mutual trust.'[29]

From this kind of comment, of which there is no shortage in the left-wing press, it is tempting to conclude that since they were less used to thinking in collective terms, women's experience of the strikes overall might be more intense than that of the men. The dramatic events of June 1936 were a bigger interruption to their lives. Some writers on women's history have argued that this was a turning point for the 'integration of women into the working class' (more properly the organized labour movement). Women's 'unprecedented militancy' was creating a new situation.[30] There is clearly some truth in this argument, but it cannot be accepted at face value.

For one thing, until the strikes, union membership was low among male and female workers alike: the explosion of membership touched neophytes of both sexes. Many men were being 'integrated to the labour movement' too. Second, if women were joining the labour movement by taking out a CGT card, as millions of workers of both sexes did, they were being recruited into a masculine world, with its own rules and customs, a world which if not positively hostile to women had certainly seen them as separate and different from the mainstream, and was far from viewing their interests as equal to men's. If they now joined this world, it was on men's terms, not theirs. Integration implies that new arrivals change the composition of the original mass in some way. It is not at all clear that this was what happened. Because the trade union records do not generally list members by sex, we do not even know how many women joined the CGT or for how long. The most thorough statistical study of the CGT's massive recruitment in the period hardly refers to women at all, no doubt because of this gaping hole in the sources (Prost 1964). It is true that by the classic norms of visibility in the labour movement, such as being elected or appointed delegate to union conferences, more women did suddenly become visible in 1936–7, as an analysis of the relevant volumes of the great Maitron biographical dictionary shows.[31] To this extent, at least, it can be argued that something changed. And there are particular instances which do seem to bear this out. For example, in the union of garment-makers, a trade where women were in a large majority, there were about 6,000 members before the strikes and about 100,000 immediately afterwards. Georgette Bodineau recalled that before the strikes it was the bespoke tailors, all men, who ran the union, whereas most women workers were in off-the-peg manufacture. But it remains unclear how many women stayed in the unions after 1937–8, when overall membership fell away rapidly. For both men and women, what happened in 1936 was not the start of a steady movement towards greater trade union consciousness, more a short-lived surge of solidarity.

Class solidarity is perhaps too readily assumed to be the dominant emotion, however, masking any potential solidarity between women or promotion of their particular interests. Madeleine Tribolati, at the time a young clerk, was one of the few women to take part in the collective bargaining talks, representing the CFTC, the Catholic trade union confederation. When she happened to meet women delegates from the CGT, 'they would find themselves on common ground defending aspects to do with "the female condition". [Their] male colleagues, whatever their union allegiance, were greatly struck by this' – understandably so, since relations between the CGT and CFTC at the time were so hostile that the CGT would not agree to the CFTC being represented in the union delegation to the Matignon talks (Launay 1981: 2,304 and note 725).

Turning from solidarity with the movement to opposition to it, if women were by and large strangers to the world of trade unions, by the same token one might expect many of them to be *less* ready to engage fully in strikes. As usual, any hard evidence is patchy, but may be symptomatic. During the autumn of 1936, when the euphoria of June was a faded memory and when the strikes were renewed in an atmosphere of bitterness and recrimination over unfulfilled commitments, there are some dramatic instances of aggression between women office workers and manual workers of both sexes in the same firm, the former being opposed to any further strikes. Sometimes hostile women workers or forewomen were singled out for a 'conduite de Grenoble', a rough ride home.[32] Qualitative evidence comes from Catherine Rhein's oral history witnesses: she found enthusiasm for the Popular Front and the strikes only among those women in her sample who had worked at Renault and Citroën, large factories where everyone joined the strikes. Some of the other respondents had antagonistic memories, or felt that they had been obliged to go along with something they did not really believe in: 'On a été syndiquées', one of them said, 'we were unionized', rather than 'we joined the union'; neither women's support nor their solidarity could be taken for granted (Rhein 1977: 280).

Nor is it clear what women got out of the strikes – in terms of the reduction in working hours, the pay rises, the paid holidays. No one has systematically examined the grievance registers for sexually specific demands. Some *cahiers*, especially in department stores, voice requests from women: the right for shop assistants to sit down for five minutes an hour; the provision of a crèche; and coded demands about arbitrary sackings (a covert reference to sexual harassment) (Couteaux 1975: 66).

What may strike us now, however, is the absence of any call for equal pay. The *cahiers* invariably call for pay rises and usually for a higher percentage rise for low-paid workers (as the Matignon agreement specified). In practice, women's wages, already low, often received a relatively larger boost than men's. But although they were still the lowest-paid workers, rarely if ever were voices raised for the principle of equal pay.

This did not pass unnoticed at the time, but it was the feminists outside the labour movement who reacted in public. Maria Vérone, of the LFDF, wrote to Léon Jouhaux, secretary of the CGT, and Roger Salengro, the Interior Minister, about the absence of equal pay from collective bargaining. Huguette Godin wrote an article in *Le Quotidien* asking whether the omission was because the employers had opposed it or because workers of both sexes had failed to raise the issue. The politician G. Lhermitte, who campaigned for feminist causes in parliament, wrote in 1938 to Daladier, pointing out that the *conventions collectives* not only enshrined the principle of unequal pay, but that if percentage wage rises were thereafter granted, the gap between men's and women's wages would grow even bigger.[33]

Equal pay was probably omitted from the strike demands not by any oversight, but because those in charge of negotiations – generally the CGT – thought it too radical and certainly not a priority. Although not unthinkable – since white-collar Post Office workers already had it, as did schoolteachers – equal pay was not yet on the trade union agenda. In practice, as noted earlier, men and women were rarely doing the same work: acceptance of the principle might not have meant a very large addition to the bill for wage increases – less than for the increase in points for low wages, from which women already benefited. One is forced to conclude that the principle was not welcome to union leaders, while women were either unwilling to promote it themselves, or too absent from the negotiating panels. There are other possible reasons. If women were paid even higher wages, would their slight advantage on the labour market vanish? The reality of the danger is demonstrated by what happened to women metal-workers after 1936, when the wage rises had started to close the gap between men and women. Catherine Rhein quotes a report of 1938:

> The difference between the male and female wage is no longer large enough for industrialists to give preference to female labour, which is less regular and less skilful (*habile*) . . . [they blame] the large wage rises for women laid down in the collective agreements as well as the difficulty experienced by women workers over a certain age in adapting to the techniques which change frequently with changes in production.
>
> (Rhein 1977: 281)

Women found themselves caught in the middle of an argument here. While men's unemployment peaked in 1935, women's unemployment peaked only later, in 1938–9, and was then submerged in the slight but general recovery. The recovery, such as it was, was partly provoked by increased arms expenditure initiated by the Blum government, and was felt most in heavy industry which employed men. At the least, this points to a differential pattern of employment and unemployment between men and women in the later phases of the crisis (Rhein 1977: 285; Sullerot 1984: 429).

There were other differences too: women suffered as much as men from the problems of the post-Matignon situation – firms closing down because they could not afford social legislation, lay-offs, further strikes and so on – but they did not always enjoy the benefits. To have two weeks' paid holiday one had to have worked for the same firm for at least a year – something not all women could demonstrate. In the first year, the special railway vouchers for travel to the sea were not made available to women heads of family or women workers with an unemployed husband (though this was changed by 1937). Berty Albrecht reported that many of her fellow-women workers in the Galeries Lafayette chose to devote their new day off (the result of the forty-hour week) to 'thoroughly doing out the house' (Fourcaut 1982: 237).

'Women strikers' cannot be reduced to any single formula, any more than men can. If anything, there was a wider range of possible roles or attitudes to the strikes among women: they could have been active participants; enthusiastic newcomers, perhaps sleeping away from home for the first time, perhaps sent home by the strike committee; reluctant recruits to the union; active resisters to the movement. As non-strikers, some wives of strikers would have been bringing in food and worrying about money – and so on. All these roles were possible within an overall experience where both class and gender interacted with each other. At the time, and later, such interaction was not openly recorded, the perception of gender taking a particularly rigid form. Union leaders often assumed an essentially domestic identity for working-class women, whether employed or not. We find Duclos calling on the 'women of France to unite for the protection of their homes' and 'the future of the race'; and the secretary of the garment-workers' federation of the CGT claiming that women's participation in the strikes 'meant it really was a matter of defending [our] bread, the home, the survival of our children', and that it confirmed 'the eminently natural character of our demands' (Birgi 1969: 51). This linked women with 'natural' demands rather than industrial ones, and assumed that the 'natural' role of women was to care for children – unmarried women workers, for instance (the majority of his new union members) did not enter this scenario. Such statements point to difficulty in thinking of women as 'proletarians' in their own right. The sexual division in the working class was simultaneously visible and invisible, and it is sometimes difficult for historians to avoid reproducing the discourse of the time.[34]

It would be wrong to suggest that such habits of mind were peculiar to men. Catherine Rhein, commenting on the memories of the women in her study, notes: 'I have to say so because they say so, and they insist on the point: the crisis, the depression, unemployment, newspapers, trade unions and politics were all domains or concepts reserved for men' (Rhein 1977: 242). Yet all these women had been employed for wages, were affected in their daily lives by the slump, read newspapers, or in some cases joined unions. In a few years they would have the vote.

They were perhaps ready to say one thing, while having lived another. But in a sense their linguistic horizons did not coincide with those of men: women heard a rhetoric addressed to them by the press, politicians, trade unionists and their own relatives, which insisted that collective action was a masculine sport. The vocabulary of unemployment and industrial action was a language that had to be learnt. Looking back over their lives, they may have found that it still seemed foreign.

CONCLUSION

At many points in this chapter, what has been at issue is the fragmented experience lying behind the terms 'working class' or 'workers'. There were other fracture lines besides those of gender: age, origin, geography, type of work, level of skill. And there were unifying factors too: broad features of working-class life and culture that affected everyone. The history of the French working class has been studied to a remarkable degree, if one considers the proportional place of the industrial workforce in French society. That history has been written in a political context, and questions of gender have been tackled in a certain order and with certain presuppositions.

To simplify a complex story, there was an early heroic history, often the work of male activists, from which women and any consideration of gender were virtually absent; then came a series of studies devoted to occupational groups. These initially concentrated on men but, with the development of the women's movement, both women workers and women in trade unions started to be studied. The earlier monographs were usually written from a class-analysis perspective and based very much on union records; they were followed by studies seeking to broaden the focus with less attention to the resolutions of trade union conferences and more to questions of working-class culture and sociology. Latterly some historians have worked to bring labour history and women's history together, and a formula that has found much favour is the 'rendezvous manqué', the missed rendezvous between women and/or feminism and the organized labour movement. Labour history, although rather massively masculinist in the past, has been one of the first areas in French historiography to recognize its shortcomings relating to gender. One sign of this has been the effort made by the editors and contributors of the Maitron dictionary of the labour movement to locate the biographical records of more women: its success can be measured by comparing the earlier and later volumes of the section devoted to the period between the wars.

The disjunction between the labour movement and the domestic world the male unionist inhabited when he crossed his own threshold was pointed out by Madeleine Guilbert, writing in 1956, but it could be applied to earlier or later dates:

We found, among the husbands of outworkers (*ouvrières à domicile*), convinced trade unionists who interrupted the conversation to complain that out-workers were not unionized and who clearly had never had the slightest idea that their own wives might be eligible. One of them realized when talking to us that he had always forgotten to tell his wife that there were unions for homeworkers.

(Guilbert, quoted in Salais *et al.* 1986: 94–5)

So the problem for the historian may be located in his or her sources. Let me end with an illustration of this problem. In September 1935, the Communist party's illustrated magazine *Regards* printed the 'Diary of a woman worker at Renault' in two instalments, containing entries dated October 1934 to January 1935. In the first extract 'Jeanine' tells how she goes to work on an assembly-line, to support her parents who are 'starving and cold'. Finding it hard to keep up, she is moved to machine operation. The woman working alongside her has no sooner told her about her son, an apprentice also at Renault, when she is called out to find him badly injured in an accident. Moving to another workshop, Jeanine suffers skin troubles from the chemicals used and is subjected to sexual harassment by the foreman, while her neighbour is struck on the head by a metal shard. In the second extract, after a further accident, Jeanine wakes up in the infirmary to discover she has lost her hand. The woman in the next bed has visitors who bring 'pamphlets and newspapers', and out of despair comes the urge to fight. 'A new world opens up before me and decides my future.' She will become a revolutionary singer, waving her mutilated arm and singing outside the Renault works: 'Let's take over Renault! Workers, my brothers! Red Front!'[35]

This so-called diary was printed during the depression and a year before the strikes. But a research student would be ill advised to use it as a genuine 'source' for the conditions of women's work at Renault. Its authenticity is highly suspect. The magazine did not even trouble to spell the author's name the same on each occasion, and the 'plot' of the diary is transparently political: after experience of exploitation, horrendously described, comes political education and a positive choice to work for revolution. That is not to say it is unrelated to real experience: all the things described are known to have existed at Renault – it is the telescoping together and fictionalizing that inspire distrust. This fiction cannot be accused of neglecting women's role in the class struggle, but it makes a romantic use of gender. The mutilation of a young girl is seen as particularly horrific, but there is no analysis of the sexual division of labour. The final cry is 'ouvriers, mes frères': we are all in this together. This apparent first-person account is actually tailor-made to convey the party's message, of a unified working class of both sexes.

It so happens that Simone Weil's factory diary, reproduced in *La Condition ouvrière*, covers almost the same period, and I have earlier quoted it, as many historians have before me, with every appearance of crediting it with authenticity. There are good reasons for so doing: it was not written to be published, and only appeared posthumously. Anyone who has held it in their hands and seen the layout of the pages cannot but be struck by a sense that Weil was trying as conscientiously as possible to set out her authentic experience. It is very different from the *Regards* concoction. But Weil herself could be a misleading witness too when she published her writing, and gender is at the heart of the trouble. During the strikes, she returned to the factory where she had worked and set down her thoughts in an inspirational article, printed in 1936. It is regularly quoted in accounts of the strike wave, as evidence from an impeccable source. Yet closely examined there is much to trouble us in this much-quoted 'first-hand' evidence of that summer of 1936. Written under a pseudonym, the piece was originally published in the left-wing journal *Révolution prolétarienne*. It began with a description of work in the factory before the strike, based closely on the relevant passages from Weil's journal and reproducing many sentences virtually intact, but with one major difference. It is impossible from the syntax in French (pronouns, adjectives, agreements) to guess the sex of the writer. The pronoun 'on' is much used ('Comme on est seul' with a masculine adjective) and some rather dextrous syntactical choices artfully maintain the neutrality. The subject matter could hardly be read by anyone who really knew the organization of the factory as referring to men: here are the familiar machines that don't work, the need to turn out 800 little metal parts in an hour, the arbitrary sackings, the all-powerful foreman. But few references are explicit. The rare mentions of women appear to be observed by the authorial eye. General references to workers are all in the masculine and one passage expressing Weil's own intensely personal feelings of docility in the face of oppression is explicitly attributed to 'un homme' (Weil 1951: 228).

The second half of the article describes the difference in atmosphere during June 1936, when the writer appears to have paid a return visit to the same factory – still omitting any syntactic markers for sex but allowing the readers to imagine that it was an all-male environment. This section contains an extremely famous passage: 'After always having bent the knee, taken everything, put up with everything in silence for months and years, what is happening is that people (*on*) are at last daring to straighten their backs, to stand up firm and speak out for a change. To feel, for a few days *that they are men*'. The first part of the quotation reflects the deeply felt reaction of Simone Weil herself – the latter has turned it into a reference to men, and indeed to virility (ibid.: 229 ff.).[36]

What is going on here? Were the people Weil met on her return to the factory the ones she had been working with or not? Were they men or women? It is quite possible that only the men remained in the workshop, since so many women workers were sent home. But part of the reason for the uncertainty is that Simone Weil carefully eliminated almost all gender marking from the passages she had taken from her diary, rephrasing her material so that the reader could easily assume the entire experience to be that of a neutral but grammatically masculine 'ouvrier'. Where the diary had made it plain in every sentence, syntactically or by content, that the writer was a woman, doing women's work among other women, these distinctions have almost all vanished from the article. And the same is true of various other reworkings of the material to be found in *La Condition ouvrière*: most strikingly perhaps in the article published in the collection as 'Expérience de la vie d'usine', sometimes referred to as 'Lettre ouvert à Jules Romains', also published under a male pseudonym.

Simone Weil's concern in much of her writing after the factory experience was to make sense of it, to valorize it and draw conclusions. She was proud of the episode, deriving pleasure from remarking to friends that neither Trotsky nor Lenin had any authentic factory work experience. But in claiming authenticity for her knowledge, and therefore authority for her analysis, she has also contrived to de-genderize and thus to de-historicize the experience, refusing to distinguish between men's and women's work in her writing for publication, although she was painfully conscious of it in her private journal. In this respect, her writings of the 1930s have been misinterpreted – but she herself encouraged the misinterpretation, by adapting her style to the discourse of the labour movement of her day, for which she had such admiration. When she wrote for public consumption, she helped to marginalize women workers by assuming that working-class experience was general – *la condition ouvrière* – only when it was expressed in terms of the dominant male experience. The price was paid in terms of historical accuracy: the downgrading of the historical specificity of women's work. Reading her work it is easy to miss the gender oppression at the heart of it, while registering oppression in the mode that apparently makes most sense: that of class oppression. But both are there.

6

THE TRUCE BETWEEN THE SEXES?

The politics of social intervention from the Great War to the Popular Front

> In those days, there was no social legislation.... In 1920, only private charity could sometimes find solutions to our problems, partial and limited solutions indeed, but we should recognize their value by trying to recall the good they did.
> (Ysabel de Hurtado, b. 1891, social work pioneer, recalling her early days, quoted in Hurtado 1966: 11–12)

> When I am appointing a new member of staff in the town hall at Suresnes, I take the candidate into a bathroom. The taps are full on and the bath is overflowing. There are plenty of buckets, cloths and mops in sight, and I ask him to take immediate action. If his first instinct is to start mopping up the water, he doesn't get the job. It goes to the one whose first move is to turn off the taps. I expect you to have the same reflexes. Always ask yourselves what are the primary causes of the repetition of the situations you face every day: sickness, poverty, unemployment.
> (Henri Sellier, Minister of Public Health, in a lecture to women social workers in 1936, recalled by a member of his audience, quoted in Knibielher 1980: 22, note)

> A formidable mechanism of social control was put into place, of which women were the instrument.
> (Del Re 1994: 166)

The last chapter explored a spectacular side of the Popular Front. This one draws attention to a less well-known aspect of its action, social work. Until recently Henri Sellier (1883–1943) was not a prominent figure in the history of the inter-war years, despite his notoriety at the time. An active member of the departmental council of the Seine (governing Paris and its suburbs) from 1919 onwards, he was also the energetic socialist mayor of one of the capital's western suburbs, Suresnes. During the Popular Front government of 1936–7, he was invited by Léon Blum to take over the Ministry of Public Health. During his brief tenure, he did not bring any spectacular piece of legislation to fruition: nothing to compare with the Matignon agreements or the raising of the school-leaving age. A longer lead time was needed for what Sellier saw as his mission in office: to co-ordinate all the disparate bodies working in the field of public health and welfare and to arrive at some national standards for dealing with the perceived social ills such as tuberculosis, infantile mortality, urban poverty-related disease or prostitution. He was not reappointed in 1937, and his grand design could not be carried to fruition.

During the last ten years, with the renewal of the history of the social services in

France, Sellier's name has emerged at almost every turn. His work in the Paris region between the wars, as well as the Suresnes experiment, both connected to what might be described as the redesign of social intervention, have been dusted off and re-explored. His tenure as Health Minister is also starting to be rediscovered. Controversial in life, Sellier remains a figure of some controversy in his 'rediscovery' too.[1]

Ysabel de Hurtado is virtually unknown, but the fact that we know anything about her at all dates from the same historiographical turning-point. The daughter of a Catholic banker, she trained as a nurse, and worked for the Red Cross during the Great War. In the 1920s she organized both the schools' nursing service and a social work service for the Parisian workers' housing schemes (Habitations Bon Marché or HBM).[2] Little in their background and nothing in their politics linked Sellier, the atheist man of the left, and this Catholic social worker. But their professional paths crossed more than once. Their contact illustrates the meeting – sometimes conflict-ridden and contradictory – between two worlds: party politics under the Third Republic, and the embryonic social services. Still in their infancy between the wars, multiform, confused and confusing, operating on the boundary between private initiative and state regulation, the social services were staffed at almost every level by women. The meeting of these worlds was therefore between a zone dominated by men and one frequented by women.

The subject of this chapter is the way gender became interwoven with the politics of social policy in this period. Disenfranchised formally, women were nevertheless pervasively present and active in the machinery of social policy-making, at both state and municipal level. 'Social policy' as a whole is too large a field to be tackled here, so I have singled out an aspect which underwent rapid change in the inter-war period, the activity covered by the term *le service social*: the social services, or social work, the executive branch, so to speak of national or local social policy. Such intervention has been defined both positively and negatively: on the one hand as the provision of help, medical aid and advice to alleviate what were known as 'scourges of society', like infant mortality and tuberculosis; or alternatively as intrusion into many households – usually the poorest – by an army of medico-social visitors and officials, seeking to operate forms of social control over the private life of the less well-off, as suggested in the third opening quotation. Until recently, social work was rather marginal to histories of the period. Partly, this might be because the sources were comparatively unexplored and preliminary research was lacking, something which is no longer the case today. It is not simply lack of source material, however, that has kept the subject on the margins of political history. There are at least two other reasons. One is disagreement over the definition of the political. For historians with an essentially narrative and adversarial view of politics, social services are not a primary concern, but part of a substructure, finding their place, if any, in background chapters on the economy, demography and society. Social service, although not exactly an area of consensus between the wars, was not one of the more obvious scenes of left–right battles. Rarely the occasion of dramatic dissent between the parties, it is not easy to fit into a chronological account. But that does not mean it was outside politics. As throughout this book, I will be arguing that we need to reassess what we mean by 'the political', using the focus of gender.

The second reason is the historiography of social work itself. As hinted above, this is not neutral territory. The social services in France had their origins largely in private charities – the *bonnes oeuvres* or good works of the nineteenth century, many of them under the auspices of the Catholic church. There is one body of literature from within the citadel, so to speak, sometimes from an explicitly Catholic perspective or by committed participants. Because of the history of clerical/anticlerical antagonism in Third Republic France, later given added edge by the divisions within the country during the German Occupation and Vichy regime of 1940–4, the study of 'confessional', i.e. religious groups remained until recently rather underexplored by academic historians.[3] What is more, the complex web of issues and discourses surrounding concepts like 'the family', family policy and pronatalism in France in this period appears particularly reactionary to many modern observers – and social work can legitimately be seen as in some sense connected to that web. The culmination of family propaganda under Vichy cast a dark backward shadow on the question in the 1930s. Worst of all, perhaps, most French social workers allowed themselves to be organized into the Vichy regime's Secours National during the war.[4]

This is a key to understanding the standard survey on the social services, by R.-H. Guerrand and Marie-Antoinette Rupp (1978), written from a 'republican orthodox' point of view. Theirs is a sharp and stimulating account, full of accurate historical information essential for any study of the subject; at the same time it is forthrightly marked by a discourse of hostility to the church and 'traditional morality', which spills over into hostility to Catholic social workers, and at some points to all social workers. The authors' viewpoint is explicitly related to political options during the Vichy period, which are regularly anticipated throughout the book. They depict most social workers of the inter-war years as naively implementing the traditional morality impressed upon them by conservative doctors and politicians, so making them ripe for takeover by Vichy.

The theme of social control is given a more firmly Marxist interpretation by Janine Verdès-Leroux (1977). In her hard-hitting survey, social work, in particular during the inter-war period, is judged in the light of its presumed intention, the maintenance and strengthening of capitalist control over the working class. A further strand of analysis, coexisting with the previous two, is the school of thought taking inspiration from the thought of Michel Foucault. Writers in this tradition have subjected to particularly sharp scrutiny the history of socially targeted medical intervention, viewing social workers as accomplices in the 'policing of families', prying into and seeking to control the private life of the working class in particular, not only in the interests of capitalism, but of hygienism and a scientist desire for regulation (cf. Donzelot 1980). The 'bourgeoisie' – whether defined economically, socially or intellectually – is in all three approaches identified as the prime mover and viewed with distaste or hostility.

Such analyses, often persuasive and stimulating, reflect moments in a long-running historical debate. They cannot be accused of ignoring gender: all of them take pains to discuss the role of men and women. It is true that they tend towards fairly similar conclusions: namely that female social workers, almost all 'bourgeois' in origin and thus foreign to the classes with whom most of their business was transacted, were the subordinate instruments of a process tending to moralize and control the working-class family – a process in which women social workers acquiesced, but had little say, since it was master-minded by male medical and political elites. As one writer stingingly puts it:

> Carried out by a fraction of the ruling class [i.e. women] that was at once dominated, yet objectively integrated in moral and cultural terms, a fraction quite willing to reproduce the arbitrary moral and cultural dictates of that class, and enjoying (within limits) the delegated authority of that class over the dominated layers of society – the whole business of social work leads us to ask questions about the legitimacy of intervention. This in turn, looked at from the point of view of the population that was on the receiving end, might lead us to consider the degree of symbolic violence required to impose it.
>
> (Verdès-Leroux 1977: 10)

This analysis subsumes gender within class. Others, Donzelot for example, have used gender as a factor operating against class, suggesting that working-class women were Trojan horses in their own households, collaborators with the invasive medical discourse against the independence of the consciously resisting male worker.

These critical approaches to the role of women social workers, while suggestive, had comparatively little empirical research to back them up. Later writers hint that that they may have over-simplified historical perceptions of the topic. Only quite recently have French scholars started to reassess the history of religious associations, philanthropy and social work, without being either unduly uncritical or overtly hostile. Not by chance, perhaps, much of this interest has to do with women's history. One of the earliest attempts to reply to the fierce criticism of social workers was Yvonne Knibiehler's compilation (1980) of primary life-history material. Knibiehler theorized her approach unobtrusively, suggesting that the texts could speak for themselves, but her sympathy for the practitioners is clear. In his preface, the political historian René Rémond wondered whether social workers might have actually raised their clients' consciousness of oppression within society, rather than simply colluding with the ruling class. That book could be seen as an early attempt to 'relegitimize' the social worker and lift the taboo. Recent researchers have picked up on such suggestions and looked in detail at aspects of social work, signalling the complexity of a question perhaps too readily reduced to a left–right, oppressor/victim argument. While reluctant to call into question too openly the view of Guerrand and others, they put forward more positive judgements of the personnel of the social services.[5]

It is with this historiography in mind that I will approach the topic, with the aim not of taking sides in the debate over finalities but of uncovering the mechanisms of co-operation, control, domination or subordination as between the *gendered actors* in this extensive field of public policy. Note however that by actors is meant 'agents of policy': one day perhaps it may be possible to study those 'on the receiving end', but the sources available so far relate overwhelmingly to those carrying out the intervention. After a brief overview of the early development of the French social services, we will look at three levels of policy-making with which Henri Sellier was directly or indirectly connected: first the local example of Suresnes; then the broader *département* of the Seine, including Paris; lastly the plans for a co-ordinated social service drawn up in the Ministry of Public Health in 1936–7.

A BRIEF HISTORY OF THE SOCIAL SERVICES

When Alexandre Bruno accompanied the Rockefeller Foundation Mission to Paris in 1917, he painted a low-profile portrait of the state of French public welfare. Nursing had long been a menial, underpaid occupation, without recognized training procedures. Although some training centres had been set up before the war, the *infirmière-visiteuse*, the equivalent of a health visitor or district nurse, was present only in 'insignificant numbers', Bruno wrote; the idea of the social services was 'almost inexistent', and as for the fight against tuberculosis, which was the mission's main concern, it was 'in a state of complete collapse' (quoted in Murard *et al.* 1987a: 463).

Paradoxically, despite the invisibility of a public service, there was no shortage of individual groups and initiatives, usually dating from the late nineteenth century. Their very proliferation made the picture chaotic. Whereas in the eighteenth century most charitable enterprises had been monopolized by the Catholic church, by the late nineteenth, public assistance had become separated from the piecemeal creation of particular associations. Urban poverty, overcrowding and poor living conditions were not new, but their increased visibility in the areas round big cities like Paris brought the 'social question' to prominence. Responses could have at least three sources of inspiration, short of revolution: traditional or social Catholicism, the latter inspired by the papal encyclical *Rerum Novarum* (1891); republican solidarism, associated with the centrist politician, Léon Bourgeois; and reformist socialism around figures like Vaillant and Jaurès. One might add to these pronatalist concern with the birth rate, and the newly emerging 'hygienist' school of medical thought, best exemplified in the TB clinics organized by Dr Calmette in Lille.[6] The French state was moving slowly towards a fuller legislative programme, with the creation of the Direction Générale de l'Assistance Publique et de l'Hygiène in 1889, and laws such as that of 1893 of assistance to the indigent. But district or town councils lacked resources to apply the laws, hence their appeal to the many private associations, of which there was no lack. It has been pointed out, with some irony, that there was a 'tangled undergrowth' of good works throughout France. In the town of Nancy alone, 'the years 1850 to 1900 saw the creation of no fewer than fifty different leagues and charities, from the Pure Milk Society to the Apprentices'

Gymnastic Group, by way of the Lorraine Tuberculosis League and the Sheet-lending Charity' (Murard *et al.* 1987a: 467).

Tuberculosis proved to be the spur to greater co-ordination, and the impact of the Great War provided the urgency. Already prevalent in cities, the disease spread rapidly among soldiers in the front line, and reached their families at home. Parliament at last took the step of setting up clinics in 1916 (though TB was not made notifiable until 1927). From 1917, the Rockefeller Mission played a crucial part in setting up and financing training centres for the nurses or *visiteuses* who were to provide the infrastructure for fighting the disease. Their function was to operate in liaison with the clinics for screening, diagnosis, treatment and follow-up, and they combined paramedical activities with education and explanation. By the time the Americans left in 1926, there were over 30 training centres in France, 170 specialized tuberculosis *visiteuses* in the Seine department alone and 42 clinics there. The man in charge of the Office Public d'Hygiène Sociale de la Seine co-ordinating them was Henri Sellier.[7]

The home-visiting agency was the origin of much of the later structure of social work in France. The principle of home visiting, from a base such as a clinic, became the preferred mode of operation. The fact that such visits were carried out among the most obviously underprivileged sectors of society (since the incidence of TB was greater there) led to an expansion of the social side of the *visiteuse's* work. Hospital social services, for example, were developed because it was argued that a narrowly medical focus would be ineffective if the entire social environment of the patient (code for 'the family'), with its poverty and associated problems, was not taken into account.

Gender was integral to the environment of social work between the wars. The point of intervention became the 'home' (*foyer*), inhabited by the 'family', identified by the presence of a woman and usually children. The individual might be the victim of tuberculosis, but the family was where the illness was socially treated. There was already a government factory inspectorate to monitor conditions of work, and the workplace was not normally the target of the social worker – unless, precisely, it was a workplace where there were large numbers of women. As a result of the employment of women in armaments during the Great War, a particular kind of industrial social worker came on the scene. The corps of female *surintendantes d'usine* was set up on the model of the British 'lady factory superintendents', to supervise the working conditions of women in factories, with special reference to their potential maternity, i.e. future families. Its own training college, the Ecole des Surintendantes, opened in 1917. Numerically far fewer than the home visitors, but more focused on a particular kind of intervention, the superintendents have been thoroughly studied from a number of perspectives in recent years, and will therefore not be the main focus of this account; but they illustrate the extent to which sexual difference was a structure in the target environment of social intervention.[8]

Home visiting was not new, but it now took on much greater proportions than before. The previous settlement model – based on a centre within the community, dispensing services and advice – was phased out. The new element in post-war France was co-ordination, promoted by the creation of a new waged profession of home visitors – as distinct from sisters of mercy or philanthropic volunteers – which gradually acquired national qualifications and status during the 1920s and 1930s. In 1922, a government decree instituted the nursing diploma with the option *infirmière-visiteuse*. What was the function of the new profession and who was recruited to it?

The term used at first, *infirmière visiteuse*, indicates the medical priorities to the fore in the immediate post-war period. Later years saw more stress on the social diagnosis to be carried out, although from the start the term *assistante sociale*, 'social worker', had coexisted alongside the early name, usually indicating a different emphasis. Different training establishments had different priorities too, and it was not until 1938 that the training for the two types of social work was formally merged. In practice one often finds the terms used interchangeably. The term *assistante polyvalente* – coined very early on – indicated a desire to combine both medical and social intervention rather than to have separate specialists. In order to avoid cumbersome use of the French terms, I will use the word 'caseworker' to describe all such visitors, since the concept of 'casework' was the theoretical novelty introduced from America, and since it covers most examples. Early caseworkers were almost all attached to particular clinics or centres, many of them specializing in TB. The caseworker would hold consultations, but also go out into the community, visiting households where there were TB patients, following up on treatment and prescriptions and giving advice to relatives about prevention. These were the days before universal state health care. Private medicine was expensive and most poorer families avoided going to the doctor. In particular, it was not commonplace for babies and children to be medically monitored from birth, hence the special effort of private charities and later of public services in the direction of mothers and young children, sometimes of course spurred on by natalist concerns. The neighbourhood clinic gave free treatment and medicine.[9]

The social services gradually extended their range, moving into schools, for example, arranging for medical examination for all children and follow-up visits to their families. On qualifying, a caseworker might be appointed to a public service, such as a municipality; a semi-public one, such as the workers' housing office (HBM); or any number of private organizations. Conditions varied: some caseworkers were strictly subordinate to clinic doctors and allowed little initiative; elsewhere, very young women might be asked to co-ordinate from scratch the entire social service for a district. The social legislation of the early 1930s on national insurance (1928–32) and family allowances (1932) created a new demand for trained caseworkers, since the independent funds set up to manage the benefits needed staff to visit claimants and process claims. State policy set up the structures of expansion, and the profession expanded accordingly.

In France, unlike other countries, the caseworker was invariably a woman. There was no ban on men training, but in practice virtually none did so before 1945. Although this is sometimes assumed to be a foregone conclusion, based on 'traditional' views of women as caring individuals, as well as on the familiar model of the Catholic 'bonnes soeurs', women were not necessarily the first choice. In Calmette's early tuberculosis clinics in the 1890s, the idea was to begin the 'practical education in hygiene of the working-class family', using the services of a 'hygiene monitor', specified as a 'man of the people' (in practice usually a co-operative trade unionist) with the aim of 'establishing true comradeship between the patient and the visitor'). At least two reasons are generally suggested for the change: first, the assumption (borne out in most cases) was that there would be a wife/mother at home in charge of caring for the sick. A woman visitor, some authorities decided, would be better able to communicate with her, and experiments were conducted with unqualified women monitors. In later years, the more medical approach in any case introduced a 'trained nurse', almost inevitably a woman, who would see that prescriptions were being observed, and who was recruited for her medical qualifications rather than her social identity. It was this model that eventually prevailed. Communication problems were seen as more easily resolved across class than across gender barriers – or perhaps the idea of men visiting women alone in the house during the day was thought unwise.[10]

One cannot of course ignore the 'common sense' ideology prevailing at the time, that this was 'natural' work for women. The visibility of nurses during the war helped, no doubt, but quotations can easily be found insisting on the devotional and self-sacrificial qualities which women alone would bring to the task. Social work, according to the conservative Professor Armand-Delille, was 'a true apostolic calling, to which religious souls will naturally be drawn' (Guerrand *et al.* 1978: 55). The stress on infant protection encouraged the idea that this was an unsuitable job for a man. The widespread presence of women in charity organizations, the feeling that social work might be an appropriate avenue for a respectable young woman who needed to earn a living, and the disappearance of the convent as a vocational possibility – all pushed in the same direction. New demands placed on the medical profession had something to do with it too. As Catherine Rollet has pointed out, follow-up advice and treatment was thought far too time-consuming for doctors to do. Even doctors interested in local clinic work (a minority of a profession still firmly wedded to private practice) saw it as no part of their function to spend time with young mothers. Discouraged from training as doctors, women were 'invited' in as helpers to cope with new needs. They were to handle the subordinate and paramedical tasks that had become more important with the philosophy of 'sanitizing society'. Regulations firmly set out the subordination of the health visitor to the doctor. As Dr Georgette Labeaume put it in a treatise on *Hygiène sociale* in 1924, the ideal caseworker would be 'intelligent, educated, committed, fond of children and capable of influencing mothers and nurses, while knowing how to remain in her role as monitor of hygiene and to be ruled by the leadership of the doctor' (Rollet-Echalier 1990: 55 and 398). This career was not designed to lead anywhere beyond casework, although some early recruits asserted themselves in administration.

Not only were the early caseworkers all women, but it is often assumed that they were unmarried and of bourgeois origin. Does the stereotype hold? The vocational aspect of the work, as a sort of lay sister in religion, was stressed by some prominent individuals, such as Abbé Grimaud, who believed that marriage was incompatible with commitment: 'The social worker is always an unmarried woman. If she takes a husband, she gives up her post: it is considered that she should devote her entire life to the mission she has taken on and that she should always be able to give it 100 per cent commitment.'[11] There was no rule in fact, but the need for celibacy was internalized by many of the early caseworkers: 'As far as I was concerned, this occupation was not compatible with marriage and bringing up children. Many of the social workers of my generation remained unmarried' (Knibiehler 1980: 30, 63–5, 73). However, as Yvonne Knibiehler remarks, the church was pragmatic enough to approve of applications to Catholic training colleges from women already married and it was not unheard of for mothers of families to take up social work. We may note that the earliest caseworkers came from a generation in which women outnumbered men, because of the war. In other words, while in practice married social workers were the exception rather than the rule, there was nothing pre-ordained about it.

As to social status, the term 'bourgeois' as ever covers a multitude of categories. Preliminary results from a quantitative study of about twenty training schools both inside and outside Paris, between 1905 and 1976, nuance the picture, but broadly confirm that, in the early days, middle-class recruitment was the norm. Later social work trainees have tended to come from a wider range of backgrounds, but in the inter-war period they came unequivocally from the better-off sections of society. Provincial recruits in the period up to about 1932 were most likely to be the daughters of *patrons*, owners of a firm, factory or farm. In Paris, their fathers were higher civil servants, engineers or in the liberal professions: daughters of Protestant ministers were disproportionately represented. This was indeed the bourgeoisie, although it has been argued that it was the most dynamic, least complacent sector of the bourgeoisie. Towards the end of the period, more daughters of white-collar workers were coming forward. Of the one-third of the sample over the whole period to 1976 whose religion is known, 54 per cent were Catholic, 12 per cent Protestant, 1.5 per cent Jewish. Protestants were particularly numerous during our period – about half of all recruits in Paris in 1930 (Crapuchet 1987: 12).[12]

One can supplement this sociological portrait of recruits by a snapshot of the social work galaxy as a whole in the late 1920s. In 1928, the new Comité Français de Service Social held its first international conference in Paris. A survey of the participants enables us to have an overall portrait of those most closely concerned with social work in France. They included representatives from the medical and political establishment – almost all male; from the administrative and voluntary 'movers and shakers' – mixed, men and women; and third, from the grass-roots social workers and health visitors – all female. Of the 1,030 French delegates to the congress, 173 were men, 857 women (whereas the representation on the more prestigious committee was 177 men, 189 women, most of the latter representing associations, or invited as the *wives* of public figures). Few delegates were in religious orders. The male delegates were doctors (about 100), or hospital administrators, and civil servants, representatives of trade unions, parliament and the League of Nations – in other words few of them were directly involved in social service and many were there ex-officio, wearing political hats. The women, two-thirds of whom were unmarried, were overwhelmingly caseworkers themselves: 96 came from the training schools for *assistantes* or nurses, 54 were *surintendantes*, 106 described themselves as *assistantes sociales*, and a large number came as caseworker representatives of welfare organizations. Overall, then, the men represented the professional classes, the women the lower practising echelons of social service. Some women did, however, address the conference and the whole affair was organized by the formidable Mme Josephine Getting (Crapuchet 1988).[13]

Guerrand and Rupp suggest, consistently with the interpretation taken throughout their book, that this conference demonstrated how women 'abdicated their responsibility', allowing men, and especially right-thinking men like Senator Paul Strauss, to dictate the ethos of the profession – i.e. the unpaid services of the lady bountiful. He told delegates: 'Every day altruism gains ground, and goodness reaches everywhere, thanks to the participation of women' (Guerrand *et al.* 1978: 62). But it could also be argued that the participants at the congress indicate that goodness and altruism were now finding new expression in the creation of a profession, rather than the *dames de bonnes oeuvres* of pre-war society. These young women might have been brought up on the ethos of philanthropy, but they were entering a paid (though not a well-paid) profession.

From this brief survey, certain structural aspects of that profession emerge. Because recruitment was only seriously launched after the Great War, we are indeed talking about a population of *young* women for most of the inter-war period, and for the most part they were also unmarried. The twenty year olds who trained in the 1920s would still be under forty when the Second World War broke out. Their numbers were swelled by veteran nurses or voluntary workers from the Great War, carrying on their trajectory into peacetime, sometimes entering training programmes as mature students. The older women (such as Mme Getting) seem to have provided a certain amount of leadership – other names will crop up below. The bulk of younger recruits were from educated middle-class homes: some were from traditional Catholic backgrounds, others from families with a tradition of public service. Determination and strength of character were minimum requirements to persist in the job, which by all accounts was a different matter from the sick-visiting of traditional philanthropy. One does not want to overstate the case in reaction to the dismissive approach of previous writers, but it is hard to see 'docility' as the chief characteristic of the profession. Political conservatism is another matter. Given their family backgrounds, the political preferences of most social workers were unlikely to be left wing. Yvonne Knibiehler has underlined the wish of most of her respondents to call themselves 'neutral' in politics. At the same time one can point to social Catholicism (and progressive Protestantism) as a motivating force for a minority of her sample, who had often been been members of youth movements. Docility is not

141

tied to any particular political preference, and some courage was called for from the early recruits, many of whom had defied their families in choosing the profession.

There was nothing obvious in the 1920s about sending young women from mostly sheltered backgrounds and with little 'street experience' into the alien, sometimes hostile environments of the problem areas of large cities and suburbs (*la zone*). They were expected to do something previously unthinkable for young unmarried women, to travel out alone, with a bicycle as their only means of transport, a uniform as chief protection. Few men of their class were placed in this kind of situation. One former caseworker from a well-to-do family, recalling her visits to the notorious slum dwelling known as the Cité Jeanne d'Arc in southern Paris, described how she surprised the writer Paul Bourget at dinner, by revealing that she went there alone, without a police escort (Knibiehler 1980: 131). Today, trainees and social workers in their first job are surrounded by a system of supervisors and monitors, and their responsibilities are carefully graded. In the 1920s, little support existed – services often had to be improvised from scratch.

This brief overview indicates that the whole field of social work as it took shape between the wars depended on a newly emergent female workforce requiring at least a minimum of practical intelligence and commitment. Its links with public policy were apparent though not always clearly articulated, and it operated in quite different modes from those of traditional philanthropy. Its connections with the world of politics will be explored in three different contexts.

SOCIAL WORKERS IN THE GARDEN SUBURB: SURESNES

Suresnes was originally a vinegrowing village to the west of Paris. By 1900 it had 11,000 inhabitants and a fairly mixed population. Henri Sellier, already a departmental councillor, came to live there during the Great War, and in the local elections of 1919 won control of the town hall for the Socialist party, SFIO. His early days were marked by political turmoil: when the Socialist party split at the Tours Congress in December 1920, he followed the majority into the new Communist party, but quickly fell out with the hard line of the PCF, and by 1924 was back in the old SFIO with most of his colleagues.[14]

It was his aim to make Suresnes a pilot town for a new vision of practical socialism, one that meant bringing about the best conditions of everyday life for its people. The *bureau d'hygiène* (health centre) was created in 1921; a schools complex was inaugurated in 1927; the municipal clinic-dispensary opened its doors in 1931; and the world famous open-air school for children with 'fragile lungs' was built between 1932 and 1935. The *cité-jardin*, a completely new housing complex planned for a mixed social population and including advanced environmental planning features, gradually took shape, reaching its target of 2,500 units in 1937.

The theory of the Suresnes experiment can be traced in the works of a man who became Sellier's close friend and collaborator: Dr Robert-Henri Hazemann, intellectual, representative of the 'hygienist' tendency in medicine and passionate planner.[15] The key to the theory lay in its 'scientific and systematic character' and in co-operation between the municipality and private charitable organisms, *les oeuvres privées*. Where the public service was distinguished by its availability to all on equal terms, by its continuity, and by its being monitored by public authorities, Hazemann wrote, private works were able usefully to complement public service by plugging the gaps. Central to co-operation was the fullest documentation: Hazemann was a devoted, not to say fanatical devotee of the card-index. 'If we were to design a statue of the director of the health centre', he extravagantly wrote, 'we would have him standing smiling between his two card-indexes' (Hazemann 1928: 44).

The practical implementing of Sellier's designs has been most minutely described by another close colleague. A former primary schoolteacher, whose wife was a caseworker in Suresnes, Louis Boulonnois was also town clerk (*secrétaire de la mairie*) and uncritical admirer of the achievements of the mayor over two decades. Both he and Hazemann stressed that the whole enterprise depended not only on some degree of political consensus but also on an integrated process of collecting, centralizing and sharing information – building up a comprehensive set of case histories: it could not be done without a committed corps of municipal employees, notably caseworkers (Boulonnois 1938).

As far back as the early 1920s, Sellier had come up with the idea that the health visitor should be 'polyvalent', able to handle both medical and social matters, as well as competent at recording and filing. To avoid the same household having to receive visits from a regiment of caseworkers it would be more effective to have one visitor fully briefed on the whole family situation. Family, private life and children were central to the Suresnes vision. As Paul Rabinow has pointed out, although Sellier was a socialist he had little to say about the workplace, seeing 'everyday life' or rather 'family life' as what happened to relieve people after work (Rabinow 1989: 325). It was this life that was to be improved and made healthy. On the other hand, the site of intervention was not exclusively the home. In this socialist Utopia, the collectivity provided much out-of-home help. Many if not most of the Suresnes initiatives were collective in focus: free milk, crèches, nursery schools, school canteens, vocational education, open-air school. There is a distinction between this approach and that of the more conservative family-centred approach of private charities.

The cornerstone of the whole plan, the caseworker, was deployed in Suresnes as perhaps nowhere else. As Boulonnois described it:

> The outstanding and certainly the earliest original feature of our organiza-
> tion was the systematic employment of the *infirmière visiteuse....* We started
> the system by applying it first where there was a legal obligation: visiting
> young mothers and nursing babies, and the school service. But since 1924, we
> have resolutely adopted 'multivalence' as a principle, and we are moving
> towards having strictly one point of contact [between family and social
> service], which we hope to achieve very soon.
>
> As of now, throughout Suresnes, visits to babies, the schools, surveys for
> public assistance, investigation of infectious diseases are all carried out by our

neighbourhood caseworkers. Every request for work, or for a service, rebate or allowance that comes to the municipality is studied by the neighbourhood caseworker who, by checking out the situation of the family, will be well placed to give, at the proper time, informed advice and views on the case. This method has the effect of considerably reducing the distant and sometimes disdainful manner in which public aid is granted, and it particularly aims to eliminate the situation in which the unfortunate have to make clumsy or begging gestures [in order to be helped], replacing this by the initiative and well-informed advice of the caseworker. We have always found this works very well and we are planning to extend and develop the zone for initiative and action by our visitors.

(Boulonnois 1938: 30)

Hazemann, too, in a pamphlet intended as a guide for caseworkers, insisted on the central role of this 'absolutely indispensable colleague', who can 'enter families on many pretexts'. In a revealingly organic image, he described the health centre as the administrative head of the social service, the assistance bureau and the dispensary as its eyes and ears; and the caseworkers as 'the two arms, enabling us to mould [developments] thoroughly (*pétrir en profondeur*) through prophylactic action – or therapeutic action, if the service arrives too late for prevention' (Hazemann 1928: 218–19).

The Suresnes experiment depended on personal loyalty and team spirit. Sellier, though dogmatic and brusque, appears to have inspired great loyalty among his colleagues, including the women schoolteachers and social workers who were closely associated with the political thrust of the enterprise. Because our primary sources are too close to him to breathe criticism, while most secondary sources view his action from a perspective critical of interventionism, it is only obliquely that one senses the political network of partisanship and hostility underlying his ambitious schemes. There was no shortage of criticism at the time: he was accused in 1929, for example, of building 'palatial schools which will inspire in the children of the common people a need for luxury which their social situation will not allow them to satisfy in later life'.[16] And Boulonnois's glowing description of the social worker is followed immediately by the admission that local doctors were unsympathetic to the health schemes: 'unfortunately. . . the local medical profession . . . never showed much enthusiasm for joining municipal initiatives in preventive medicine, and did not particularly favour the immunization programme, the cancer screening, nor the dispensary of the Office Publique d'Hygiène Sociale' (Boulonnois 1938: 30). Sympathetic doctors from outside Suresnes were consulted (including Jean d'Alsace, pioneer of the birth control clinic).

To participate in the programme was not just a job, then; in context it was a political act. To what extent was the woman social worker, deprived of the vote at municipal level as at parliamentary level, not entitled to all her civil rights, nevertheless a political actor in this kind of experiment? Suresnes was not the only locality where it was taking place. Hazemann refers to similar programmes in

Vanves, and Vitry-sur-Seine. Yvonne Knibiehler quotes examples of social workers, such as Madeleine Delbrel, who became closely committed to the municipal team in the communist suburb of Ivry, whose politics she was far from sharing. But Knibiehler also points out that in their self-descriptions, many of her correspondents did indeed claim that the social service was 'politically neutral'. She argues, convincingly in my view, that what they saw as 'politics' was the party confrontation at election times, the 'politicians' who might recuperate their work if they were not careful. No doubt the degree of near-political commitment found among Suresnes social staff was uncommon. The 'politically neutral' social worker often *preferred* to think of her sphere as a technical one, above – or below – politics, and one where she had some autonomy. Regarding her work as problem-solving, apolitical, she could have argued that similar welfare policies were introduced by municipalities of different political complexions. Yet if one reads the disclaimers collected by Knibielher, it is apparent that some self-deception was at work. Like it or not, the caseworker was swimming in an entirely political environment of which she was perpetually made aware and to which she inevitably tailored her actions:

> In those days, the elected councillors were highly politicized and for them the social services were an electoral springboard. We had to be careful. I realized that the only solution was strict neutrality.

> The pejorative adjective 'reformist', to which I was constantly exposed, irked me. Some colleagues, without any training but more committed politically to the party that ran the town hall, or another colleague, on the contrary very competent professionally but quite indifferent to politics, did not have to put up with the same kind of remark. I left my job after three years.
>
> (quoted in Knibiehler 1980: 138–43)

If one is trying to establish some kind of typology of the political in this context, the Suresnes caseworker must represent the grass-roots level: the point at which decisions taken in the town hall interacted with the local population. In the hierarchy of decision-making, the ordinary caseworker was on the lowest rung. But that did not mean an abdication of responsibility: the very novelty of the service meant that there were no precedents, and caseworkers had to use initiative and take decisions, often having an input into the shape of the service at local level. Nor was it happening in a political vacuum, as some preferred to think.

STRONG-MINDED INDIVIDUALS: CO-OPERATION AT EXECUTIVE LEVEL

In the second example, the role to be investigated is the interaction between 'women of initiative' and politicians or decision-makers. The theatre of such co-operation was usually broader than a single municipality. The Paris region, with its ever-growing population and visible social distress, was the scene of several co-ordinated projects.

The mushrooming of the Paris inner and outer suburbs since 1900, and the striking poverty of the 'zone' as well as of some of the working-class quarters of Paris itself, meant that the *département* of the Seine was a special focus of concern. Private charity was before long supplemented or replaced by public service. The new composition of the population after 1918 brought left-wing majorities to the town halls of the industrial suburbs of the capital and once the Communist party came into existence in 1920, it embarked on its conquest of what came to be known as the 'red belt', eventually making significant gains at the 1935 local elections. The majority on the departmental council of the Seine had long been socialist (cf. Fourcaut *et al.* 1992: 12–37).

A cluster of initiatives was associated with the new low-cost housing, the HBM. These were an innovation of the wartime and immediate post-war period, and once again we find Sellier as one of the prime movers in the decisions taken by the public authorities to buy up land and vote funds for constructing what would now be called 'grands ensembles', projects or estates, in the outer *arrondissements* and inner suburbs of the city (Fourcaut *et al.* 1992: 186). The rehoused population brought together a number of issues previously scattered or neglected, and the rehousing process itself created new problems. Ysabel de Hurtado, as one of Knibielher's informants, described early efforts to set up a special social service for the HBM as poorly co-ordinated. For example, an enquiry into whether mortality from bronchial diseases had diminished revealed that the new larger lodgings were often colder than people's previous cramped living quarters. Calls were made for better heating. But social workers were often only temporarily concerned and their interventions episodic (Knibiehler 1980: 165).

A critical turning-point for co-operation between different bodies came with the new laws on social insurance and family allowances in 1928–32. The funds relating to sickness benefits, family allowances, etc. were administered by independent funds (*caisses*), which had to employ agents, from municipal services or private charities, to visit claimants and their families. In the Paris region, some of the women who had been organizers of independent social charities or of semi-public services responded to the appeal made by the Red Cross, among others, that private associations help with the workings of the new legislation. Both Ysabel de Hurtado and Léonie Gillet volunteered and a particular form of collaboration had as its focus a pilot organization concerned with the protection of perinatal health and that of young children.

When the Caisse d'assurances sociales de Seine et Seine-et-Oise was set up in the wake of the new legislation in 1931, its director was Marcel Martin, a friend and colleague of Sellier, and like him a socialist. He too was in favour of enlisting private charities to co-operate. 'Of extraordinary intelligence, bubbling with ideas, generous and visionary', as an admirer put it, Martin set out to implement a public service model for the new fund (Hurtado 1966: 25 ff.).[17] Instead of creating a dedicated service available only to those who were insured, he planned to co-ordinate existing services to provide comprehensive coverage for all who needed it. Infant mortality seemed to him the most urgent practical field in which this could be tried. His plans at first provoked alarm among the existing private charities. Fearing competition, they decided to practise some co-ordination themselves, carrying out a pilot survey in 1931, in the *XXe arrondissement* and the inner suburb of Montreuil, to co-ordinate services for the newborn, protecting against the commonest causes of mortality. In the meantime, Martin's board, with more generous resources, was pursuing the same aim in the other nineteen *arrondissements*. After a few months of separate activity, it was agreed to merge these two initiatives. A pre-existing association, the Office de Protection Maternelle et Infantile (OPMI) was the umbrella under which they came together. Renamed after a while the Office de la Protection de la Maternité et de l'Enfance de la Seine (OPMES), it was officially asked to monitor the health of all children from birth to three years under the auspices of the social insurance fund. Mlle de Hurtado was put in charge of its social services – an executive post. This was neither a private nor a public organism but a 'semi-public service, not supplanting existing services but complementing and co-ordinating them' (Gourlet 1947: 83). The hundred or so 'polyvalent' caseworkers attached to OPMES were funded three-quarters from the social insurance budget. On its council sat representatives from public life, including Sellier and Senator Paul Strauss, the titular head of the pre-existing OPMI.

The brains behind OPMI/OPMES was its *comité technique* – three men and three women – meeting weekly with Senator Strauss in the chair. The other two men on it were Martin as director of the Caisse and Hazemann, by now director of the Public Office of Social Hygiene for the Seine département. The three women were Ysabel de Hurtado, Léonie Gillet for the Red Cross and Madeleine Hardouin for the family allowance board.[18] 'To describe these weekly meetings, directed towards a constant search for better methods and animated by passionate discussions, would take too long,' wrote one participant. 'Dominated by the vigorous personality of Marcel Martin, the technical committee established all the regulations for maternity allowances within the insurance Caisse, as well as its work for OPMES' (Hurtado 1966: 27). Incompatibility might have been expected, with Martin and Hazemann crusading for social hygiene in a context of political collectivism, whereas the women would see things from a more 'good works' perspective. All three women are described as having come from a background of 'ardent piety'. But according to more than one account, the committee worked well: the three women were described by one informant as 'very well informed, very determined, very authoritarian'. Mme Gillet in particular was a good intermediary between the positions. Hazemann is quoted as saying: 'She was extraordinary: she was always surprising us. She had ideas and found ways and means to do things' (Reverdy 1972: 96).

These included the establishment of a vast corpus of documents registering every young child in the Paris area, and the co-ordination of the appropriate caseworkers, who had themselves to be trained to new standards of record-keeping and versatility. All the associations in the capital had their own way of doing things, jealously guarding their methods and prerogatives.

> We had to visit every institution, see every caseworker, make an appointment
> to see someone in every town hall [for each *arrondissement* or suburban
> *commune*] and if one thinks of the range of political parties we had to confront
> to get the participation of the 80 *communes* in the Seine *département*, and
> remembers that the OPMES, although backed by the Caisse and approved
> by several offices in the prefecture, had no real administrative authority, it will
> be seen that much tenacity was required to get the desired results.
>
> (Hurtado 1966: 29)

By the outbreak of war, OPMES could claim at least some tangible results. It had its
team of caseworkers, a secretariat and a working index system. It was claimed that
infant mortality had fallen from 10 per cent to 6 per cent.

The political questions arising from this example differ from that raised by the
professional social worker in the case of Suresnes. It is the encounter on far more
equal terms than one might have supposed, of responsible and motivated men and
women, in a context which can hardly be described as outside politics. It is only one
example among literally thousands: the French Republic had a dense and, to the
historian, confusing plethora of semi-official and official advisory councils, committees of all sorts. On these bodies, particularly if they were in any way concerned
with welfare, children or education, women were frequently invited to serve.
Private charities drew even more upon the voluntary work of women. By the inter-
war period, partly as a consequence of wartime arrangements, the ramifications of
the state or of local authorities reached deep into the fabric of organizations which
might not see themselves as having a political function, yet which took decisions
governed by new legislation and provided feedback that was translated into policy
decisions. The actual relations between men and women as groups, or as
individuals, within the mass of organizations, and the effectiveness of this mixed
committee work must remain opaque to historical enquiry until researchers
undertake the patient investigation of minutes of meetings – but there can be no
denying that 'committeewomen' had a say in many decisions.

OPMES was a particularly visible case of this widespread phenomenon. Thanks
to biographical research, we now know something about all those on the technical
committee of OPMES, both men and women. The men have formal careers,
traceable through the usual reference books. Hazemann in particular has recently
attracted scholarly attention. Of the three women, while none of them is a
household name, all form part of a nebulus now arousing new interest in historians
of social work. Informal sources (relatives, oral history) have to be explored to
discover the stages of their itineraries through the corridors of the social service.
They are representative of a particular generation of women best described as
strong-minded rather than feminist. They tended to have wartime experience.
Often formidable characters, they were well-known in welfare circles and slightly
two-edged tributes to them are frequently found from the pens of male colleagues.
Their 'careers', if that is the right word, often had erratic beginnings – a surprising
number entered some form of paid or unpaid activity as a result of personal

circumstances, perhaps the death of parents, husband or child: in other words, they were strongly motivated to look beyond the family circle, and in some cases had actually broken with it. They were often well connected enough to find the right opening for their talents. To the three mentioned above could be added the names of Léonie Chaptal (1864–1934), Juliette Delagrange (1880–1936), Josephine Getting (1877–1943), Berthe Milliard (1877–1924), Berthy Albrecht (1893–1943), and many more.[19] They would make a tempting study for a collective biography, since their trajectories are often similar: they were sometimes of strong religious faith, often remained unmarried, and had that sort of tough innocence of a generation of secular nuns. Those who are best known are those who have left traces in the archives. Others are remembered only by chance, like Mlle Lannebit who initiated the social service of the HBM:

> She was astonishing: I can see her now, she seems ageless, with no private life, having devoted her existence to the children's nursery she had established in the Cité Jeanne d'Arc, putting into it all her own money, going short herself if necessary, begging and browbeating her friends and others, preaching, persuading, and sometimes really wearing them out. She produced marvels out of thin air. She looked like a poor old bag-lady, but she was in fact a remarkable person.
>
> (Knibielher 1980: 164)

Mlle Lannebit is a more humble example than Mme Getting, but both are examples of strong-willed women entering an arena where they had to conduct negotiations with male politicians over resources and funding.

This kind of dedicated and unpaid committeewoman or tireless organizer did not entirely disappear after the Second World War, but later expansion of employment opportunities for women made it less likely that the pattern would go on being repeated. What one has between the wars is a historical high point for such activity, linked to the 'home front' experience of the Great War and the unique situation offered by the embryonic social services in post-1918 France. Sociologically and historically this generation can be seen as a transitional one between the philanthropic lady of good works and the professional woman. Politically, such women were operating within the machinery – local, regional and national – of the Third Republic, although they had little or no official standing. Paradoxically, the lack of firm frameworks gave them elbow-room. Middle class, articulate and unwilling to be intimidated, they were sometimes prepared to work closely with politicians of various parties – whatever their own views – or, by contrast, to stand up to them. As will be noted below, some of those who worked closely with Sellier were very far from sharing his political views. There is a parallel here with the more modest caseworker seeing her job as 'not political'. For the Hurtados, Gillets, Hardouins, it was perhaps more a case of the higher pragmatism – the desire to put into effect plans they had come to cherish. But their investment of time and energy in negotiation and discussion was comparable to that required by their male counterparts in political milieux.

HENRI SELLIER, SUZANNE LACORE AND THE WORK OF THE HEALTH MINISTRY UNDER THE POPULAR FRONT

The last example takes us deeper inside the corridors of power. One of the many innovations of Léon Blum's cabinet of June 1936, after the victory of the Popular Front at the polls, was the appointment of three women as junior ministers: Cécile Brunschvicg and Irène Joliot-Curie were attached to the Ministry of Education, and Suzanne Lacore joined the new Minister of Public Health, Henri Sellier. The broader context of the appointments will be returned to in Chapter 7; here it is the Health Ministry and its connections with the world of social service that most closely concern us.

Suzanne Lacore (1876–1976), although little remembered today, was the woman minister on whom most press attention focused at the time.[20] Her official designation, *sous-secrétaire d'état à la protection de l'enfance*, was a quite new title, corresponding to public concern about the ill treatment, poor health and poverty of many of France's children, especially in and around Paris. There was much sympathy for her appointment, though at first she might seem an eccentric choice: a simple primary schoolteacher from the Corrèze, with no Parisian profile of public office, already sixty years old, tiny and demure in appearance. She soon made her mark as a passionate speaker, however, as press reports testify. Reading them, one might assume that she had freedom of action, for she took to publicity like a duck to water, taking photocalls, opening crèches, making speeches of an intensity that contrasted with her appearance. 'Anyone who has not heard Suzanne Lacore speak will never know what true faith is. [Photographs show] a timid self-effacing figure. But that figure stands up to speak and suddenly the light shines.'[21] But this does not tell us what her relationship was with Sellier, or whether she had much real influence within the ministry.

Sellier himself was by now a man with a mission, dominating his immediate subordinates. He has been called the 'first real Health Minister', although the post had officially existed since 1930. Sellier immediately appointed Hazemann as director of his private office. They formed a powerful team. Sellier was famous for his brusque no-nonsense manner (he ruffled many feathers) and for his absolute dedication to public welfare services. Hazemann was now a leader of the 'hygienist' tendency in public medicine. The philosophy they shared, 'social hygiene', is set out in the joint paper they gave to the Second International Conference of Social Work in London in July 1936. For both of them, the Health Ministry was the chance for which they had been waiting.[22] Jules Moch later said of Sellier:

> I am sure that he saw in his ministerial functions above all a way of extending to the rest of the country the initiatives successfully introduced to his own town of Suresnes . . . . He remained in government what he had been all his life, a technician of the provision of housing and schools, an animator of social life at local level, a passionate believer in the welfare of the family and of assistance to childhood.[23]

Lacore was directly attached to Sellier's office. She had not been chosen by him, and was not part of 'the team'. But they were both lifelong socialists and one would not *a priori* expect much disagreement. If there was any difference of opinion, the minister's view would have prevailed. Sellier was quoted in his local paper as saying, 'Just a door separates the offices of the two ministers [himself and Lacore]. This door often opens since in fact anything to do with childhood has to do with public health: the child must above all be protected against physical handicap and sickness.'[24]

Lacore will almost certainly have been integrated into the ministry's overall planning rather than encouraged to branch out on her own. Sellier's attitude to the confusing network of private and public approaches to welfare which existed by 1936 was characteristically pragmatic, if not exactly tactful. He wanted to bring order into things. One can see in the ministry a replication at higher level of the negotiations Sellier had already taken part in at regional level. He was prepared to work with private organizations if necessary – and if he was impressed by their competence. But he could be outspoken against the many would-be do-gooders or nursing staff, if their only qualifications were 'confessional', i.e. religious. And he was irritated by the chaotic proliferation of agencies. His desire was to co-ordinate and to get results, and to that end he was prepared to work with like-minded souls – even if they were wealthy Catholic women from whom all his convictions separated him. This did not go unremarked among his political allies, whose anticlericalism was more absolute than his own. A press report in September 1936 made it known that 'a Mlle X, sister of a bishop [this identifies her as Mlle Chaptal], who is not in any sense a civil servant, and whose role at the Health Ministry is as the agent and protector of confessional, [i.e. Catholic] charities, still has an office at the Ministry, granted her by Louis Marin [Sellier's predecessor] in contravention of all the rules.'[25] An inter-ministerial letter from Sellier to Cécile Brunschvicg gives a clear example of his appreciation of another such woman, Juliette Delagrange: 'I have worked with her for a long time. I thoroughly appreciate her knowledge of the problems of social protection, the intelligence with which she looks for solutions and the objective spirit which dominates her concern; she could be an excellent liaison agent between your administration and mine.'[26]

Neither Sellier nor his close political associates were soft on the Catholic church: Martin and Hazemann were both freemasons, and Suzanne Lacore is likely to have taken the same line, as an *institutrice* and long-standing militant of the anticlerical SFIO. There may have been some prickliness in the team's exchanges with their Catholic counterparts. By the same token, their interlocutors also sometimes had strong feelings about the risks of becoming too involved with 'state' representatives. Ysabel de Hurtado, in her account of this period, explains that Léonie Gillet in 1936, foreseeing 'a state takeover of philanthropy' – which she viewed with hostility if not horror – suggested setting up a co-ordinated Union des institutions privées, 'which was quickly agreed to by many of the Paris-based organizations' (Hurtado 1966: 30).

Conciliation broke out. Mme Gillet and the marquise de Ganay did not hesitate to put their scheme to Sellier, whom they already knew from OPMES, and 'although a militant socialist, he gave them his support. In fact he went further and . . . in a series of circulars of August–September 1936, made it obligatory for any private institution which wanted a subsidy from the Ministry to join the Union.' In fact Sellier went further than they liked in the rather strong anticlerical tone of the circulars. However, the Union was set up and worked for about two years. After that, with Sellier no longer at the Health Ministry, it had lapsed by the outbreak of war. This entire episode could be viewed as a preliminary contact between two wary camps, neither inclined to underestimate the other, before a more prolonged negotiation (Hurtado 1966: 30 ff.; Rollet-Echalier 1990: 272 ff.).

This was not long coming. Over the summer of 1936, a serious start was made by the ministry to co-ordinate welfare services and private charities at departmental level.[27] There was little time to implement, let alone monitor the measures, and the disruption and reorganization of the war years covered the traces of all existing projects in a centralized social service under the auspices of Vichy. But the ideas of Sellier and Hazemann epitomized advanced thinking of the 1930s. (As 'social hygienists', they have come under criticism today for the element of social control that their regulatory approach contained, but that is another story.) As they saw it, they were seeking to bring coherence into the piecemeal development of the social services, and this meant collaborating with many charities run by women. There is a hierarchical and perhaps gendered subtext here of bringing republican order and rationality to the haphazard if well-intentioned plethora of 'good works'.

It is not always possible to see what part Lacore herself played in the results that came out of the Health Ministry in this area – some of the relevant decrees, such as those of January 1937 on the inspection of children's agencies, do not carry her signature, suggesting she may have been at some remove from the real centres of decision. But she adopted the prevailing ministry style: circulars and surveys poured out of her office asking for information. In the short term, a number of practical measures were taken, mostly increasing resources for particular groups or tightening up the inspection of health services affecting children. Lacore seems to have been instrumental in making it possible for the first time for women to be full inspectors of the Assistance publique (previously they could only be deputy inspectors), and there are signs she thought women especially suitable for social work. In her own pronouncements, she used the rhetoric of 'difference': 'woman will add her qualities of generosity and delicacy which particularly single her out for dealing with children and in particular unfortunate children.'[28]

When the journalist Hélène Gosset reported on Lacore's first six months, she began with a seemingly random list of small-scale measures: increased aid to lone mothers in need; improved conditions for taking in abandoned babies; increased surveillance of children in state care ; adoption; improved facilities for breast-milk donors; survey of infantile mortality; supervision of children of travelling parents; *colonies de vacances* for children of the unemployed; a survey of handicapped children. A later article commenting on the overall work of the ministry added further examples to the list. She noted that Suzanne Lacore had set up three commissions for child protection: one to handle children in 'moral and physical danger' (what would today be called child abuse); one to deal with backward and handicapped children; the third concerned with children's out-of-school activities – playgrounds, *colonies de vacances*, books, films, etc.[29]

The composition of the commissions was the familiar mix: records of the first show that it contained representatives from the ministries concerned (Health, Justice, Education, etc.) and from the medical profession – all men; plus a number of women, mostly from charitable organizations, with the exception of Alice Jouenne, Suzanne Lacore's *chef de cabinet* (who seems to have acted as co-chair some of the time) and one or two journalists. The commission was chaired by Hazemann, a sign that it was integrated into the overall plan, and not an initiative of Lacore's.[30]

What is clear, though, is that the work of child protection was perceived as important, that Lacore was firmly identified with the co-ordinated ministry approach to it, and that a start was made in tackling this major social problem. Complaints were nevertheless heard that there had been few tangible results. Alexis Danan, a well-known press campaigner for measures against child abuse, later wrote that 'when Mme Suzanne Lacore was secretary of state for the protection of childhood, she envisaged the creation of supervisory committees in every *arrondissement* and canton, but her plans never came to fruition.' The women's weekly journal *Minerva* commented that there had been adverse remarks on this record in the press, to the effect that there were 'still' many children suffering physical abuse. It added the rider that the women ministers had met some resistance, not from their ministerial colleagues, but from the permanent civil servants.[31]

Such hints, and some of the archive papers, suggest that it was not so easy for a woman to move straight into a position of authority – a point to be taken up in a later chapter. If Lacore's position was a little precarious within the ministry, Sellier's was precarious within the government. When the Blum government resigned in June 1937, Sellier, despite his popularity and unquestionable energy as Health Minister, was not reappointed to the new government. (Neither Lacore nor Brunschvicg, the two serving women ministers, was reappointed either.) The health portfolio went to the radical Marc Rucart. Partly the change of personnel was simply a reduction of the socialist ministers, but there is evidence concerning Sellier that suggests more than this, and it is a point relevant to the substance of this chapter.

There are many hints that one of Sellier's initiatives, his attempts to eradicate or reduce prostitution, aroused hostility to him in political circles. The so-called 'French system', whereby it was compulsory for prostitutes in *maisons closes* to register with the police and undergo regular health checks (while their clients were subject to no such control) had long been a cause of concern to activists against prostitution. Between the wars strong feelings were regularly expressed on both sides of the question. Sellier lent his authority as minister to the campaign for closure, spearheaded by various organizations concerned for morality and welfare, many of them philanthropic or with religious patronage. His personal archives in

Suresnes contain massive documentation on the campaign behind the bill he presented to the Assembly in November 1936, a measure which had the apparent backing of both Lacore and Brunschvicg.[32] While it might be popular with the Catholic church and with many women's organizations, the bill did not command support among deputies and senators. The whole affair was eventually buried, apparently after pressure from the organized and well-connected lobby known euphemistically as the 'landlords of furnished properties'. It is sometimes hinted that this ruined Sellier's career. He had attacked 'the occult power of the knights of prostitution. This brave audacity cost him his portfolio.'[33]

This may not have been the only reason for his going, but it may have combined with disillusion about the possibility of achieving change at national rather than municipal level. His local paper reported that 'close associates of the mayor of Suresnes, in whom he sometimes confided, were well aware how disillusioned he was with his ministerial functions and the total powerlessness he felt, how much he suffered from . . . the pressure on him not to meet commitments he had entered into, the difficulties he experienced having to move in parliamentary and political circles so contrary to his practical mind.'[34]

CONCLUSION

Whatever the truth of the allegations over the prostitution bill, Sellier's initiatives were in some sense at odds with the polarized politics of left and right at this fraught time. He took pains to try to keep health measures out of the party political arena, but his contacts with the private charities were frowned on; his moralizing stance on prostitution was not greeted with enthusiasm by his own party; and he chafed at the obstacles preventing 'common sense solutions' at national level comparable to those he had enacted in Suresnes.

It would be going much too far to see the (well-attested) misogyny of parliamentary milieux as a central reason for Sellier's misfortunes. But it may be clear from the foregoing account that he was closer than his party colleagues to the concerns that mobilized the articulate but socially conservative and often devout Catholic women whom he met regularly in the pragmatic context of social welfare. They were not on the whole concerns that mobilized politicians (with the exception of the pronatalist lobby, and that was not chiefly concerned with welfare). One of the arguments regularly advanced by women's suffrage movements was that social problems would move up the agenda once women were able to vote. The experience not only of the Health Ministry, but also of the OPMES and the municipality of Suresnes was one of increasingly necessary co-operation with women in various capacities: Sellier's associate minister, her women advisers (see the names of Suzanne Lacore's *cabinet*), philanthropic committeewomen, like Mme Getting, and the whole army of less well-known social workers and health visitors who participated in the welfare services. The tensions and conflicts surrounding the figure of Sellier, and the non-reappointment of the women ministers, are surface signs that, perhaps more than at any previous time in French history, two conflicting agendas were coming into contact: that of the predominantly male political world and that of the predominantly female world of social services.

The three different levels of interaction between these two worlds which have been surveyed here call for more detailed research. As noted at the start of the chapter, the dominant interpretations of social work in this period have hitherto stressed the element of social control, and that is undeniably present. The most recent writers nuance their views: thus Susan Pedersen, writing of the fund which administered family allowances in the Paris area, the Caisse de Compensation de la Région Parisienne, notes that

> a genuine concern among CCRP social workers for both public health and domestic morality dovetailed neatly with employers' desires for access to the employees' families.... Employers worried about the disruptive and potentially revolutionary influence of the heavily male, heavily communist Parisian unions thus attempted to remake the Parisian working class through a direct appeal to women.
>
> (Pedersen 1993: 173)

The CCRP, managed by businessmen, is perhaps a special case. But clearly the recipients of social workers' visits were broadly speaking the urban poor, while the dispensers of social work were the relatively privileged, whether we are talking about middle-class caseworkers or socialist town councillors. Whether it was simply a class conspiracy shot through with symbolic violence is less demonstrable. It is after all possible to envisage the outcome of social intervention as enabling people in hardship to regain more control over their lives, whether in terms of improved health for their children or in less quantifiable ways. But, in any case, what was visibly happening between the wars was that private philanthropy was yielding ground to intervention by local authorities (on both left and right). Temporarily, they coexisted in an uneasy sort of truce.

Politicians like Sellier on the left and Strauss on the centre-right needed the co-operation and expertise of strong-minded women like Getting, Hurtado and company, and the commitment of trained caseworkers. To see such women as inevitably doomed to be manipulated and having no influence on decision-making seems to me over-dismissive, given the available evidence. Retrospectively we may not always share their ideas. But they had practical experience and knowhow that was not available to the great majority of men. It was not expertise that brought much in the way of rewards: men were not jockeying to build careers in social work. But it was capable of being used to set up new structures, those of the embryo welfare state. The overall context, it is true, deprived such women of collective authority. Ironically Henri Sellier himself, while prepared to work with women he trusted, was appalled at the idea of granting the vote to all women.

7

THE PERMEABILITY OF PUBLIC LIFE

Mainstream and alternative politics

Naturally, since she was excluded from *le pays légal*, woman [*la femme*] would rarely be a political activist or even a member of a political party. Even if she was a wage-earner, she was hardly more likely to have joined a trade union.

(Borne and Dubief 1989: 205)

Le pays légal is the official nation as opposed to *le pays réel*, the 'real' one. If the politics of social work often masqueraded as 'non-politics', or could be viewed by participants as 'politically neutral', that was partly because of the way politics was encoded during the Third Republic. Weighing a baby at the neighbourhood clinic might not look like part of the political process, either to the child's parents or the health visitor operating the scales; but with a broad definition of the political, the historian has no problem arguing that that is just what it was. This chapter looks critically at the politics/non-politics boundary: on one hand, surveying some of the formal mechanisms of decision-making, within *le pays légal*; on the other, noting the diversity of pressure group politics with roots in *le pays réel*. As the quotation suggests, one might expect to find men in charge of the former, with women appearing, if at all, in the latter.

But is the frontier as watertight as such categories suggest? With a suspicion that it isn't, I have chosen to approach the subject through the notion of permeability. In what ways can political life be seen as *infiltrated* by people formally excluded by the rules of gender? In a watercourse, the movement tends to be one way. The new element between the wars, I shall argue, was that more women than ever before were taking part in something we can call 'politics', and that this movement was becoming irreversible. Some men took the initiative in inviting them to do so; others bitterly resisted any such steps; many men, and women, barely noticed the change. Rather than discuss issues such as the cause of peace, the subject of Chapter 8, or even the formal exclusion of women from voting rights, tackled in Chapter 9, I mean to devote this chapter to some structural features of political activity, to see what infiltration might mean. Three sites of enquiry suggest themselves: political actors; the politics of association; and political culture.

Women had more opportunities than one might suppose to become actors in the political arena of inter-war France. Their action could be formally recognized (as co-opted 'municipal councillors' for example); or it might be exerted through informal channels of communication, ranging from journalism to private influence; or it might mean no more than joining a party or an association with political aims. In the first two cases, this meant directly working with or alongside men; in the last instance, there might be a choice between single-sex or mixed political groupings. In all three, it implied either adapting to an already existing political culture or, as sometimes happened, creating a new one.[1]

POLITICAL ACTORS I: CO-OPTED INTO OFFICE: RESPONSIBILITY WITHOUT POWER?

To assume that decision-making bodies in inter-war France were all-male is understandable, but not quite true. France under the Third Republic contained several tiers of *elective government* (municipal, departmental, national) formally open only to men. But it had a wealth of semi-official *non-elected* committees and other bodies, which could co-opt women. By 1918, there was even a third category of local and some national *elective bodies* for which French women had been both eligible and/or voters, in some cases since the 1880s. These included departmental primary education boards and local industrial tribunals, as well as chambers of commerce and agriculture (Albistur *et al.* 1977: 578). Both the latter categories would repay research, but this section concentrates on co-option, which was increasingly practised between the wars. There was a range of possibilities. Members of *non-elected* councils and committees (*conseils* and *commissions* – what would be called 'quangos' in Britain today), were recruited essentially through patronage. We have already noted the activities of committeewomen in welfare and social work. In these domains, it was not uncommon for a woman or two to be appointed to quite high-level bodies. Even so, they were never more than a tiny minority: only one woman sat on the Conseil Supérieur de la Natalité set up straight after the war (Marguerite de Witt-Schlumberger).[2] They were better represented on the Renoult commission created in 1926 to discuss revision of the *Code Civil* as it affected married women: this was composed of nine men and seven women, mostly lawyers.[3] The career of one participant, Marcelle Kraemer-Bach, illustrates another possibility open to women well qualified or well connected enough to have access to political circles: appointment to the *cabinet*, or private office of a government minister. She was briefly a member of Edouard Herriot's private office when he was Prime Minister in 1932. Such nominees had official status on a level with senior civil servants – and their equivalents are still powerful today. But the two examples of co-option I shall look at in more detail were peculiar to the inter-war years: the appointment of women as municipal councillors and as government ministers.

The practice of inviting women to sit on local councils began at least as far back as 1926 (a communist initiative) but became widespread after the local elections of 1935, which resulted in many new left-wing councils, though it was not confined to the left. The mechanisms for co-opting and the titles given to the co-optees varied. The term 'councillor' itself, widely used in the press in the 1930s, is misleading. In many cases, women had already been invited to sit on local subcommittees discussing welfare or hygiene. But only after the 1935 elections did they seem to acquire more formal status. In Dax and Reims, for example, they were now described as 'adjointes'; in Lorient, Villeurbanne, Colombes and Beaune as 'consultantes' either 'privées' or 'techniques'; sometimes they were known as 'auxiliaires'. In some municipalities, they were elected by a male electorate; in other places, a female electoral college was convened; most often of all, women already known to the men of the majority group on the council were simply appointed. Their numbers were small but not negligible: six in Dax, Versailles and Louviers (in the last example, fifty candidates stood for election) – but as many as twenty in Paris. They had the opportunity to discuss relevant issues, but were not allowed to vote in full council.[4]

Feminists were divided over whether the initiative was a step forward or a step back. While *La Française* regularly mentioned the appointments favourably, the long-established Ligue Française du Droit des Femmes (LFDF) opposed the whole principle of co-option, referring to the great 'swindle that lies behind the famous experiment with women as pseudo-local-councillors' (Bard 1995: 675). The pro-suffrage socialist *député* Bracke declared that it was 'not even getting in by the back door, it is simply gaining entry to some side-balcony. It is the recognition of accepted inferiority.'[5]

One can see why they were doubtful. The women in question were hand picked, and if not party members, often the wives of party members. Almost invariably, they sat on welfare and education committees, handling such issues as childcare and delinquency, health and social problems, with which women were considered by their political patrons to have 'natural affinities'. As noted earlier, given the structures of the social work and nursing professions, there were pragmatic reasons for asking women to help councillors deal with welfare issues. Later historians, feminists in particular, have taken a dim view of this practice, dismissing it as type-casting. It did not go unchallenged at the time either. As Marguerite Grépon wrote in 1936:

> Women are generally agreed to be indispensable in [the sphere of] public hygiene and all aspects of public assistance. But it means we are still in the infirmary. Eternally devoted to the task of repairing things that have gone wrong, never the task of creation.[6]

There is much force in this complaint, but it can be given a different slant, if we follow the logic of the last chapter. After 1918, the state at both national and local level was increasingly viewed as shouldering some responsibility for welfare. But only a minority of male politicians was professionally interested in such questions: traditional assumptions that women were more suited to discuss issues like child-care were thus not hard to reconcile with the need to recruit them for the growth of the modern social services. Many left-wing mayors, following the lead of pioneers like Sellier, saw it as their role to improve the conditions of life of the working class, providing 'cradle-to-grave' care if possible, demonstrating their awareness of social evils such as infantile mortality, alcoholism and avoidable disease. Viewed this way, it could be argued that these initiatives marked a dawning perception among politicians that existing arrangements were inadequate in areas that were beginning to arouse public concern, voiced in the press. Women were approached because politicians thought they were the experts. It was, of course, an undervalued area of expertise, but simply to deplore that is to fail to historicize the episode. It fits into the long process whereby the boundaries of state intervention and private charity were being renegotiated. The point also bears repetition that women in public life, whether feminists, social work pioneers or left-wing activists, kept drawing attention to social problems. Suffrage campaigners regularly argued that these would receive serious attention only when women had the vote. The rhetoric of difference – stressing traditional aspects of women's domestic concerns – was not necessarily seen by everyone as conflicting with that of equality in terms of equal rights. While welfare politics was not an obvious career path for men, it could offer a real, if limited, chance for women to achieve social mobility – and political visibility.

The most striking example of co-option in the period was the appointment by Léon Blum of three women as junior ministers in his cabinet of June 1936.[7] One of the most vaunted innovations of the Popular Front, this was a personal initiative by Blum, who took the view that women would come into politics 'from the top'. He had difficulty persuading his first two choices, Irène Joliot-Curie and Suzanne Lacore, but they eventually yielded to his personal appeals. Lacore, whom we have already met, was a member of Blum's own party, Joliot-Curie a more recent adherent (often assumed to be closer to the Communist party). The third woman, Cécile Brunschvicg, was the choice of the radical leader, Blum's coalition partner, Edouard Daladier. On hearing Blum's proposals, he had asked for a government post for a woman from his own party. Brunschvicg accepted the post readily.

The details of these appointments need not concern us here, but they raise several relevant points. In the first place, they clearly come under the heading of the *politics of gesture*. They may have been inspired by the co-opting of local women councillors, but the evidence suggests that, unlike the latter who were called on for their competence, to meet a perceived need, the women ministers were seen by Blum as more ornamental than functional, as a symbol of his theoretical support for women's rights, rather than bringing special expertise into the government. His letter to Suzanne Lacore is particularly revealing: to her protest that she had no previous experience Blum replied: 'You will not have to command, but to inspire (*animer*). Above all, you will just have *to be there*, since your presence alone will mean a great deal' (emphasis in original).[8] This aspect of their appointment – just being there – has tended to choke off any detailed scrutiny of the episode. While it figures in virtually all accounts of the Popular Front, the appointment of these women is rarely analysed. The magic number of three is not queried (whereas one of the three barely served more than a couple of months); the women's party affiliations escape notice (although they correspond to a spectrum of Popular Front opinion); their non-reappointment has attracted no comment. The politics of gesture proceeds by symbol, and historiography has faithfully reproduced it here, often with the gloss that the episode *was* a gesture and no more.

The detailed record nuances the picture. In Lacore's case, as we have seen, Blum knew that slotting her into the team at the Health Ministry under Sellier would effectively be giving her more of a public relations role than a decision-making one. As he guessed from her oratory at Socialist party congresses, she would best be employed making affecting public speeches, where she indeed proved effective and popular. Her policy function within the Health Ministry was to follow rather than to lead.

The same was probably even more true of Joliot-Curie. That she was an ornament to the government can hardly be denied. With her husband Frédéric, she had won the Nobel prize for chemistry in 1935, and was a heroine of French science. One of the youngest ministers, mother of two young children, she was much photographed at first. As a politician, however, she made only the most ephemeral of appearances. She worked at her post for scientific research during June and July 1936, but her immediate superior, the Education Minister Jean Zay, wrote of her that 'she seemed ill at ease in ministerial offices. She was literally languishing. Only her laboratory really attracted her. And she was in a hurry to return there. In official meetings, over administrative files, one sensed she was not really there, she had no taste for it' (Zay 1987: 229–30). When her husband left the Sorbonne for a chair at the Collège de France in August, she wrote to Blum offering her resignation, in order to take up Frédéric's post so that their joint scientific work could continue. Her resignation was held over at government request until late September, but she had effectively worked in the ministry for only two months. Her appointment had brought the government a burst of welcome publicity, and although her resignation was noted by contemporaries, it was overshadowed by other events. Most historians do not mention it, tacitly assuming that she served for the length of the government, so the 'ornamental' effect has proved powerful enough in her case to obscure the reality.[9]

The third woman, Cécile Brunschvicg, raises a rather different point: that of the problem of authority. She too could admittedly be seen as playing a part in the public relations side of the appointments. But unlike the other two, she was well used to public life at a number of levels. As a sixty-year-old committeewoman, a veteran suffrage campaigner and a long-standing member of the Radical party (which she had joined in the vain hope of converting it to women's suffrage), she was neither reluctant to serve nor inclined to leave all decisions to her senior minister – also Jean Zay, who was only half her age. Her approach to the job was to try hard *not* to be an ornament. All the traces left by her on the record show evidence of personal investment and initiative. To a journalist in November 1936, she said: 'There is so much to do that I have given myself two or three essential tasks. When I have successfully completed them, I shall attack other problems.'[10] Her brief was welfare within the the Education Ministry, and a general overseeing of women's rights. Her achievements were of a piecemeal kind, and hardly dramatic, but not entirely negligible either. It must, however, have been from her that the hints came, later picked up by the feminist journal *Minerva*, of difficulty in grappling with the machinery of government: 'We know what hostility our women ministers met, not from their ministerial colleagues, who were sympathetic and charming, they tell us, but from certain heads of large administrative sections.'[11] By taking a pragmatic approach, Brunschvicg revealed where the greatest problems lay: an ornamental woman might be accepted, one who wanted to give orders within a ministry met more opposition.

The problem of authority was inevitable and built into the episode. Without any apprenticeship in government, pitched into an environment which could not be assumed to be friendly, women were at an even greater loss than their male colleagues of the Popular Front cabinet. Some of the men in Blum's cabinet had little or no ministerial experience, and one or two were very young – but they did benefit from the support system offered by familiarity with parliamentary and administrative affairs, acquired in a conventional career. Brunschvicg once remarked that she dared not speak in the debate on married women's civil capacity, 'in front of all those lawyers'. Both Lacore and Brunschvicg recruited close women friends or colleagues, some of them legally qualified, to their private offices: in Brunschvicg's case her own daughter, in Lacore's case the formidable Alice Jouenne. This was one means of defending themselves.[12]

A third point about these posts is the question of women's suffrage. Although Blum was not personally opposed to women's right to vote, he knew that many of his fellow-socialists, not to mention the Radical party, were firmly against it. He had no intention of throwing government weight behind a suffrage bill in the first session. At the time, and later, the women ministers were criticized for not doing more to promote women's rights: some thought they should have made entry to government conditional on Blum's promise to bring in a government suffrage bill. Since the Popular Front received favourable publicity from their appointments, this is a fair point, but it was unlikely that at least two of the three would have considered it. Both Joliot-Curie and Lacore were on record as expressing the standard left-wing reservations about women's votes – that at this dangerous time in French history they might vote the 'wrong way'.[13] As for Brunschvicg, her case is trickier. She had written only in May 1936:

> Of course we would like to see a woman minister, but what we want most of all from the new government is a bill on political equality for women such as the Socialist party has called for at every conference. What disappointments we have had to put up with in our struggle, after promises and commitments from politicians![14]

She had, however, stood down, at Daladier's request, from her presidency of the UFSF while she was a minister, and although not entirely silent on the issue, as is sometimes suggested, she does not seem to have been an active campaigner for the cause while in government. Ever a pragmatist, Brunschvicg assumed that argument by demonstration would gradually convince politicians of women's competence

161

and good sense. Writing two years later, she felt able to say, rather complacently, that she saw the experiment as a 'happy precedent for the future'.[15]

Was she right? Léon Blum seemed to think so when, in May 1937, he made a speech celebrating women and hoping that his initiative would lead to greater things: 'By taking two women into the government, the Socialist party has virtually made the equality of the sexes a reality.[!] But the paradox whereby women can be ministers without being *députés* cannot and will not last' (quoted in Bard 1995: 680). On the positive side, the women ministers did shatter some taboos. The favourable, indeed warm reaction of the press and public opinion to their appointment, and the courtesy shown by most parliamentarians to them, indicates that some symbolic barriers were crumbling. Brunschvicg claimed that her postbag was full of appreciative letters, many from women who were being drawn to take an interest in politics at last. Three surviving women activists of the period, when interviewed recently, agreed that they had all felt the incident had 'done something' for women's rights (Adler 1993: 120–1).

On the negative side, the appointments were completely exceptional. The fact that few voices were raised about the non-reappointment of the women ministers in 1937 shows that no immediate precedent had been set. The feminist charge, that both this and the co-opting of councillors was a display of tokenism, is hard to argue with. Whether co-opted to a ministry or a town council, 'token' women would have found themselves in a very awkward position. Subordinate to men, with little freedom of manoeuvre, and no independent power base or resources, they were assigned to policy areas men were unlikely to covet, since they carried little prestige and no career promise – areas corresponding to the supposedly 'natural' concerns of women. Owing their appointment to patronage left them vulnerable to short-term change: when their patrons lost office, they went too. In short they had responsibility without power.

In terms of the argument of this chapter, however, the negative aspects of the co-option model, while they should not be glossed over, do not seriously damage the notion of the permeability of the political arena. Co-opted, patronized, stereo-typed, marginalized or cold-shouldered though they may have been, and little though the episode did in the short term for the cause of suffrage, the few women parachuted into office were setting precedents, puncturing the all-male line-up of political personnel. The innovation met surprisingly little protest or hostility from the political class, the press and public opinion. Women 'councillors' gave their views on local welfare measures, women ministers signed decrees published in the *Journal Officiel*, received all the formal marks of respect accorded ministers, chaired committee meetings of politicians and public servants, and so on.[16] Responsibility without power maybe, but even minimum responsibility for political decision-making had previously been denied to women. To see their role as 'merely symbolic' is both to miss the potential for destabilizing the *symbolic order* that they embodied, and to overlook their experimental position as forerunners of later generations of women nominees, who have also had to learn to handle authority within the *pays légal*.

POLITICAL ACTORS II: POWER WITHOUT RESPONSIBILITY?

The starting point for our second category, the informal exercise of power, could be seen as the other side of the same coin. Often noted by historians, mentioned in memoirs, strongly disliked by feminists and indeed everyone else, political 'Egerias' were women who had power without responsibility. All politicians' families and intimate friends, of both sexes, no doubt exert more influence over public figures than we can ever know. Men can exercise informal power over their colleagues too; but particularly sinister connotations are attached to the women behind famous men. One British observer rather exaggeratedly described late Third Republic France as 'strikingly similar to the Bourbon era in this respect' (Spears 1954: 90 ff.). He was thinking of the marquise de Crussol and the comtesse de Portes, respectively the 'Egerias' of Édouard Daladier and Paul Reynaud, the last two Prime Ministers of the Third Republic. There is no shortage of comment on these two women, who came to symbolize the phenomenon of the power behind the despatch box during the last years of the regime.

Edouard Daladier was a widower with two young sons by the early 1930s and did not remarry until after 1945. He became a visitor to the 'salon' of Mme de Crussol, 'la marquise rouge' as the right-wing press had dubbed her. Born Marie-Louise Béziers in 1906, heiress to a Breton canning business, she had married the marquis de Crussol, of the Uzès family, but her passion was republican politics. During the 1920s, she was part of the 'Geneva set' of whom more later, and an active member of the UFSF. In the early 1930s, 'courteous, friendly and attentive, she held one of those salons that no longer exist, where parliamentarians of every party rubbed shoulders with diplomats, civil servants, intellectuals and socialites.' The polarized politics of the Popular Front made such eclecticism difficult or impossible to maintain, but it was during the late 1930s that she is supposed to have exerted the greatest influence over Daladier. Daladier's biographer found little serious evidence of her political role, but concedes that 'her influence was possibly not as negligible as it appears at first sight' (Réau 1993: 289). The most damaging allegation was that, during the phoney war, her feud with Hélène de Portes, whom she had known since girlhood, led to dangerous disagreements between Daladier and Reynaud.[17]

Hélène de Portes, born Hélène Rebuffel in 1902, daughter of a *polytechnicien*, had married count Henri de Portes, but the much older maverick conservative politician, Paul Reynaud, whom she met in the late 1920s, became her grand passion. It is essentially in the critical years 1938–40 that she is supposed to have been most influential. Reynaud's circle, which met around dinner-tables presided over by his companion, was originally united by its opposition to German expansion and to Nazism, and its wish for greater rapprochement with Britain to oppose the dictators. But it became divided during 1939, and Hélène de Portes was assumed to be closest to those who favoured a degree of appeasement. The most virulent accusations against her relate to the dramatic period of Reynaud's

163

premiership, from March to June 1940, when she was thought to have had a hand in key appointments and dismissals. At the height of the débâcle, in June, she strongly favoured an armistice, which was not Reynaud's own choice. Her dramatic death, in a car accident in which Reynaud was injured, on 28 June, just after the armistice, caused maximum distress and embarrassment for the ex-premier, and helped contribute to a black legend.[18]

Both these women, despite eye-witness testimony to their shrewdness and political nous, and notwithstanding their political differences, are credited with having had a nefarious influence on government politics. Parallels with previous eras, references to the Bourbons and to salons, seem to locate them in a timeless zone peopled by the mistresses of kings. Mme de Portes was described as 'la Dubarry 40' (Guichard 1991: 186). But despite these tempting references to times past, it makes more sense to see them in terms of a structural imbalance which can be historicized. Women living in close proximity to powerful men have no doubt often been tempted, if they had any ambition or political interest, to intervene privately. Between the wars, however, a particular kind of frustration can be seen at work in many of the French women whose names are known to us through their political activity. The perpetual discussions of women's enfranchisement (see Chapter 9) created the illusion that it was just around the corner, yet it was perpetually postponed. 'Egeria' roles were one response to this irritating situation. Even well-connected feminists were not above exerting unofficial pressure through their 'society' positions. Cécile Brunschvicg, married to the philosophy professor Léon Brunschvicg, was hostess to Parisian academic society, and at the same time hoped to influence the Radical party from within on the 'woman question'. Her fellow-radical, Suzanne (Crémieux) Schreiber is an even clearer example of a woman to whom politics mattered much, and who trod the line between being a 'femme politique' and a 'femme du monde' or an 'Egérie', operating in both formal and informal modes.

Suzanne Schreiber has been better treated by posterity than other Egerias, in the sense that available memories of her are positive, though her name has all but vanished from the mainstream record. Yet this was a woman who 'lived intensely through each ministerial crisis, those exciting moments when she made and unmade ministerial appointments, having this prefect allocated to that private office, diverting this councillor somewhere else, hiring one and firing another' (Guichard 1991: 164). Family links helped. Born in 1895, the daughter of a republican senator, she had married her *filleul de guerre*, Robert Schreiber, founder of the financial paper *Les Echos*. During the 1920s she was a *femme du monde* of a new type, dividing her time between the Radical party, her philanthropic work and her feminist activities in the UFSF. Within the Radical party, paradoxical as it might seem, given the opposition of the radicals to women's suffrage, a small number of well-connected women became quite prominent at this time: Cécile Brunschvicg, but also Suzanne Grinberg, Marcelle Kraemer-Bach, Eliane Brault. But 'the most successful career' was Suzanne Schreiber's: elected to the party's governing body in 1925, she was one of its vice-presidents by 1929. Specializing in child welfare, she was not so much stereotyping herself as choosing an area where she would have no male competition. But official politics combined with salon politics: the grand dinners in her apartment in the avenue Montaigne were legendary, and her personal knowledge of the Radical party was encyclopedic. Mediating between factions, she was consulted during every cabinet reshuffle or new government, since the radicals were crucial to almost every coalition. Alas, the *éminence grise* was better at cabinet-making than at finding herself a job: she might seem an obvious choice for a portfolio when Blum appointed women ministers but, for whatever reason, she did not get Daladier's nomination. After 1945, Suzanne Crémieux, as she was now known, became a senator, remaining faithful to the Radical party until her death in 1976, and achieving the official recognition lacking during her youth. Her example shows the thin dividing line between regular party politics and that unofficial world of power and influence behind the scenes, where *éminences grises* of both sexes played roles unsuspected by the public.[19]

Journalism too is on the borderline between official and unofficial politics. Mention should be made here of a group of 'exceptional' women, whose role can readily be historicized: women journalists, a newish phenomenon in the 1920s and 1930s. They were not entirely unknown before and during the Great War. But the spread of wide circulation newspapers after the war, combined with greater numbers of educated women prepared to seek a living, made it a more possible career after 1918. The newspaper world was of course overwhelmingly male. Not many women would have felt at home in the smoky newpaper offices of the *IIe arrondissement*. Significantly, the few women who became really famous were columnists or foreign correspondents, operating as freelances, rather than working their way up through the ranks of hacks. Geneviève Tabouis (1892–1985) was one of the few.[20] By any standards, she exerted influence on public opinion both inside and outside France: she had the ear of her country's politicians, and was read by an interested and loyal public. As foreign correspondent for the Paris liberal daily *L'Oeuvre*, she became one of their best-known columnists in the 1930s. Her articles urging resistance to Hitler were translated in the British press and she describes in her memoirs arriving in London by train to see a billboard claiming in large letters 'Madame Tabouis says no!' Well connected, since she was a niece of Jules Cambon, she benefited from a good start, but owed her career (which came after marriage and children) largely to her unusual determination. She built up an extraordinary network of sources of information, some of them in inner councils at Berlin. She famously irritated Hitler for knowing what he would do next and, perhaps inevitably, she was nicknamed Cassandra, thus according her some kind of magic status, as a sybil or a clairvoyant, names rarely applied to a man. But she was not a unique figure: during the Third Republic, but particularly between the wars, several serious women journalists of comparable fame were active: Séverine, Andrée Viollis, Louise Weiss.[21]

The last of these combined several of the characteristics under discussion. Had she been born twenty or even ten years later, Louise Weiss (1893–1983) might have found herself in parliament after 1945. She came from a 'dynasty' of public servants, but the family was not enthusiastic about her own career. After a good education, in France and abroad, she passed the *agrégation* on the eve of the First World War, then volunteered for hospital work during the war. In 1918, she co-founded a weekly paper, *Europe Nouvelle*, and was its director until 1934. Devoted to the cause of international understanding, the journal was closely identified with the views of Aristide Briand. Weiss was a woman of action: on her own initiative, she arranged for the evacuation of over a hundred French governesses from Russia after the revolution in 1921, and in 1938 she was instrumental in finding refuge for the Jewish passengers of the steamer *Saint-Louis*, who were in danger of becoming stateless. But she was also prepared to play the society hostess. Her slightly Bohemian 'salon' in the 1920s was a centre of Briandist and League of Nations politicking. During the 1930s, despairing of the cause of European peace, she flung herself into a high-profile campaign for women's suffrage, founding a group called Femme Nouvelle and attracting much media attention. During the Second World War, she edited a clandestine newspaper, and thereafter devoted herself to a prolific writing career. After an unsuccessful campaign to become the first woman member of the French Academy in 1974, she was elected to the European Parliament on a Gaullist ticket in 1979, becoming the 'doyenne' of the assembly, achieving just before she died the official political role that had eluded her all her life.[22]

Louise Weiss may not seem in retrospect the most likeable of people, but her case is full of interest. Her frank, lively and far from objective memoirs are sharply critical of others, more rarely critical of herself. Some historians have drawn on them for evidence about women's attitudes, others have registered their distrust of her reporting and their distaste for her self-aggrandizing style. But politics is not about being nice – let alone reliable. Weiss's interest for us is that she provides an excellent illustration of someone at the interface between official and unofficial politics, a frequent place to find women during this period as perhaps in no other age. Whether campaigning for official recognition or using influence when she could not achieve her ends otherwise, she was a thoroughly political animal. In retrospect, she strikes one as a woman who was, in Simone de Beauvoir's famous expression, 'flouée', cheated of the life she might have led. Intelligent, well educated and with a talent for lobbying, well connected nationally and internationally, she contemplated with some exasperation the male politicians, with whom she shared certain qualities and not a few foibles. As a representative of a transitional generation – women who were highly educated, had learnt independence during the First World War, earned their living in the inter-war years, knew the ropes of public life but never had a chance to hold official posts – she encapsulates some of the qualities and the pent-up energy that helped to puncture, if not to penetrate, the closed world of male politics.

The contrasting models of co-option and influence illustrate the separation of the reality of power from the appearance. Women's political aspirations might be directed, with their own consent, into special areas where they were visible, like the three ministers, but lacked real power. Or else they might be forced underground into the murky world of influence, where their power might be surprisingly real but unacknowledged, if not frankly deplored. It would be foolish to claim that the examples quoted above add up to a major incursion by women into the male world of politics. But they are the tip of an iceberg: the army of wives of men in every political party, for example, were in close proximity to the official structures of the republic. There is enough evidence to show that automatic exclusion from the sites of power no longer worked. It was being nibbled away, increasingly, through the 1920s and 1930s. Sometimes the infiltration was officially sanctioned and provided with the trappings of office; sometimes it took the time-honoured forms of pillow-talk or salon-holding; what is different here is that a generation of women with cause to feel particularly impatient, cheated of the rights they fully expected, might combine both approaches, without necessarily antagonizing the men in power. Public life was made of porous material: it could be infiltrated by outsiders, so long as they kept to certain channels.

THE POLITICS OF ASSOCIATION: PARTIES AND CAMPAIGNS

So far our examples have come from the inner circle of politics – local or national office, proximity to ministers and parliamentarians. If the notion of political personnel is extended to cover membership of groups with broadly 'political' objectives, we could be talking about a very large number of people, many of whom might not think of themselves as 'politically active'. France is conventionally regarded as a country with a high number of associations and rather low membership, even for high-profile bodies like political parties and trade unions. But even a roll-call confined to the chief office-holders and most energetic activists of the groups operating during this period would list thousands of people, mostly concentrated in Paris and the big cities. Political parties, which had come into serious existence by the beginning of the twentieth century, are only part of the picture. The inter-war period saw unparalleled expansion of the number of associations, in particular of those run by or with women.[23] Some were born at particular times during the inter-war years in response to international events: anti-fascist associations, or groups taking sides during the Spanish Civil War. Others were active or developed throughout the whole period: the major and minor political parties, the peace movement in all its forms, groups concerned with civil or civic rights, such as the Ligue des Droits de l'Homme (founded during the Dreyfus affair), associations for the defence of interests of immigrant workers, women's suffrage movements. How far were these minor political waterways infiltrated by women?

With the partial exception of the Radical party – which actually forbade women to be members until 1924 – mainstream political parties were not officially single sex. But their membership was overwhelmingly male. It is true that women had always been able to join and attend meetings of the various socialist parties before 1905 and this continued within the unified SFIO after that date. The Communist party, created when the socialists split at Tours in 1920, proceeded likewise. But all

167

parties, even revolutionary ones, were increasingly drawn into electoral politics, all-male by definition, and in that context saw little urgent need to recruit or even address women.

Comparatively little work has so far been done on parties of the right (cf. McMillan 1988: 355). The authors of a catalogue of women's associations between the wars found little material on political parties in general, and almost nothing on those of the right (cf. Blum *et al.* 1984: 621–7). When one recalls that it was an article of faith for many left-wing politicians in France that women would give their votes to right-wing parties, this might seem surprising. At all events, the evidence is scant. In 1935, however, possibly because of the threat from the Popular Front, two women's sections were created by parties of the moderate right. The Section Féminine of the Fédération Républicaine de France, mixed despite its name, was presided over by the women's suffrage campaigner Louis Marin. Claiming branches in fifty *départements* by 1937, its stated aims were 'to bring together Christian women desiring to serve their country by collaborating with men in the public domain as they do at home . . . and to prepare them to vote for unalterable principles'. Its bulletin, *Le Devoir des femmes*, lasted until 1940. The right-centre parliamentary group known as the Alliance démocratique set up a women's association in 1935, Femme Française, on the initiative of P. E. Flandin. There seems to have been some overlap between both these party affiliates and members of two right-wing suffragist groups, the Fédération Nationale des Femmes (FNF) and the much larger Union Nationale pour le Vote des Femmes (UNVF). Mme Lescouvé appears both as president of the FNF and as co-president of the women's section of Louis Marin's party, while Paul Smith suggests that the FNF was virtually absorbed by Femme Française.[24]

No doubt the anticipation of women's voting rights had something to do with these initiatives. If they remain rather under-researched, so *a fortiori* do the extreme right-wing leagues from the point of view of gender. Some of them openly favoured women's suffrage, making opportunistic if not necessarily well-founded assumptions about its impact. Individual members of both the UNVF and FNF were said to be close to Pierre Taittinger's Jeunesses Patriotes. The Croix de feu opened its ranks to the sons and daughters of the war veterans who were its original constituency. The leagues did have women members, massively outnumbered by men however. What was more, the whole symbolic apparatus of most leagues was masculine and paramilitary, in itself something presumably alien to women's experience. To find a clear example of a political association of the right which women joined in any numbers, one has to look outside both leagues and parties to an autonomous phenomenon, and an all-women one: the largest women's association in France, neither a party, nor officially attached to one: the Ligue Patriotique des Françaises (LPF).[25]

Its origins within nationalist opinion went back to the Dreyfus affair and its aftermath. The Ligue was founded in 1902 by Catholic women of the right. While claiming to be apolitical in nature, the LPF was quite close to Jacques Piou's Catholic party, Action Libérale Populaire, up to 1914, energetically helping in election campaigns and combating the anticlerical left. Its membership became extraordinarily large by French standards, reaching 585,000 by the outbreak of the First World War, and 1.5 million by 1932. According to one of its historians, 'rechristianization was [its] fundamental raison d'être', both before and after the war, and much of its commitment was to Catholic social action, including charitable works and morality campaigns. Its pre-war leaders had rejected any hint of feminism, refusing to be grouped with the Catholic women's suffrage movement. But its stand on this matter seems to have been influenced by Papal policy: once Benedict XV had indicated tolerance of women's suffrage in 1919, the LPF campaigned publicly for the vote. As in so many cases where activity by or on behalf of women is combined with a socially conservative outlook, the label 'feminist' is disputed. Anne-Marie Sohn, along with other French feminist historians, is unwilling to apply it to a movement so committed to women's traditional role, whereas James McMillan, who argues that the LPF enjoyed autonomy from the hierarchy, has suggested that by throwing its powerful weight on the side of suffrage, it 'ultimately served to provide a route to feminist consciousness' (McMillan 1988: 362).

If rather than measure feminist consciousness we are seeking to identify the extent to which associations including women intervened on the political stage, the Ligue looks a promising case – although far less appears to be known about its activities in the post-1918 period than in its early years, reflecting the drying up of police reports about it in the 1920s. Was its membership, as one report of a 400-strong meeting in 1927 suggests, 'mainly confined to old ladies' (and does that make it politically insignificant)? At its congress, held in April the same year, one of its speakers, Mlle Bavelier, nevertheless set out what one could read as a blueprint for political action, stopping short of casting the vote:

> She first insisted on the important role that woman has always played in the life of a country, on the greater role she will play once she has been invited to vote, and on the need to prepare her for the new duties which will be hers. Then she explained the opportunities the Ligue offered for training through its civic delegates and civic commissions, more of which should be created throughout the country. She also pointed out the opportunities Ligue members had for action, whether working within municipalities, or organizing campaigns on themes likely to modify the mentality of voters, using the press, posters and pamphlets.

This is taking part in politics to be sure, but along the lines encouraged by Pius XI himself.[26]

It seems likely that membership of the Ligue overlapped with a whole range of Catholic conservative associations, aligned against the republican left. In this respect, it was an active part of the right-wing political universe, having some impact on public opinion, and without any exact equivalent on the left.[27]

If right-wing politics offered a twofold model based on the somewhat phantom women's section, alongside an autonomous but incalculable feminine league, the model detectable on the left is rather different. The radical party was in the odd position of having several well-known feminists prominent on its own governing body, while remaining opposed to women's suffrage. Before 1924, the party constitution simply excluded women. Until then, a convenient channel of communication for women in sympathy with the politics of radicalism was the Ligue des Droits de l'Homme.[28] Its leaders, committed republicans and former Dreyfusards, were mostly sympathetic to women's suffrage; some of them were married to prominent feminists; and women's rights were regularly discussed at its meetings. It was under the aegis of the LDH that the broad-based feminist association, the Conseil National des Femmes Françaises (CNFF) tabled two resolutions at the Radical party congress of 1924, calling for admission of women to the party and for women's suffrage. The second was duly rejected, the first, more surprisingly, accepted. The radicals thus embarked on a model not unlike that of parties further to the left: a sympathetic welcome for 'trusted' women, that had nothing to do with suffrage for all. By 1925, ten women found themselves on the executive committee. Ironically, as we have seen, it was quite easy for women, if they were well connected, to make a career within the party, using the mechanism of 'vice-presidencies' and committees. No fewer than thirty-seven women served on the executive over the next twelve years. As Serge Berstein has pointed out, their prominence was not reflected in grass-roots membership: of 6,984 conference delegates over the same period, only fifty-three were women. Many of the 'stars', such as Suzanne Schreiber and Cécile Brunschvicg, were urged to specialize in social affairs, not exactly a priority for radicals. And the 'entrism' explicitly favoured by these feminists, in an effort to change the party from within, remained unsuccessful. Both Herriot and Daladier sat on the fence over the suffrage question. Brunschvicg's faith that example would win her colleagues over seemed to other feminists like a triumph of hope over experience.

The question presented itself very differently to women in the Socialist party, though the result was much the same in the end. For the majority of women socialists, feminism – for which read 'bourgeois feminism' – was the enemy. The SFIO offers a clear example of the famous *rendezvous manqué*, the failure of feminism and socialism to meet in this period. In the SFIO, while anticlericalism was powerful in shaping the party's views, the class struggle was also specifically made a priority by the women's group within the party in the early period, the Groupe des Femmes Socialistes (GDFS). In a pamphlet called *Socialisme et féminisme* written in 1914, its author 'Suzon' (now known to be Suzanne Lacore) stated her firm faith that women's emancipation would come about only as a result of the proletarian revolution, and described dissident feminists as 'Valkyries and viragos'. During the inter-war period, nothing like as many women joined the Socialist party as one might have expected, while those who controlled the women's section resolutely opposed any form of 'gender identity politics'.[29]

The Socialist party cannot fairly be described as misogynist, but neither did it encourage women and numbers were very small. In 1933, when the women's section was reorganized into the Comité National des Femmes Socialistes

(CNDFS), they numbered 2,995 (2.17 per cent of the total); a year later it had risen a little to 3,376, or 2.57 per cent. Party numbers rose generally during the enthusiasm for the Popular Front, but men remained 97 per cent of the membership. Patricia Hilden, in her study of working-class women and socialist (mostly Guesdist) politics in northern France before 1914, argues that 'it is not sufficient to adduce women's low membership figures in socialist parties or unions as conclusive evidence for the argument that working women were apolitical', and her remarks may apply to the later period too (Hilden 1986: 277). As we saw earlier, strikes during the 1930s mobilized women who never show up in the statistics for union membership. Charles Sowerwine's broad study of women in the Socialist party, which concentrates on the period to 1914 but includes some pages on the inter-war period, stresses the absence of autonomous women's groups, and lays particular responsibility for the stagnation of the socialist women's section on its leading spirit for many years, Louise Saumoneau, whose hard core of supporters 'all shared identical views on the danger of feminism and the need to maintain the GDFS as a socialist group, however small, rather than risk the danger of penetration by feminists' (Sowerwine 1983: 167). Members were obliged to join a (male-dominated) party section before joining the GDFS, a rule that was maintained, thanks to Lacore and others, after 1933. Sowerwine comments that 'to come to a male section, to find oneself the only woman in a smoke-filled room where the main topic of discussion was electoral politics from which one was barred . . . was an heroic undertaking for a woman in the Third Republic' (ibid.: 189). At the same time, the Socialist party had its share of strong-minded women. Again, it is important not to confuse women's political activism with feminism. The two might be kept in separate compartments of the mind. Germaine Picard-Moch, Alice Jouenne, Suzanne Buisson and others all played important roles in Socialist party politics; Louise Saumoneau herself was a formidable character. But their policy of integration within the party benefited only an inner core of women activists, while preventing any serious appeal to the mass of potential women members outside. The socialist women ended up rather like the radical women, as an old guard, on cosy terms with the party leadership, but to some extent just as isolated from most working-class women as the 'bourgeois feminists' they despised.

Were matters any different in the Communist party? The same distrust of 'bourgeois feminism' might be assumed to affect it, but in spades: 'the women of the PCF had little time for feminism' (Smith 1991: 114). Not that there were many women in the party during its early tumultuous years after 1920. Only twelve sat on the central committee between 1920 and 1936, and only two on the smaller *bureau politique*. The party's early membership of 100,000 melted away as it moved into its 'Bolshevization' period, and by 1929 there were no more than 35,000 members, falling to a low of 32,000 by 1932. The percentage of women members was always tiny: the 1929 congress was informed that while there were 3.5 million wage-earning women in France, 2 million of them in industry, only 40,000 were in the CGTU and a mere 200 in the party.[30]

The PCF, male dominated though it undoubtedly was, took a different line from the socialists and radicals. During the 1920s, paradoxically, its policies came close to those of the bourgeois feminists, at least on paper. In the Chamber of Deputies, it regularly supported women's suffrage bills, several proposals being sponsored by the group leader, Marcel Cachin. Several reasons were possible. Most obviously, for the PCF, revolution and class struggle were the way forward, so the working class of both sexes was its target. (Its radical opponents accused it of being cynically prepared to see the bourgeois republic collapse through the feared increase of pro-clerical votes.) But to see the party as having a principled belief in equality of the sexes is not entirely far-fetched. Of all the parties until about 1934, and in some ways even after that, the PCF was least sexist in its discourse, while still distancing itself from the political feminism it regarded as bourgeois. Much influenced by the Soviet critique of the family during the 1920s, the party regularly campaigned for collective solutions to women's domestic role: collective laundry, childcare and canteens. The weekly paper it published aimed at women workers, *L'Ouvrière*, encouraged the idea that all women should take part in production. It defended Henriette Alquier when she was prosecuted for advocating contraception, and was in favour of medicalized abortion, although even at this stage it did not make contraception a priority.[31]

After the 'turning-point' of 1934, however, and the attempt to woo outsiders during the Popular Front, the Communist party did something of an about-turn on the family. Paul Vaillant-Couturier's articles in *Humanité* praising family values were a sign of the times.[32] *L'Ouvrière* ceased to appear, its place taken by a women's page in *Humanité* dominated by recipes and other homely items. Cécile Vassart in an article in *Cahiers bolchéviques* entitled 'Il nous faut gagner les femmes', urged communists to

> make the party hospitable to women; don't forget that [our woman comrade] has family duties, don't let's ask too much of her, or overwork her, for if our male comrades find their soup ready when they get home, their wives have to prepare it, and we must always bear this double shift by women workers in mind.

(quoted in Dab 1980: 75)

Sandra Dab comments sarcastically that this was the extent of the work required of a 'Stalinist woman party militant during the Popular Front according to the party leadership'. Other commentators have argued that women were perceived by the party leaders at this time as a *masse de manoeuvre*, a group in society to be recruited and exploited, like young people or national servicemen. As noted in an earlier chapter, the Union des Jeunes Filles de France was created at this time, in order to handle the increased recruitment of the Popular Front heyday, without alienating those sectors of French society who preferred a traditional approach to gender.

It cannot be gainsaid that the Communist party itself encouraged a fairly traditional discourse about women in the 1930s. For all that, it seems to me that generalizations in this vein are misplaced and that left-wing politics and women's political activity were not incompatible, although they are sometimes resistant to historical detection. One of the major sources for the political history of the left in this period is the *Dictionnaire Maitron*.[33] Whereas the earlier volumes of this unique biographical database probably do underestimate the number of women activists, the inter-war volumes reflect both improved recording techniques and a rise in left-wing activism after 1936. But even before this, anti-fascist women had been mobilized in the active French section of the Comité Mondial des Femmes contre la Guerre et le Fascisme, resulting from the communist-dominated Amsterdam–Pleyel movement of 1932–4.[34] Renée Rousseau (1983) suggests that this movement has been underestimated as a focus for the energies of many women communist sympathizers, and points out that its programme was not confined to anti-fascism, but contained calls for women's rights. Some of the same women were joined by others on committees of support and aid for Republican Spain. Women in the communist galaxy, not always party members, provided a large reservoir of committed people. When, in 1939, in the wake of the Nazi–Soviet pact and the outbreak of war, the party was outlawed in France, its male militants had to lie low. Rousseau suggests that it was their wives and other women sympathizers who managed to reconnect the networks in clandestinity. One could place this point alongside the work of Dominique Loiseau, who has argued that the wives and companions of left-wing militants (socialist, communist, trade union) played an essential but virtually unsung role in this period.[35] There are signs that the historiography of the left is altering its approach to gender history.[36]

POLITICAL CULTURE: GENDERED MODES OF BEHAVIOUR

The political – or rather the electoral – culture of the Third Republic developed out of nineteenth-century patterns of male sociability. 'In small towns and villages, the *cabaret* [i.e. café, where alcoholic drinks were also sold], the place where people could read the papers, became the centre of political life' (Mayeur 1984: 37). Republicans in particular held their meetings in cafés. Masonic lodges, although demonized by their opponents, covered only a small bourgeois clientele. 'More important were the debating societies, reading or learning groups for the people [*populaire*], places of social intercourse which might be more or less politicized' (ibid.). At the turn of the century, electoral politics was still very much, as Mayeur puts it, 'a matter for men', *une affaire d'hommes*: local notables, mayors and councillors, the local *député* and senator, and their supporters. Women simply had no presence in these milieux, although the families of politicians had more political awareness than other families, as is reflected in political dynasties from which women activists might later emerge. Women from Dreyfusard families – many of them Protestant, Jewish and free-thinking – were often enthusiastic feminists. Police reports of political meetings regularly remark on whether any women were present or not.[37]

After 1919, women were to be found not so much in parties but in mixed associations and running their own groups, in far greater numbers than before the war. It is at this stage that one can really start to speak both about their integration into male political culture, and/or the creation of an alternative culture. The total of national (i.e. Paris-based) organizations, run by women and of a broadly political nature, listed by the most comprehensive catalogue to date, comes to 144. Of these, thirty-three were concerned with the suffrage and related causes and twenty-four with peace; there were groups with religious affiliations; trade union groups; only seven women's sections of political parties were noted, as compared to thirty-four 'miscellaneous' groups. This is almost certainly an underestimate, and the catalogue deliberately excluded groups with philanthropic aims, which would have made the total unmanageable. In addition, many women took part in other mixed groups not listed. The founding dates of a large proportion of the groups shows them to have dated from just before, during or after the First World War (cf. Blum *et al.* 1984: passim and 516).

The topography of women's politics could hardly at this stage be identical with men's.The educational background and social training of men and women had remained very separate. Single-sex schooling, as noted in Chapter 2, kept the sexes apart during their teens. Youth movements, for the inter-war generations, would have done the same. Men would mostly have done their military service, in yet another all-male milieu, before moving into a political world where women had no formal place. Men met each other informally in newspaper offices, on racecourses, at masonic lodges, in cafés, all venues difficult of access, if not actually out of bounds to women in the years after 1919. To give some idea of the cultural segregation that marked the biographies of most male politicians of these years, one need look only at the early years of the three 'leaders' of the Popular Front: Blum, Daladier and Thorez. All three served apprenticeships, professional or political, in ways that would scarcely have been open to women.

Daladier's career is perhaps the most archetypical Third Republic story. Born in 1884 to a modest family – his parents had a baker's shop in Carpentras – he was a scholarship boy. Picked out at primary school by an inspector (as Jaurès and Herriot had been before him), he went to the *lycée* in Lyon where Herriot was his mentor. Having failed the entrance exam to the ENS, he studied history at university, passed the *agrégation* in 1909 and for the next few years taught in a boys' *lycée*. Politically, his apprenticeship was through a youth organization attached to republican and masonic circles, the Fédération des Jeunesses Laiques. His eloquence led to an invitation to stand for the local elections on a Union Républicaine ticket, and he found himself mayor of Carpentras at the age of twenty-seven in 1911. Mobilized in 1914, he was wounded several times and had a good war record, which stood him in good stead when he ran for parliament in 1919. His political career really took off then, as *député* for the Vaucluse. Educationally his cursus had taken him through a series of all-male institutions, and the examinations on which his academic career was based were not yet open to women. His political milieu corresponds almost exactly to Mayeur's description of all-male republican politics in the early years of the century; the patronage of Herriot was beneficial; and his war service (yet another area closed to women) gave him the necessary *gravitas* to hold his own in the *chambre bleu horizon* (i.e. the 'ex-servicemen's parliament', elected in 1919).[38]

Blum's career was less typical, but some of the same characteristics emerge. Born in 1872, the son of a Jewish family from Alsace living in Paris, where his father had a small fabrics business, Blum was also an educational prodigy. The Lycée Charlemagne was followed by a year at the ENS. Here he met his mentor, the librarian Lucien Herr, whose influence was to mark him for life, and who introduced him to Jaurès. Blum's stay at Normale ended abruptly when he failed his exams, but that was no great setback, since he embarked on a dual career combining law and belle-lettriste journalism, writing for the *Revue Blanche* and earning his living comfortably as a member of the *conseil d'Etat*. The Dreyfus affair completed his political apprenticeship and he later followed Jaurès into the reunified Socialist party, the SFIO. During the war, he became *chef de cabinet* to Marcel Sembat, and was elected to the assembly for the first time in 1919, alongside Daladier.[39] This Parisian career was based more on professional capacities and ideological allegiance than Daladier's classic cursus through local politics, but in both cases the early rungs of the ladder would have been hard for a woman to climb. One has only to think of Cécile Brunschvicg, who also came from a prosperous Jewish family, but who had to study in secret because her father disapproved of girls' education.[40] Or of Suzanne Lacore, who despite making her mark in the SFIO, remained a primary schoolteacher in the Dordogne and could not aspire to local political office – the normal way to enter politics in the provinces. Neither could a woman seriously expect to become the protégée of a patron, because of the equivocal situation that would create.

Maurice Thorez's beginnings were different again. No woman could have written the famous opening words of his biography *Fils du peuple* (1937): 'Mineur et fils de mineur', 'a miner and the son of a miner'. This self-description may have been a shade economical with the truth, but his career would still be difficult for a woman to emulate, rooted as it was in the trade union and Communist party culture of the northern mining areas. This was an alternative path to politics, different from that of republican or socialist meritocracy. Succeeding his father-in-law as a party official, Thorez had a chequered time in the 1920s, dodging the police but eventually being groomed for the party leadership by Moscow. Most commentators refer to the powerful influence on him of Jeannette Vermeersch, who eventually became his second wife: a formidable character, but one who could not aspire to party leadership, instead being a sort of communist Egeria.[41]

None of these career paths was really open to women, hence the diversity of background of the few hundred women whose names survive in the inter-war registers of political groups. It is true that (as with Blum and Daladier) they mostly came from the middling ranks of society, and that the 'meritocratic' professions which predisposed to public life – teaching and the law – were well represented. Family links (as in the case of Thorez) could be as important to women as to many men. The wives of men in public life were often members of parties or groups. If they were to play any part in the political world, women were obliged in many respects to imitate men. If they entered political parties or mixed associations, they had to learn the ropes. The apprenticeship they received there was usually their first taste of the conventions of public life, from minute-taking to public speaking. The latter was a particular hurdle, since it represented a break with behaviour expected of women. There are examples dating back to the nineteenth century of forceful women orators, such as Louise Michel; and exceptionally, as in the revolutionary episodes from 1789 to 1871, women's political clubs had been formed. But it is the *routinization* of public speaking for women which marks the inter-war years. Advice and practice, such as aspirant male politicians received, was not available. Unsurprisingly, women lawyers and teachers adapted best to public speaking. To help others, feminists organized 'public speaking courses' (*écoles d'oratrices*).[42]

Although some women might adapt to the dominant (patriarchal?) discourse, imitating men was not necessarily the best policy on a platform, and there are occasional hints that women gained by cultivating their difference. A rare comment on this point, in a pro-League of Nations journal in the early 1920s, is instructive. The writer remarks that he has often seen a platform party composed of several men and one woman. To spare her supposed shyness, the woman is rarely asked to speak first, so a man will open the evening with 'dialectic, erudition , rhetoric' – the male attributes of eloquence. When the woman is invited to speak,

> with her very first words, she has won the audience's sympathy. What she says is simple, unaffected and without coquetry. She allows her common sense to speak and her heart to vibrate and the audience is charmed, surprised and won over. The other male speakers would be well advised to save their breath.[43]

This observation could be read two ways. Couched in admiring terms, it is also a comment on the artlessness, not to say simple-mindedness of women speakers. Given their inexperience, it may well have some truth in it. But some women orators in inter-war France were well versed in the rules of male politics, and might have devised a style contrasting with that of their male colleagues. Contemporary press comments on Suzanne Lacore's speeches as minister in 1936 stress the emotional impact she made as a fragile elderly figure, dressed in black and speaking from the heart. This cast her as a 'simple and natural' orator. But Lacore was a seasoned speaker at Socialist party conferences (Blum had heard her perform 'brilliantly' shortly before he appointed her) and not as naive as people imagined. A 'womanly' presence might be turned to advantage in mixed company.

If, on the other hand, women set up associations of their own, they were unlikely to set out to disrupt the prevailing pattern. Associations under the law of 1901 had to have a constitution and membership rules. Groups created by women modelled themselves on past practice, with their *comité d'honneur* (list of patrons) and their executive committee, president, secretary and treasurer. Minutes were taken and records kept. They hired halls and speakers for meetings, published bulletins if they could afford it, and advertised their actions. All this might seem straightforward enough: the bread and butter of interest group politics. Where women joined mixed groups, their apprenticeship lay in adapting to the rules formulated by men. But all-women organizations were different in their financing and their staffing, in their conventions and practices from the male political world. While many of their members were 'bourgeois' in the sense of being middle class, they did not as a rule have personal incomes sufficient to finance an association that relied on its membership for funds. What they could give was voluntary unpaid time, since paid officials were out of the question. The burden of administration fell on a restricted group of the most committed. The secretary of an association might remain at her post for many years. From the voluminous archives of a Gabrielle Duchêne, one of the most active women in France – or from the equally copious records of the less-known Jeanne Mélin, who ran one small peace group and belonged to many – one can see how much paperwork was left to the 'hon. sec.'. The gargantuan correspondence generated by even a tiny group must have cost a fortune in itself.[44]

The peace group organized from someone's writing-desk was part of an informal culture that spilled over into private life. What would today be called networking went on between different kinds of groups, in Paris and elsewhere. Meetings were held not in committee rooms in the town hall but often in the secretary's front room. The context encouraged dismissive remarks about 'chattering over teacups', an image that sticks like velcro to all-women groups. But reading the correspondence of the secretaries of these associations is a sobering experience. This was truly the politics of commitment, for there was no career to be made, no glittering prizes to be won. By the same token, women's politics were free of any suspicion of corruption such as lingered round the parliamentary politics of the Third Republic. The worst that might be said of them was that some social climbing might go on there. But the demands made on serious activists, whose commitment had to be its own reward, were great: the strains revealed themselves in illness, discontinuity and exasperation.[45]

Exasperation and frustration can be motivating forces, of course. Because they were excluded from the mainstream of political life – electoral meetings, assembly debates – all-women's associations, like other extra-parliamentary movements, sometimes resorted to direct action. The male-dominated paramilitary leagues, which depended for their impact on a masculine identity, used the repertoire of parades, marches, drive-pasts and fly-pasts, drawing on the standard male symbols of warfare and technology. Women's groups drew on a similarly constructed 'women's rhetoric', usually decorous, but sometimes more flamboyant, and often dependent on dress codes and feminine attributes.

Plenty of examples of this alternative politicking can be documented. There is a file of haphazard police reports, consulted by everyone studying the French feminist movement during the inter-war years, which provides plentiful evidence of various actions carried out in Paris by 'feminist' groups, mostly in the late 1920s and early 1930s. The catalogue of events one can extract from it includes *inter alia*: entering the Senate through the public gallery (with inside help, via family networking) and showering the senators with leaflets reading 'To fight alcoholism, women need the vote'; hiring buses, covering them with banners and driving round Paris (street demonstrations were banned at the time, a point sometimes overlooked by

177

historians who have remarked on the absence of mass action); silent demonstrations by teams of women relaying one another outside the Senate at the opening session; war widows hiring taxis and hoisting banners protesting at the tax law; campaigners wearing green suffrage ribbons and badges on their hats; talking energetically to the policemen who tried to move on silent demonstrators (the report notes that young working-class policemen were rather intimidated by the formidable, middle-aged, articulate bourgeoises they confronted); flyposting all over Paris maps showing countries where women did or did not vote, depicting France as hopelessly backward. And so on.[46]

Much of this activity deliberately stressed sex difference. Similarly, women's peace movements of the 1920s and early 1930s devised symbolic actions designed to attract press attention. In the late 1920s, several peace groups organized an anti-war toys campaign, with women posted outside toy stores, especially at Christmas, to dissuade parents from buying toy weapons for their children. It received regular publicity, though history does not record how effective it was. Demonstrators handed out tracts and particularly postcards – a favourite form of propaganda at the time. One group organized a Saint Nicolas day demonstration, in which a child symbolically broke a gun barrel. On armistice day 1931, the same group organized a peace ceremony on the Champ de Mars at which an 'alternative', non-martial Marseillaise was sung.[47]

From time to time individual women campaigners with a keen sense of publicity emerged. Marthe Bray toured the provinces with a cine-projector, showing humorous pro-suffrage films, rather a novelty in villages and small towns. She also ran a stand at the annual Paris fair, and in 1930, with the permission of the Health Ministry, ran an anti-syphilis day. Her helpers, wearing suffrage badges, handed out tracts warning of the danger of syphilis. This might seem to fulfil a stereotypical role, both caring and moralizing, but the campaigners had to be embarrassment-proof and keep their nerve.[48] Even more spectacular and even more 'feminine' were the tactics of Louise Weiss, whose Femme Nouvelle suffrage campaign in 1934–6 left few stunts untried. Her initiatives included having famous women (such as aviatrixes) head parades; demonstrations by society women on the racecourse at Chantilly; releasing balloons; presenting senators with socks (to show that 'women would still darn their socks when they had the vote'); a banquet for wealthy women taxpayers, a sort of latter-day Boston tea party; alternative women's ballots at election. Her gimmicks were not only feminine but resolutely upper class – holding champagne parties, wearing a Molyneux gown to be arrested in, using hat-boxes for ballot boxes.[49]

None of these tactics, even the last mentioned, were in the end particularly outrageous or extreme – there were no hunger strikes, no incendiary devices, no deaths on the racecourse. But these small acts of rebellion, regular and frequent, were carried out against a steady background of well-behaved lectures, meetings and handing out of tracts, mostly centred on Paris, but taking place in provincial towns as well. Numbers were never large, but their cumulative force is considerable. The inter-war generation of women contained hundreds – at times thousands – of committed individuals, prepared to engage in political action, conventional and unconventional, in the interests of conviction politics, usually the suffrage or the peace movement, but covering other causes as well. Their actions often have something rather amateurish about them – the mark of zeal. Louise Weiss advised her demonstrators to turn up looking elegant, then to pull out banners (or chains, or leaflets) from under their coats to surprise passers-by. These were the weapons of people with more imagination than resources (no party headquarters to provide posters and banners) and were often the brainchild of a single individual. Alongside the loud masculine paraphernalia of the leagues, much recorded for posterity, they might seem insignificant, yet they mobilized just as many people. Nor were they undertaken routinely or half-heartedly: it was a repertoire of political action carried out with conviction – not to say desperation.

This is perhaps the place to say a few words about the political presence of 'feminism' (cf. Chapter 10). Many of the women active in various interest groups could be describable as feminist, in the sense that women's rights were something they valued, even if they might not use the word of themselves – and even if historians are sometimes reluctant to use it of them. Christine Bard is surely right to point out that 'feminism cannot be reduced to suffragism or to its battles, won or lost'. Women, not all nominally feminist, who campaigned against social problems like prostitution, syphilis, alcoholism and so on, often did so because they saw women as the front-line victims of such ills. They often found themselves fighting on several fronts at once: such as the schoolteacher Pierrette Rouquet, an official of the Groupes Féministes de l'Enseignement Laïque, who during 1927 found herself co-ordinating both the campaign for Henriette Alquier ('it has taken up my energy for almost a year') and the campaign against the Paul-Boncour law which called for the official mobilizing of both sexes to war work in an emergency, a measure opposed by communists and pacifists.[50] Women teachers like Rouquet and Alquier formed a sort of counter-culture, one of many in inter-war France, which mobilized energies episodically for different political causes, but without the official support systems of large pressure groups or political parties. Both Christine Bard and Paul Smith have argued energetically against the dismissal of feminism at this time as 'weak and anaemic' or 'ridiculous and extravagant but fortunately few in number',[51] as some historians have put it. Nor is the label 'bourgeois' particularly meaningful, since most political activists in these years, unless specifically within the labour movement, came from the middle classes of society. To mobilize large numbers of women for causes like the vote, year after year, was not easy: the correspondence of secretaries of associations is full of complaints at the difficulty of recruiting and maintaining interest. And if measured by the immediate success rate, the record of suffrage agitation in itself is not encouraging.

But such activities have to be located within a polity where many policies, in theory backed by powerful organizations, came to nothing – defence policy to name but one. These were years when bills languished in committee, where the decisions of one government might be reversed by the next, where even the apparently pathbreaking innovations of the Popular Front might run into the sands.

To speak of politics in the last twenty years of the Third Republic is to speak of an arena in which few politicians enjoyed a long run of power, and in which negotiations between competing groups rarely had predictable outcomes. Yesterday's outsiders might be tomorrow's insiders and vice versa. In such a context, the women who tried to obtain the ear of Radical party elites might be closer to power in some respects than the leaders of the CGT, and limited progress might be made on some aspects of social policy by non-elected committees within the Health Ministry. Whether we like the form taken by such politics or not, we are surely neglecting a large area of political life if we fail to notice them. Joan Scott has argued that one way of rewriting history from the perspective of gender is to look at political communication: 'We must find out how people interpreted and used the language of politics, how official pronouncements resonated with various publics, how people articulated their understandings of war and its consequences, how opposition was expressed and silenced' (Scott 1987: 29). This is a daunting agenda, but a start can be made. In this chapter, some attention has been paid to oppositional or alternative politics; the next one looks more closely at a whole culture which overlapped with official policy at times, and at others sharply diverged from it; a culture in which women were openly, visibly and undeniably concerned: the culture of the peace movement(s) between the wars, or to put it another way, 'how people articulated their understandings of war and its consequences'.

8

WAR AND PEACE
Assent and dissent

As a woman, I have no country; as a woman, I want no country. As a woman, my country is the whole world.

(Virginia Woolf 1938: 125)

If we employ only the conventional ungendered compass to chart international relations, we are likely to end up mapping a landscape peopled only by men . . . . We don't need to wait for a 'feminist Henry Kissinger' before we can start articulating a fresh, more realistic approach to international politics. Every time a woman explains how her government is trying to control her fears, her hopes and her labor, such a theory is being made.

(Enloe 1989: 201)

The chancelleries of Europe between the wars might seem unpromising terrain for gender analysis. But to stop short because those who sat round the conference tables at Versailles or staffed France's embassies abroad were almost all men, is to close one's eyes to the possibility that international history, like political history 'has been enacted on a field of gender' (Scott 1988: 49).[1] Examples are easy to find. Nationality, for example, is not gender-free: married women's nationality was long construed as that of their husbands in international law, and in most countries they had no right to separate passports. Or take war and peace: gender is built into the structures of warfare. For much of history, young male troops have been mobilized, leaving behind or defending a civilian population of adult women, with the children and elderly of both sexes. And the figurative use of metaphors of marriage and sexuality (courtship, alliance, divorce) is commonplace in international relations. France is regularly allegorized as a female figure.[2] There is nothing 'natural' or fixed about these examples. Neither nationality laws nor the military draft have resisted change in the twentieth century; even linguistic agendas shift over time. But they are part of the shared culture that has shaped our perceptions of diplomacy and contact between nations: we readily assume them to be 'the product of consensus rather than of conflict' (Scott 1988: 53).

History is not without examples of women taking an active part in relations between countries. But the international history of the twentieth century contains little reference to gender, and it is easy enough to see why. Foreign and defence policy are often studied separately from domestic politics. Diplomats and civil servants in the foreign office usually form a separate corps and, between the wars, both diplomacy and the military were firmly closed to women because of their sex. Whether we write about the Maginot line or the Dawes Plan, whether we study Locarno, Stresa or Munich, that infernal sequence of dates familiar to every student, we are talking about a relatively autonomous elite of male decision-makers (or non-decision makers). That need not reduce the question to one of monopoly and absence. The approach of this chapter takes its cue from Cynthia Enloe: it seeks to uncover the presence of both sexes where only one has until now been visible. Far from operating in a vacuum, the men in suits who looked out gloomily across Swiss or Italian lakes were surrounded by the 'ambiance' of public and political opinion (Milza 1988: 337).[3] From that 'ambiance' no adult was protected. Public opinion is as yet too undocumented a notion, so it is with articulated opinion that we must deal, and in particular with the politics of peace-seeking. As a recent study puts it, the forms of commitment to peace 'may be understood as varied responses to the perceived inadequacy of traditional political leadership'. It is not surprising that on this issue voices were heard from 'alternative' quarters, from 'groups who refused to accept the established structures of the political arena.... These included ex-servicemen, Catholics, women and intellectuals' (*Matériaux* 1993: 53). Renewed interest in formerly underestimated groups may have helped the recent revival of research in peace studies.

In France that revival could not be taken for granted. Munich has cast a long shadow. This chapter would have been more difficult to write twenty or even ten years ago. Although the two decades covered here were obsessed with the avoidance of war, until recently there was some reluctance to relate the study of peace movements to that of diplomacy and conflict, and 'pacifism' was a subject rather avoided by French historians, saturated as it was with memories of appeasement and of collaboration during the Vichy regime. Yet, as René Rémond points out,

> of all the feelings that roused, disturbed and mobilized hearts and minds [in inter-war France] there is probably none that was so widely shared, or had such a decisive impact on political choices and behaviour, as the attachment to peace and the desire to maintain it.
>
> (*Matériaux* 1993: 1)[4]

It is still difficult to write about peace movements without judging them by subsequent events. Some pacifists, Rémond continues, were 'blind' to the rise of Nazism, others 'more far-sighted, saw that the coming of the Third Reich had created a situation so new that they were obliged to convert their original pacifism into anti-fascism'. Far-sightedness is always in greater supply after the event. The purpose here is not to indict the political judgement of contemporary actors, but to consider the connections between the diplomats, mostly men, and the people of either sex who tried to make their voices heard in the concert of nations.

We might even speculate that gender as a component of the symbolic order has not been quite absent from the collective amnesia about inter-war pacifism. A common term to describe pacifism before the war is 'bêlant', 'bleating', the sound made by sheep and associated with female weakness. French pacifism in retrospect has seemed misguided, cowardly, naive or supine: characteristics later associated with attitudes towards the German Occupation of 1940–4. I have suggested elsewhere (1990) that an unexamined theme of Marcel Ophuls's *The Sorrow and the Pity* was that Resistance was at heart a 'masculine' activity, while unthinking acceptance of the Vichy regime or collaboration with the occupiers, was 'feminine'. Alain Brossat's remarkable study (1992) of the French women who had their heads shaved at the Liberation for sleeping with the enemy, points out the symbolic nature of the retribution. Between the wars, while women may not have formed the big battalions of pacifism, their participation in peace campaigns was clear to see. Is it too far-fetched to argue that the historical focus on the extreme right-wing or fascist leagues, 'nasty but virile', along with study of the Popular Front as a reaction to fascism, has been a way of avoiding looking too closely at peace movements whose behaviour (non-violence, fraternization) was associated symbolically with the feminine? The peace movements which provided the context of inter-war diplomacy – 'paralysed it', according to one historian – have attracted less notice than the process of diplomacy itself, or the clash of left–right forces. The absence of women from political narrative finds partial explanation here.[5]

With the lapsing of fifty-year rules, the death of the inter-war generation, the reappraisal of the Occupation years and the rise of women's history, pacifism has now come in from the historical cold.[6] Long under-researched and perhaps too schematically dismissed, the landscape of peace campaigning in inter-war France is now becoming one of some complexity. The sheer volume of material is bewildering: a yearbook published in 1936 listed about 200 French associations – many no doubt fragile, short-lived or virtually non-existent. But there is enough to be going on with. In May 1931, when an indefatigable peace campaigner, Jeanne Mélin, wrote to over 180 associations and countless individuals to publicize a new group, she received a testy reply from Gaston Moch:

> During the forty years I have spent campaigning for peace, I have never ceased to protest at the wasted effort that results from this proliferation of associations, which seems to go on increasing all the time. Not a week goes by without my being invited to subscribe to one or more new organizations, all more or less repeating the work of already existing groups, and your proposal seems to be no exception.[7]

During the 1932 election, the Ligue des Droits de l'Homme, campaigning for peace, approached a variety of organizations 'directly or indirectly committed to the cause of peace': they included war veterans, feminist groups, trade unions, youth movements, civil servants, co-operatives, teachers' groups.[8] Anyone who read a newspaper or belonged to an association was likely to be touched by such campaigns. 'Defence of peace was a popular cause, won in advance, as long as one stuck to general sentiments' (Offenstadt 1993a: 39).

It is with people active for peace that this chapter is concerned: not with outcomes, but with actors, not so much diplomats as ordinary people who scanned the newspapers. The typology suggested in Norman Ingram's pioneering study of the French peace movements makes a useful starting point. He distinguishes between 'legalistic' or 'conditional' peace campaigning on one hand, and 'integral', or 'unconditional' pacifism on the other. Pointing to a chronological dimension, he describes the former as 'old-style', the latter as 'new-style' pacifism, since the dynamics of the peace movement were determined by world events. 'Old-style' refers to the approach which put faith in traditional diplomacy, while placing new hope in the League of Nations. 'Integral' or new-style pacifism refers to more militant movements, for whom peace was a priority. Their members often refused personally to take up arms and were willing to engage in direct action. Ingram took as his example of the former the Association pour la Paix par le Droit (APD), founded in 1887, which he describes as old-fashioned and academic in its approach; and as an example of the latter, the French branch of the LICP, founded in 1931, an uncompromising 'new-style' movement. Both were open to both men and women but, significantly, Ingram's third example is the French branch of the Women's International League for Peace and Freedom (WILPF), founded in 1915. (The French acronym LIFPL will be used here to distinguish the French branch from the transnational association.) There were several all-women peace movements at the time, but Ingram explains that he sees LIFPL as moving between the two types of pacifism. Christine Bard, on the other hand, though using a similar typology to Ingram's, chooses to describe LIFPL – at least in its later years – as a group of a third kind, a 'politicized' peace movement. This useful distinction will be used here. For a politicized peace movement, peace was an issue of capital importance, but one that fitted into a longer-term political agenda: it was not an end in itself.[9] These categories – legalistic, unconditional and politicized – can be used to examine the ways in which gender interacted with questions of war and peace. Respecting chronology, which is critically important, the first section will cover the 1920s and the creation of the League of Nations; the second the dedicated peace campaigns straddling the inter-war decades; and the third the tensions between pacifism and anti-fascism in the 1930s.

RATIONAL THINKING, OR PEACE BY AGREEMENT: THE GENEVA YEARS

'Legalistic' may seem a dismissive term for the approach in which many people placed their trust in the 1920s. Alongside the near-unanimous *desire for peace* among French people after the war, there was also serious *support for peace*. The stronger term 'pacifism' may not be appropriate, since support for peace after 1918 did not necessarily imply opposition to the war. Stalwarts of the APD took the view that the Central Powers had been responsible for the outbreak of war in 1914 and guilty of unprovoked crimes such as the invasion of Belgium. They supported – at least at first – the disputed clauses of the Treaty of Versailles, such as reparations, the provisions for the Rhineland and the Saar, and reduction of Germany's military power.

The Paris conference which had produced that Treaty resulted in the founding of the League of Nations as an international forum or 'standing conference', with the aim of averting future conflicts. At first, membership of the League was confined to the victorious powers which wished to join, plus thirteen neutrals. Further admissions could only be granted by a two-thirds majority. The defeated powers were temporarily banished to a waiting-room (Germany was eventually admitted in 1926). Britain and France were founder members, but the United States, despite Woodrow Wilson's sympathy, chose not to join: throughout the League's history, America sent only observers to its sessions. The USSR also remained outside the League, joining only in 1934. The headquarters of the League was to be at Geneva, on neutral Swiss territory.[10]

For some years after the war, Franco–German tension persisted over the territorial and the reparations clauses of the Treaty of Versailles. Only after the episode of the occupation of the Ruhr, and the compromises of 1924–5, was there a period of relative stability, with Geneva the focus of greater hope than in the past. With Aristide Briand at the Quai d'Orsay from 1925–31, the so-called 'Briand years' saw the flowering of official dialogue between French and German delegations to Geneva.[11] But from the start, the Foreign Ministry had subsidized support groups for the League. In France, these were never as popular as the League of Nations Union in Britain. But small groups like the APD reached a slightly wider audience during these years. Its journal *La Paix par le Droit* expanded its circulation of 5,000 in 1920 to 8,000 by 1924 (Ingram 1991: 24).

The identity of the APD was serious, academic and intellectual – the pacifism of the pedagogues, as Ingram calls it. There were not many women in its ranks but it made targeted appeals to them, devoting a special issue of its journal to 'Les femmes et la Société des Nations' in 1922. The indefatigable Marie-Louise Puech, whose husband was APD secretary, and who herself was the moving spirit of a women's support group for the League, the Union Féminine Française pour la SDN, wrote many articles calling for women, especially feminists, to take an interest in the League of Nations as a potential site of equality for women.[12]

Legalistic moves for peace held great appeal for the mainstream French women's suffrage groups. During the Paris peace conference of 1919, women's suffrage groups from the allied countries had held a conference alongside it. Well represented there was the French UFSF which had strongly supported the French war effort (refusing to attend the separate women's peace conference held at The Hague in 1915). A delegation of women suffragists led by Lady Aberdeen lobbied strongly for women to be represented within the new League of Nations. Following private audiences with leaders such as Clemenceau, they were granted 'permission to be received at a plenary session of the peace conference [where they] asked for women of all countries to have the right to collaborate with men in the new League of Nations'.[13] 'How many French women still do not know', asks Marie-Louise Puech in an article in 1922, 'that while they may exert no direct influence on their own parliament or even their local council, they have the right to sit in the international parliament, the League of Nations?'[14] By supporting the League, it was possible to reconcile both the cause of peace within a legal framework and the cause of women's rights: many French suffragists regarded them as linked anyway. The League provided certain French women with a political platform denied them at home. An 'international parliament' was something quite new, so old rules (such as an all-male diplomatic corps) might be side-stepped. Thanks to the women's lobby at Versailles, Article VII of the League's charter stated that 'all functions of the League of Nations and the attached services, including the secretariat, are equally open to men and women.' Member states could nominate women as delegates, or permanent officials. The same applied to the International Labour Office (ILO), also based in Geneva. Whether women would be appointed depended on the member states. Countries which had already granted rights to women were readiest to entrust them with national affairs at Geneva. In this respect France was no pioneer, but at first French women hoped pressure would come from outside.

Most member countries, as well as senior League officials, saw the question of women's rights as a matter for each country to deal with domestically. The primary function of the League was to promote peace. But the League had after all sponsored the Mandates Commission with attention to the rights of minorities, as well as conventions on slavery and trafficking in women, 'on the principle that there were fundamental individual rights which should be protected through international law' (Miller 1994: 221). Some women's groups accordingly pressed for the League to sponsor an 'equal rights treaty', in order to codify international law on women's rights. During the inter-war years, Geneva became 'the international centre of the women's movement. The major transnational women's associations [including WILPF] set up permanent or temporary headquarters in Geneva and in several cases remain based there today' (ibid.: 220). To put it another way, in Geneva between the wars, 'everyone was "getting together" and all the "get-togetherers" would get together once again centrally and all-embracingly' (Rupp 1994: 1,576).

For all these reasons, Geneva was attractive to French women activists. If in France they were still excluded from parliamentary politics, they were welcome in the international forum. The League's headquarters were on France's doorstep, French was one of the working languages of the secretariat and assemblies, and was spoken in the streets of Geneva; and women met no discrimination inside the League's offices. Practical advantages combined with the prestige of the League in the early days to make it an alternative focus for political pressure, and its chief concern – world peace – was one already high on the agenda of many of the French women's associations.

The presence of French women at Geneva can be traced historically in at least three distinct milieux. The first and most familiar from memoirs and biographies, but perhaps most remote from peace campaigning, was the 'international set', which gathered at Geneva in September for the opening of the General Assembly, especially after 1924, the year of the Protocol.[15] Prominent in the colourful crowd of 'unofficial delegates, impostors and Amazons' (quoted in Guichard 1991: 140) were a number of leading lights of Parisian society such as Claire Boas de Jouvenel, 'queen of the peace conference', the duchesse de La Rochefoucauld, and Anna de Noailles (Jouvenel 1979: 32). All three took a genuine interest in international politics and had some influence on susceptible French politicians, but collectively such 'hostesses' have been the target of much contemporary and retrospective sarcasm, and a stream of anecdotes about the Hotel des Bergues, home of the French delegation, where the barman offered 'Protocol cocktails' and 'Arbitration orange fizz'. Even the more nuanced descriptions of this milieu are dismissive of the 'twittering female admirers' of Briand and Herriot: 'There were many women in Geneva: wives, mistresses, Egerias, genuine women journalists like Geneviève Tabouis and Louise Weiss, others a little less authentic, high society ladies and *demi-mondaines*' (Oudin 1987: 516–17). The 'genuine journalists' and feminists themselves passed harsh judgements. Maria Vérone, in an article calling for more women delegates, referred in 1928 to the 'snobinettes' and adventurers who hung around the delegations,[16] and Louise Weiss was scathing about the 'Parisiennes', who only arrived when Geneva had become well established as a fashionable venue: 'They couldn't have cared less about peace. Indeed they played a part, though one shouldn't over-emphasize it, in discrediting the whole Institution, which was eventually to crumble through lack of moral courage or respect for the truth' (Weiss 1980, vol. 2: 184). Some of the remarks made about unofficial politicking in the last chapter no doubt apply here too. Still, given the immense role played at Geneva by unofficial contacts, it can be assumed that sexual politics was not insignificant, though it may be resistant to historical enquiry without detailed study of personal papers.

Less ambiguously, some women were official delegates or advisers to specialized permanent commissions. The annual assembly lasted only a few weeks: birds of passage flew. But the secretariat and commissions stayed all year round. The chance to appoint women delegates was not enthusiastically seized. Most of the few women appointed were substitutes, and only the Scandinavian countries made regular nominations. Some French women did get postings in Geneva: Mme de Witt-Schlumberger was nominated in 1921 to the standing commission on children and the family, and Adrienne Avril de Saint-Croix followed her there in 1922. In the same year Marie Curie became the first official French representative with a seat on the commission for intellectual co-operation. But by 1931, after about ten years of the League's existence, there were still only nineteen women delegates to the Assembly in all, and only one full delegate.[17] Stereotyping was characteristic of these appointments. Virtually all French women were asked to tackle 'family' issues. Jo Vellacott has argued that the Inter-Allied Suffragists of 1919 encouraged this focus on 'definable women's issues', confining themselves to a separate international women's agenda, just as some wanted a separate domestic women's agenda.[18]

What of the permanent officials? The League gradually built up a large secretariat. But most jobs were for translators or secretarial/clerical staff – Roneo operators and file clerks for the immense quantities of paperwork. French-speaking women were eligible for these, but they remained at subordinate levels, with only about a hundred women reaching higher executive posts. In 1932, under pressure from women's associations, a resolution was passed calling for ways of 'intensifying women's participation in the League's work', but even by 1937 little serious progress had been made: 'women are secretaries, typists and deputy heads of section, while men still hold the control levers and the most interesting jobs.'[19] Still, the French director of the ILO, the 'feminist' Albert Thomas, who believed in promoting able women, appointed a number of senior French women colleagues. They included the industrial inspectress Gabrielle Letellier, and one of the most senior ILO officials, Marguerite Thibert. As *chef de section* responsible for the employment of women and children, Thibert was highly influential, although her name remained hidden in the anonymous reports she wrote over the years. Her only signed article in those days was the hard-hitting piece about women's work during the depression (cf. Chapter 5).[20]

Lastly there were the representatives of transnational women's associations such as the International Women's Suffrage Alliance (IWSA), International Council of Women (ICW) or WILPF. The latter had its headquarters at Geneva, where its secretary-general for many years was the Frenchwoman Camille Drévet, while the president and secretary of the French section of WILPF, Gabrielle Duchêne and Andrée Jouve, were both on the international executive committee.[21] Neither the parent organization, given its own radical origins in 1915, to be discussed below, nor the French branch, LIFPL, can exactly be described as 'legalistic'. But particularly during the 1920s, they yielded to the general optimism and, besides, their leaders were well aware of the potential of Geneva for what would today be called 'networking', meeting both national politicians and representatives of other international associations.

The contrast between the official silencing of women's voices in France, particularly at election times, and the steady flow of women's initiatives at Geneva – demonstrations, petitions and so on – was a point French campaigners did not fail to make. When, in 1929, Aristide Briand made an explicit appeal to the women of the world to support his peace policy, Maria Vérone writing in *L'Oeuvre* asked sarcastically how women in Briand's native country could possibly respond to his call. In 1930, the International Women's Peace Crusade sent a delegation to the London Naval Conference with a petition in favour of naval disarmament. The Frenchwoman Mme Rudler told the British Prime Minister, Ramsay Macdonald, that she was speaking for 'millions of wives and mothers in France' who had no voice at the conference.[22] Women peace campaigners operating outside France could claim independence from party politics. And exclusion from national politics gave a certain desperate energy to French women's participation in international initiatives taken seriously at the time, such as the parallel disarmament conference in 1931–2. Such energy points, however, towards the conclusion that women's presence at Geneva could be a displaced form of participation in national politics. Peace, while both important and desirable, was often less the centre of their preoccupations than the question of women's rights over the long run.

The League of Nations is more famous for what it failed to achieve than for its positive successes, but if we are scanning these years for structures rather than outcomes, it can be seen as playing a structurally equivalent role in both the peace movement and feminism: at Geneva faith was placed in the power of sweet reason to remove obstacles in the way of desirable objectives. The leading lights of suffrage organizations often sincerely believed that women who had the vote would make peace a priority, but in some ways it suited their own agenda well to stress their support for the official efforts of their government (rather than rock the boat). Women working within the international institutions tried to be a good advertisement for responsibility. Journalists like Louise Weiss and Geneviève Tabouis set out to show the seriousness of their attachment to informed debate, and their trustworthiness as sources of information. Both spent most of their time with men. The feminists who gravitated to the League were making the case for equality – for example in the campaign over the nationality of married women (Miller 1994: 226 ff.). They were making a conscious appeal to men in power to be taken seriously, and they assumed a common interest in peace. Reasonable, educated and fairly privileged people themselves, they mostly seem to have hoped that in the sex war, as in shooting wars, it was all over bar the shouting. Assuming inevitable progress towards equality, they probably underestimated male resistance to women's rights, much as they underestimated the forces ranged against peace.

SEXUAL DIFFERENCE AND IDENTITY POLITICS IN THE PACIFIST MOVEMENT: ANCIENS COMBATTANTS, MOTHERS AND FEMINISTS

Sweet reason was not so evident elsewhere in peace-minded circles. 'Militant', 'extreme', 'integral', 'unconditional' – all these adjectives have been applied to the pacifism summed up in Félicien Challaye's defiant slogan, 'rather a foreign occupation than war', echoing Bertrand Russell's famous words: 'Not a single evil that one should like to avoid by war is greater than the evil of war itself.' These pacifists were energetic in the cause of peace rather than simply hopeful of the resolution of conflict by the goodwill of nations. For them peace took precedence over any other political goal. Typical of the approach was the Ligue Internationale des Combattants pour la Paix (LICP), which included enthusiasts of both sexes. Founded in France in 1931, at a time when faith in international mechanisms was starting to wobble, the LICP is generally regarded as the most intransigently pacifist group of all.[23] Through mass demonstrations, festivals and the media it reached a wide audience, although its paid-up membership was never more than 10,000. The LICP deliberately sought to locate itself outside party politics, painting an unflattering portrait of national leaders ('deceivers in the pockets of the arms manufacturers'). It was a forum where mavericks, veteran peace campaigners and intellectuals, rather than known politicians, would be the speakers, and its audience was not necessarily the electorate (male) but 'the people' (mixed). Eleven women were on its 77-strong committee, and women speakers were given special prominence in its effort to reach 'ordinary people'. Records survive of the birth

189

control campaigner Jeanne Humbert touring central France with her lecture 'against the approaching war' in 1932, and of many public speeches by Marcelle Capy, a 'peace professional' whose personal magnetism is attested for throughout the period: 'Her simple eloquence, well served by a strong warm voice, had an extraordinary impact on audiences made up of ordinary people' (*Matériaux* 1993: 36; Ingram 1991: 140).

This kind of remark alerts us to the use of a specifically womanly rhetoric. Even clearer stress on sexual difference (or complementarity) is found in the existence of some separate men's and women's peace movements, each stressing gender-specific reasons for joining the cause. A further distinction that may be made is that between a specifically *women's* pacifism – based on an assumption that peace was essentially a women's issue; and a *feminist* pacifism, based on the idea that the two philosophies were logically linked. Both were to be found in inter-war France.

Much was made in some quarters of the supposedly 'natural' links between women and peace, since the harrowing experience of the Great War had created a consciousness of the gender divide which underpinned much post-war bitterness. One sentiment voiced in France after the war was that women were collectively to blame for not having done more to halt the conflict. On the outbreak of war, organized women's movements in most combatant countries, including Britain and France, had unanimously supported the war effort. Individual distress or bereavement did not prevent women from joining the wartime industrial labour force, or volunteering in large numbers as nurses and auxiliaries to tend the wounded. Praise for their 'war work' was accompanied by calls to grant them new rights such as the vote. From here it was but a short step to seeing the war as something that emancipated women. The reverse side of the coin was a sentiment which developed remarkably quickly among combatants and others: hostility to women for 'profiting' from the slaughter on the battlefield and/or failing to raise their voices to prevent it. In Britain, this approach was summed up by the famous *Punch* cartoon showing two women factory workers saying: 'This war is too good to last.' In France, the malaise had many causes: the reaction of enlisted men to what they saw as folly and frivolity on the home front; fear of adultery by lonely wives; the enforced infantilizing of wounded men dependent on the care of healthy young nurses; apprehension about jobs in industry being lost to women. Some of these fears were voiced during the war; some of them took time to emerge in works of literature; almost all such feelings were articulated by men.[24]

The publications of the French peace campaigner, Fernand Corcos, are an often-quoted example of this stance. His books reproached women with having signed up for war work for love of gain, and accused them of lukewarm support for peace campaigns. He called for a move away from the 'egalitarian education' Frenchwomen were receiving, and back towards their 'true beings'. He had hoped that 'being sensitive to suffering, woman would have rebelled at the idea of so many deaths: "war is detested by mothers". Mothers, I thought, will put a stop to it. I was mistaken' (Corcos 1929: 286). This disgust, rather than praise, for women's wartime patriotism was shared by certain trade unionists, not without some ulterior thoughts about post-war employment (Robert 1989: 517). And it met up with a feeling widespread among the *anciens combattants*, the war veterans, that they alone had paid the full price of the war.[25]

Antoine Prost's study of ex-servicemen has stressed both the trauma which virtually all his correspondents had experienced (and often repressed for many years) and their pacifism. He has argued that the tiny minority of veterans who joined aggressive movements like the Croix de feu have received far more historical attention than the three million or so registered ex-combatants who expressed pacifist sentiments throughout the 1920s and even in the 1930s, many of them joining anti-war associations. The pacifism of the veterans was a reflex of revulsion at the horror: ('Plus jamais ça!') after 'the war to end wars', but it was also partly inspired by hostility to those who had not seen combat – elderly politicians or civilians. Theirs was not an objection in principle to fighting, but it contained anti-militaristic feelings expressed in a deliberately virile rhetoric, stressing the comradeship of the trenches compared with the light-heartedness of the home front (and in some cases the irresponsibility of the commanders).

Prost describes the veterans' pacifism as 'patriotic', and in this respect they must be clearly distinguished from the 'unconditional' pacifists who would refuse to fight under any circumstances. But for former soldiers, peace was still a value to be placed above all others. They too supported the League of Nations, and played a role in its support societies in France. They admired Briand, as René Cassin explained in a letter to Prost:

> not, as has been suggested because he offered them an easy road to peace without sacrifices, but because in 1922 he was the only one who spoke frankly about the dangers that would threaten peace after 1935 [given France's birth rate] and about the twin necessity of settling as best one could the temporary causes of irritation (reparations, armaments, occupations) in order to concentrate our efforts on the long term: a League of Nations which would be *powerful* enough to ensure peace ... through collective security when the bad times came.
>
> (Prost 1977, vol. 3: 114)[26]

The patriotic vision of the war veterans surveyed by Prost was a traditional, indeed a patriarchal one, centred on the family to be defended – the 'France where you open a bottle of wine on Sunday afternoon when friends come round', as he describes it. Theirs was a specifically male pacifism, based on shared experience under fire, and of having taken responsibility for others.

Its counterpart as a gendered movement was the 'maternal' pacifism called for by Corcos and duly delivered by some of the women's peace campaigns. Virtually all women's peace groups at some time or another used the rhetoric of maternity to promote peace – it was part of the common coin of available imagery. But some women used it purely tactically, whereas what was new was the militant use of motherhood by previously 'apolitical' women who would once have lived by their maternal identity rather than give it political voice.

191

Womanliness was an essential ingredient of such groups' image. Thus an early example, Madeleine Vernet's Ligue des Femmes contre la Guerre, founded in 1921 at the orphanage which she ran at Epone, laid special emphasis on the education of children. At meetings, its speakers appealed to women as 'creators of life, who must defend it'. Its members undertook 'not to do any war work, of any kind, directly or indirectly', thus implicitly criticizing women who had not withheld their labour during the war. This small group (never more than 300 members) lasted only a few years.[27] Its place was taken in 1928 by an organization with similar aims but a much wider audience, the Ligue des Mères et Educatrices pour la Paix. Its president, Mme Eidenschenk-Patin, made full use of the rhetoric of maternalism:

> Women, and particularly mothers, who have a horror of war, constitute a great force not yet aware of its strength . . . . Mothers are an incomparable force, firstly because they are the early educators of men . . . and secondly because motherly love is the same in every woman's heart, and can and must unite women across frontiers to save their children.
>
> (Blum *et al.* 1984: 585)

The LIMEP had branches in several countries but was based in Paris and the bulk of the membership was French. By 1932 it claimed 65,000 members and by 1938 100,000. It sent toys to the children of the unemployed in Germany, issued tracts against war toys, and directed anti-war propaganda at children. In a pamphlet issued in 1934, it explained that 'the five founders of the League are mothers of families. Three of them between them lost FOUR sons in the last war.' The LIMEP recruited particularly in the countryside, 'where before our efforts no systematic publicity for peace had ever reached'. The suggestion is that, unlike the other groups such as LIFPL which recruited 'among intellectual women', LIMEP recruited among the thousands of peasant women who had lost sons in the war, 'les masses féminines populaires'.[28] Active and apparently well supported, claiming to be 'apolitical', the LIMEP is described as naive by Christine Bard (1995: 309; in 1936 it wrote to Hitler protesting about nationalism in German school textbooks). It continued to hold to its ultra-pacifist line right through to the summer of 1939, when its members were still beseeching Daladier to seek any means of avoiding war. It offers a clear example of a single-issue campaign, undeflected from its hatred of violence by political change, and deliberately embracing the identity of the nurturing mother. It may have been naive, but it was not minded to allow male governments to speak in its name.[29]

Very different, despite a similar rhetoric from time to time, was the LIFPL, the French section of WILPF. The odd history of this group makes it sensible to look at its early history in this section, under 'identity politics', its later history in the next, 'politicized pacifism'. There is no doubt that the original thrust behind the foundation of WILPF was a campaign for peace, even 'integral pacifism', and that it was exclusively a women's movement with the style, rhetoric and approach of identity politics, inspired by early revulsion against the wartime slaughter. In March 1915, when it was already clear how costly the war would be in lives, women's suffrage associations from both combatant and neutral countries, including the United States, called a conference at The Hague, comparable to the better-known Zimmerwald conference of socialists in September 1915 and the Kienthal/Berne conference, also socialist, of April 1916. All such conferences were strongly opposed by the French and British national authorities, and delegates had difficulty obtaining passports or crossing frontiers. Few reached Zimmerwald or Berne, and no French woman went to The Hague at all. The official French suffrage movement sent a strongly worded letter explaining that if German and Austrian women were present, French women could not attend, because of the atrocities allegedly committed by the Central Powers in northern France. 'A dangerous encounter had to be avoided.'[30]

The Hague conference did not see itself simply as a gathering of mothers and Antigones deploring the slaughter, but as a meeting to discuss serious proposals for bringing it to an end. Experience gained in the pre-war suffrage campaign enabled the delegates to contemplate such a controversial undertaking, running the gauntlet of a Channel blockade among other things. The conference placed an embargo on speeches apportioning blame for the war, and allowed only positive proposals on to the agenda. Its final resolutions were circulated to heads of states, including Woodrow Wilson, and initially encountered some sympathy. There is little dispute about the convergence between many of its proposals and what later emerged as Wilson's Fourteen Points, but the time was far from ripe.

Not all French women suffragists condemned The Hague conference: 'I am in extraordinary mental turmoil trying to work out where French women's duty lies over this,' Marguerite de Witt-Schlumberger wrote to Jeanne Mélin (Bard 1995: 95). Some went further. After the conference, emissaries from The Hague were welcomed to Paris by a group of women later known as the 'Comité de la rue Fondary'. Wishing to set up a French branch of the International Committee of Women for a Permanent Peace formed at The Hague, they issued a short pamphlet, *Un devoir urgent pour les femmes*, arguing that conditions for an honourable peace should be explored as quickly as possible. Two aims only were declared: voting rights for women and peaceful settlement of all international conflicts. Drafted by Jeanne Halbwachs and Michel Alexandre, the pamphlet was published at the group's expense over the address of a flat in the rue Fondary in Paris, rented by an active campaigner, Gabrielle Duchêne. The rash decision to send it to deputies and senators drew down upon the tiny group the wrath of the French state. The whole committee was summoned by the police, the scandal reached the press and the 'defeatist' enterprise was widely condemned.[31]

In 1919 the committee formed at The Hague, renamed the Women's International League for Peace and Freedom (WILPF), planned to hold a parallel meeting alongside the peace conference. Disconcerted by the Allies' decision to hold a victors' conference in Paris, instead of on neutral territory with all parties fully represented, WILPF met in Zurich in spring 1919 and invited women from the defeated countries. In this, it set itself apart from the inter-allied women's suffragist conference meeting in Paris. The difference between the two conferences was extreme, since German and Austrian delegates to Zurich were directly affected by the Allied blockade. (Other delegates were shocked by their condition and one woman from Germany died soon after the conference.) This time, French delegates were not prevented from attending, though only four made it, and in a highly charged atmosphere the Frenchwoman Jeanne Mélin was presented with flowers by the German delegate, Lida Gustava Heymann, and the two embraced on the platform.[32] Draft copies of the document containing the Versailles peace treaty arrived in Zurich during the conference and were thought deeply disappointing. WILPF leaders drafted a critical response, dwelling on what they saw as the folly of reparations, and the refusal to allow Germany to join the League of Nations; in short, on the departure of the treaty from the Fourteen Points. This approach became the foundation of WILPF's future action (Vellacott 1993: 37).

However 'alternative' the Zurich conference might seem, this was not simply an example of 'womanly pacifism'. The main thrust of this gathering, attended by professional lawyers, journalists and teachers, meeting as campaigners for women's rights rather than as wives and mothers, was that women should be included in future deliberations over international relations, not to represent a 'feminine' point of view but as adults who would take responsibility for their actions. Part of their explicit aim was to understand war in order to prevent it. While the energy and passion of early WILPF activists distinguished them from the more polite pragmatists of the mainstream women's suffrage groups, it was their relative sophistication in political terms that set them apart from some of the ultra-pacifist maternalist groups. During the 1920s, however, WILPF was 'absolute for peace': this was the driving force behind it, although some campaigners, notably in France, moved away from this position later, and one can perhaps begin to see why.

In absolute pacifist politics, differences between the sexes were often underlined to create an effect. There was from the start some ambiguity about the WILPF's attitude to this kind of essentialism. Ingram maintains that there was something very distinctive about women's pacifism in the 1920s, and that this was sacrificed by the French branch of WILPF when it became 'politicized' in the 1930s. Bard, on the other hand, argues that it was the militant internationalism and lack of religious sentiment that distinguished the French branch. To explore these suggestions, we need to turn to the difficult choices confronting pacifists after the breakdown of Briandism.

POLITICAL PEACE CAMPAIGNS: ANTI-FASCISM AND THE TURMOIL ON THE LEFT

If by politicized pacifism is meant a peace campaign that is neither pragmatic (after the manner of diplomacy), nor absolute (after the manner of ultra-pacifism), but which takes its cue from pre-existing political choices, then the term will do quite well to describe the contradictory pacifism to be found on the French left in the 1930s, in which anti-fascism was a major component.

Some of the new movements of the 1930s were linked to established political parties. When this was the case, women were likely to be more removed from central decision-making. Recent research on the 'umbrella' organization, the Rassemblement Universel pour la Paix, for example, founded in 1935, suggests a limited role for women, given the RUP's identity as an elite, inter-party and inter-movement peace campaign. The reasons had to do with the networking at its centre, concentrated in circles close to one of its founders, the radical politician Pierre Cot (cf. Mazuy 1993: 40–4). Women were included in the RUP for the sake of completeness, in itself not insignificant, but they were more prominent in other anti-fascist movements.

Of all the established parties, the Communist party was most active in the politics of anti-fascism. Many French socialists were 'gut-pacifists', but pacifism was not an issue in itself for communists. As one commentator puts it, 'pacifism was out of order if it hindered the spread of communism and the defence of the Soviet fatherland, but recommended when it weakened the imperialist enemy' (Defrasne 1983: 99). Since Soviet Russia was the enemy of the French state during the 1920s, the PCF waged an unremitting anti-militarist campaign inside France in these years, drawing on some of the old anti-army reflexes of the extreme left: its propaganda sought to destabilize conscripts and to dissuade working-class youths from joining the regular army.[33]

It was in the 1920s too that there occurred a particular burst of women's pacifism, encouraged by the Communist party. In March 1927, the French National Assembly gave approval in principle to a military bill sponsored by the socialist Defence Minister, Joseph Paul-Boncour, 'Briand's right-hand man at Geneva' and a supporter of entente and the League. It proposed that in time of war 'all French citizens, irrespective of age or sex [be] bound to participate in the defence of the nation and the maintenance of its moral and material existence'.[34] Boncour was not suggesting that women should do military service. Rather, with the memory still fresh of the haphazard and piecemeal arrangements of the previous war, the idea was that women should be prepared from the start to take over men's office jobs or to staff medical, paramedical and civil defence services. On the bill's first reading, the chamber voted in favour by 500 to 31, the only opponents being the communists. But the Senate had second thoughts about its 'socialist' implications, the socialists in the chamber in turn refused Senate amendments, and during the 1928 elections the measure was quietly dropped. Throughout 1927, however, reaction to it was strong in certain circles.

Some feminists, even when committed to peace campaigning, regarded the logic of the bill as perfectly acceptable, even helpful to women's rights. Hélène Brion, who had been taken to court for pacifism during the war, Madeleine Pelletier and Marguerite Durand, non-conformists in other contexts, all took this view. Pelletier argued that 'the current logic of conscription for men is in fact implicitly based on the exclusion of women from citizenship.'[35] Durand similarly pointed out that if women were actually subject to mobilization laws, they could not be refused citizens' rights. But the majority of feminist or women's peace groups, while picking up on the word 'citizens', strongly opposed the law, arguing that women would have no choice in the declaration of war. The committee of the French section of WILPF prepared an open-letter to Paul-Boncour to be sent as from the international headquarters:

> It is with pained astonishment that we see a French politician claiming to be a convinced pacifist using his rhetorical gifts to urge the passing of a law as militaristic as can be imagined, and even boasting of the part he has played in its drafting.... And when that politician plays an important role at the League of Nations and within the Preparatory Commission on disarmament, such an attitude takes on a particularly tragic character.... Refusing women the right to vote [French law] disposes of their lives and their consciences without their consent.[36]

The fiercest opposition by far came from the Communist party, now at the height of its anti-militaristic period. The stress on women which the press had highlighted, with varying degrees of shock or jocularity, inclined the party to launch a special initiative directed at women: the creation of a new women's peace organization to oppose the bill. Known at first as the Union Fraternelle des Femmes contre la Guerre Impérialiste, by 1928 it was claiming 4,000 members divided into 180 sections. The secretary was Antoinette Gilles of the CGTU. The sworn enemy of 'Christian women's peace organizations . . . which are carrying out the policies of bourgeois war under the mask of pacifism', the UFF aimed its appeal at 'working women'. In the words of one pamphlet 'the least politically-minded of working women will instinctively say that she is against war: we must start from here and bring her to work in the struggle against imperialist war' (Blum *et al.* 1984: 588).

The UFFCGI was, if not exactly a communist front organization, then at least explicitly close to the party. It held joint meetings with the CGTU, and in some ways foreshadows the development of the anti-fascist associations in the 1930s. Yet one can see that traditional notions of womanly identity were deliberately being mobilized against the Paul-Boncour law. It must be recognized that one did not have to be a communist to be opposed to the measure, heartily disliked as it was by many women's peace groups, and by 'integral' peace campaigners such as Fernand Corcos.[37] The Paul-Boncour proposals did not go away. After a few years' quiescence, they were tabled in 1935, again to no great enthusiasm. By the time they were finally debated, in March 1938, things had changed: the communists were now among their strongest supporters, so they were approved unanimously in both houses of parliament. For all that, French civilian defence appears to have been comparatively underprepared, having been given little practical thought until late in the day. Those women who actually volunteered for duty in the early months of the war were given little to do.[38]

The anti-Paul-Boncour agitation of 1927 was momentarily energetic, but confined to comparatively few people, and the communist campaign was transparently manipulative. All the same, the echoes it met signalled an immense undertow of passive resistance to any form of mobilization for war, which helps to explain the real difficulty of anti-fascism in converting from a movement for peace into a movement for resistance. As the significance of Hitler's rise to power became apparent, the anti-fascist movement of the 1930s grew from small beginnings to reach many. The two conferences for peace held in Amsterdam in 1932 and in Paris at the Salle Pleyel in 1933, under the aegis of communist intellectuals Romain Rolland and Henri Barbusse, were the starting point for a broader movement (known for short as 'Amsterdam–Pleyel') which took on its full significance after Stalin's about-turn of 1934, when the Soviet Union joined the League of Nations, and more especially after the Stalin–Laval agreements of 1935.[39] The Communist party now came round to favouring French national defence and its anti-militarist campaign gave way to an anti-fascist one. That women were present in considerable force in anti-fascist peace campaigns cannot now be doubted, as historians are beginning to recognize. Again, the most detailed research has initially concentrated on the LIFPL, one reason being that its archives in the Duchêne papers at Nanterre give a remarkably full account of its troubled life during the 1930s.

Although LIFPL was not a large association in France – possibly with only 4,500 members at its peak[40] – it was a key player. It took an active part in the creation of the much larger Comité Mondial des Femmes contre la Guerre et le Fascisme (CMFCGF), closely tied to the Amsterdam–Pleyel movement and claiming thousands of members in France, possibly as many as 600,000 by 1936. The headquarters of the Comité Mondial were in Paris and Gabrielle Duchêne, secretary and leading light of LIFPL, was one of the Comité's four secretaries. Having worked on the Duchêne papers myself, my conclusion is not quite the same as that of the two historians who have so far studied LIFPL most closely, Michel Dreyfus and Norman Ingram. In slightly different ways, each of them has concluded with some regret that this group lost its autonomy in this period, becoming embroiled in the contradictions between pacifism and anti-fascism. Dreyfus nevertheless regards this as an interesting period in LIFPL's life, seeing its failure as a reflection of what was happening in other broadly left-wing peace movements, whereas Ingram regrets that the Ligue lost the originality and independence it had shown in the 1920s: 'what was inherently new, exciting, innovative and unique in the feminist contribution to peace in the immediate post-war world was lost in France by the 1930s . . . the French section of LIFPL became a shadow of what it might have been.' He goes on to talk of the 'Stalinization of Gabrielle Duchêne', its leading light and secretary-general, and argues that in the 1930s 'whilst laudable in itself [her] demand for action became a reflection of the policies of the Amsterdam–Pleyel movement and hence of the Third International' (Ingram 1991: 307).[41]

At one level, no one would quarrel with this reading. Gabrielle Duchêne certainly tried to lead the Ligue firmly off towards a pro-Soviet stance, and in so doing succeeded in tearing it apart. She had always been a communist sympathizer, although so far as is known she never joined the party. There is plenty of evidence of her increasing support for the PCF's position after making a visit to the Soviet Union during the late 1920s. Her activity in the Comité Mondial from 1934 on led

197

her to formulate more and more clearly a preference for the Soviet Union. In 1936 she gave a lecture on 'the two kinds of pacifism', which she labelled 'integral pacifism' and 'realistic pacifism', the latter meaning moral support for the Soviet Union in an attempt to protect it from German aggression. The assumption was that the 1935 pact would mean France coming to the defence of the USSR, not the other way round. By contrast, the Lyon branch of LIFPL, under the influence of the Trotskyist schoolteacher Berthe Joly, took a thoroughly critical view of the Popular Front, precisely because of its sympathy for the USSR. Joining forces rather incongruously with the ultra-pacifists still in LIFPL, who simply abhorred taking sides and wanted to reassert the primacy of peace, the Lyon group challenged Duchêne and the LIFPL leadership in 1936, but ended up being expelled. Ultra-pacifists such as Jeanne Alexandre and Madeleine Vernet, after two years of uneasy incompatibility, left to form a more absolutist Ligue des Femmes pour la Paix in September 1938. Duchêne was unrepentant about the turn of events, remarking that 'more had been achieved in two years for the cause of peace and liberty in the Comité Mondial than in twenty years of the Ligue' (quoted in Ingram 1991: 297). If we look at outcomes here, however, there were certainly no winners, and the Ligue was in the same situation as every other peace campaign which saw war overtake it (including the CMFCGF). It had no direct influence one way or the other on the French government, although it contributed in no small measure to assumptions made about public opinion. By 1938–9, its leaders began to see war as inevitable, as did many anti-fascists, a stance much at odds with the movement's history. What is more, and this certainly seems to have been felt as a loss, LIFPL was less minded to foreground its feminism as the skies darkened. It invited male speakers to its meetings and the feminist content of its literature declined.

Seen from a different perspective, however, what has most struck me about the Duchêne papers is the glimpses they give of the political energy (divisive and self-mutilating though it might turn out to be) of women completely outside the formal political system. At the same time, they were not isolated from the currents of opinion flowing through France at the time. What Ingram finds depressing seems to me to be evidence that women's peace movements were not all of a piece; that they were not confined to any particular politics, 'womanly identity' politics in particular. While the irrepressible Duchêne's own texts and those of the leadership group are the most forceful in tone, some of the most interesting letters in this voluminous collection come from rank and file provincial organizers and members, expressing a variety of reactions, from the very naive to the very well informed. One organizer wrote as early as 1933 with a warning against 'the revolutionary or communist element . . . the words "revolution" and "assassins" do not go down well'.[42] In 1935, Madeleine Vernet asked Jeanne Challaye to pass on a message to Duchêne:

> I have not left the Ligue yet, because I am still attached to some of the people in it, but I don't like the French section's attitude. To speak in favour of

dictatorship and civil war can't be the role of an organization with our name . . . . Since 1932, the Ligue has become an echo of Amsterdam, losing its own personality. It's stopped the campaign for disarmament and is actively putting out propaganda against Hitler.[43]

Marthe Pichorel of the strongly pacifist Syndicat National des Instituteurs penned a furious letter in July 1935: 'the French section is still identical with the Rassemblement Mondial . . . I get the feeling that we pacifists are being cheated, no more no less.' Many of these letters are hostile, threatening or notifying resignation, yet even from correspondence criticizing the leadership there is a striking sense of political involvement. Sometimes this comes from members evidently venturing for the first time into anything that might be termed politics, torn between wanting to have a view and a sense that as women they are barely entitled to do so. One woman resigned from the League on the grounds that the new line is too 'political': 'it has always seemed to me over-reaching oneself to meddle in things one has not experienced or even studied.'[44] Another writes:

> I do not entirely share the views of the Ligue (on the Saar and the Rhineland) and besides, if I had known that in this Ligue the orders came 'from the top' and were taken by an international executive committee, I would never have joined it . . . . I think that for some time now the cause of peace has been too closely identified with the crusade against Hitler and the defence of Russia, and I can't go along with that.[45]

In one instance, a sort of index of commitment is provided by a local secretary: listing her membership of about fifty (for the town of Caen), she has annotated most of them with comments such as 'very, very loyal', 'only joined to do me a favour', 'very left-wing'. Of this mini-sample, eight or nine are described as Catholics (some of the 'Sangnier' tendency, others simply identified by their religion); another eight or so are identified as 'on the left'. Some women joined 'after reading my article in the paper', one 'is very frightened of war, we can count on her'. Of those whose professions are listed (a minority), seven or eight were postal or telephone workers, and about the same number were primary schoolteachers. The branch treasurer, a shopkeeper, was a member of the Communist party, unusual for 'this reactionary town'.[46]

These fifty women were no doubt only episodically drawn into any sustained campaigning, but they offer a snapshot of grass-roots interest which was multiplied all over France in a modest way. Their activity – or lack of it – is symptomatic of the tensions within French society at the time: anguish over the international situation, powerlessness to affect it. Their branch secretary despaired of getting members to come regularly and in sufficient numbers to meetings: they pleaded sick children, their work, trade union business, distance and lack of transport, sometimes their own exhaustion. The communist treasurer, kept at home by the shop and an invalid child, still found time to let it be known, however, that 'since Germany was now rearming, she was in favour of French rearmament'. Like the others, her case shows that the everyday life of women had room in it for political thinking, as did that of the men around them.

Christine Bard rightly argues that the pacifism of women's groups is striking not so much for its numbers or rate of militancy, both of which fluctuated, as for the variety of attitudes to be found there, reflecting those in the peace movements as a whole. In the LIFPL, socialists, communists, left-wing Catholics, Trotskyists and ultra-pacifists came together to argue. The minutes of the national council of LIFPL, held in July 1935, show in miniature the fault lines at the heart of left-wing pacifism at this time. In a series of lively debates (over support for pacts of mutual assistance, over unilateral disarmament, over relations with the Comité Mondial or with the WILPF headquarters, and especially over the perceived intentions of the USSR), the committee was divided time and again, along lines indicating the future break-up of the French section. Duchêne's strong personality made itself felt, oozing contempt for 'le pacifisme bêlant'. Of the British section of WILPF she reported that 'some people joined, thinking they were going into a pacifist outfit operating on a sentimental basis, and took fright when they discovered the reality.'[47] In miniature, the debates in LIFPL reflected those carried on elsewhere, but that is not to say they were directed from outside. The disagreements were heartfelt, the *désarroi* near-universal.

In the examples of politicized pacifism quoted here, we can see not only the strains inflicted by the difficult circumstances of the late 1930s, but also the way women were drawn regularly into the major issues of international politics. Sexual difference *was* widely used for propaganda purposes at various times, echoing the strong maternalist strain in 'women's pacifism'. It was sometimes spontaneous, sometimes stage-managed. The 1927 Union Fraternelle des Femmes was created by the Communist party in an early version of its 'sector' tactics: selecting a particular group as a *masse de manoeuvre* in order to reach categories within society. No doubt the women PCF members and sympathizers who joined the UFF were whole-hearted in their resistance to the Paul-Boncour proposals, as were many other women, but the rise and eclipse of this particular campaign were ultimately determined by other things than the desires of its members. Comparatively little research has been done on the later and much larger Comité Mondial des Femmes contre la Guerre et le Fascisme, which might seem to have much in common with the UFF. But this raises different questions, if only because it seems to have mobilized far more women and because it seems likely that a younger generation, less given to maternalism, and more inclined, during the Popular Front, to join left-wing political movements, provided the constituency for the anti-fascist peace movement. To take one major example of the CMCGF's activity, it was the younger generation of women who, like the young men of their age, reacted to the Spanish Civil War, providing volunteer nurses or sometimes combatants in not negligible numbers, and creating support committees for refugees, where women played a central role.[48]

In the small but key case of LIFPL, we surely see an inner-directed group, whose origins were quite independent from political parties, and untrammelled with relations with male-dominated groups, whatever the later political options of its members. The fact that its leadership came increasingly to support a party line was a reflection of the political choices open to all in the period: after all, Duchêne was far from alone in her move towards a pro-Soviet kind of anti-fascism. But the interesting thing is that the Ligue put up a fight, tearing itself apart in the process, with views being openly expressed in written or spoken form by a genuine constituency of women who were most unlikely to be found writing in the same way to their local party headquarters, or standing up to speak at a mixed political meeting. As was later to be the case in the 1970s, an all-women organization provided a place where 'ordinary women' could express their views without risk of being intimidated by the men who were thoroughly at home in political debate. (Who needed men, one might ask, when Gabrielle Duchêne was around.) There is great unevenness in the political experience and education of these women, as one might expect by the 1930s: both naivety and sophisticated manipulation existed side by side within LIFPL.

CONCLUSION

Historians have sometimes referred to the naivety of the public at large in this period. Another way of saying the same thing is that both men and women felt anxiety over international affairs, even if their views on the topic were ignorant or biased. Of all the developments in French politics in the inter-war period, that of the peace campaigns is one of the most important. Neither before 1914, nor after 1945, were peace campaigns so active an element in French history. These movements impress by their range, variety and intermittently conspicuous campaigns. Yet in narrative histories of these years, their existence is muffled and obscured. Approaches to political history concentrate on the left–right split. Parties and extra-parliamentary movements of both extremes have received regular attention, even when their membership was insignificant, since they contribute to the structuring of long-term left–right distinctions. Pacifism had an awkward tendency to ignore left/right distinctions or to shift between them. Its troops waxed and waned with the changing temperature of international relations. It will no doubt be some time before it is integrated into narrative history, yet no useful purpose is served by pretending it did not exist. More particularly, anyone interested in teasing out the gender implications of peace campaigning will have realized that it mobilized the unpolitical, the amateurs rather than, or as well as, the professionals, women as well as men. There is no need to overstate the case: women were overall in the minority in these campaigns. But it was a significant minority when we relate it to subsequent events.

The evidence from even a rapid overview of peace campaigning is that no simple assumptions can be made about whether peace is automatically a 'women's issue'. To put it rather schematically, there are at least three possible reponses to this question. The first is to deny any necessary connection between pacifism and women as such. This response would point to the many women and certain feminists who supported the war effort and who, while certainly favouring peace after the war (as who did not?), did not make it a priority. The second response is to assert that all women, whether feminists or not, *ought* to be in favour of peace, as mothers, daughters, sisters and wives. Evidence of support for this view comes from the many women who did characterize war as the ultimate evil, in the name of motherhood. Lastly, a specific connection might be made between feminism and pacifism, provided both words are carefully defined. The admittedly small numbers of pacifist-feminists of the founding conference of WILPF argued that men and women should together discuss the problems of international peace, rather than consign women to sex-specific aspects of international gatherings. Pacifism and feminism both had roots in a philosophy of humanism. French women between the wars did not necessarily take up unshakeable positions within any of these lines of thought, but in quite substantial numbers, they did begin to take issue with the question.

We also need to ask how women compared with men on these issues. Some of the evidence suggests that generation and milieu may well be as powerful a factor in political behaviour as sex. At different historical moments, French men and women of various generations reacted differently. The ageing war veterans and the mothers of sons lost in the First World War still wrote anguished letters to the press in 1939, but a younger generation of men and women was more involved in anti-fascism and much influenced by the Spanish Civil War. At the same time, men and women of all ages in milieux strongly committed to peace, such as the primary schoolteachers' union, will have favoured peace in changing contexts across the two decades. Did all-women groups, meeting separately from men, engage in specific ways with the political issues of the day? Did the fact that they downplayed their feminist agenda in favour of international affairs mean that they were losing autonomy, or was it simply evidence of the impossibility of maintaining the same priorities in changing and increasingly fraught circumstances? We do not necessarily have to make the greater or lesser autonomy of women in the peace movement, or the extent to which they explicitly included feminist goals in their aims, important though these things are, the only significant aspect of their participation in the political movements of the day.[49] What is important is that any overview of political history should recognize the peace movements, since if they are omitted, a significant sector of political activity for both sexes goes unremarked.

In terms of the overall argument of this book, which is cumulative, my purpose in this chapter is to insist that there were powerful forces at work in the inter-war years to draw women into public life in a multitude of ways, sometimes emphasizing sexual difference, sometimes burying it in common causes with men, sometimes insisting on the campaign for women's rights. The energies of many of these women were directed into several causes which do not neatly fit left–right divisions: social welfare, feminism and peace, all of which have been referred to in earlier chapters, and all of which are sidelined in political narratives of the period. This is not through some conspiracy by historians, but neither is it completely accidental and inadvertent. It proceeds from a dominant historical narrative of the Third Republic, governed by a republican perspective, articulated round the politics of left and right. This narrative has been built up over the years to the point where it is difficult to think differently about the Third – or any other French – Republic. For this reason, the final chapter will look directly at the relations between gender and the republic.

9

RIGHTS AND THE REPUBLIC
The inter-war years as antechamber to democracy?

If one had to pinpoint the centre of political life in France between the wars, the 'inner sanctum', most people would choose the Palais-Bourbon, the classical building that looks across the Seine towards the Place de la Concorde. Etched in gold on its façade were the words *Chambre des Députés*. Inside is the 'house without windows' or *hémicycle*, in which the directly elected *députés* sat during the Third Republic, as they do under the Fifth, their political views reflected in the seating arrangements from left to right, echoing the origins of these terms during the Revolution of 1789. Behind the debating chamber is a warren of corridors and committee rooms, the *coulisses* in which unofficial politics can take place. A mile to the east, the Palais du Luxembourg houses the Senate, the senior assembly of the French republic. Indirectly elected, the senators have always had longer terms of office than the *députés*, and are less affected by short-term political change.

In the years between the wars, the corridors of both buildings were thronged with men in the parliamentary uniform of the double-breasted suit. Women secretaries and clerks might enter the buildings, visitors to the public galleries were of both sexes, but membership of the inner sanctum depended not only on election, but on having been born male. No woman ever sat as elected representative, nor cast any vote to put anyone there, although as we know three women did take seats on the government benches in 1936, thanks to Léon Blum's unprecedented initiative. Access to the centre of the French political universe was defined not by class, race or creed, but by the shape of one's body. All over France, elected councils in town halls mirrored the national assemblies. Formal politics was reflected in the informal milieu which later historians describe as 'la sociabilité républicaine', centred on the café and the committee room; not formally barred to women, it was an environment unwelcoming to them, both by the sale of alcohol and by the discussion of affairs in which they were pronounced to have no part.

History has not been kind to the politicians of the late Third Republic. One of the earliest and most lucid analyses was Marc Bloch's memoir *L'Etrange Défaite*, written in the aftermath of the débâcle of 1940. Writing much later, Jean Mayeur saw the seeds of trouble in the deep divisions following the Dreyfus affair when, in addition to the rift between Catholics and anticlericals, signs of splits on social and foreign policy became evident. The regime somehow survived the Great War, and even managed an 'Indian summer' until about 1932, he writes, but once the post-1929 crisis struck there was a

> loss of support from the middling classes; a collapse of faith in the virtues of parliamentary liberalism and in political democracy; general exasperation with the struggle between the two blocs [left and right], aggravated by new rifts over foreign policy; a breakdown in communication between political parties and public opinion which had little to do with the parties and which they sought to address in outmoded rhetoric; recourse to decrees instead of legislation; and a chronic inability to take decisions. Such was the spectacle presented by the republic as it drew to a close.
>
> (Mayeur 1984: 402–3)

Most observers agree that while the inter-war years produced a series of tough challenges, the assemblies of the Third Republic were by any standards unequal to such tests of will and nerve. Over the special case of the Popular Front, which in some respects seemed an attempt to break the deadlock, opinions are divided. Some historians have agreed with the analysis associated with Alfred Sauvy, namely that the last thing France needed at this time was a demobilization of the workforce through shorter working weeks and more holidays. In its extreme form, this view concurs with Pétain's famous attack on pre-war politicians for encouraging 'l'esprit de jouissance' rather than 'l'esprit de sacrifice'. Others have argued that the Popular Front deserves credit for taking the first measures to rearm and revitalize French industry. Others again have taken a mixed view. Henri Dubief ended his study of the years to 1938 with the half-romantic reflection that Blum's measures were unfortunate in the short term, beneficial in the long term, that the future belonged to those 'non-élites' who were inspired by 1936: the 'young trade unionists, the new peasant associations, the social Catholic movement, the intellectuals, artists and militants who would bring about the renaissance of the country when the élites had given in to the enemy'.[1] Dubief is here reflecting a widespread reproach levelled at the mature politicians of the 1930s. As James Steel points out, 'the idea that France – the France of the apéritifs and the radical party congress – had become corrupt and decadent, was not confined to the "bien-pensant" or neo-fascist right. It was already abroad in the 1930s on both right and left' and was to be held by Gaullists and Resisters during the war as well as by Pétainists (Steel 1993: 5).

Whatever the justice of these severe remarks, is all this a history to which gender is simply irrelevant? One would think so from the judgments quoted above, for none makes any attempt to relate gender relations to any overall analysis of the politics of these years. (Dubief's comments on the 'non-élites' could refer equally to both sexes, but one suspects that in practice he was thinking only of men.) What exactly is the 'France' referred to above, and sometimes simply assimilated to the Third Republic? 'La classe politique' is often said to be 'cut off from opinion'. This is clearly an over-simplification: politicians for rural areas were regularly attentive to the views of 'la France profonde'; socialist and communist politicians can be assumed to have been in contact with their working-class constituencies. If politicians failed to agree, it was in large measure because opinion among French voters, that is French men, was deeply fractured. Gender division is not usually thought of as part of that splintered consciousness. Although common sense tells us that male voters did not live in some all-male vacuum, and contemporaries were well aware that they did not, republican history is not so sure. Since women were not voters, in most retrospective analysis of republican politics they do not seem to be part either of the 'classe politique' or of public opinion: their own political opinions may or may not have been as divided as men's, but they were in neither *le pays légal* nor *le pays réel*.

Yet as I have been at pains to argue throughout this book, women were not outside politics, even politics as formally defined, let alone the politics of work-place, family and culture. We have noted the interaction of the sexes in several public contexts. As the end of the book approaches, it is time to tackle the question often taken to be central to political identity: the right to vote. If it is agreed that in a polity with representative parliamentary institutions, such as the French Third Republic, the right to vote matters, then it is impossible to discuss the workings of the system without reference to the terms of inclusion and exclusion. We would not dream of embarking on a history of South Africa, for example, without referring to the people who were banned from voting until the mid-1990s. Between the wars, to judge from the amount of parliamentary time devoted to it, the most discussed aspect of political rights within the French republic was whether or not persons of the female sex could be allowed to vote and stand for election. This was not the only potential issue: the question of voting rights for French servicemen was sometimes raised by the Communist party; and resident foreign workers repre-sented a major disenfranchised group. There was a gendered aspect to both these groups of non-voters, since serving soldiers were by definition male, while the majority of immigrant workers were men. But neither of these groups was at the centre of such a prolonged and emotional debate as the one that raged over women.

The long campaign for women's suffrage and the history of feminism in France between the wars have been the subjects of much scholarly enquiry.[2] Both of these will be touched on in what follows, but the agenda is a little different. Its first item is the problem as usually posed. Most writers who have approached it, myself included, have sought to explain 'le retard français', France's lateness in 'granting the vote to women', or as I would prefer to call it, introducing universal suffrage. The inter-war period seems at first sight to be the age when France fell behind other countries in this respect. It will be argued here that the issue conceals more historical complexity than a simple backwardness model might indicate. The second part of the chapter will turn the question around: instead of asking 'why was universal suffrage postponed until 1944/5', it will ask 'why *did* it happen then?'. This may prompt the suggestion that instead of being a time when 'nothing happened' on this front, the inter-war years can be seen as the time of collapsing male monopoly: the antechamber to democracy.

'LE RETARD FRANÇAIS' AND THE GENDER GAP

Under the Second French Republic, all French men over twenty-one were granted the vote by the decree of 5 March 1848. They voted in elections immediately afterwards on 23 April (Rosanvallon 1992: 248–9). Universal suffrage for both sexes did not come until a century later, after the Third Republic had foundered. It proceeded from the ordinance of 21 April 1944 enacted by the Comité Français de Libération Nationale, later known as the Provisional Government of the French Republic, sitting in Algiers. The long gap between these two dates, during which many other western and some non-western countries had granted women voting rights, has understandably caused comment. The famous 'retard français' has most recently been formulated in Rosanvallon's study of universal suffrage. How did it come about that

> a whole century separates the recognition of male suffrage (1848) and female suffrage (1944) whereas the gap is much smaller everywhere else? How can we explain why the political rights of women were recognized in France much later than in many other countries which have a less clear democratic heritage or unconvincing feminist credentials... such as India (1921), the Philippines (1937), or Turkey?
>
> (Rosanvallon 1992: 393)[3]

The question has two parts. If we take first the question of France as compared to other countries, the inter-war period is apparently the time when France really fell behind. Elsewhere, a wave of female emancipation followed the First World War. Whether as a result of women's war work or suffragist arguments or both, 1918–20 saw women receive the vote in no fewer than twenty-one previously all-male polities such as Britain (for women over thirty only, until 1928), the United States, Germany, etc. France was on the verge of joining them when the Chamber of Deputies voted in May 1919 for full political rights for both sexes. As is well known, the Senate eventually blocked this proposal in 1922, and went on to do the same to several similar bills in the inter-war period, thus providing the short-term explanation for the 'French delay'. The Senate's opposition is generally taken to have been inspired very largely by fears of 'the clerical vote', that is, fears that women would vote for parties closer to the church, and opposed to the anticlerical republicanism which was the principal belief of the Radical party. Since the radicals were partners in most government coalitions of the period and since groups incorporating them held an unshakeable majority in the Senate, they were able to block women's suffrage for twenty years or so, aided by more conservative opponents.

All this seems undeniable. With hindsight, however, it can be argued that France's backwardness vis-à-vis other countries, though real, loses much of its significance if placed in context. In the twenty-five years between the Assembly vote in May 1919 and the decree of 1944, Europe had been through a major series of convulsions and many Europeans, men or women, had been deprived of the chance to vote in a regular democratic process. No elections were held in France for nine years, between 1936 and 1945, because of the outbreak of war in 1939, and the same was true of other parliamentary regimes such as Britain – where in any case all women over twenty-one had been free to cast their votes only during the brief interval from 1928 to 1936. Several of France's neighbours had had totalitarian regimes, where no free elections were held for much of the period (Germany after 1933); Italian women had never voted, even before fascism; Spanish women had been briefly enfranchised in the early 1930s but the Civil War had put an end to all that. The period 1919–45 was, in short, one of patchy enfranchisement and disenfranchisement, followed by war, rather than the age of regular electoral history which an unexplained recital of dates might suggest.[4]

In context and in practice, then, French women did not lag quite so far behind their European contemporaries as one might think. It may also be remembered that the fifty years after the Dreyfus affair (1894–1944) formed a long-drawn-out but ultimately finite period in French history, during which the clerical–anticlerical fervour was at its height.[5] With unfortunate timing, women had begun to press seriously for their rights at the turn of the century, just when the governing parties of the republic, having waged an unremitting battle against the church before and during the Separation of 1905, felt most vulnerable to attack, fearing the impact of a clerical backlash. It is not particularly fruitful to ask whether their fears that women voters would contribute to some clerical revival were remotely justified. No doubt the never-quite-exorcized demons of 1848–51 lay behind the apprehension among some republicans that women would destroy the Third Republic, just as the newly enfranchised male peasants of France had destroyed the Second (Rosanvallon 1992: 411–12). At all events, it is no accident that most parliamentary support for women's suffrage, despite Senate reluctance, came in the 'Indian summer' of the 1920s when the danger to the republic appeared to recede, and as France returned to normal after the war. But the storm clouds of the 1930s and the polarization of left–right politics made even those most in favour of women's suffrage once more reluctant to make it a priority. That is in no sense to 'excuse' the delay, merely to relativize it. In context, the short-term aspect of the 'French delay' can be explained *to some extent* by the special circumstances marking this period of French history, while the 'advance' of other countries turns out on scrutiny to be less striking than strict chronology might suggest.

The second part of the question is the gap between France's early granting of rights to the male half of the adult population and its tardy recognition of those of the female half. Here longer-term arguments about the philosophy of republicanism seem quite appropriate. Was the republic constructed not so much without women as against them, as I once suggested? (1986). It has variously been argued by feminist historians that a masculine religion of republicanism, based on fear of occult women's power, made the republic a gendered regime from the start (cf. Landes 1988). Rosanvallon, using not dissimilar arguments, has suggested that the very boldness of the extension of rights to all men, many of them owning little or no property, created the need for a category of non-citizens or dependents, outsiders from citizenship, whose role was precisely to confer all the more value on it for its proud possessors. During the French Revolution, neither domestic servants nor women were 'active' citizens. With some nuances, his approach can quite easily be reconciled with a feminist analysis when applied to the early periods, 1791 or 1848 (Rosanvallon 1992: 130–48).

But the stress on long-term factors is less helpful for the inter-war years. Rosanvallon's key argument is that those countries like Britain, which granted some women some rights earlier than France (the municipal vote, for instance, or making rights conditional on property or age qualifications), held to a philosophy of representation of interests, whereas French republican theory is based on universalism. Women were admitted to the polity in Britain, he suggests, not because they were equal, but because they were different, representing a different set of interests. In France, by contrast,

> The obstacle to women's suffrage was more philosophical than political. Over and above temporary and partisan objections, the granting of limited suffrage in the municipal arena was not available as an alternative approach to citizenship in the framework of French principles. . . . Citizenship cannot be divided up in French public law. *The French delay is not the consequence of greater anti-feminism in France than elsewhere. It proceeds instead from a restrictive and demanding conception of the citizen-individual.*
>
> (Rosanvallon 1992: 409–10, my italics)

The claim here is that France was the home of a universalism not found elsewhere – certainly not in the gradualism of Britain. It is an interesting claim, but hard to substantiate in practice. Not only does it underestimate the recorded willingness of plenty of male republicans to offer women voting rights in France, it also excuses, in the name of a 'philosophy of rights', the anti-feminism (or misogyny) of those who refused to do so. The inter-war years, far from being a time of monolithic and principled opposition to women's political rights by republican purists, were, when closely observed, an age of bitter confrontation between feminists and anti-feminists (of both sexes), most of whom claimed to be republicans.[6]

One has only to look at the number and range of different propositions for women's political rights that came up for debate in the French parliament, to see that by now women's suffrage was a regular feature on the agenda. Prominent politicians whose republican credentials are above suspicion repeatedly proposed granting rights to women, whether on the same terms as men or, for the sake of compromise, with all kinds of variations and half-way houses presumably incompatible with universalism. The arguments put forward by these men, who might have been assumed to have universalism at heart, were often just as 'pragmatic' as the British were supposed to be: they too argued that women would bring something different to politics, a concern for different issues in society, for example. That proposals of this kind did not survive to reach the statute book was a measure of the strong opposition to them, but their frequency and variety do not support the view that they were unthinkable for republicans.

Paul Smith has pointed out, in his very thorough account of the parliamentary campaign for the vote, that the question was practically never off the political agenda between 1919 and 1936, as the briefest summary will illustrate. In May 1919, the Chamber of Deputies voted 344–97 in favour of a clear and all-encompassing proposal, the Bon-Dumont bill, that all electoral laws should apply to citizens of both sexes. This war-worn assembly, elected in 1914, was, like its British counterpart, explicitly minded to 'reward' women for their war work. Both Aristide Briand and René Viviani spoke strongly in favour. The Senate, however, showed no sign even of discussing it, despite a vote by the Chamber in October 1919, asking it to do so. While the upper house postponed its debate, two partial proposals were discussed in the newly elected and now much more conservative lower house: the family vote and votes for war widows. In November 1922, in a climate of expectation, the Senate finally debated the question in general, but refused by a fairly narrow majority, 156 to 134, to pass to discussion of the articles. During 1923 the Chamber considered favourably two further proposals, one for votes for all women over twenty-five (later reduced to twenty-one) and one for universal adult suffrage plus a family vote representing children (Roulleau-Dugage). During 1924 the communists in the Chamber put forward another proposal for equal electoral rights for women, while the conservative campaigner Louis Marin went for the compromise of the municipal vote, with the aim of enfranchising women for the 1925 local elections. In April 1925, the newly elected Chamber considered several proposals concerning the municipal vote and passed one by 390 to 183, but without recommending urgent implementation. During 1926, two further proposals, one from Léon Blum and the socialists, were sent to committee by the Chamber. In 1927 the communists and centrists made another request to have the matter discussed in time for the 1928 parliamentary elections. In July 1927 Poincaré as Prime Minister declared the government in favour of a proposal for the municipal vote, which the Chamber passed by 396 to 24, but despite several requests from the Chamber in 1928 and 1929 it did not appear on the Senate agenda. In February 1932 an amendment to the electoral law enfranchising women was vetoed by the Chamber by 307 to 0, with 283 abstentions (explained by political reasons). Yet again, the veteran socialist Bracke pressed the government 'to use all its influence with the Senate so that that Assembly may discuss the texts voted on this subject by the Chamber of Deputies and several times communicated to the Senate' (approved 463–38). In July 1932 the Senate did consider the question, but concluded that there was 'no urgency', and further attempts to rouse the senators were unsuccessful. Before the 1935 local elections another attempt was made in the Chamber to have the municipal vote granted to women (won 305–236), and a further 'full rights' proposal from Bracke was sent to committee. In 1936, with the newly elected Popular Front government and an Assembly further to the left than the previous one, the indefatigable Louis Marin brought what was to be the last suffrage proposal to the Chamber. Calling for full electoral and eligibility rights, it was passed by the largest margin ever, 488 to 1 (the one was an error). Government ministers were among the 93 abstainers, thus indicating their unwillingness to give it priority. This bill too was buried by the Senate until the outbreak of war. The first and last of these proposals were broad enough to be compatible with republican universalism: most of all the others represented some form of compromise.[7]

What does this extraordinary catalogue suggest? Setting aside the possibility, by no means implausible, that many *députés* cynically voted in favour of women's rights, safe in the conviction that the Senate would carry on blocking them, it nevertheless tells us that parliamentarians were perfectly content for their constituents to see their names regularly appearing for the cause, whether or not their support was half-hearted. It also tells us that support was not confined to one or other part of the political spectrum (although it is clear that the most consistent opposition came from the Radical party and other anticlericals on the left). It tells us that some of the leading politicians across the board (Briand, Poincaré, Blum, Cachin, Marin, etc.) spoke in favour of the cause. It tells us that partial and pragmatic proposals were made alongside calls for all-out enfranchisement, with the aim of seizing opportunities such as impending local elections. The regular gaps in the stream of proposals tell us that political contingency sometimes sidelined this issue in favour of other more pressing ones but, for all that, the impression cannot be escaped that women's suffrage had secured a regular place in the timetable of every assembly since 1919, with greater enthusiasm being shown during the 1920s, and a corresponding decline after 1936. It also tells us that formidable powers of opposition were vested in the intricate system of delays and debates that marked the parliamentary politics of the republic, and that the motivation for the delay was strong on the part of the comparatively few, but very powerful men who consistently blocked the reform. (It was not, of course, the only 'reform' they blocked.) Christine Bard has argued that 'we ought to relocate the problem: it was the force of resistance lined up against any reform that explains the "French delay", rather than the weakness of the women and men fighting for reform.'[8]

So at the most formal level, not to speak of political life outside parliament, the inter-war years witnessed prolonged, if irregular, pressure for women's enfranchisement and correspondingly fierce rearguard resistance to the idea. In that respect, this was a period like no other in French history. While many other countries had put the issue behind them or out of mind altogether, France went on worrying away at it for twenty years. It might therefore be argued that 'le retard français' is a slightly misleading concept. It pushes us to look for reasons for France's backwardness, whereas if we turned the question round and asked why the men of France could *no longer resist* giving women the vote in 1944, we find ourselves obliged to put more emphasis on the stimulus to change – a perspective in which the years leading up to the decree of 1944 gain in importance. Rather than start the clock in 1848 (or 1791), as many histories do, or trace the history of the campaign for women's suffrage, as has been done in some detail elsewhere, it now seems to me that an account with gender as a focus might start by seeing 1944/5 as a key turning-point in French democratic and republican history and work backwards.

In this perspective, the inter-war period, rather than simply one when 'nothing happened', becomes the last episode of ferment and uncertainty about political rights as between the sexes. In the course of reassessing the inter-war period, however, the entire historiography surrounding the coming of universal suffrage in France cries out for scrutiny. In my view, it has been ideologically constructed in a way that needs to be decoded.

IRRESISTIBLE FORCE OR MOVABLE OBJECT?

Ten years ago I wrote an exploratory essay about the misremembering of the events of 1944/5, as they related to the republic and universal suffrage. Today it still seems to me that the historiography of these events remains a major problem for anyone hoping to introduce gender as a concept into French history. It spills back into the pre-war years and forward to our own time, and until we have found a way to handle it, the gender-blind will go on leading the gender-blind. To grapple with this issue will mean making a brief excursion forward from the inter-war period, in the interests of putting it into context. In other words, one needs to reconsider the breaks between 'the inter-war years', 'wartime' and 'the post-war years', which it is so tempting to see as major historical divisions.

Many political surveys of the Liberation analyse the years 1944–6 in terms of whether or not they marked a 'new beginning', a break with the past.[9] In one respect, at least, there is a short answer to that. The ordinance of 21 April 1944 provided the principle of universal suffrage, which was put into practice at the local elections of spring 1945, followed by elections to the National Assembly in autumn that year. (In fact after ten years of no elections, the French people voted half a dozen times in quick succession between 1945 and 1946.)[10] This is not generally how this significant development has been recorded by historians. A brief survey of all the most obvious places to look for mentions of it suggests that it represents an aporia, or difficulty, of major proportions. Almost without exception, the event is elided, or referred to only in passing. In particular it is viewed as entirely concerning women.[11] Can this be the reason why the information is so often conveyed in an aside or a subordinate clause, or literally in parenthesis to the main narrative: 'besides, the electorate had been considerably enlarged, after the establishment of female suffrage' (Becker 1988: 17); 'the female vote (established by the ordinance of 21 April 1944), political events under the Popular Front and Vichy, and the desire for change broadly explain the results [of the local elections of 1945]' (Sirinelli 1993: 240); 'Frenchmen and Frenchwomen (who were voting for the first time) had to reply to two questions in a referendum' (Berstein and Milza 1983: 94). In a well-established tradition, several writers use the rhetoric of the gift: women were given, granted or allowed something they had not 'received' before: 'For the first time women were allowed to vote' (Price 1993: 302). In the popular mind, one person, General de Gaulle, 'granted women the vote', something for which he was often thanked after the war: 'the eclipse of the Radical party and the suspension of parliament enabled General de Gaulle to introduce the female vote by decree in

1944' (Zeldin 1973: 360); 'Frenchwomen were given the vote in 1945 by the reformist Liberation Government under de Gaulle (not noted for his feminism)' (Ardagh 1982: 348). A gift may be a quid pro quo, in this case for good behaviour during the war, such as joining the Resistance. 'The share of women [in the political arena], with the food crisis, and the obtaining of the right to vote for the municipal elections, was intimately linked to their Resistance activity' (Rioux 1980, vol. 1: 78). There seems to be no clear consensus on exactly how to present the information; but no major history describes it as 'the introduction of universal suffrage'.[12]

What all these rhetorical strategies do, one way and another, and surely with no malign intent, is to resist the idea that this event was important to men. By so doing, they deprive it of historical significance. History, they imply, is somewhere else – in the constitutional debates about whether parliament or president should have more power, whether or not the coal mines were to be nationalized. One reason may be that the sequence of events themselves is a little untidy: there was no clear date evident to contemporaries, as was the case in 1848. But beyond that, historians are the prisoners of their own terminology. I have found it quite hard myself to avoid referring to 'women getting the vote'. If, on the contrary, the same thing were called, quite accurately, the coming of universal suffrage, one suspects it would have more claim on universal curiosity. Historians would feel obliged to ask why it happened, why it happened *then*, who was responsible, and to find out as far as possible what facts underpin the accuracy or otherwise of the sentence 'General de Gaulle granted women the vote in 1944'.

As with any major event, a mixture of short- and long-term forces may turn out to be at work. Short-term factors must include the politics of the Free French in Algiers in 1944. The famous ordinance of 21 April 1944 was a long document, proposing constitutional arrangements for France after the Liberation. Women's suffrage, mentioned in only three of its articles, was by no means the chief preoccupation of the drafters of the text. After the Allied landings in North Africa in November 1942, de Gaulle, as head of the Free French, had transferred his headquarters from London to Algiers and by the end of 1943 had reimposed himself as the leader of the Comité Français de Libération Nationale with whom the Allies were obliged to do business. Before the CFLN could be transformed into a provisional government, de Gaulle needed to demonstrate the legitimacy of the institutions he had created, and to convince the Allies that a liberated France would adopt its own democratic institutions, with no need for an Allied Military Government such as was established in Italy and planned for Germany. Given the long-standing distrust of the Free French (and of de Gaulle in particular) expressed in word and deed by the United States from 1940 to 1943, it was important to show that he could draw on support from all quarters of the French Resistance.[13]

To this end the Consultative Assembly held its opening session in the Palace of the Algerian Assemblies in Algiers on 3 November 1943. Hardly representative in any arithmetical sense, it included delegates from the Resistance inside and outside

France, parliamentarians who had not supported Vichy, and local notables. One woman, Marthe Simard, was present at the opening session, in itself a symbolic rupture of former taboos, and she was later joined by one or two others, such as Resistance worker Lucie Aubrac. Although the political parties of the 'old republic' were to some extent discredited, care was actually taken to see that they were present, since they stood for pre-war democracy, and indeed their parliamentary practices soon imposed themselves upon the Assembly.

A committee on 'legislation and the reform of the state' was created, chaired by a Corsican Radical party ex-*député*, Paul Giacobbi. When the question of women's votes was raised, he was quick to wave it aside as inopportune and far from urgent, a view that was not at once challenged. Eventually, on 8 January 1944, which perhaps deserves to be called a historic date, the committee voted in favour of the principle of women's suffrage, but decided that this would not be enacted until all the prisoners of war and other deportees had returned to French soil. Any Constituent Assembly to be elected immediately after the end of the war would have to be the result of male votes only. Reflecting pre-war thought processes, the committee allowed that women might become local councillors in the interim period (and as they actually were at the time inside Vichy France). It was not until the debates of 22–4 March 1944 that these 'safeguards' were removed. Local elections were due to be timetabled as the first after Liberation and, in the first move for change, a Christian democrat, Robert Prigent, persuaded the committee to grant women the right to vote, as well as to stand in these elections. Then, on 24 March, Fernand Grenier, the communist ex-*député* and mayor of Saint-Denis, argued strongly for granting women the vote purely and simply on the same terms as men. The communist presence, according to Grenier's first-hand account, was an essential element at Algiers, and the anticlerical argument had never cut much ice with the party anyway, as we have noted. Most socialists present, whose own programme still included women's suffrage, voted in favour, as did most gaullists. Radical party members continued to oppose it, but the days when the radicals had controlled the middle ground were over. The final voting in committee was 51 votes to 16. A month later, the CFLN published the ordinance in full. Article 1 said that a Constituent Assembly would be elected by 'all French men and women over the age of majority'; Article 9 enjoined local authorities to see that women were enrolled on the electoral register; article 17 said that 'Women will be voters and eligible for election on the same terms as men.'[14]

Albert and Nicole du Roy, in one of the fullest available accounts of these proceedings, accept that the communists played a leading role. Grenier was the man who 'gave the measure a push in the right direction at the right time', they point out, agreeing with him that it is inaccurate to say that de Gaulle 'granted women the vote'. De Gaulle's position in 1944 is clear enough: he was in favour, but left the debates to the commission. What cannot be known is what he would have done if the commission had not allowed women's suffrage. It was certainly not at the centre of his preoccupations, but he regarded it as more or less settled well before 1944, as can be judged from his often-quoted message to the Resistance on

23 June 1942: 'Once the enemy is driven from our land, all French men and women (*toutes les hommes et toutes les femmes de chez nous*) will elect a National Assembly which in the full exercise of its sovereignty will determine the country's destiny' (de Gaulle 1954, vol. 1: 430). This text was intended to reassure the Resistance inside France that de Gaulle was committed to restoring republican democracy after the war, and was not the authoritarian dictator some suspected. Subsequent comment has often hinted that de Gaulle and the gaullists favoured women's votes because parties of the right, or with clerical connections, would benefit, and such a calculation cannot of course be entirely discounted. What is less often remarked on is the international pressure, of which de Gaulle was acutely aware, for France to prove its democratic credentials. Since the pressure came from Britain and the United States, countries where women's suffrage was not in doubt, the non-enfranchisement of women would almost certainly be seen as a black mark (although to my knowledge there is no documentary evidence to indicate this).[15]

If de Gaulle's position is clear, that of the internal Resistance is not, or rather the indications all run the other way. Allied opinion was not a particularly potent factor inside France, where traditional politics rumbled on in the Conseil National de la Résistance, the umbrella organization on which all movements were represented by late 1943. Since the notion had wide currency after the war that women were granted their vote in recognition of their role in the Resistance, it is ironic that the official Resistance made no such call at any time. Like the committees in Algiers, the CNR had begun work on drafts of post-war constitutional reform. A small committee had surveyed opinion among resisters and drafted proposals which went to Algiers in autumn 1943. These did mention the possibility of women voting, though in cautious terms. But the official programme adopted by the CNR in March 1944 specifically says that its aim is to 'ensure the establishment of the broadest possible democracy, by restoring the means of expression to the French people by *reinstating* universal suffrage' – without indicating any change in the definition.[16] The same divisions as were occurring in Algiers had made themselves felt within the Resistance, with socialists and communists in favour, and radicals, rather stronger inside France, against. Interestingly, one difference was the desire, expressed by the committee in its proposals sent to Algiers, that a future government would introduce the family vote, i.e. extra votes granted to heads of families depending on the number of children. The family vote had also been a strong feature in the various constitutional proposals framed by the Vichy authorities, culminating in the eighth and last draft constitution drafted in January 1944, which also granted women the vote under certain conditions. It is clear from these debates that there were not as many rigid distinctions as one might suppose between Resistance thinking and Vichy over some aspects of the desired state reforms. In the end, republican orthodoxy of the one-citizen-one-vote variety prevailed, with the crucial redefinition of women as citizens finally enshrined in the constitution of the Fourth Republic in 1946. But this had not been a message clearly transmitted by official representatives of the internal Resistance. Retrospectively, the change has sometimes been represented as a logical development of Resistance, but some sleight of hand is involved. Hanna Diamond could find little trace of calls for women's political rights in the clandestine literature of the Toulouse area which she surveyed for her thesis.[17]

All the above can be seen as part of the short-term context of women's citizenship. When considered in detail, it adds considerable qualification to the (to my mind) inadequate assumption that the war years were the key and that women's Resistance activities provided the trigger. Women's resistance was certainly invoked in Algiers, and Grenier specifically described feeling ashamed that the heroic women he had encountered during the war might have no rights in the new France. Women of course participated in the Resistance, in ways which have even now not been fully recognized, but this point has to be treated with caution. The small number of women formally honoured by male colleagues for Resistance work sits uneasily with the readiness of the same men to explain the granting of the vote entirely in terms of this argument.

More seriously, the short-term context was itself embedded in both the medium and the long term. All those involved in debating the question in 1944 were extremely familiar with the debates over women's rights from before the war: the idea did not spring unbidden into the minds of the committee in Algiers. In fact it is historically more plausible to see women's Resistance activity as itself part of a longer continuum of women's activities, reaching back into pre-war years. Despite the temptation to see the years 1940–4 as a watershed in French consciousness, wartime politics, including those of the Resistance, did not come from nowhere, but had their roots in the pre-war years, sometimes quite specifically in the confrontational politics of the Popular Front era.

This is not the same thing as arguing for explicit continuity between pre-war feminism and the Resistance. It is true that comparatively little research has been done of the prosopographic kind on the generation straddling the years before and after 1940.[18] But in any case, the established leadership of the feminist movement in particular had been dominated by an older generation, already grown-up during the Great War. Many of these women had died (Maria Vérone, Marguerite Durand) or faded from active politics by the time of the war (Cécile Brunschvicg). Those who were Jewish (Brunschvicg again or Marcelle Kaemer-Bach) went into hiding, some being deported. Even some of these older women played a part in Resistance activities. But active resisters were more likely to be younger women whose political commitments in the 1930s were not necessarily, or not primarily, as feminists. Christine Bard found very little continuity between the feminists she studied and the Resistance, and she also argues that women in the Resistance tend to describe their motivation as having very little to do with being 'women' or 'feminists' anyway (Bard 1995: 439 ff.).

But membership of a feminist association was only one form of political activity open to women before the war. As we have seen, youth movements, anti-fascist groups, committees for aid to Spain, the strike movement of 1936 and so on were all possible preparations for Resistance, even setting aside personal or family connections. The evidence is fragmentary and for obvious reasons relates to the politics of the left, but examples can give hints of continuity. Hanna Diamond's local study, based on oral history, had available only the testimony of younger women; the oldest of those whom she interviewed in the 1980s had been thirty-eight in 1940, and the great majority had been in their teens and twenties. Among her sample, twenty-five had been actively involved in the Resistance, and of those most were single women, too young to have had much in the way of pre-war commitments. Eight respondents did, however, have pre-war political experience, mostly in organizations attached to the Communist party.[19]

A similar pattern emerges from another recorded sample, the first generation of women elected to parliament after the war. In the first three elected National Assemblies of the post-war period (October 1945, April 1946, October 1946) a total of forty-nine women was elected to parliamentary seats (most of them were re-elected in all three Assemblies, but the total includes a few names who sat in only one). The percentage of women *députés* was not to rise as high again for many years and it is customary to refer to these pioneers as 'the Resistance generation', since many of them had played some role in Resistance and Liberation committees. However, when examined more closely, many of these women can also be shown to have been politically active in the years before the war. Most of them were too young to remember the First World War or to have been active in the 1920s (only nine of the forty-nine were born before 1900, twenty-four were born between 1900 and 1910, sixteen between 1910 and 1920). Even so, of the twenty-seven communist women, who do of course skew the sample somewhat, sixteen had some kind of recorded political activity before the war, mostly as party activists or members of the communist youth movement, one or two in the peace movements closely linked to the party. Among the others (socialists and MRP), the majority had some kind of pre-war link with politics, whether party activism, activity in a trade union or youth movement, or occasionally in the feminist movement; they included a number of journalists and lawyers. Some were members of political families, with husbands or fathers who had held political office, and one or two had been professionally associated with family members in politics. Unsurprisingly, most of the sample are recorded as having some kind of Resistance activity. But, of these, only eight did not *also* have records of pre-war activism. In other words, Resistance activity alone does not explain their selection.[20]

The women parliamentarians were a special group, selected by the parties from among the most prominent and competent women known to them at the Liberation. But one might legitimately conclude that participation in the Resistance (whether by men or by women) was likely to be in some way linked to the (mostly left-wing) political culture of pre-war France. In the case of either sex, one is talking about a very small minority. But such threads of continuity as there are did not depend on the right to vote so much as on political participation in exactly the less official or more committed kind of politics we have been surveying. This medium-term context should not be overlooked.

Finally, although personal membership of the feminist movement cannot easily be shown to have a direct link with post-war politics, the long-term influence of feminism as a philosophy and a thinkable idea is a different matter. Most commentators have played down considerably the influence of feminism both before 1918 and between the wars. Rarely if ever is the decision of 1944 seen as having anything to do with organized campaigns by women, and pre-war suffragism was at one time routinely dismissed as variously feeble, unrepresentative, bourgeois, over-timid and without any impact on opinion.[21] The early studies of French feminism have tended to highlight its theoretical and militant origins in the nineteenth century and its 'peak' in about 1914. Little detailed work had until recently been done on the movement between the wars. This has now changed, in particular with the massive thesis by Christine Bard which amounts to an attempt to rehabilitate inter-war feminism as a strong force, active across a whole range of women's experiences – work, sexuality, citizenship and peace.

Bard does not attempt to argue that feminism mobilized large numbers of French women. Her arguments are relative: the maximum number of people (of both sexes) who could formally be described as feminists – i.e. favouring a change in the status of women – was probably no more than about 200,000 to 300,000 at any time. In a France where membership of political movements was in any case low and prone to fluctuation, where even the trade unions in the years 1919 to 1935 had historically low membership, these numbers are still far from negligible and their visibility from time to time meant that people were aware of them. Second, there is no doubt that the movement was extremely diverse, both in its philosophies and in its objectives, so much so that Bard's thesis speaks of 'féminismes' in the plural. Such divisions have often been described as regrettable, but she argues that they merely reflect the political divisions so evident throughout French politics and society at the time. The division of the movement is not necessarily a sign of weakness any more than of strength. Bard identifies three possible types of feminism: first, a radical, avant-garde, usually left-wing consciousness, closely associated with neo-Malthusianism and not necessarily concerned with suffrage; second, a reformist, pragmatic feminism, grouping the majority of the official organizations such as the CNFF, the LFDF and the UFSF – for such women the suffrage, although a central demand, was not the only cause to be fought for; and third, a more 'moderate', i.e. conservative form of feminism, associated more closely with the suffrage as a way of representing women in their traditional role, and represented by the Catholic UNVF. The very fact there there were divisions meant that feminism had several faces, appealing to different sectors of society. To measure its influence is far from easy, whatever date one picks. The point is that these ideas were available and thinkable in pre-war society, not new in 1944.

To estimate the impact the feminist movement as a whole had in French society between the wars means recognizing the range of possible arenas for intervention. Suffrage was not the only issue dear to the hearts of militants. As has already been noted, apart from a wide range of issues connected with social problems and with civil rights, many women activists devoted more of their efforts to the peace movement at certain times. But the suffrage issue was a goad to action – it inspired two or three generations of inter-war women to keep up the pressure at the heart of the parliamentary system, operating both at a pragmatic and a symbolic level. The argument can be made that the movement kept on applying pressure where it mattered:

> The circumspect approach of the UFSF [for example] which envisaged a campaign for the vote in stages, beginning with the right to the local vote, the Union's republican and philanthropic image, its insistence on linking the suffrage with the battle led by women against social evils [*les fléaux sociaux*] ... and lastly the personal links some of its leaders had with *députés*, mayors and senators, help explain its success with a non-negligible fraction of the *classe politique*.
>
> (Bard 1993: 66)

The political pressure exerted by suffragism in the short term was arguably more qualitative – in the sense of being applied at strategic points – than quantitative, attempting a mass consciousness-raising campaign. It was unsuccessful in the short term, but given the arena in which the decision was likely to be taken, not impractical. Its long-term impact within French society is harder to estimate. The decision of 1944 was taken neither by the French population at large nor by the directly elected single-sex Assemblies of the Third Republic; it was taken instead by a haphazard and only notionally representative selection of people (of both sexes, although women were a tiny minority) which had not yet even taken the name of 'provisional government'. To explain this decision therefore may not require us to demonstrate the impact of feminism on French society as a whole, but it does imply noting the particular past experience of the group in question, which can quite specifically be related to short-, medium- and long-term factors. The delegates to Algiers had not been living on some other planet before the war.

Most crucially of all, when that decision was taken, and when it became generally known, there is no record of open opposition to it, whether from politicians or the electorate in the post-war period – on the contrary it was broadly welcomed in the press and in articulated public opinion. Some commentators have expressed the view that the right of women to vote was a 'ripe fruit' ready to be harvested. 'The reform had become inevitable,' as Christine Bard puts it. Andrée Lehman wrote in the 1960s that 'hearts and minds had been prepared for it'. A street poll in October 1944 found that everyone asked a view was in favour of it.[22] It might be suggested that if the measure met so little explicit resistance from either men or women, the argument had largely been won during the long-term war of attrition before 1939. As to how readily the post-war political world adjusted to welcome women politicians, that is another story. In some ways the 1940s and 1950s could be argued to be a more difficult period for women's political participation than the 1930s, when the absence of political rights was in some sense a stimulus to action. Perhaps, then, 'le retard français' is a false problem which needs reformulating in relation to post-war France.

CONCLUSION

The decree of 1848 had been accompanied by a brave statement: 'Dating from this law, there are no longer any proletarians in France, *il n'a plus de prolétaire en France*' (Rosanvallon 1992: 286). No such ringing testimony greeted genuine universal suffrage when it appeared in 1944 or 1945. The argument of this chapter is that the relationship between this important event and the way it was perceived at the time and afterwards by historians is more complex than one might expect. We can sympathize with historians faced with an apparently confusing sequence of events at the Liberation, but not with their general failure to recognize that by any standards this was an important moment in republican history, and their disinclination to explore the causes and history behind it.

We are apparently faced with two approaches to the events of 1944–5, one from women's history, the other from men's. Women's history cannot avoid taking this date to mark something important, a watershed in the history of rights. Yet, at the same time, most modern feminist historians, with the advantage of hindsight, have gone to some pains to argue that it did not greatly change the political face of France, and that it did not in itself lead to immediate major change in women's lives. Françoise Thébaud has been quoted earlier in this book pointing out that both before and after the vote, a policy of pronatalism and family legislation, which had little to do with notions of individual citizenship, sought to define the family roles of men and women. Despite their new rights, it seems that French women did not see politics as a world in which they could identify themselves, rather as a 'male club that means to remain so'. Hanna Diamond's sample of women in Toulouse mostly reported that they did not find voting a very liberating experience, nor did they express any interest in the 'politicking' of the post-war years. Feminist political scientists, putting it slightly differently, argue that 'in western political discourse, citizenship remains defined as an activity practised in an androcentric field of action and represented through the codes of a phallocentric discourse' (Jones 1990: 781). In recent years, the fact that every French parliament since the war has been over 90 per cent male has led to campaigns for quotas or for parity of representation of the sexes.[23] Arguments originating both in equality and difference have been marshalled in favour of rethinking the concept of representative politics. Marie-Victoire Louis has, for example, pointed out the contradictory definitions of public and private and of sexual offences that emerge from analysis of the revision of the French Penal Code, a revision carried out by parliamentary committees containing virtually no women (Louis 1994).

In one sense, then, the argument that 1944–5 was a watershed has been challenged by the very people to whom it remains a significant date: whether or not women were formally citizens of the republic, feminists have argued, politics and man-made laws have been carried out without or against them. The republic has remained single sexed, in continuity with the situation before 1939. Looked at from another perspective, that of the historian who pays scant attention to 1944–5 by failing to note that it saw a momentous change in the nature of the French republic, the idea of a watershed never seems to have been considered in the first place. The extension of the vote to women, when analysed within 'men's history', is seen as making no serious difference to politics, political life or the republic. And in the writings of such historians, women's very existence remains equally under-recorded in French political history, whether they are referring to the years before the vote or after.

These two otherwise opposing groups of historians seem to converge in down-grading the importance of the 'granting of the vote'. My view is that 1944–5 was not a solution to anything, but became part of the problem, and in that sense I too would argue that there is some degree of continuity in practice between the inter-war years and those that followed. But my conclusion differs from the two interpretations above. First, whatever its immediate impact, the arrival of universal suffrage is incontrovertibly a major development within the logic of French republicanism. For historians professing republican values, it is therefore incomprehensible that they should fail retrospectively to grant it importance, or to explore its circumstances. Second, the continuity I would underline is that before and after this event, both men and women existed within the 'magnetic field' of politics. Their relations were complex and extremely unequal, but they simply cannot be either taken for granted or described as if one of the sexes were not present.

They can be historicized in a number of ways – for instance by suggesting that there may actually have been *more* political activity by women in the inter-war years than immediately after the war, since formal exclusion from politics was a spur to action for those of the earlier generation. The suffrage question itself, as was argued earlier in this chapter, received more concentrated attention from more people during the two inter-war decades than it ever had before or would ever again. In that sense, the male monopoly was perhaps being breached. Should we then see these years as an antechamber to a new democracy, rather than a time when women stood in complete outer darkness? Yes, I think we should. But perhaps the image, like all images, is not perfect. If the old order was showing clear signs of crumbling, it is not evident that a new one took its place. The idea of an antechamber suggests that entering the 'house without windows' would represent complete success. Instead, the way politics developed after the war suggests that the culture of parliamentary and representative politics had been profoundly moulded by the practices created when it was an all-male space. Fears expressed before the war that the republic would be changed or threatened by the admission of women turned out to be misplaced, at any rate in the short run. Such fears reposed on the firm belief that the republic stood for something intrinsically good, rather than something flawed from within by its exclusion of half the population. By assuming that 'granting the vote' solved all ills, I would argue, the flaws originating in the man-made system have not been analysed, and perhaps in a way, by misremembering what happened at the Liberation, historians have helped to prevent them even from being addressed. The inner sanctum itself is not yet visibly the home of a double-sexed democracy.

CONCLUSION

Writing in the summer of 1940, when France had been overcome and occupied by Hitler's forces, the historian Marc Bloch set down his thoughts about the 'strange defeat'. War in modern times, he wrote, spared nobody and was the concern of all:

> In the face of national peril and the duties it presses on us, all adults . . . are equal and it is a strange misunderstanding to claim that any of them can be recognized as having some kind of privilege of immunity. . . . As for the nation, there can be no worse tragedy for it than to be compelled to sacrifice the existences on which its destiny depends. Alongside these living forces, others weigh very little. I would not exempt even women from this, at least apart from young mothers whose safety is indispensable to their children. Our women companions of today laugh at the fainting-fits of their grandmothers. They are quite right to do so and I do not see why courage should be any less natural to them than to us, or less obligatory. In the days of professional armies, the soldier, whether lord or mercenary, shed his blood for those who had contracted with him. In exchange, non-combatant populations maintained him out of their taxes or paid him a wage. If he allowed their safety to suffer, they would have legitimate cause for complaint. The contract had not been kept. In our time, anyone who is fit enough becomes a soldier, no one in the threatened city [*personne dans la cité menacée*] escapes mobilization, with its obligations and risks. That is the only clear way: anything else is sentimentality or cowardice.
>
> (Bloch 1990: 163–4)

This was not quite the view taken by the French air force or army in 1939, but the idea of the nation being mobilized, men and women alike, was not completely unthinkable, as the Paul-Boncour bill of 1927 had suggested. The same year had seen Henriette Alquier stand trial on a charge which was in a sense related to the idea that all French people, men and women alike, were responsible for all: she was thought to have contravened the law restricting free speech on contraception, and thus indirectly to be damaging France's future armies in the field. Significantly, Bloch used the word 'cité' when he referred to the threatened city, not the more ordinary word 'ville'. *Cité* implies the *civitas* or state, rather than just an urban

222

settlement. The *cité* is the *pays légal* if you like, as opposed to the *pays réel*. French women were in the *ville* but not in the *cité* at the time he wrote.

Michèle Riot-Sarcey, reviewing the story so far of 'women's history in France', also uses the term *cité* when she argues that the history of women has been tolerated so long as it remains within certain bounds:

> [But] its interference in the field of political history in particular is not accepted, because the presence or absence of women in the city [*la cité*] is not admitted in political thought, which is dominated by the concept of the universal. The neuter or neutral, which is peculiarly masculine, determines the presuppositions accompanying this mode of thought.

Despite much research that demonstrates beyond reasonable doubt that the exclusion, subjugation or separate (generally worse) treatment of women is readable from almost every historical document, she maintains, 'women's destiny remains a sort of a-historical given, whereas men's is developed in a cultural, social and political context which can be restored in all its historicity.'[1]

Whichever way one turns, political history seems to be the test case for altering the historical agenda. Throughout this book, the concept of the political has deliberately been used in a fairly restricted sense: to refer to the kind of activity that most of us would recognize as related directly or indirectly, but at no very great remove, to the common-sense meaning of the word 'politics'. If we look at aviation, we are bound to consider government defence policy; social work and childcare relate to welfare policy; peace campaigns and civil rights associations, even youth movements, are part of the network of interest groups openly putting pressure on legislators – and so on. When primary sources have been used, they are the usual sources for political history – the press, reports of parliamentary debates, archives of associations, personal papers of politicians and public figures, and so on. This study has not drawn upon those sources of 'unofficial knowledge' that a broader social or cultural portrait of inter-war France might have assembled. It might have been possible to approach the subject from another direction and have written a completely different, and no doubt fascinating, history about the politics of everyday life. But I wanted to look rather at the everyday life of political folk – of both sexes – hoping to find a way of challenging definitions of politics from which the unpowered, or those deprived of a historical voice, were absent. No very big deal, these days, this is one form of the 'return of the repressed' which Raphael Samuel sees as having become part of the inescapable politics of history.[2]

At my elbow throughout the time of writing have been the mainstream histories of France that I use regularly for teaching, the authors I consult about 'what happened'. In the introduction, they were described as a classic corpus, and for all their variety, whether produced inside or outside France, they display a number of constants in terms of language and priorities. It bears repeating that I admire and find useful a great deal of what they have to say; and refer to them all the time. But, in the course of writing the book, what seemed to become clearer was that the obstacle to a gendered analysis of these years in France was something more specific than absent-mindedness or just 'forgetting about women'. The real problem was a particular form of gender-blindness related to French republicanism, arising from allegiance to a particular model of the republic. In other countries and other histories, different versions would probably apply.

Because of the vocabulary it adopts and the priorities it gives certain subjects, French republican historiography takes a broadly left-wing approach: grafted on to an economic analysis of society, today's republicanism regularly uses the language of class. But comparatively few historians writing today are explicitly Marxist, and it is to some extent as Marxism has waned as an intellectual force in France that republicanism has survived more generally in society as a more impregnable philosophy, distinguished by the importance it gives to the concepts of liberty and rights. What is more, the post-1970 reappraisal of the Occupation years has encouraged historians to reassert republican values, with Vichy seen as the counter-model for which responsibility is simultaneously accepted and refused. Another understandable boost to republicanism has been the rise in recent years of the Front National.

Viewed from across the Channel, French republicanism seems entirely admirable in many ways, not least for its everyday vocabulary. I remember seeing in a Paris street a sign forbidding anyone to leave bicycles on the pavement. Over a defiantly parked bicycle, its owner or someone else had written in chalk, 'Le citoyen a tous les droits': the citizen (in the masculine) has every right. But this grammatically gendered example reminds us as forcefully as anything can that while a philosophy of rights may exist in the abstract, the French republic is not and never has been a set of timeless principles, it has a real history and has had real exclusion zones.

In a recent book devoted to analysing 'the republican model', a number of authors set out to explore why 'the Republic is not just a régime, but a true political model, corresponding to the aspirations of the French [*les Français*]' (Berstein *et al.* 1992: 7). They agree in locating the 'golden age' of the model very precisely in French history, between about 1900 and 1930–9, dates that cause one to reflect. They run broadly from the Dreyfus affair, the 'founding myth' of the Third Republic as Michel Winock rightly calls it, to the Vichy regime, 'that rape of the Republic' (ibid.: 32). The threats to justice (posed by the Dreyfus affair) and to freedom (posed by Vichy) have had the counter-effect of creating an apparent golden age when justice had indeed been defended and liberty was not yet under threat. But whose liberty? These were exactly the years when debates raged sporadically over the admission of women to the city, a question that always got the answer no. Republican theory, which regularly makes obeisance to Condorcet, should allow citizenship to all sentient and reasonable adults (cf. ibid.: 229 ff.). The practice of the Republic seems in this case to have been more powerful than the theory, rather than the other way round as argued by Pierre Rosanvallon (1992). No historian of France writing today would now dream of denying the right of women to be full citizens. But a degree of shared amnesia about this aspect of the quite recent republican past cannot be entirely without effect on the way the history of that precise period is approached.

The neutral citizen of liberal democratic theory has been challenged by feminist political scientists in several cultures,[3] but there is a particular resistance in France to abandoning the vocabulary of 'les droits de l'homme' – for historical reasons which should not be underestimated. The Rights of Man are nothing less than a *lieu de mémoire*, a well-spring inspiring the discourse of the educational and scientific establishment. Writing from within the French context, Nicole-Claude Mathieu argues that

> the question of language is far from superficial, in that ideological representations of the two sexes are expressed in a manner that is quite unconscious, yet very concrete, whether in the syntactical and lexical structure of scientific pronouncements or in everyday speech. The general and the masculine are purely and simply identified as the same thing, and unconsciously obliterate the female category as a social subject.[4]

In writing about inter-war France, then, to return to our sheep, it may be easier to recognize why certain patterns run through any political narrative. The clash between left and right is the main plot of the opera, defence of the republic and its particular form of democracy is the side taken by the good guys. Hence the large numbers of graduate students who have worked on the implantation of the Communist party during the Popular Front years (generally from a sympathetic stance), or on the extreme right-wing leagues (practically always from a non-sympathetic stance). Some subjects are awkwardly positioned in relation to left and right and have only recently started to find chroniclers who are not bound by a rather rigidly manichean approach: I am thinking in particular of peace move-ments and social intervention where, as we have seen, right and left might overlap and in which, not by chance perhaps, women happened to be particularly involved. It has also proved particularly difficult to bring feminism into the political spectrum, since it so awkwardly straddled left and right, and since its leaders were mostly 'bourgeois', as republican historians often remark. Examining the cam-paign for women's suffrage seriously as a political force would bring one up against the embarrassing clash between the theory and the practice of republicanism. But instead of investigating the quandary of gender and republicanism within a political narrative, most histories restrict the question to a section on women. The historiographical disturbance surrounding the events of 1944–5, discussed in the last chapter, is the logical conclusion of that choice. This is neither sexism, nor accident: it is largely the result of structural priorities.

All of us who work on French history, even or especially outside France, have been deeply influenced by French republicanism: we mostly appreciate its virtues. Perhaps we have not always appreciated, speaking for myself, quite how strongly its narrative structures may affect how we view certain periods in French history. It is not so much the 'what' that changes, but the 'why' and the 'how'. I do not have any particularly revolutionary theory about public events in France between the wars: much of what has been narrated here does not contradict the versions of French history we already have. The terms of the Treaty of Versailles are not going to be altered by knowing that a parallel women's suffrage conference was being held alongside. But the second conference, and the associated women's meetings in favour of peace do have claims on our attention if we see it as the task of history to analyse the context of finite events not only in terms of geopolitics or class, but also of gender. Women as a group set out on this occasion to influence international thinking. It was one sign that, during the early twentieth century, and more particularly between the wars, a shift was occurring in relations between men and women. Less dramatic perhaps than some recent changes, it contrasted quite strongly with the nineteenth-century context – whether the issue was going to school, going on strike, flying aeroplanes or travelling to international conferences. The male monopoly of politics in France at this time was not secure, as we might have assumed if we paid no attention to what women were doing. It was being infiltrated, amended, influenced in a multitude of ways, some visible, like the appointing of women ministers, others less obvious but perfectly discoverable once one starts looking. It is the 'starting looking' that this book has tried to do, thinking this history through differently, adopting the particular – but at the same time enabling – perspective of 'gender-encompassing history'.

NOTES

INTRODUCTION

1 Pierre Nora interviewed in *Le Point*, 13/2/93.
2 On Lavisse, see ibid. On the historical debate over the Occupation and Vichy regime, see Rousso (1991); cf. special number of *Annales E.S.C.* (1993, vol. 48), 'Présence du passé, lenteur de l'histoire: Vichy, l'occupation, les Juifs'. The quotation about a 'clear and well-informed guide' is taken from the cover of Price (1993), chosen at random.
3 Much of what follows relates to history written inside France. In most English-language publications, the inter-war period is part of a longer historical survey. Alfred Cobban's *A History of Modern France* (Harmondsworth: Penguin, 1957), 3 vols, was the chronological account most used by students for many years; Theodore Zeldin's monumental study (1973 and 1977) took a pioneering thematic approach. More recent general histories have some affinities with the textbook, in that they are chronological and designed for students: Larkin (1988); McMillan (1992); Price (1993).
4 The inter-war years are covered by vols 12 (Becker and Berstein 1990) and 13 (Borne and Dubief 1989) replacing earlier versions by Philippe Bernard and Henri Dubief. French publishers have produced many multi-volume histories subdivided chronologically: Rémond (1990), is vol. 4 in *Histoire de France*, ed. Jean Favier; Agulhon (1990) is in the Hachette *Histoire de France*. Examples of recent French *textbooks*, identifiable as such by their layout and design, are Abbad (1993); Berstein (1988); Sirinelli *et al.* (1993).
5 The other contributors to the volume are Jean-Pierre Azéma, Jean-Jacques Becker, Serge Berstein, Aline Coutrot, Jean-Noel Jeanneney, Philippe Levillain, Pierre Milza, Antoine Prost, Jean-Pierre Rioux, Jean-François Sirinelli, Michel Winock – all familar names who have also contributed to a large reference work: Sirinelli (1995).
6 For obvious reasons, index references register more men than women (about 12 women to 500 men in Sirinelli *et al.* 1993). The rhetoric of referring to women has altered a little in recent years, sometimes criticizing past sexism, but the syntactical structures and proportion of text devoted to women remain unaltered. For well-intentioned but unsatisfactory separate sections on women see Becker and Berstein (1990: 363–4) and Borne and Dubief (1989: 203–6).
7 Archive collections particularly rich in inter-war material are: the papers collected by Marie-Louise Bouglé in the Bibliothèque Historique de la Ville de Paris (BHVP), catalogue by Maité Albistur; the Fonds Gabrielle Duchêne, at the Bibliothèque de Documentation Internationale Contemporaine (BDIC) at Nanterre; and many particular collections in the Bibliothèque Marguerite Durand (BMD), Paris. For an overview of women's history, see Perrot (1994); for a monumental series see Duby and Perrot (1988–92) especially the volume on the twentieth century (Thébaud 1992). Cf. Bouchardeau (1977); McMillan (1981); Klejman and Rochefort (1989). Apart from

Bouchardeau's survey, which has many virtues, and Dominique Desanti's readable but lightweight book (1984), there is so far no full-length historical study of women or gender concentrating on the inter-war period, but Christine Bard's recently published thesis on the feminists of these years is an indispensable landmark (1995). Paul Smith, 'Women's social and political rights in the French Third Republic 1918–1940' (D.Phil., Oxford, 1991) is due for publication shortly.

8   The outstanding recent publication in this area is Roberts's cultural history of the post-war period (1994) which takes Gilbert, 'Soldier's Heart', as one of her starting points. The question of whether or not 'women were emancipated' by the war is discussed in the latter section of McMillan (1981) and by several contributors to Higonnet *et al.* (1987).

9   The word was used as a foreign term by Michelle Perrot (1994: 14), but in the collective article by seven women historians (Dauphin *et al.* 1986) the concept is expressed as 'la différence des sexes'. Cf. Duchen (1994b: 229 and notes 6 and 7).

10 See bibliography under Scott for the various texts which, along with Denise Riley's famous essay (1988), provided the starting point for copious debate. For a helpful bibliography up to 1994 of the 'post-Scott' debate, from a position sympathetic to Scott's view, see Canning (1994). For an example of the sometimes very hostile passions raised, see Hoff (1994). For a more dispassionate account, locating this debate within the broader context of post-modernism and relativity, see Appleby *et al.* (1994: chaps 6–8). The term 'the social science view of gender' is used by Scott (1991a: 56–7), to differentiate it from her own definition. Cf. Bennett (1989) and Jane Rendall writing in Offen *et al.* (1991).

11 See review by Joan Scott of Linda Gordon's book *Heroes of Their Own Lives*, Gordon's reply, and Gordon's review of Scott's book *Gender and the Politics of History*, all in *Signs* (1990, vol. 15: 848–60).

12 Whether in the Annales school or the new political history, this remains a problem. On the Annales cf. Fauré (1980); Davis (1992); Stuard (1981: 139). Cf. Perrot (1994: 53). It is instructive to compare recent surveys of French social history by Antoine Prost (1992) and James McMillan (1994): gender is practically absent from the former, very prominent in the latter.

1   DEMOGRAPHY AND ITS DISCONTENTS

1   *Journal Officiel, Débats Parlementaires* (11 October 1919), quoted in many secondary accounts, e.g. Tomlinson (1986: 132); Dupâquier (1988: 187).

2   Also much quoted, cf. Dupâquier (1988: 192).

3   For an overall survey of pronatalism, see Ogden and Huss (1982); cf. Huss (1990). For details of the 1920 and 1923 laws, see Dupâquier (1988, chap. 4); cf. Guerrand and Ronsin (1990: 69 ff.). For state policies to encourage higher birth rates see Spengler (1976); Talmy (1962, vol. 2); Glass (1967: sections on France); and introduction and chap. 4 of Laroque (1986). On family allowances, but also on pronatalism in general, see Pedersen (1993b). For a brief but instructive resumé in the context of women's rights, see Offen (1991). Anne Cova's thesis on maternity policy in France under the Third Republic was not yet available when preparing this chapter.

4   Summary of the Alquier case based on the following sources: documents in the Dossier Henriette Alquier and the Dossier Groupes Féministes de l'Enseignement Laïque, both in the Bibliothèque Marguerite Durand (BMD), Paris; documents in Archives Nationales (AN), F^7 13749; documents in the Bouglé collection, Bibliothèque Histor-ique de la Ville de Paris (BHVP), especially Fonds Marthe Bray, III, Correspondance (includes a copy of the incriminated number of the *Bulletin*); cf. Maitron dictionary, for biographies of principals; Bernard (1968, vol. 2: 46–53). Case summarized in

Guerrand and Ronsin (1990: 93–5). On the GFEL, see Sohn (1977) based on her 1973 doctoral thesis, 'Féminisme et syndicalisme: les institutrices de la FUE de 1919 à 1935' (University of Paris-X, Nanterre). On Guillot, see Liszek (1995).

5   Cf. Pedersen (1993b: 370). For full details of the political context (but without mention of Alquier affair), see Becker and Berstein (1990: 301–10); Mayeur (1984: 307).

6   On the 'demographic lament', see Ogden and Huss (1982: passim); the most recent compendium of French demographic thinking on the twentieth century, and one of the fullest secondary sources available, is Dupâquier (1988). Cf. Spengler (1976).

7   The history of INED is critically approached in Le Bras (1991) and from a feminist perspective by Jaspard (1992).

8   The most striking example of the rhetoric of dichotomy is Berstein (1988: 5–7): in the space of a page and a half he includes the terms: *stagnation, baisse, insuffisante, faiblesse, diminuer, inquiétant, pays de vieux, usé, exsangue, sans dynamisme*; see ibid. (170–1) for a contrast with the years 1940s–1980s: *bouillonnement, solutions, réflexions pionnières* etc. Larkin (1988) also opens with a discussion of demography, and Rémond (1990) includes the topic in the introduction. Both Larkin (1988) and McMillan (1992) use the term 'stalemate society' to refer to the inter-war years. For 'un pays de vieux', see Brunet and Launay (1974: 102). Borne and Dubief (1989) contains a good example of the rhetoric of *faiblesse* versus *vigueur*, but also a comprehensive survey of the demographic question.

9   On the Alliance, see Tomlinson (1986); Thébaud (1985).

10 For an example from the far left, see Tartakowsky and Willard (1986: 27). For evidence of the persistence of the debate see *Le Monde*, 12 April 1995, 'La politique familiale oppose les candidats à l'Elysée'.

11 With Guerrand (1971) and Guerrand and Ronsin (1990), Ronsin's book is central to the libertarian tradition. Cf. Ronsin (1980: 198): 'as a result of the [1914] war, women acquired a more important place in social life and some of them *refused to submit* to repeated pregnancies.' The voluntarist approach is similar to that taken by two generations of feminist historians: cf. Bouchardeau (1977); Sohn (1992, 1993), a good example of emancipation discourse; Klejman and Rochefort (1989). On the 1970s context cf. Duchen (1986, chap. 3).

12 See Berstein (1988: 5–7) for an analysis of the pyramid entirely in terms of the loss of men. Cf. Dupâquier (1988: 96) for a longer discussion, but still expressed in negative demographic terms. For full figures for age-groups in 1921 divided by sex, ibid. (97–8).

13 The late 1980s saw renewed interest in immigration between the wars. See, for example, Noiriel (1988); Milza (1986). The chapter on 'L'entre-deux-guerres' by Maurice Garden and Hervé Le Bras, in Dupâquier (1988) recognizes this literature and stresses the positive aspects of immigration for population growth.

14 The notion of 'the golden age' is developed at length in S. Berstein and Odile Rudelle (eds) (1992) *Le Modèle républicain* (PUF); cf. Chapter 9 below.

15 On the UFCS, see Talmy (1962, vol. 2: 197 ff.); Pedersen (1993b: 393–6 and references). Offen (1988) opened up a debate about the possibility of a 'relational feminism', sparked by the difference she saw between her own findings on French feminism and the 'Anglo-Saxon' model. Black (1989) uses the terms 'social feminism and 'equity feminism' to mean something similar. Other feminist historians take the view that women strongly favouring a traditional role for women do not rate as 'feminist' at all. Pedersen (1993a: 254 ff.), gives a critical account of the UFCS women, 'devout and courageous' perhaps, but naive and no match for the secular natalists. Rather than 'feminists' I prefer to call members of the UFCS 'politically active'.

16 See, for example, Laroque (1986, chap. 4); Ceccaldi (1957: esp. 46 ff.) for statistics; Glass (1967); and relevant sections of Dupâquier (1988). This literature has now been enriched by Pedersen's comparative study of Britain and France (1993b). She describes

the 1932 act as 'the single most important piece of legislation passed in inter-war France' (ibid.: 372) (and this one does get into the chronologies).

17 Pedersen (1993a: 261). The question of payments to mothers is also discussed in Glass (1967: 436) and by Offen (1991: 150 ff.). The 1932 act specified that officially the allowance was payable to the 'wage-earner who supported the child'. If both parents worked, it went to the father, who 'could pay the person actually caring for the child', thus enabling funds to send the money to mothers in practice. The 'stay-at-home mother' allowance of the 1939 Code was payable to the mother, as was the first-child bonus, but regular family allowances under this Code could be paid to the father.

18 Cf. McLaren (1983) based on his numerous articles; cf. Roberts (1994: 263, note 1) for problems over abortion statistics; for details on abortions from testimony in legal archives see Sohn (1993, chap. 12: 780–6), evidence covering a long timespan.

19 Cf. Simone de Beauvoir, *Lettres à Sartre* (Paris: Gallimard, 1990, vol. 2: 211), letter in 1940 referring to a named male friend who 'refused to go in for all the "gymnastics" engaged in by men who don't want children' and left it to the woman to deal with the consequences. On present-day France, cf. Le Doeuff (1989: 270–1).

20 On Strauss and the *carnet de santé*, see Rollet-Echalier (1990: 263–73), a mine of information, but mostly for the years before 1914; cf. also Stewart (1988); Cova in Bock *et al.* (1991); Thébaud (1986). Much empirical material is also to be found in Knibiehler and Fourquet (1980), but less on the inter-war period. French state policy has been analysed from various perspectives. Cf. Jenson (1986); Offen (1991) suggests some positive effects of family policies on the later welfare state; cf. Gisela Bock, 'Pauvreté féminine, droits des mères et états-providence' in vol. 5 of *Histoire des femmes*.

21 This section draws on my earlier research – Reynolds (1990) – where fuller references will be found. On the earliest crèches, see J. B. F. Marbeau, *Manuel de la crèche*, 2nd edn (Paris, 1886), copy in dossier 'Crèches' at Musée Social, Paris; and the same author's pamphlet *Des crèches* (1845, ibid.). Figures from F. Lédé, *Les Crèches, budget et utilisation* (Paris, 1925); see also L'Héritier (1984); and on the workplace crèches in the north, Smith (1981: 142–3 and index). For details on crèche provision see Rollet-Echalier (1990: 87–97, 218–22, 526–39, 576–81); in the 1930s there were perhaps 11,000 places in France, almost 4,000 of them in the Paris region.

22 On wet-nurses, see Sussman (1982); on mortality in crèches, L'Héritier (1984) cites 222 deaths among 512 children in 14 crèches in 1853.

23 Lecture given in aid of Société Maternelle Parisienne on 15 December 1901, published as brochure, 1902; in MS dossier 'Crèches'.

24 On trade union distrust see Knibiehler and Fourquet (1980: 260); for reactions of town councils in the north, Smith (1981: 154); for distaste expressd by feminists, *La Fronde*, report on 26 October 1899. On the church–state quarrel as it affected crèches, Rollet-Echalier (1990: 531–5).

25 On wartime provision, see L. Bernard, *La Défense de la santé publique pendant la guerre* (Paris, 1920: 297 and 303). See also McMillan (1981: 133 ff.); Dubesset *et al.* (1977), and Thébaud (1984: 169 ff. and 270 ff.). On the law of 1917, see Marcel Frois, *La Santé et le travail des femmes pendant la guerre* (Paris, 1926: 128 ff.). Cf. Abel Crissac, *Rapport sur l'allaitement maternel au magasin et à l'atelier* (Paris, 1916, brochure in Archives Nationales, (AN) F^{22} 447).

26 Factory inspectors' reports are filed in AN F^{22} 447; cf. Mlle Letellier's 1928 report on fourteen establishments in the Nord.

27 Cf. the series of articles 'Helping the family' by Paul Vaillant-Couturier appearing almost daily in *L'Humanité*, from 21 November to 16 December 1935; summarized in part in Bouchardeau (1977: 127–9). These articles did not praise the crèche, but expressed doubts about its value.

28 Included in Union Féminine Civique et Sociale, *Le travail industriel de la mère et le foyer ouvrier, documents pour le Congrès international* (Paris, 1933, copy in Musée Social: 283–4).
29 *Oeuvre nouvelle des crèches parisiennes*, brochure (1925), Archives of the Prefecture de Police, dossier 'Crèches', B/D203; Strauss's speech is on p. 35.
30 Cf. note 29 above: the two conferences are bound in the same document.
31 Text of plan dated 28 January 1920, in papers of J.-L. Breton, AN, 398 AP (21).

2 FROM KINDERGARTEN TO YOUTH HOSTEL: GROWING UP BETWEEN THE WARS

1 For a discussion of the concept in a francophone context, see Baudoux *et al.* (1992); Le Doeuff (1989), part 4, considers the political and philosophical content of the term.
2 Since Philippe Ariès's pioneering *L'Enfant et la vie familiale sous l'ancien régime* (1960), childhood in France has been much studied, but the inter-war period is not well served: cf. Heywood (1988); Prost and Vincent (1987b: 77 ff.). The most helpful book is Crubellier (1979).
3 Cf. the Ozoufs' article, 'Le Tour de la France par deux enfants' in Nora (1984, vol. 1); and J. P. Bardon (ed.), facsimile edition (1977), of this classic by 'G. Bruno' (Augustine Fouillé). Cf. Cavanna (1978: 150–1), whose mother had read this book while minding the sheep.
4 On early nursery schools cf. Zeldin (1977: 186–7); Crubellier (1979: 213 ff.); Luc (1994: 858 ff.). In 1921, the educational content of the nursery school was reduced and a half-century of legislative silence followed (ibid.: 915). Prost *et al.* (1987b: 82) says that until the 1950s 'nursery schools or the baby classes [in primary schools] took the children of the poor, whose mothers were obliged to go out to work. The nursery school was a . . . kind of baby-sitting service.' Cf. Cavanna (1978: 53): 'Poor people's kids get a real start in life. No sooner hatched than in the crèche, next stop the *maternelle*. Broken in for school, no problem.' But cf. also *Mémoire de Paris* (1993: 59).
5 On 'domestic science' or 'home management and puericulture' in the syllabus for girls in the primary sector (up to age thirteen) in France, see Lelièvre (1991); when compulsory schooling was extended to the age of fourteen by the Popular Front, the new syllabuses for the higher primary schools stressed practical education: 'for girls this meant that nine hours of a thirty-hour week would be devoted to "elements of applied sciences", "practical works" and drawing' (Clark 1982: 692).
6 Cf. P. J. Hélias, quoted in Crubellier (1979: 60). Cf. *Mémoire de Paris* (1993: 67): 'Separation of boys from girls was very strict . . . . Even during the holidays, relations [between the sexes] were awkward and false, with unpleasant undertones. There wasn't the freedom between boys and girls that there is today.' The schoolteachers who provided evidence for Ozouf (1992: 277–8) claimed not to have made any distinction between girls and boys, though one would like to see their claims questioned a little; on the 'mixing' in catechism class, allowed because of the watchful eyes of the priest and no doubt those of God, see ibid. (278) and Bonheur (1963: 201).
7 On literacy, see Furet and Ozouf (1982). On book production, see Chartier and Martin (1991), the chapters on schoolbooks, children's books, comics and bibliography. On textbooks, see Citron (1991); Bonheur (1963) is an engaging compendium of primary school culture in France before 1939; on gender in textbooks cf. Clark (1984); Decroux-Masson (1979).
8 Cf. Sartre (1964); Beauvoir (1980); Cavanna (1978); Kriegel (1991). The autobiographies of intellectuals usually mention books read in childhood but are subject to memory lapses: Cavanna, b. 1923, claims to have read as a child Saint Exupéry's *Le Petit Prince*, published only in 1943. Diaries would be more reliable, but are lacking.

9   This library, founded in 1924, and still in existence in the rue Saint-Séverin, ex-rue Boutebrie, Paris Ve, was part of a US-funded initiative after 1920. There were only about a dozen such in France in 1931. For details, see Renonciat (1991), a fund of information based on the holdings of L'Heure Joyeuse: a 'fonds ancien' of children's books from between the wars and a collection of archives, including a home-made *Journal des lecteurs* (1926 and 1932–4).

10   On comics, see Ory in Chartier and Martin (1991: 495–503); Fourment (1987); Michel Pierre, 'Illustrés' in Barrot and Ory (1990: 111–26).

11   Simone de Beauvoir's childhood and adolescent reading is recorded in many places in her memoirs (1980). See pages 33, 52, 66, 70–2, 84, 98, 101, 111, 114, 116, 122, 145, 151 ff., 182, 194, 198 in the 1980 Folio edition.

12   Kriegel comments that she was not alone in being forbidden to read comics, quoting the memoirs of Cardinal Lustiger. Cf. Henri Troyat, *Un si long chemin* (quoted in Renonciat 1991: 28) on being caught with an *illustré*. Cf. also Cavanna (1978: 186), on his library books: 'Jules Verne, the Bibliothèque verte, the Jungle Book'. On the popularity of Malot's *Sans famille*, see David A. Steel, 'Hector Malot, *Sans famille* and the sense of adventure' conference paper, BCLA, 1994.

13   On animal literature and the Père Castor series, see Renonciat (1991: 44–55; 68–9); Chartier and Martin (1991: 485, 493).

14   Archives of L'Heure Joyeuse, *Journal des Lecteurs* (1926 and 1932–4); NB *Les quatre filles du Docteur March (Little Women)*, beloved by Beauvoir, is listed as a favourite in 1932.

15   On the eve of the First World War, there were 2.4 million boys and 2.1 million girls altogether in state schools, and about 370,000 boys and 700,000 girls in private, mostly Catholic, schools (Prost 1967: 218; a useful reference work despite its age). On the separation of primary and secondary sectors in the inter-war period, see ibid., chap. 16, 'Les instituteurs de la République'. See also Zeldin (1977, vol. 2, chap. 6). Cf. Lelièvre (1991: 93) for further figures. NB *Collèges* were funded by local authorities, *lycées* by the state: in this section, no distinction between them is made. Both co-education and the *école unique* eventually came about at broadly the same time, in the 1960s and 1970s.

16   Mayeur (1977) is essential. Cf. Crubellier (1979: 287): 'Françoise Mayeur's book is the best of guides. We need only summarize it' – which he usefully does.

17   Figures from McMillan (1992: 82). The number of girls doubled between 1913 and 1939, but so did that of boys. Not until after the Second World War were the sexes equally balanced in secondary education. These larger issues cannot be tackled here: see Lelièvre (1991), the conclusion to this chapter and Lagrave (1992). It is too sweeping to say, as Furet and Ozouf do (1982: 146), that by the 1880s, 'one of the major inequalities in French education – inequality between the sexes – had almost disappeared . . . there were now almost as many girls in primary school as boys.'

18   On the history of the boys' *lycée*, see Prost (1967), relevant chapters, and the wealth of detail in Zeldin (1977, vol.2, chap. 6): 'Privilege and culture', which is devoted to boys' secondary education.

19   Cf. also Mayeur (1977) passim and Offen (1983), an admirably lucid article on a complex subject.

20   On all the foregoing, see Mayeur (1977: 387 ff.), and Lelièvre (1991), the section 'Une école d'état spécifique'.

21   On women entering university, Charrière (1931) has a number of detailed statistics. By 1929, about 16,000 women were in French universities, 12,500 of them French, and of those about 5,000 were studying for literary degrees. Cf. Lelièvre (1991: 141), graph, and Crubellier (1979: 292), slightly different figures but same ratios. On the difficulty of women entering the ranks of the professorate in literature despite these changes, cf. Charle (1994: 217 ff.), 'La femme indésirable'. On women and scholarship, cf. Davis (1992).

22 The difference between the intellectually ambitious boy and girl school-leaver could be copiously illustrated by a comparison between the prestigious Ecole Normale Supérieure in the rue d'Ulm (for men) and the school of the same name in Sèvres (for women), impossible here for lack of space. Cf. Sirinelli (1988); Mayeur (1977: 410 ff.); Moi (1994, chaps 1 and 2: a brilliant dissection of the *non-dit* in Beauvoir's academic record). Ulm was 'the apex of the whole academic hierarchy' (Bourdieu 1988: xix); Beauvoir rejected Sèvres, because 'I didn't want to shut myself up outside Paris with a lot of women' (1980: 221–2), for the Sorbonne. She ended up a tolerated outsider in Sartre's ENS coterie, but according to Moi (68 ff.) failed to see how, as a woman, she 'was marginalized by the intellectual field with which she identified'.

23 Most of the work has been done by the team working with Gerard Cholvy. See Cholvy and Hilaire (1986, vols 2 and 3); Cholvy *et al.* (1991) contains several *témoignages* and a useful bibliography. For a general overview of youth movements, see *Jeunesse et ses mouvements* (1992: 95 ff.), chapter on France by N. Chaline *et al.*

24 Cf. Baudoux *et al.* (1992: 216–22), contribution by Christine Bard. On the initials of the JOC/F and reflections on women in militant families, cf. Dominique Loiseau, 'Les militantes de l'ombre: femme de . . .', paper given at conference on 'Les Dictionnaires biographiques du mouvement ouvrier', November 1993, Centre Malher, Paris, p. 13.

25 On scouting and guiding in France, see Effenterre (1947); Cholvy *et al.* (1991), relevant chapters; Cholvy (1986, vol. 2: 374 ff.): 'L'essor du scoutisme' and references.

26 The JOC and associated organizations are discussed in all the general studies cited above. The best single study is Pierrard *et al.* (1984). Rolande Trempé's chapter is a model of how to integrate gender into analysis of the movement. See also the more partisan Aubert (1991) for fervent *témoignages* from former members; cf. Debes and Poulat (1986) on origins. Cf. bibliographies in Cholvy's collections; for founding dates of all JOC-based movements, see Crubellier (1979: 317).

27 Monique Luirard, 'Eléments en vue d'une histoire de la naissance et de l'implantation de la JOC dans la region stéphanois au cours des années 30', unpublished paper given to the conference Vie Quotidienne et Front Populaire, Centre Malher, Paris, September 1986, p. 2. See also Jean Nizey's chapter on the JOC in Saint-Etienne in Cholvy (1985).

28 Jean Nizey, 'Les militants de la JOC dans le Maitron', paper given to international conference at Centre Malher, Paris, November 1993 on 'Dictionnaires Biographiques du Mouvement Ouvrier'.

29 On the history of the youth hostels movement (hostellers were called *ajistes* from the acronym AJ = auberge de jeunesse), see Kergoat (1986: 312–15), drawing on the thesis by Heller-Goldenberg (1984). Heller's thesis is summed up in her paper to the conference Vie quotidienne et Front Populaire (Paris, 1986): 'La jeunesse ajiste au temps du Front Populaire, culture et loisirs'. There is a substantial section on the youth hostel movement in Ory (1994: 776–88). The AJ are described in Jackson (1988: 231–2; 1988: 133–6). Cf. Dufrasne (1991); Cacerès (1981) also has chapters on *colonies de vacances* and the creation of the programme for *animateurs*, the CEMEA, dating from this time and overlapping with the *ajiste* movement.

30 Figures from Eugene Raude and Gilbert Prouteau, *Le Message de Léo Lagrange* (Compagnie du Livre, 1950: 105).

31 See Jackson (1988: 135) for a quotation from André Chamson in the weekly *Vendredi*: 'If we were to give a face to the Popular Front, as artists have given one to liberty [presumably an allusion to Delacroix] it would be that of a young man, bronzed by the sun, muscular, used to hiking in the open air, his soul innocent and yet not naive, singing "Allons au devant de la vie"'.

32 Kergoat (1986: 314), reference to unintended pregnancies. Cf. Ory (1990: 1,538): the CLAJ began to be accused of laxity, and the Ligue took steps to stop mixing the sexes.

Ory suggests that the mixed emphasis of the CLAJ was intended to distinguish it from the 'military' atmosphere of some youth movements (1,553–4). (This section has been dropped from the published version of his thesis.)

33   Summary of Violette Nozière's case based on contemporary newspaper reports (*L'Oeuvre* etc. in BDIC, Nanterre) and Nozière dossier in Bibliothèque Marguerite Durand, Paris.

3 'A SLIP OF A GIRL CAN FLY IT': THE FALSE PROMISES OF AVIATION

1   Some material in this chapter appears in Reynolds (1989). For the screenplay of *Le Ciel est à Vous*, see Grémillon (1981: esp. 44). The plot concerns Thérèse's attempt on the women's long-distance record in a plane adapted by Pierre. See the Fonds J. Grémillon, Bibliothèque de l'Arsenal, Paris, carton 13, several dossiers, esp. no. 013; cf. Semple (1985).

2   On the literature of flight, see Wohl (1988); Zeldin (1977: 358); cf. *Humanité* (14 September–13 October 1935).

3   See Petit (1981); Chadeau (1987); Christienne *et al.* (1981) and references.

4   There is nothing quite as broad in range as Corn (1983), but see Petit (1977), a mine of information, and the special number of *Mouvement social* (1988, no. 145); cf. also Marck (1990); all contain fair-minded references to women.

5   The motor car could also have been a fruitful topic. 'Short skirts, short hair, flat shoes and a sporty style' for women were all associated with motor transport (1928): dossier of press cuttings on 'Automobilisme' at the Bibliothèque Marguerite Durand (BMD), Paris. Cf. Roberts (1994: 78), quoting *Le Figaro* from 1925 on 'la femme moderne': 'Nothing stops her, nothing fills her with dread . . . . Intrepid, she drives her own car while waiting to pilot her airplane.'

6   Aka the Baronne Raymonde de Laroche; she was killed in a crash in 1919. For early licence holders of both sexes in the US, and information about the international context, see Corn (1983, chap. 1). For details of the early days in France, see Petit (1977).

7   See Petit (1981: 44) for figures of machines; on figures for licences, Petit (1977: 60); cf. article in *Le Matin* (15 October 1926), for the estimate that there were ten women to about 12,000 men. In Grémillon's film, Pierre has been the 'fidèle mécanicien' (Petit 1977: 99) of the French First World War ace, Guynemer, as the real-life M. Dupeyron was. The point about men's access to training was put forcefully by the pilot Madeleine Charnaux in *La Française* (September 1939).

8   On Marthe Richard's proposal, cf. her own, possibly romanced autobiography (1974: 99–100). Cf. *Le Figaro* (27 September 1915), 'Nos aviatrices s'ennuient', in dossier 'Femmes dans l'aviation', BMD (hereafter 629 Avi, BMD). Richard (1889–1982) campaigned to close licensed brothels in France after 1945. Cf. dossier on Marie Marvingt in the BMD. On *l'aviation sanitaire* little information was found. Cf. Janine Devillers, *L'Aviation sanitaire au point de vue du droit international* (Paris: Editions internationales, 1933), copy in BMD.

9   On barnstorming in general, see Corn (1983: 12–13): Lindbergh began as a barnstormer. On the exceptional Adrienne Bolland, see obituary in *Le Monde* (18 March 1975); dossier in BMD; Slava Liszek, 'Femmes à l'assaut du ciel', *Antoinette* (no. 259, March 1987). She is also celebrated in many 'women in the air' books such as Lauwick (1958).

10   On Madeleine Charnaux, Maryse Hilsz (1903–46) and Hélène Boucher (1908–34), see Lauwick (1958); on Maryse Bastié (1898–1952), see ibid., and Bart (1981); Hélène Boucher flew solo to Saigon at twenty-one and broke four world speed records in a day in 1934 shortly before her fatal crash. Cf. dossiers under all these names in BMD, as

well as the general dossier (629 Avi). The New Zealand flyer Jean Batten (1909–82), who was honoured in France, is a textbook case: she sold her piano to buy flying lessons; her first plane was a fifth-hand Gipsy Moth in which she flew to Australia; and she made 'frequent trips to the pawnbroker in order to keep up my solo flying' (Batten 1979: 12).

11 629 Avi, BMD

12 Corn (1983: 75). 'Duck soup' means 'easy-peasy, nothing special'. See ibid., chap. 4: 'Making flying thinkable: women pilots and the selling of aviation'. Cf. ibid.: 89–90 – the concept of the stewardess is similar: a young, vulnerable woman who flies regularly allays passengers' fears.

13 Cf. memo from Flandin to the feminist Jane Misme, Fonds J. Misme, BMD (copy in Bolland dossier). French women pilots never formed a pressure group like the 'Ninety-Nines' in the USA: see Corn (1983: 80 ff.).

14 On Aéropostale, cf. the still-growing literature, from the heroic and elegiac to the demystifying and financial. Daurat was thinly disguised as Rivière in Saint-Exupéry's *Vol de nuit*. Cf. Petit (1981: 47–50; 1977: 188 ff.); Marck (1990: 521–4) on the 'myth' of Aéropostale. Exploits of its pilots were followed by 'every schoolchild in France'. Cf. Heimermann and Margaud (1994). Financial scandal killed off the enterprise which was absorbed into Air-France in 1933. Cf. Webster (1993), one of many biographies of Saint-Exupéry.

15 See Christienne and Lissarague (1981); Christienne (1977a; 1977b; 1979). See Chadeau (1987) for the history of manufacture; Petit (1977: 170) on competition and corruption.

16 On the 1920s in general, and the famous 'politique des prototypes' (1928–33) which ended in incoherence, see Chadeau (1987: 147 ff.): 'Never was the glorification of the pioneering entrepreneurs so pronounced, never were their achievements so limited and mediocre.' On the 1930s, see ibid., chap. 7. The story is much the same whoever tells it. Cf. Christienne *et al.* (1981: 29); Kirkland (1982: 108), on how French aviation 'languished' for much of the period; Young (1974 and 1978).

17 Pierre Cot (1895–1977), controversial Radical party politician, one of the 'young Turks'; cf. the article on him in Sirinelli (1995); Berstein (1982). Of Cot's three initiatives, nationalization has attracted the most attention, cf. Chadeau (1987: 323 ff.); Christienne (1981: 47 ff.), argues that nationalization was positive on balance but brought much short-term disruption; Frank (1981) takes a more positive line. Cot's own book (1939) was written to defend his own position.

18 *L'aviation populaire* has been surprisingly little studied by historians. It figures marginally in most histories of Popular Front policy on sport and leisure, or of the French air force, but see Christienne (1981: 55 ff.); Ory (1990: 1,462 ff. and 1994: 742–7); Vincent (1993) is the first post-graduate study and has unearthed many details. (I am grateful to his supervisor Claude Pennetier for bringing this thesis to my attention.)

19 On private flying, see Petit (1977: 177). The left-wing aviator Sadi-Lecointe is quoted in the magazine *Vu* on 25 July 1936 as saying the aim was to 'extend to the children of the people what was only yesterday the privilege of the well-off classes: the right to fly'. On the Croix de feu, see article 'La ligue' in Sirinelli (1992, vol. 2: 61–111); Mermoz was their most famous recruit. Christienne (1981: 39 ff.) claims that, contrary to popular belief, the air force was not 'acquis à La Cagoule'.

20 On German aviation policy as perceived in France, see Vincent (1993: introduction); Christienne (1981: 39 ff.). On l'Aile Tendue, see Vincent (1993: 10).

21 On the budget of *l'aviation populaire*, see Ory (1990: 1,466 and 1,470); Vincent (1993: 13 ff.) Cf. Chadeau (1987: 261): '260 light aircraft were acquired by the ministry… and given to the flying clubs'. Costs were kept low by buying small planes in kit-form to be made up by clubs: e.g. the Farman Moustique and the Renault Luciole. On the

intended structures, see Ory (1990: 1,462 ff.); Christienne (1981: 57 ff.): a possible target was to 'constitute an exceptional pool of trainee pilots for the air force'. Vincent (1993: 66–7) comments that the project depended on the forty-hour week, since a day and a half a week was the minimum for a serious course of flying lessons.

22 Cf. photographs showing both boys and girls making models of aeroplanes at school in AN 312 AP (Abraham papers). For the 1937 clarification, see Vincent (1993: 124).

23 Ory reckons that in 1937 about 10,000 people in all were involved. By the end of 1938, 3,500 young pilots had their first certificate and 1,250 the second (the serious one). But only a fraction of these entered the air force.

24 The 'Jeunes Ailes de Villejuif et du Kremlin-Bicêtre' had as its aim 'To practise engineless flight, and to develop in as many people as possible of both sexes a feeling for and love of the air' – Vincent (1993: 125). Cf. ibid.: 129: *all* the girls in one junior section had signed up for parachute jumping.

25 The figures for licences appeared occasionally in the press. See *Le Temps* (28 May 1932): Louise Faure-Favier gives comparative figures for several countries; *La Française* printed an article on 4 November 1933 asking why there were so few airwomen in France.

26 Grémillon (1981: 47). Cf. Jean Batten's statement: 'It was my intention to establish at least *a women's record* for the journey [to Australia] realising that my aeroplane was not suitable for anything faster at this stage [1934]' (Batten 1979: 15; my italics).

27 On Boucher and press comments on her death, see dossier 629 Avi, BMD.

28 Commandant Dauchy, quoted in *Minerva* (9 July 1939).

29 Charnaux in *La Française* (September 1939); the anonymous article in *Le Journal*, 'Aviatrices au Chômage' appeared on 5 October 1938, just after Munich. Both in 629 Avi, BMD.

30 Cf. Bolland dossier, BMD; on Bastié and Charnaux, see Lauwick (1958: 174 and chap. 8 passim). Cf. *Le Journal* (19 September 1931) on the special flying suits made in leather to match the plane's colours for Bastié and others, to 'protect the formal clothes they wore on stopovers'.

31 Changes took place in the 1970s. Women were admitted to ENAC (the Ecole Nationale de l'Aviation Civile) in 1974, the words 'de sexe masculin' being dropped from its statutes (*Journal Officiel*, 8 March 1974); by then two women were flying passenger planes for Air-Inter. In the military, there were 6,275 candidates for the 216 places made available in 1976. By 1978, there were 149 women officers and 3,500 NCOs (Beauregard 1992: 228–9). In 1995, the British RAF promoted Jo Salter as its first woman bomber pilot to be 'combat ready'; at this date women were in all three services in France, but there was said to be 'doubt' over using them in combat (*The Guardian*, 22 February 1995).

4 WHAT DID PEOPLE DO ALL DAY? THE SEXUAL DIVISION OF LABOUR IN FRANCE BETWEEN THE WARS

1 On definitions, especially across national accounting systems, see Glover (1994) and references. This chapter is not based on analysis of the primary census material, but of the terms in which it is discussed: it is an essay, not an empirical study. See bibliography for the large number of secondary works on work, employment and economic activity between the wars; Marchand and Thélot (1992) is the most recent and accessible general presentation of the data to date.

2 Robert (1989: 451–2). This quotation is chosen simply because it conveniently summarizes the analysis to be found in virtually all secondary accounts, not to single out Robert, whose thesis is an invaluable source. On women's work in the period, see Dauriac (1933: esp. 91); Daric (1947); Guélaud-Léridon (1964); Guilbert (1947: 754–72).

3   On the history of the census, Marchand and Thélot (1992: esp. 14); Dupâquier *et al.* (1988, vol. 3, chap. 1, and equivalent chapter in vol. 4).

4   Lewis (1984: 175). For essays and references to the debate both on the informal economy and domestic labour, see Thompson (1984) and Jenson *et al.* (1990), esp. chapter by V. Beechey. Jan Windebank's work on the informal economy (1991) has been particularly drawn on here since her material relates to France, albeit since 1945 (cf. her bibliography 236–44).

5   The figures used here are all from Marchand and Thélot (1992: esp. 176–7); Sauvy (1984, vol. 3: 292 ff.) gives slightly different figures and age-groups. Several writers have pointed out that, historically, higher percentages of married women in France were economically active than in other European countries, partly because of the decision to count wives of small farmers and shopkeepers, partly because French women in the late nineteenth century and later did not automatically give up waged work on marriage, though there were regional variations: cf. Hilden 1986 (278–9). This debate is not entered into here, since our concern is the women classified as inactive – most of whom were probably married or as good as.

6   Françoise Cribier, Equipe de géographie sociale et de gérontologie, University of Paris-VII, survey material consulted with permission: the corpus consisted of a sample from the Caisse Nationale d'Assurance Vieillesse des Travailleurs Salariés, CNAVTS-CORDES, 1978; interview LGH 1704.

7   These paragraphs clearly owe much to Christine Delphy, whose original analysis was prompted by the survival in the 1960s and 1970s of small farms and family firms in France, and fits well the context of the inter-war years; cf. Delphy (1984, chap. 5, and 1988, interview). Delphy asks not whether the arrangement is willingly accepted or not, but who benefits from it. Answer: not 'men' as such, but all family members – children, old people, etc. But of the adults capable of doing the work, women rather than men have historically done so.

8   Cf. Pember Reeves (1993), and Spring Rice (1981).

9   Cf. Sullerot (1984); Frost (1993); Furlough (1993); Martin (1987). Paulette Bernège was the expert on good housekeeping.

10 White-collar work is surveyed in Zerner's thesis (1985), summarized in an article (1987). Cf. also Marchand and Thélot (1992: 174–5); much useful detail in Thuillier (1988); cf. Pézerat *et al.* (1984); Bachrach (1987) on the Post Office.

11 For interesting speculation about 'political vetting' in relation to women civil servants, see Larkin (1995: 167).

12 When the then Foreign Minister, Georges Bidault, granted Borel her posting he countered it with another proposal: 'instead of [sending me to Kiev], he married me, put me on unpaid leave, with my full consent of course, and as mother acidly remarked, ruined my career'.

13 On doctors, see articles by Lorillot and Pequignot in *Pénélope* (1981). On Madeleine Pelletier, see Gordon (1990); Sowerwine and Maignien (1992). Cf. Largillière (1981).

14 This section is based on my paper 'The face on the cutting-room floor: women editors in French cinema in the 1930s', Birmingham conference 'Sound Bites and Silent Dames', 1992, to appear as 'Proceedings', ed. Susan Hayward, 1996; cf. also Reynolds (1992); 'Les femmes et la technique du cinéma' in *Revue du Cinéma: Image et Son* (1974, no. 283: 23 ff.); 'Actualité du montage', *Technicien du film* (January 1960); 'Les monteurs', *Cinématographe* (special no. 1985).

15 On the training, conditions and *mentalités* of primary schoolteachers, the best overall study is now Ozouf (1992); on the inter-war period in particular, see Trouvé-Finding (1987). On secondary teachers, see Cacouault (1987); Mayeur (1977). For a thorough study of the first *sévriennes*, many of whom were still in post between the wars, see Margadant (1990).

16 On labour in France the most recent general studies are Noiriel (1986) and Magraw (1992), which both contain full bibliographies. Jean-Louis Robert's thesis (1989) covers workers of both sexes: since it is based on trade union records, the story is told broadly from the point of view of men. On women workers between the wars, apart from Sylvie Zerner's thesis and the articles in *Le Mouvement social* (1987, no. 140), see Fourcaut (1982); on women and the labour movement, see below, Chapter 5.

17 On Taylorism, see Noiriel (1986: 128 ff.); Montmoullin *et al.* (1984). Cf. Downs (1993, esp. note 1); Schweitzer (1982).

18 To take one specific example among many, in an employment report of 1927 from the Isère, women were specifically requested for chocolate factories and for metal-working: AN F^7 12993.

19 Simone Weil's 'Journal d'Usine' and contemporary letters, articles and fragments were in the collection put together for Gallimard in 1951, now in an Idées paperback (1979). Some of the material is now published, with notes, in Simone Weil's complete works (1991) but the page references used here are to the Idées paperback for convenience, since not all the texts are yet available in the collected works; cf. Chapter 5 below and Reynolds (1993b) for a more extended analysis of *La Condition ouvrière*.

5 FROM THE DEPRESSION TO THE STRIKES: *OUVRIERS* AND *OUVRIÈRES*

1 On the 'social' crisis, cf. *Le Mouvement social* (1991, no. 154). On women, see Del Re (1994, esp. chap. 6); on the depression, as well as the works by Sauvy (1984), Jackson (1985), Marseille (1980) and Scot (1988), see the full account in Borne and Dubief (1989: 11–43), based on Sauvy's work of the late 1930s. For an earlier version of this section, see Reynolds (1993a).

2 Gabin played working-class roles in *La Bête Humaine, La Grande Illusion, La Belle Equipe, Pépé le Moko, Quai des Brumes, Le Jour Se Lève*, all made in the late 1930s; cf. Guillaume-Grimaud (1986) which, like many books on French cinema, features a cloth-capped Jean Gabin on the cover. In several films, e.g. Carné's *Hôtel du Nord*, the actress Arletty was cast as a prostitute, suggestive of 'timeless' roles for women.

3 Noiriel (1986: 172–4) claims that women were, after immigrants, 'the other major victims' of unemployment, explaining this by the notion of the family wage. Both he and Kergoat (1986: 12), quote the overall census figures, a rather blunt instrument, as evidence. The overall drop in numbers of 'economically active' women between 1931 and 1936 (about 500,000 in all) is not in question. But the assumption that those laid off were all 'employed married women with children' is a stereotype which cannot be sustained. Cf. Scot (1988: 93) for more slippage of terms: referring to the same census statistics, he writes that '*the working class* was proportionally more adult, masculine and French, more concentrated, more stable, during the crisis, than it had been during the 1920s' (my italics). The statistics refer of course to the full time *industrial workforce*.

4 The account is no doubt heightened by invention, but the situation was a common one.

5 Cf. Marseille (1980: 656); Chenut (1987: 83 and note). Records were kept only after 1931, but short-time working started earlier. According to Letellier *et al.* (1938, vol. 1: 58), those still in work were doing on average four hours less in 1935 than in 1931.

6 The point is developed in Letellier *et al.* (1938, vol. 1: 68–9). NB at Hispano-Suiza, men earning 7 Fr 50 were replaced by women at 4 Fr 75, a counter-case (*Vie Ouvrière*, November 1931).

7 Oral evidence in documents deposited by Simone Petrément in the Fonds Simone Weil, Bibliothèque Nationale, Paris. NB this was a crisis-recruitment pattern, not a sign of upturn. On *La Condition ouvrière* as evidence, see note 36 below.

8   Fanny Clar, 'Chômeuses', *Vu* (December 1933: 82). 'Will they try for jobs in metal-working? Many have.' She comments on the hard work and low pay.

9   Interview transcript, consulted by permission of Françoise Cribier, Equipe de géographie sociale et de gérontologie, University of Paris-VI. Cf. Weil (1951: 50) and Letellier *et al.* (1938, vol. 3: 103), where regret is expressed at the need for mothers of children to work, but no mention is made of married women as such.

10   *Le Matin* (5 November 1931). Richet, Nobel prizewinner and previous feminist sympathizer, under the headline 'Women's work increases unemployment and harms the family', wrote in strong terms against 'women' working, providing a good example of the assimilation of women to mothers of young children: 'women are abandoning their toddlers . . . to work as much as men'. On feminist reactions, see Bard (1995: 313 ff.).

11   See Thibert (1933 passim). The essentials of this article are summarized in Sullerot (1984), the best short piece of writing on Frenchwomen's experience between the wars.

12   Regulations are summarized in Letellier *et al.* (1938, vol. I, part 3); given in full in Bonnet (1939).

13   On Calais, see Archives Nationales (AN) F^{22} 682 Chômage (9 March 1933) and see other documents in the same carton: requests were also made for benefits in kind, such as children's clothing and for more representation of women on the committees administering benefits. Quotation on outworkers from the excellent and gender-encompassing Salais *et al.* (1986: 95).

14   The ministry circular said: 'there is reason to suppose that charwomen (*femmes de menage*) employed for only two or three hours a day, or about 20 hours a week, cannot earn a living from their work' (Bonnet 1939: 66–7).

15   Interview transcripts, courtesy of Françoise Cribier. On the break between work and non-work, cf. Salais *et al.* (1986: 92–4).

16   Catherine Rhein, 'La vie dure qu'on a eue', unpublished memoir, Bibliothèque Marguerite Durand, 41; see the same author's doctoral thesis (Rhein 1977: 242 ff.).

17   Cf. Rhein (1977: 281) on the problems of older women finding work after the industrial wage rises.

18   This section of Noiriel's study, 'Les raisons d'un déclin', provides a subtle and interesting discussion but one that hardly mentions women workers, although they closely fit his analysis.

19   The best short survey of women and the labour movement is Rebérioux (1988); cf. also Guilbert (1966); Zylberberg-Hocquard (1978 and 1981). For new perspectives, cf. Laura Frader's article on the family wage and the French labour movement in L. Frader and Sonya Rose (eds), *Gender and the Reconstruction of Working-class History* (Ithaca: Cornell University Press, 1996, forthcoming). On the CFTC, see Launay (1981); Bard (1993).

20   On the election campaign, see Jackson (1988, chap. 1); Kergoat (1986, chap. 3).

21   Prost rightly points out that union membership was low in metals, food and textiles, but nowhere relates this to the sexual division of labour. Cf. Noiriel (1986: 187): the strikers were mainly 'not very skilled workers [*des ouvriers peu qualifiés*, in the masculine] from large-scale industry, without any tradition of resistance and no experience of the labour movement'.

22   Figures in Guelaud-Léridon (1964), quoted here from Laura Frader, manuscript article, 'Working women and working mothers, gendered identity at work and in the French labor movement', note 6.

23   Cf. Jackson (1988, chap. 2); Kergoat (1986, chap. 4). Tilly (1986: 327) gives the figure of 2.4 million strikers in 16,709 separate strikes. On women, Birgi (1969) and Couteaux (1975) provide much empirical detail. *Humanité* (30 June 1936), carried an article on 'Les femmes dans les grèves'. For an earlier version of this section, see Reynolds (1989).

24   *Humanité* (5 June 1936).
25   ibid. (6 June 1936).
26   ibid. (26 May 1936); but cf. an example of a mixed factory where all workers took eight-hour shifts at occupying, AN BB^{18} 3009, Besançon. These documents (Correspondance des procureurs généraux relative aux grèves de 1936, Series BB^{18} 3007–3012) were consulted with permission and provide some of the few available archival records relating to the strikes.
27   AN, BB^{18} 3011.
28   *Humanité* (9 June 1936). NB on 29 June 1935 *Humanité* had reported that a dressmakers' strike was closely watched by workers in department stores; for detail on *les grands magasins*, see Couteaux (1975: 40–5) on low pay and compulsory make-up and nail varnish. According to *Excelsior* (6 June 1936), there were c.100,000 white-collar workers on strike, a third of them in department stores. Cf. M. Colliette's testimony, in Lefranc (1965: annexe).
29   Henriette Nizan in *Vendredi* (25 June 1936).
30   Birgi (1969) puts forward this argument, which is picked up by e.g. Colin (1975: 116 ff.).
31   Personal checking of the Maitron *Dictionnaire* for the inter-war years showed that many of the entries under women's names were for trade unionists recorded as active after 1936.
32   E.g. AN BB^{18} 3009, Bordeaux region (11 December 1936); BB^{18} 3011 (the famous 'Cusinberghe affair', in which an employer shot a striker); BB^{18} 3007, Aix; BB^{18} 3012, Grenoble (July 1936) – all cases where women workers were at odds with strikers, some reports of violence between groups of women.
33   AN F^{60} 246, letter from G. Lhermitte (Maria Vérone's husband) to Daladier, then Prime Minister, about women's suffrage and equal pay. Cf. *Droit des femmes* (July 1936); on the question of equal pay, see Colin (1975: 116 ff.); Couteaux (1975: 79). Cf. Bard (1995: 326 ff.).
34   For unwitting exclusion of women from 'the working class', cf. Dupeux (1976: 212): 'The CFTC before 1936 had drawn most of its support from office workers and women; now it had more support from *the working class*' (my italics). Many women in the CFTC were textile workers, both before and after 1936.
35   'Journal d'une ouvrière de chez Renault', *Regards* (19 and 26 September 1935) (copies in BDIC).
36   The question of gender in Simone Weil's writings in general is one which has scarcely been addressed, and seems to be of great complexity. The title of the published article in *Révolution prolétarienne* uses the term 'ouvrières', in contrast to the syntax; in many bibliographies, it becomes 'ouvriers'. I have discussed the factory experience texts collected in *La Condition ouvrière* at greater length in an article (Reynolds 1993b). See for full details of publication etc. the new edition of complete works (Weil 1991). The manuscripts are in the Fonds Simone Weil in the Bibliothèque Nationale.

6 THE TRUCE BETWEEN THE SEXES? THE POLITICS OF SOCIAL INTERVENTION FROM THE GREAT WAR TO THE POPULAR FRONT

1   For details of Henri Sellier's career, see the article on him in the Maitron dictionary and Burlen (1987). Cf. Lhemanne (1977); Rabinow (1989: chap. 10); Pennetier *et al.* (1992). Sellier's personal and political archives are deposited in Suresnes, Service de Documentation de la Mairie; this vast collection has been explored very selectively for this and the next chapter.

2   On Hurtado, see 'Quelques figures féminines' (1993) and her own account: Hurtado (1966). She is also transparently the 'Y.H.' among Knibiehler's informants (1980).

3   Cf. Rollet (1948). For details and a bibliography of 'the revival of religious history in France', see Cholvy (1991: 211 ff.)

4   For a balanced discussion of the Secours national, see Eck (1992: 194 ff.). Cf. Hurtado (1966: 39) for a brief reference which fails to problematize it.

5   For a careful account of the debate and a cautious indication of the next step, 'without trying to resolve the problem either of the "ultimate aim" of social service or of its "effectiveness"', see Gradvohl (1987). Del Re's recently published thesis (1994), though a little schematic in form, contains much useful survey material and some stimulating ideas about women and social citizenship. Her analysis of social work is in the Guerrand tradition.

6   See Knibielher (1980: 17–19) for a summary; on Bourgeois, cf. Zeldin (1973, vol. 1, chapter on 'Solidarism'); cf. Guerrand and Rupp (1978). On Calmette, see Murard and Zylberman (1987a: 473).

7   On the Rockefeller mission, see Rollet-Echalier (1990: 394 ff.); Guerrand and Rupp (1978: 44 ff.); on Sellier, see ibid. (68).

8   On the *surintendantes d'usine*, see Fourcaut (1982); Gradvohl (1986 and 1987); cf. Downs (1993). Debate centres on how far they were a mere 'tool of the employers'.

9   On caseworkers' training, see Knibiehler (1980: 78–125); Guerrand and Rupp (1978: 68 ff.); Del Re (1994: 159–66). Guerrand and Rupp (1978) suggest with some reason that the pre-1914 *maison sociale* (modelled on the 'settlement') was a more 'feminist', less intrusive approach than the later home-visiting norm.

10 Rollet-Echalier (1990: 398) gives as reasons both the Anglo–American precedent and the notion of 'family casework', leading to the woman visitor who could approach all members of the family. The 'moniteur' approach of Calmette is described by Murard and Zylberman (1987a), with the suggestion that Solidarism moved the emphasis towards 'educating from above'.

11 Abbé Ch. Grimaud, quoted Guerrand and Rupp (1978: 65). Cf. Del Re (1994: 145) for a quotation on similar lines from Céline Lhotte. Prescriptive quotations need handling with care.

12 On Catholic social work, see also Fayet-Scribe (1990), a mine of information; Protestantism and the social services is also currently being explored; cf. Bard (1995: 241 ff.), on Protestant dynasties and feminism.

13 On Josephine Getting (1877–1943), see 'Quelques figures féminines' (1993: 71–6). Born Rothschild, married to an industrialist, Josephine Getting was well off, but not over-rich. Personal tragedy pushed her into fundraising and nursing during the Great War; Dr Cabot of the American Red Cross prompted her to found the Service Social Hospitalier in France, and she was a prime mover of the Comité Français du Service Social which organized the conference. Refusing to leave Paris during the Second World War, she was deported and died at Auschwitz, aged sixty-six.

14 On Suresnes, see Burlen (1987: esp. 195–245); Rabinow (1989: 339 ff.); Lhémanne (1977: passim).

15 On R. H. Hazemann's career, see Murard and Zylberman (1987b: LIX–XCI).

16 Anon., *Il y a 50 ans H. Sellier installait la première municipalité à direction socialiste à Suresnes* (Saint-Ouen, n.d., but 1970: 7); copy in Musée Social.

17 Hurtado (1966: 25 ff.); cf. Reverdy (1972: 86–8). A comparable institution was the Caisse Régionale de Compensation de la Région Parisienne, for administering family allowances, run by Gustave Maignien; see Pedersen (1993: 269 and 273 ff.).

18 On OPMES, Rollet-Echalier (1990: 414 ff.): 'the organism that best reflects the hopes of the age'; on Strauss and his history of interest in natality and childcare, ibid. (128–30); Strauss, Rollet argues, was not a populationist, but a welfare campaigner. On

Hurtado, see note 2. On Gillet, see Reverdy (1972); on Madeleine Hardouin, see 'Quelques figures féminines' (1993: 53–7).

19　On Léonie Chaptal, see 'Quelques figures féminines' (1993: 31–5); a devout Catholic and sister of a bishop, she founded several charities and a school of nursing. On her death, Sellier wrote to her brother 'What a warm friendship I, the atheist, had with this admirable representative of the evangelical life.' On Juliette Delagrange, see ibid. (37–42); she was instrumental in getting the state diplomas of the caseworkers' profession on to the statute books. 'Used to dealing with men, she judged them very coolly and sometimes with biting sarcasm.' On Josephine Getting, see note 13 above. On Berty Albrecht, see 'Quelques figures féminines' (1993: 81–6); Fourcaut (1982: esp. 221 ff.) as well as her daughter's biography of her – Albrecht (1986).

20　For more details on the women ministers, see Chapter 7 below, and Reynolds (1994). On Suzanne Lacore, see ibid. (201, note 20), and the entry on her in Maitron. A lifelong militant, she was active in the SFIO women's section; for useful references to her early party activity, cf. Sowerwine (1982); see also cuttings file on Lacore in Bibliothèque Marguerite Durand (BMD).

21　*Minerva* (n.d., but December 1936), BMD file on Lacore.

22　The Sellier-Hazemann paper is reproduced in *Revue d'hygiène* (July 1936). Cf. Murard and Zylbermann (1987b: LXIX–LXXI): 'It was a *coup de foudre* at first sight: "another myself", the politician would later say of the expert'. Cf. also Sellier's radio broadcast on taking office, quoted in Lhemanne (1977: 43).

23　Quoted in Anon, 'Il y a cinquante ans' (1970: 25). On the history of the Health Ministry, see Rollet-Echalier (1990: 292–4).

24　*Le Suresnois* (19 December 1936), carton Presse 1936, Archives Henri Sellier, Service de Documentation de la Mairie (SDM), Suresnes.

25　ibid., cutting from *La Lumière* (and not the only one in this vein). Mlle Chaptal died very shortly afterwards. Sellier had not innovated in letting her have an office there.

26　On Juliette Delagrange, see letter to Brunschvicg in Archives Nationales (AN) 312 AP (2), papers of Marcel Abraham, Jean Zay's *directeur de cabinet*.

27　On co-ordination, see circular of 26 September 1936, *Journal Officiel* (3 October 1936); see also AN F^{60} 608, Protection de l'enfance.

28　On Lacore's rhetoric of difference, see for example the brochure *Femmes socialistes* (1932), copy in Musée Social (thanks to Karen Offen for this reference).

29　*L'Oeuvre*, reproduced in *Minerva* (8 November 1936).

30　On the commission, see minutes in Archives Henri Sellier, SDM, Suresnes, file on 'Enfance 1936–7'.

31　Brochure in AN F^{60} 608; cf. *Minerva* (8 November 1936).

32　On Sellier's campaign on prostitution, see the many files on the subject in his archives at Suresnes. For an overview, Corbin (1978); Tardieu (1984). On the well-backed Union temporaire contre la prostitution et la traite des femmes, see Blum *et al.* (1984: 652–3).

33　Anon, *Il y a cinquante ans* (1970: 41).

34　*Le Suresnois* (26 June 1937).

7　THE PERMEABILITY OF PUBLIC LIFE: MAINSTREAM AND ALTERNATIVE POLITICS

1　This chapter develops material from two earlier publications (Reynolds 1993c and 1994).

2　Mme de Witt-Schlumberger (1853–1924), granddaughter of Guizot, was president of the UFSF. Cf. Henriette Coulmy of the CGT, the first woman to sit on the Conseil

Supérieur de l'Enseignement Technique: Correspondence of H. Coulmy, Bouglé Collection, BHVP.

3   Part I of its report was discussed by the Senate in 1936 but Part II, on marriage contracts, was not discussed before the war, reducing the impact of the 1938 law giving married women civil capacity. For details, see M. Kraemer-Bach, 'La capacité de la femme mariée en droit français: la loi du 18 février 1938', *Revue pratique de droit international* (1938), in dossier Kraemer-Bach, BMD, and relevant pages of Kraemer-Bach (1988); cf. Blum and Horne (1988: 351 ff.); Smith (1991).

4   On early women councillors, see *Humanité* (30 May 1926); *La Française* (February and December 1936), on the post-1935 appointments. Cf. Bard (1993: 675 ff.); Weiss (1980: 88). See Maitron dictionary entries for Marie A. Lefevre, Louise Durand; photo of *conseil général* of the Seine, 1936 (ibid., vol. 33: opposite p. 33) (three women included). These municipal councillors should not be confused with symbolic candidatures, a frequent tactic at election time.

5   *Le Droit des Femmes* (July 1936). The episode, if mentioned at all by historians, is normally dismissed as without interest; cf. Borne and Dubief (1989: 205).

6   Marguerite Grépon, 'Les femmes dans la cité des hommes' in *Esprit* (special no., June 1936).

7   For a detailed overview of the women ministers' appointments, see Reynolds (1994). Cf. Spencer (1984) and Adler (1993: 119–28). A Ph.D. dissertation is being written by Claire Sanders.

8   Blum to Lacore, May 1936 (undated), reproduced by Lacore in *Vétéran socialiste* (1960: 18). Cf. Smith (1991: 136). Blum told a meeting (30 June 1936) that he was applying the programme of the Popular Front, where women's suffrage did not figure, not that of the SFIO, where it did.

9   Papers in Curie Archive, Institut Curie, Paris, include Irène Joliot-Curie's draft letter of resignation, letters from Jean Perrin and Jean Zay, and her diary for 1936. Despite speculation about other reasons, her resignation was dated August, and motivated by the wish to succeed her husband at the Sorbonne. From late July until late September she was at the ministry only a few days. Thanks to Mme Bordry, the curator of the Archive. Details in Reynolds (1994: 200 and n.).

10 Interview with Anne-Mathilde Paraf for *La République*, reproduced in *Minerva* (9 November 1936) (in dossier on Brunschvicg in BMD). For more details, see Aubrun (1992).

11 *Minerva* (8 November 1936). Cf also note 23 below.

12 Cécile Brunschvicg appointed a UFSF stalwart, a young male lawyer and her own daughter, Aubrun (1992: 88). Suzanne Lacore appointed two SFIO women, Alice Jouenne and Yvonne Demène (see Maitron entries for these names); neither was a lawyer. On the problem of authority, thanks to Karen Offen for her helpful commentary on my paper to the Berkshire Women's History Conference, Vassar College, 1993. On Brunschvicg's reticence, see Blum and Horne (1988: 359).

13 Joliot-Curie is quoted in *La Française* (23 November 1935) as saying that 'the massive arrival of women voters [would] risk producing political change of which women would be the first victims'; Lacore shared the SFIO women's section view that women might vote for the right. Weiss (1980: 245) dismissively refers to Lacore as in thrall to Sellier but there was probably no dissent between them; Sellier himself tabled a proposal for the *municipal* vote – Smith (1991: 137).

14 *La Française* (30 May 1936).

15 *La Française* (30 May 1938); see the Brunschvicg cuttings file in BMD for evidence that, as a minister, she did occasionally call for votes for women, e.g. at a prize-giving in November 1936.

16 For reactions to the women ministers, see Reynolds (1994: 206). Detailed records survive of a meeting of university rectors held at the Ministry of Education, chaired by Cécile Brunschvicg: she got her way by determined chairing; papers of Marcel Abraham (Zay's chef de cabinet), Archives Nationales, AN 312 AP (6). Cf. Zay (1987: 182) on being a new minister.

17 On the marquise de Crussol, see Guichard (1991: 192 ff.); her first name is variously given. Cf. Réau (1993: 289). Discreet in public, she was widely assumed by the right to be pro-British.

18 On Hélène de Portes, see Guichard (1991: 185–92). Spears (1954: 90 ff.) is representative of the negative opinion of contemporaries.

19 On Suzanne Schreiber, née Crémieux, see Guichard (1991: chap. 8); details in Rustenholz et al. (1993), alas not indexed. Cf. chap. 13 on her links with the 'young Turks' of the party. Her recent separation from her husband could have been why she was not chosen as a minister in 1936. On women in the Radical party, see Berstein (1982, vol. 2: 237); Smith (1991: 91–101).

20 On Geneviève Tabouis, see the file in BMD and her own books, Tabouis (1942 and 1953). In the 1930s her book Le Chantage ou la guerre, translated as Blackmail or War?, a Penguin Special in 1938, gave her great notoriety. Cf. the obituary in Le Monde (24 September 1985).

21 Séverine (Caroline Rémy, 1855–1929) had made her name on Jules Vallès's Le Cri du Peuple in the 1880s, worked on La Fronde before 1914 and wrote for the left-wing and feminist press until her death. Andrée Viollis (1879–1950) was reporter and columnist for L'Oeuvre and other dailies and and co-founder of the Popular Front weekly Vendredi in 1935. Madeleine Jacob covered the Violette Nozière case; see her Quarante ans de journalisme (Paris: Julliard, 1970).

22 On Louise Weiss, see her six-volume memoirs (1980), but handle with care.

23 The essential starting point for any research in this area is Blum et al. (1984).

24 See Blum et al. (1984: 626–7) for the women's section of the Fédération Républicaine de France, and ibid. (627 and 566) on Mme Lescouvé; cf. Smith (1991: 119–23).

25 Little has been written on women and the extreme right. Smith (1991: 128 ff.) for overview. See also Soucy (1986); its sequel (1995) could not be consulted in time for this chapter. On the LPF, see McMillan (1988) and Sohn (1984). Records of the LPF are to be found in police reports in AN F^7 13215/6 and in the Archives de la Préfecture de Police (APPo) Paris, BA 1651.

26 AN F^7 13216, report on 'jubilee meeting' of the LPF.

27 The only possible contender is the anti-fascist movement, animated by the Communist party but including members from the broad left, the Comité Mondial des Femmes contre la Guerre et le Fascisme. Cf. Blum et al. (1984: 575–7).

28 Of the Ligue des Droits de l'Homme founded in 1898, there is no recent history, and the organization's archives were lost (and recently found in Russia, but are not yet accessible). Much information is, however, contained in Basch (1994). Victor Basch was president of the Ligue from 1926 until the war. Police reports of meetings are to be found in AN F^7 13089.

29 On 'Suzon', see Hilden (1989). For identification, see the article on Lacore in Maitron et al., and for Lacore and the turn of the century socialist party (ies) in general, see Sowerwine (1983). Cf. Germaine Picard-Moch's article in Le Populaire (14 March 1935), 'Sacrifier les femmes pour sauver la République', typical of Socialist party feeling. Cf. Smith (1991: 112).

30 On women in the PCF, see Smith (1991: 114 ff.); Dab (1980); Rousseau (1983); Blum et al. (1984: 625–6). There are very few references at all to women in Jacques Girault (ed.), L'Implantation du parti communiste français dans l'entre-deux-guerres (Paris: Editions sociales, 1977).

31 On Henriette Alquier, see above, Chapter 1. During the 1928 election, just after the Alquier case, Pierrette Rouquet, who had organized the campaign for her within the GFEL, wrote to Marthe Bray, a 'bourgeois feminist' in the following terms: 'The communists are certainly the ones who have come out most clearly for votes for women [but] I know them well enough to know that they would not sign your poster; they have a very rigid discipline and rather special understanding of feminism': Fonds M. Bray, carton III, in Bouglé collection, BHVP.

32 The Vaillant-Couturier articles were published in *Humanité* in 1936, cf. Chapter 1 above, and rediscovered by Bouchardeau in her pioneering work (1977).

33 Personal sampling of the Maitron dictionary. At the conference held on completion of the inter-war volumes, it was noted that available records influence the choice of names for a reference work: party records, union lists, the archives of the volunteers for Republican Spain and so on, have all provided entries. A major source for women was Sohn (1975).

34 On the Comité Mondial, see Blum *et al.* (1984: 575 ff.); cf. Bruley (1986: esp. 138–9). Bruley argues that in Britain, unlike France, the Communist party was unsympathetic to women's rights or issues in the 1920s, but became more so in the 1930s – she interprets this as a manoeuvre to recruit women, comparable to what was happening in France with the UJFF.

35 Dominique Loiseau, 'Les militantes de l'ombre: femme de...', paper given at the conference on the Maitron dictionary (Paris, November 1993), based on local research at St Nazaire. Loiseau argues that parties and unions wanted members' wives to sympathize with the movement. To that extent they were 'controlled', but she also sees the Comité Mondial and the UFF as offering them some autonomy. For single women in the families of dockyard workers, political activity was often a duty. On anarchist families, see Auzias (1993), and contribution to *Bulletin de Institut d'Histoire du Temps Présent*, 'Problèmes de méthode en histoire orale' (special no., 1980).

36 In the Paris conference of 1986 on 'Daily Life and the Popular Front', the papers were overwhelmingly about men. By contrast, the 1993 conference celebrating the completion of the Maitron dictionary for the inter-war years included many papers on women and gender.

37 On women and the Dreyfus affair, cf. Maire Cross, 'Dreyfusardes', unpublished conference paper (Paris, December 1994), and see Bard (1995: esp. 227 ff. and 235 ff); for family ties between feminists and politicians, see ibid. (384 ff.).

38 Details on Daladier from Réau (1993) and cf. the same author's brief piece in Sirinelli (1995).

39 On Blum's early life, see Lacouture (1977), and the entry on Blum in the Maitron dictionary.

40 For details of Brunschvicg's early career, see Aubrun (1992).

41 On Thorez, see Robrieux (1975); entries in the Maitron dictionary and Sirinelli (1995). Thorez's autobiography *Fils du peuple* (Paris: Editions sociales, 1937) appeared during the Popular Front for propaganda purposes.

42 The term 'écoles d'oratrices', schools for women speakers, referred to initiatives mostly taken by feminists: in 1932, the UFSF set one up on the urging of Marguerite Durand; Marcelle Kraemer-Bach did something similar. See the file on her in BMD, and Blum *et al.* (1984: 617).

43 Theodore Ruyssen, in *La Paix par le Droit*, special issue on women in 1923, in BMD dossier 'Paix'.

44 Cf. files at the BMD, Bouglé collection at the BHVP, and the Duchêne collection at the BDIC which contain ample evidence of the activity of women's and mixed organizations. This section is chiefly based on reading in the Jeanne Mélin and Marthe Bray

papers in the Bouglé collection, and the sections of the Duchêne papers devoted to peace organizations.

45 See previous note: the Fonds Marthe Bray contains repeated references to exhaustion and illness. Bray herself wrote to a correspondent in 1927, 'We have made enormous sacrifices of money, time, fatigue [*sic* for energy?] and even health . . . everything must be tried.' In 1935, Colette Reynaud was writing to Bray to offer help since she was 'alone and ill' .

46 Examples from papers in APPo BA 1651, which have their counterparts in AN F[7] 13266 (also containing provincial records) NB circular from the Prefect of Police, August 1927, banning processions or marches on the public highway except for funerals and commemorations.

47 The anti-war toys campaign was a feature of the Ligue d'Action Féminine (Marthe Bray). See Bouglé collection, Groupes et associations, boîte 1, and APPo BA 1651. 'As every year in the festive season,' the police reported, 'members of this group stood outside department stores, handing out leaflets' (23 December 1930). The symbolic demonstrations were the brainchild of the indefatigable Jeanne Mélin: see Bouglé collection, Melin papers, esp. boîte 38 (1927–32).

48 For a running commentary on the frustrations and frenetic efforts of this outsider, starting a campaign from scratch, see her correspondence in the Bouglé collection.

49 Weiss (1980) gives many details; see also the file on Femme nouvelle in BMD and the police reports in BA 1651. Blum *et al.* (1984) is uncharacteristically uninformative about this group.

50 Bouglé collection, Fonds Marthe Bray, III, correspondence, letter of 27 May 1927. Bard (1995) gives a wealth of detail about the feminist campaigning milieu and the styles of action.

51 Cf. for example Adeline Daumard, in E. Labrousse and F. Braudel (eds), *Histoire économique de la France* (Paris: Seuil, 1980, vol. 4: 450).

8 WAR AND PEACE: ASSENT AND DISSENT

1 For perspectives on women and international relations, apart from Enloe's original and stimulating book (1989), see Grant and Newland (1989, esp. chaps 2 and 6); Watt (1992).

2 Cf. De Gaulle (1954, vol. 1: 1) and on allegory Warner (1985): many French examples.

3 Cf. Léon Blum's reference to the view shared by both government and 'the French people' over the invasion of the Rhineland in 1936, that 'peaceful regulation' was the way to proceed; quoted in Borne and Dubief (1989: 58).

4 The word 'pacifism' is still handled with care in France. Rémond distinguishes between 'pacifism' as an 'ideological movement' and 'attachment to peace' as a widely shared sentiment. The editors of *Matériaux* (1993) describe the French people as 'pacific', i.e. peace-loving, and pacifism as 'militant activity in favour of peace'. Cf. Blum *et al.* (1984: 515) for similar caution: 'instead of the term "pacifism", which has strong connotations, it is better to use the broader description "anti-war movement".' Cf. note 9 below.

5 For an indication of priorities, cf. the bibliography of Borne and Dubief (1989), a fair reflection of coverage. In the past, the left was much studied; recent years, no doubt because of the rise of the Front National, have seen the publication of more works on the right such as Sirinelli (1992).

6 *Matériaux* (1993) is a symposium of studies of mostly left-wing pacifist organizations, based on recent graduate theses; cf. the bibliography in Offenstadt *et al.* (1993b). The major study of French pacifism in English is Norman Ingram's Ph.D. thesis (University of Edinburgh, 1988); references here are to the published version (Ingram 1991).

7 Jeanne Mélin papers, in Bouglé Collection, Bibliothèque Historique de la Ville de Paris (BHVP), Correspondance, 1931, cf. boîte 37, Cercle Pax Occident-Orient 1931–2.

8 Archives Nationales (AN) F^7 13089, Ligue des Droits de l'Homme, 2 February 1932.

9 Cf. Ingram (introduction) for definitions of pacifism and their relevance to France. LIFPL gives him his biggest headache in terms of classification since he excludes from 'pacifism' groups associated with the Amsterdam–Pleyel movement of the 1930s, discussed below (Ingram 1991: 8–9). On LIFPL's position, cf. Bard (1993), original thesis now published as Bard (1995: see esp. 289–312). Cf. M. Vaisse's distinction between 'post-war pacifism' of the 1920s, bent on avoiding a repetition of the Great War, and 'pre-war pacifism' arising from the threat posed by the dictators, in his article 'Pacifisme' in Sirinelli (1995). For further definitions, e.g. the use of 'pacifism' for the belief that all war is wrong, 'pacificism' as a version that sees war as sometimes necessary, see Caedel (1980, 1987).

10 On the League of Nations, see Walters (1965, chaps 1–7).

11 Cf. Becker and Berstein (1990: 210–22, 250–9). 'Stability was achieved in the years 1925–30 on the basis of the 1924–5 compromise' (Watson 1984: 89–104). On Aristide Briand (1862–1932) the most recent biography is Oudin (1987); cf. article on Briand in Sirinelli (1995).

12 On Marie-Louise Puech, see dossier in Bibliothèque Marguerite Durand (BMD), Dos 327 SOC (Société des Nations).

13 Marie-Louise Puech manuscript, in BMD, Dos 327 SOC; see also Dos 327 Uni (Union féminine pour la SDN); for details and names of French delegates to this conference, see Bard (1995: 131, note 2; 242 ff.). Cf. Vellacott (1993: 30).

14 M.-L. Puech, 'L'action féminine et la Société des Nations', supplement to *La Paix par le Droit* (1922: 3–4), copy in BMD dossier, 327 UNI.

15 On the Protocol, a proposal for compulsory arbitration, eventually buried, in which French premier Herriot had played a prominent part, cf. Walters (1965, chaps 22–4), Becker and Berstein (1990: 253 ff.): 'The basic features of the Briand years were negotiated settlement of reparations, rapprochement with the Allies, reconciliation with Germany and faith in collective security.'

16 Maria Vérone, article in *L'Oeuvre* (October 1928), copy in BMD dossier 327 SOC.

17 *Minerva* regularly printed news of appointments, and cf. Bard (1995: 135, note 3).

18 Cf. the appointment of Germaine Malaterre-Sellier in 1932, once more to the 'family' commission – Guichard (1991: 153 ff.); Bard (1995: 135–6). Cf. Vellacott (1993: 30). Vellacott's sympathies are with the feminists of WILPF who did not want to be confined to a 'womanly' agenda, but NB 'women's issues' covered topics in which women's rights were regularly being violated worldwide: trafficking in women, forced marriages, etc.

19 Walters (1965: 79) comments that the British official Dame Rachel Crowdy was 'the only woman who ever held a post of high responsibility in the secretariat'. On Crowdy, see Miller, (1994: 71): the British envoy Helena Swanwick, a specialist on disarmament, despaired at being assigned to the inevitable Fifth (family) Committee: 'As a woman I was predestined for the Fifth Committee, a sort of ragbag of miseries and forlorn hopes' (ibid.: 68). Cf. Enloe (1989: 121) on the present-day UN: in 1984, while women held 83 per cent of clerical and secretarial posts, they held only 22.3 per cent of the professional international civil service posts.

20 On Marguerite Thibert (1886–1982), see the special supplement to no. 28 of *Citoyennes à part entière* (the magazine of the Ministère des Droits de la Femme) (February 1984), devoted to her.

21 On the overall history of WILPF, see Bussey and Tims (1965) and Vellacott (1993).

22 Vérone, *L'Oeuvre* (11 September 1929); Rudler, quoted in BMD dossier DOS 327 PAIX.

23 On the LICP, founded by Victor Méric, 'the Dick Sheppard of French pacifism', see Ingram (1991: 134 ff.) and Offenstadt (1993a). The LICP was particularly concerned about the new technology of warfare, such as chemical weapons.

24 See Thébaud (1984: 135) for some literary examples, and compare Roberts (1994, chap. 1). Not all the voices were men's; cf. Andrée Jouve writing in a pamphlet in 1918 that 'all women accepted the war and sought to play a part in this monstrous crime', cited in Bard (1995: 129).

25 'Civilians didn't care, they had no idea of the carnage we were living through. The war could go on, the home front would be OK. The cinemas were open . . . . Girls wouldn't look as us, poor squaddies home on leave: we weren't smart enough in our civvies' – Prost (1977, vol. 3: 74).

26 Becker and Berstein (1990: 255) quote Briand: 'I am following the policy dictated by our birth rate.'

27 On Vernet's league, see Bouglé Collection, BHVP, Groupes et Associations, boîte 1, dossier on Vernet; cf. APPo BA 1651, on the Ligue. In 1922, it brought together twenty-two other organizations in its campaign against war toys. Many core members were communist sympathisers (Hélène Brion, Colette Reynaud). Vernet (1878–1949) became a 'professional peace campaigner'.

28 On LIMEP, see Blum *et al.* (1984: 585) and papers in Bouglé collection, BHVP, G & A, boîte 1, December 1934.

29 Cf. AN F^{60} 246, letters to Prime Minister's office, letter from LIMEP of 22 May 1939, calling for a general non-aggression pact.

30 Cécile Brunschvicg, quoted by Bard (1995: 94). On the 1915 conference, see Vellacott, (1993: passim); Liddington (1985) and Wiltsher (1985). On LIFPL in general see Ingram (1991, chaps 10 and 11). The papers in the Fonds Gabrielle Duchêne at the BDIC, Nanterre, are the essential primary source for any study of the French branch.

31 On Jeanne Halbwachs and Michel Alexandre, both long-term peace campaigners, see the entries in Maitron. On the comité de la rue Fondary, see Bard (1995: 99–102); Ingram says very little about the early days of LIFPL, and the Duchêne papers are silent. Duchêne was asked to resign from her post in the CNFF and her daughter was invited to resign from her school's former pupils' association. Cf. the long police report on the feminist groups during this period in APPo, BA 1651, October 1915. On the extraordinary life of Gabrielle Duchêne (1870–1954), one of the most active women on the left in this period, see references for LIFPL and Anon, *Gabrielle Duchêne : In memoriam* (Paris: LIFPL, 1954).

32 Letter from Jeanne Mélin to Cécile Brunschvicg, 22 May 1919, correspondence, Fonds Jeanne Mélin, in Bouglé collection, BHVP; cf. Bard (1995: 137). On the Zurich conference, see Vellacott (1993).

33 See AN F^7 13350, antimilitarisme 1928–30, for police reports on this campaign.

34 See Challener (1955: 197) for text and further details. Originally proposed by the Conseil supérieur de la défense and sponsored by Maginot and Painlevé, it went with the defensive strategy of the French military high command. Paul-Boncour, however, saw it as compatible with Jaurès's vision of the nation in arms.

35 Quoted in Bard (1993: 268); on Brion's trial for 'defeatism', see Bard (1995: 102–8). Brion was always more of a feminist than a pacifist, however; cf. ibid. (141–4).

36 Text in Fonds Jeanne Mélin, Bouglé collection, 18 March 1927.

37 AN F^7 13089, February 1932, speech under the aegis of the Ligue des Droits de l'Homme.

38 Challener (1955: 229 ff.); cf. Nicole Dombrowski, 'When the generals were impotent and the mothers virile', paper given at the Ninth Berkshire Conference on Women's History, Vassar, 1993, on the absence of state-organized civil defence during the phoney war and the exodus of 1940. In 1938, a committee of women in the Légion

d'honneur set about encouraging voluntary civil defence: Bouglé collection, BHVP, Groupes et Associations, boîte 5, brochure 'Le service national féminin'. Backers included G. Tabouis, L. Weiss, S. Grinberg.

39   For the context of the Stalin–Laval agreement and the rise of anti-fascism after February 1934, see Jackson (1988: 195 ff.) and Kergoat (1986: 58 ff.); Borne and Dubief (1989, chap. 4, 'La crise diplomatique').

40   For numbers, see Ingram, (1991, 259–62); Fonds Duchêne, BDIC Nanterre, FΔRes 206, September 1935.

41   See Ingram (1991, chaps 10 and 11) for details on LIFPL and cf. Dreyfus (1982, 1988, 1993). Dreyfus regards LIFPL as a good litmus test for changes in left-wing opinion. Ingram agrees that LIFPL showed 'remarkable clear-sightedness . . . with regard to the danger posed by Hitler', but argues that its leaders were abandoning both their pacifism and to some extent their feminism in embracing anti-fascism so whole-heartedly.

42   Fonds Duchêne, BDIC, FΔRes 208 (22), letter from Jeanne Lenormand, April 1933.

43   ibid., FΔRes 208 (16), correspondence of 1935, letter of 5 July.

44   ibid., FΔRes 208 (17), 10 November 1936.

45   ibid., FΔRes 208 (17), correspondent from Valence, 12 October 1936.

46   ibid., FΔRes 208 (22), Caen branch; cf. comments on the same papers by Ingram (1991: 260–1).

47   ibid., FΔRes 208 (15), July 1935.

48   The role of women in the support organizations for the Republican cause during the Spanish Civil War has not to my knowledge ever been explored thoroughly, although there is plentiful if very scattered information in the various archives. There were many humanitarian groups providing aid for refugees, taking in orphans etc., as well as more active forms of participation such as military action by both men and women. The Maitron dictionary includes entries for men and women who volunteered for action, taken from the archives of the Association des Vétérans de l'Espagne Républicaine. The Duchêne papers contain a mass of documentation on the Comité international de coordination et d'information pour l'aide à l'Espagne républicaine, FΔRes 251 (1-8); FΔRes 104. The Comité Mondial des Femmes was particularly active.

49   For theoretical approaches to these questions, see Elshtain (1987), Pierson (1987: see esp. essay by Carroll).

9   RIGHTS AND THE REPUBLIC: THE INTER-WAR YEARS AS ANTECHAMBER TO DEMOCRACY?

1   Cf. Dubief (1976: 222); Sauvy (1984, vol. 2: 191–201, 297–305); Frank (1982); the various interpretations are fully discussed by Jackson (1988). NB The legend on the Palais-Bowbon now reads: *Assemblée Nationale*.

2   On suffrage, see Hause (1984). On the inter-war period Smith (1991; forthcoming as a book) and Bard (1993 and 1995) are essential. For longer-term perspectives, see Roy (1994); Klejman *et al.* (1989); McMillan (1981). On origins, see Moses (1984), and on post-war feminism Duchen (1986 and 1994).

3   Rosanvallon's book, although I do not agree with all he says, is unusual and admirable among works by French political scientists, in that it pays serious attention to the relation between women and 'universal suffrage'.

4   For details of the dates of women's suffrage in other countries, see Hause (1984: 18–27, 253 ff. and references).

5   Mayeur (1984: 8) warns against anachronistic readings of this period: 'for a long stretch of the history of the Third Republic, attitudes towards the régime and *laïcité* formed the

true demarcation line between left and right' – something he sees as shifting seriously only in 1936.

6   Discussed further in my paper 'Le Sacre de la citoyenne: réflexions sur le retard français', given at colloquium 'Féminismes et cultures nationales', Lyon, 1994, forthcoming in Proceedings.

7   This account is a partial compilation from several sources, including Bard (1995), Smith (1991), Hause (1984) and drawing in particular on the useful summary in Pascal (1990: 13–28). The voting figures vary in secondary accounts. It should be remembered that since the Senate was elected by indirect suffrage, granting women the vote in municipal elections would have made them indirect electors of the Senate. This was not always made explicit.

8   Christine Bard, 'Les luttes contre le suffrage unisexuel sous la Troisième Ré-mi-publique', *Modern and Contemporary France* (1995, vol. NS3: 146).

9   For an overview from a political science perspective, see Berstein (1992: 357–81). Despite the promising title, this article contrives not to mention the change in the electorate between these two republics.

10 For full details of this period, see Williams (1972). The April ordinance was confirmed in 1944, and regulated elections until the final Constitution of the Fourth Republic was adopted in October 1946: this enshrined the principle of equal citizenship for French people of both sexes.

11 Cf. *Les grandes dates de l'histoire de France* (Paris: Larousse, 1986 edn: 229 – 'April–May 1945, left wins local elections (women vote)').

12 Some historians do choose their words more carefully than others. See, for example, Larkin (1988: 143) (a slightly quirky version, however).

13 On the different bodies which played a role in the Algiers debate, see Roy (1994: 225–64); Grenier (1977) is an extremely influential first-hand account.

14 Details based on Roy (1994) and Grenier (1977: 259–60).

15 Neither Shennan (1989) nor Wall (1991) refers to Allied pressure. Shennan (68) regards it as 'almost inconceivable' that women would not be included in the post-war institutions, but remarks that the April 1944 ordinance made it a *fait accompli* from which retreat would be difficult.

16 On the omission of women's suffrage from the various drafts of the Charte de la Résistance, see Andrieu (1984: 35, 76 and 152).

17 On the Vichy proposals and the CNR committee, see Roy (1994: 225 ff.). On women in the Resistance, apart from first-hand accounts, recent surveys include Rossiter (1986), Guidez (1989) and Bertin (1993). For a seminal analytical approach, see Paula Schwarz (1987). Cf. Diamond (1992: esp. 250, note 10).

18 But NB unpublished master's thesis by Paula Schwarz, 'Precedents for politics: pre-war activism of women in the French resistance' (Columbia University, 1981), which could not alas be consulted for this book.

19 Diamond (1992): see esp. chaps 5, 6, 8 and appendix on the oral history sample.

20 Data compiled from Pascal's biographical listings (1990). For details of the first *députées*, cf. Footitt (1995), kindly sent me by the author before publication.

21 'History has been churlish towards the inter-war feminists, the "deserving pupils" of the republic' (Bard 1995: 458); cf. Borne and Dubief (1989: 205): feminism was 'weak ... anaemic and divided'; for choicer terms ('ridiculous, extravagant ... of easy morals'), see Adeline Daumard in Braudel *et al.* (1982: 450).

22 Cf. Bard (1995: 449); Diamond (1992: 249–52 and 1995). The question is fully addressed in Duchen (1994, chaps 1 and 2) and Jenson (1987).

23 The campaign for 'la parité' was launched in 1994 during the commemoration of the fiftieth anniversary of women's voting rights. Cf. press reports and conference held in University of Paris-VII and at the Assemblée Nationale, November 1994, Proceedings

to be edited by Eliane Viénot. Cf. Gaspard *et al.* (1992). The problems facing women entering a male culture are fully aired in Mariette Sineau's perceptive book *Des femmes en politique* (Paris: Economica, 1988).

CONCLUSION

1   Michèle Riot-Sarcey, 'L'histoire des femmes en France: un objet mal identifié', article read in manuscript before publication (1, 3).
2   Raphael Samuel, *Theatres of Memory*, vol. 1, *Past and Present in Contemporary Culture* (London: Verso, 1995: 444). This passage continues as follows: 'The influence of feminism, which in the space of twenty years, has...put all our taken-for-granted categories into question, hardly needs arguing, though in the field of political history, it still seems possible for all-male academics to assemble.' For the term 'unofficial knowledge', see ibid., 'Introduction' .
3   See, for example, Anne Phillips, *Engendering Democracy* (Cambridge: Polity, 1991).
4   Nicole-Claude Mathieu, 'Critique épistémologique de la problématique des sexes dans le discours ethno-anthropologique' (IRESCO, 1985) in *L'anatomie politique, catégorisations et idéologies du sexe* (Paris: côté-femmes, 1991: 104) cited by Riot-Sarcey, 'L'histoire des femmes', manuscript p. 13.

SOURCES AND BIBLIOGRAPHY

Full references to primary sources will be found in footnotes, using the abbreviations listed here:

AN: Archives Nationales (CARAN), Paris.
APPo: Archives de la Préfecture de Police, Paris.
Bouglé (BHVP): Collection Marie-Louise Bouglé, Bibliothèque Historique de la Ville de Paris (BHVP); catalogue by M. Albistur.
BMD: Bibliothèque Marguerite Durand, Paris: named dossiers of documents and press cuttings.
BDIC: Bibliothèque de Documentation Internationale Contemporaine, Nanterre: Duchêne collection.

BIBLIOGRAPHY OF WORKS CITED IN TEXT

General works are listed in the first section and may be referred to throughout the book, otherwise secondary sources are listed by theme, referring to chapters or groups of chapters. Short Harvard-style references in both text and notes refer to this bibliography, which includes unpublished theses. Only works cited are listed here: books marked with (B) carry very full bibliographies for further reference. Unless otherwise indicated, all French titles were published in Paris, and all translations of quotations are my own.

GENERAL WORKS ON FRENCH HISTORY AND ON WOMEN'S/ GENDER HISTORY, PLUS REFERENCES FROM INTRODUCTION

Abbad, Fabrice (1993) *La France des années 20*, Armand Colin.
Agulhon, Maurice (1990) *La République de Jules Ferry à François Mitterrand*, Hachette.
Appleby, Joyce, Hunt, Lynn and Jacob, Margaret (1994) *Telling the Truth about History*, New York/ London: Norton.
Bard, Christine (1995) *Les Filles de Marianne: histoire des féminismes 1914–1940*, Fayard. (B)
Becker, Jean-Jacques and Berstein, Serge (1990) *Victoire et frustrations 1914–1929*, Seuil. (B)
Bennett, Judith (1989) 'Feminism and history', *Gender and History* 1, 3: 251–72.
Berstein, Serge (1988) *La France des années 30*, Armand Colin.
Bock, Gisela (1989) 'Women's history and gender history: aspects of an international debate', *Gender and History* 1, 1: 7–30.
Borne, Dominique and Dubief, Henri (1989) *La Crise des années trente*, Seuil. (B)
Bouchardeau, Huguette (1977) *Pas d'histoire les femmes?*, Syros.

Bridenthal, Renate, Koonz, Claudia and Stuard, Susan (eds) (1987) *Becoming Visible: women in history*, Boston: Houghton Mifflin. (B)

Brunet, J.-P. and Launay, M. (1974) *D'une guerre à l'autre 1914–1945*, Hachette.

Burguière, André and Revel, Jacques (eds) (1989–92) *Histoire de France*, 4 vols, Seuil.

Canning, Kathleen (1994) 'History after the linguistic turn: historicizing discourse and experience', *Signs* 19, 2: 368–404. (B)

Citron, Suzanne (1991) *Le Mythe national: l'histoire de France en question*, Eds Ouvrières.

Dauphin, Cécile *et al.* (collective article) (1986) 'Culture et pouvoir des femmes, essai d'historiographie', *Annales E.S.C.* 41, 2: 271–93.

Davis, Natalie Zemon (1992), 'Women and the world of the "Annales"', *History Workshop Journal* 33: 121–37.

Desanti, Dominique (1984) *La Femme au temps des années folles*, Stock.

Downs, Laura Lee (1993) 'If woman is just an empty category, then why am I afraid to walk alone at night? Identity politics meets the post-modern subject' in *Comparative Studies of Society and History* 35: 414–38.

Duby, Georges and Perrot, Michelle (1988–92) *Histoire des femmes en Occident*, Plon, 5 vols, translated by A. Goldhammer (1992–5) as *A History of Women in the West*, Cambridge, Mass: Belknap, 5 vols. (B) Page references to French edition.

Duchen, Claire (1994a) *Women's Rights and Women's Lives in France 1944–68*, London: Routledge.

—— (1994b) 'Gender', *Paragraph*, 17: 227–35.

Farge, Arlette (1984) 'Pratique et effets de l'histoire des femmes' in M. Perrot (ed.) *Une histoire des femmes est-elle possible?*, Marseille: Rivages.

Fauré, Christine (1980) 'L'absente' in *Les Temps modernes* no. 410: 502–13 (in English (1981) in *Signs* 7, 1: 71–80).

Gilbert, Sandra (1987) 'Soldier's Heart: literary men, literary women and the Great War' in M. Higonnet *et al.* (eds) *Behind the Lines*, q.v.

Gildea, Robert (1994) *The Past in French History*, New Haven/London: Yale University Press. (B)

Higonnet, Margaret, Jenson, Jane, Michel, Sonya and Weitz, Margaret C. (1987) *Behind the Lines: gender and the two world wars*, New Haven/London: Yale University Press.

Hoff, Joan (1994) 'Gender, a postmodern category of paralysis', *Women's History Review* 3, 2: 149–68.

Jenkins, Keith (1991) *Rethinking History*, London: Routledge.

Klejman, Laurence and Rochefort, Florence (1989) *L'Egalité en marche: le féminisme sous la Troisième République*, eds des femmes.

Larkin, Maurice (1988) *France since the Popular Front 1936–86*, Oxford: Clarendon Press.

Le Doeuff, Michelle (1989) *L'Etude et le rouet: des femmes, de la philosophie etc.*, Seuil.

Lequin, Yves (1983–4) *Histoire des Français XIXe siècle–XXe siècle*, Armand Colin, 3 vols.

McMillan, James F. (1981) *Housewife or Harlot: the place of women in French society 1870–1940*, Brighton: Harvester.

—— (1992) *Twentieth-century France: politics and society 1898–1991*, London: E. Arnold. (B)

—— (1994) 'Social history, "new cultural history" and the rediscovery of politics: some recent work on modern France', *Journal of Modern History* 66, 4 : 755–72. (B)

Maitron, Jean and Pennetier, Claude (eds) (1982–93) *Dictionnaire biographique du mouvement ouvrier français*, Part IV (1914–39), Editions ouvrières (referred to in text as 'Maitron').

Mayeur, Jean-Marie (1984) *La Vie politique en France sous la Troisième République*, Seuil.

Nora, Pierre (ed.) (1984–92) *Lieux de mémoire*, Gallimard, 7 vols.

Offen, Karen, Pierson, Ruth and Rendall, Jane (eds) (1991) *Writing Women's History: international perspectives*, London: Macmillan.

Ory, Pascal (1994) *La belle illusion: culture et politique sous le signe du Front Populaire*, Plon.

Perrot, Michelle (1984) *Une histoire des femmes est-elle possible?*, Marseille: Rivages (translated by F. Pheasant (1992) as *Writing Women's History*, Oxford: Blackwell).

—— (1994) 'Où en est en France l'histoire des femmes?', *French Politics and Society*, 12, 1: 39–57. (B)

Perrot, see also Duby.

Pomata, Gianna (1993) 'History particular and universal: on reading some recent women's history textbooks', *Feminist Studies* 19, 1: 7–50. (B)

SOURCES AND BIBLIOGRAPHY

Price, Roger (1993) *A Concise History of France*, Cambridge: Cambridge University Press.
Prost, Antoine (1992) 'What has happened to French social history?', *Historical Journal* 35, 3: 671–9.
Rémond, René and Bourdon, Janine (eds) (1978) *La France et les Français 1938–1939*, FNSP.
—— (ed.) (1988) *Pour une histoire politique*, Seuil.
—— with Sirinelli, J.-F. (1990) *Notre siècle*, Fayard.
Reynolds, Siân (ed.) (1986) *Women, State and Revolution, essays on power and gender in Europe since 1789*, Brighton: Harvester.
Riley, Denise (1988) *'Am I That Name?' Feminism and the category of 'women' in history*, London: Macmillan.
Roberts, Mary Louise (1994) *A Civilization Without Sexes? Reconstructing gender in postwar France 1917–1927*, Chicago: University of Chicago Press. (B)
Rosanvallon, Pierre (1992) *Le Sacre du citoyen: histoire du suffrage universel en France*, Gallimard.
Rousso, Henri (1991) *The Vichy Syndrome: history and memory in France since 1944*, translated by A. Goldhammer, Cambridge, Mass: Harvard University Press.
Sauvy, Alfred (1984) *Histoire économique de la France entre les deux guerres*, Economica, 3 vols.
Scott, Joan Wallach (1986) 'Gender: a useful category of historical analysis', *American Historical Review* 91, 5: 1,053–75.
—— (1988) *Gender and the Politics of History*, New York: Columbia University Press.
—— (1991a) 'Women's history' in P. Burke (ed.) *New Perspectives in Historical Writing*, Cambridge: Polity.
—— (1991b) 'The evidence of experience', *Critical Inquiry* 17, 4: 773–97.
Sirinelli, Jean-François (1988) *Génération intellectuelle: khagneux et normaliens entre les deux guerres*, Plon.
—— (ed.) (1995) *Dictionnaire historique de la vie politique française au XXe siècle*, PUF.
——, Vandenbussche, R. and Vavasseur-Desperriers, J. (1993) *La France de 1914 à nos jours,* PUF.
Stuard, Susan Mosher (1981) 'The Annales school and feminist history: opening dialog with the American stepchild', *Signs* 7, 1: 136–43.
Tartakowsky, Danielle and Willard, Claude (1986) *Les lendemains qui chantent? La France des années folles et du Front populaire*, Messidor.
Thébaud, Françoise (ed.) (1992) vol. 5, *Le XXe siècle* in Perrot, Michelle and Duby, Georges, *Histoire des femmes en Occident*, Plon. (B)
Zeldin, Theodore (1973 and 1977) *France 1848–1945*, Oxford: Clarendon Press.

DEMOGRAPHY (CHAPTER 1)

Becker, J. J. and Berstein, Serge (1990) *Victoire et frustrations 1914–1929*, Seuil. (B)
Bernard, F. *et al.* (1968) *Le Syndicalisme dans l'enseignement*, Grenoble: IEP.
Berstein, Serge (1988) *La France des années 30*, Armand Colin.
Biraben, J. N. (1981) *Les Berceaux vides de Marianne: l'avenir de la population française*, Seuil.
Black, Naomi (1989) *Social Feminism*, Ithaca: Cornell University Press.
Bock, Gisela and Thane, Pat (eds) (1991) *Maternity and Gender Policies: women and the rise of the European welfare states, 1880s–1950s*, London: Routledge.
Borne, Dominique and Dubief, Henri (1989) *La Crise des années trente*, Seuil. (B)
Bouchardeau, Huguette (1977) *Pas d'histoire les femmes?*, Syros.
Brunet, J.-P., Launay, M. (1974) *D'une guerre à l'autre 1914–1945*, Hachette.
Ceccaldi, Dominique (1957) *Histoire des prestations familiales en France*, UNCAF.
Cova, Anne (1989) 'Cécile Brunschvicg (1877–1946) et la protection de la maternité' in *Actes du 113e colloque des sociétés savantes*, Strasbourg.
—— (1990) 'L'assurance maternité dans la loi de 1928–30' in *Actes du 114e colloque des sociétés savantes*, Strasbourg.
Davidson, F. (1964) *Day-care centres in Paris and its suburbs*, Geneva, WHO papers, no. 24.
Dubesset, Mathilde *et al.* (1977) 'Les munitionnettes de la Seine' in Patrick Friderson (ed.) *L'autre front*, Editions ouvrières.

254

Duchen, Claire (1986) *Feminism in France from May 1968 to Mitterrand*, London: Routledge.

Dupâquier, Jacques (ed.) (1988) *Histoire de la population française*, vol. 4, *De 1914 à nos jours*, PUF.

Fuchs, Rachel (1988) 'Morality and poverty: public welfare for mothers in Paris 1867–1900', *French History* 2, 1: 288–311.

Glass, D. V. (1940, revised 1967) *Population Policies and Movements in Europe*, London: Frank Cass.

Guerrand, Roger-Henri (1971) *Libre maternité*, Castermann.

—— and Ronsin, Francis (1990), *Le Sexe apprivoisé: Jeanne Humbert et la lutte pour le contrôle des naissances*, La Découverte.

Hantrais, Linda (1992) 'La fécondité en France et au Royaume-Uni: les effets possibles de la politique familiale', *Population* 4: 987–1,016.

Huss, Marie-Monique (1990) 'Pro-natalism in inter-war France', *Journal of Contemporary History* 25, 1: 39–68 (see also under Ogden).

Jaspard, Maryse (1992) 'Mythes et réalités de la démographie française', *Nouvelles questions féministes* 13, 3: 5–28.

Jenson, Jane (1986) 'Gender and reproduction or : babies and the state', *Studies in Political Economy* 20: 9–46.

Knibiehler, Yvonne and Fourquet, Catherine (1980) *Histoire des mères*, Montalba.

Larkin, Maurice (1988) *France since the Popular Front 1936–86*, Oxford: Clarendon Press.

Laroque, Pierre (ed.) (1986) *La Politique familiale en France, depuis 1945*, Documentation française.

Le Bras, Hervé (1991) *Marianne et les lapins*, Olivier Orban.

Le Doeuff, Michèle (1989) *L'Etude et le rouet*, Seuil.

L'Héritier, J. (1984) 'Le jour où l'on mit les enfants à la crèche', *Histoire* no. 67.

Liszek, Slava (1995) *Marie Guillot : de l'émancipation des femmes à celle du syndicalisme*, L'Harmattan.

McLaren, Angus (1983) *Sexuality and Social Order: the debate over the fertility of women and workers in France 1770–1930*, New York: Holmes & Meier.

McMillan, James (1981) *Housewife or Harlot*, Brighton: Harvester.

—— (1992) *Twentieth-century France*, London: Arnold.

Mayeur, Jean-Marie (1984) *La Vie politique sous la IIIe République*, Seuil.

Milza, Pierre (1986) *Les Italiens en France de 1914 à 1940*, Rome: Ecole française de Rome.

Noiriel, Gérard (1988) *Le Creuset français: histoire de l'immigration XIXe–XXe siècles*, Seuil.

Offen, Karen (1984) 'Depopulation, nationalism and feminism in fin-de-siècle France', *American Historical Review* 89: 648–76.

—— (1988) 'Defining feminism: a comparative historical approach', *Signs* 14, 1: 119–57.

—— (1991) 'Body politics: women, work and the politics of motherhood in France, 1920–1950' in G. Bock and P. Thane, *Maternity and Gender Policies*, q.v.

Ogden, Philip and Huss, Mari-Monique (1982) 'Demography and pronatalism in France in the nineteenth and twentieth centuries', *Journal of Historical Geography* 8, 3: 283–98.

Pedersen, Susan (1993a) 'Catholicism, feminism and the politics of the family during the late Third Republic' in Seth Koven and Sonya Rose (eds) *Mothers of a New World: maternalist politics and the origins of welfare states*, London: Routledge.

—— (1993b) *Family, Dependence and the Origins of the Welfare State: Britain and France 1914–1945*, Cambridge: Cambridge University Press. (B)

Perrot, Michelle (1984) *Une histoire des femmes est-elle possible?*, Marseille: Rivages.

Rémond, René, with Sirinelli, J.-F. (1990) *Notre siècle*, Fayard.

Reynolds, Siân (1990) 'Who wanted the crèches? Working mothers and the birth rate in France 1900–1950', *Continuity and Change* 5, 2: 173–97.

Roberts, Mary Louise (1994) *A Civilization Without Sexes? Reconstructing gender in postwar France 1917–1927*, Chicago: University of Chicago Press. (B)

Rollet-Echalier, Catherine (1990) *La Politique de la petite enfance sous la IIIe Republique*, INED.

Ronsin, Francis (1980) *La Grève des ventres: propagande néo-malthusienne et baisse de la natalité en France 19e–20e siècles*, Aubier.

Scott, Joan W. (1987) 'Rewriting history' in Margaret Higonnet *et al.* (eds) *Behind the Lines: gender and the two world wars*, New Haven: Yale University Press.

Sirinelli, Jean-François *et al.* (1993) *La France de 1914 à nos jours*, PUF.

Smith, Bonnie (1981) *Ladies of the Leisure Class: the bourgeoises of northern France in the nineteenth century*, Princeton: Princeton University Press.

Sohn, Anne-Marie (1977) 'Exemplarité et limites de la participation féminine à la vie syndicale: les institutrices de la CGTU', *Revue d'histoire moderne et contemporaine* 24: 391–414.

—— (1992) 'Entre deux guerres' in Françoise Thébaud (ed.) *Le XXe siècle*, vol. 5 of *Histoire des femmes en Occident*, Plon.

—— (1993) 'Les rôles féminins dans la vie privée à l'époque de la IIIe République', doctoral thesis (doctorat d'état), University of Paris-I.

Spengler, J. J. (1976, original edition 1938) *France Faces Depopulation*, postlude edition 1936–76, Durham: University of North Carolina Press.

Stewart, Mary Lynn (1988) *Women, Work and the French State: labour protection and social patriarchy 1879–1919*, Montreal: McGill/Queens University Press.

Sussman, Gerald (1982) *Selling Mother's Milk: the wet-nursing business in France 1715–1914*, Urbana: University of Illinois Press.

Talmy, Robert (1962) *Histoire du mouvement familial en France 1896–1939*, Aubenas: UNCAF, 2 vols.

Tartakowsky, Danielle and Willard, Claude (1986) *Les lendemains qui chantent? La France des années folles et du Front populaire*, Messidor.

Thébaud, Françoise (1984) *La Femme au temps de la guerre de 14*, Stock.

—— (1985) 'Le mouvement nataliste dans la France de l'entre-deux-guerres: l'Alliance nationale pour l'accroissement de la population francaise', *Revue d'histoire moderne et contemporaine* 32: 276–301.

—— (1986) *Quand nos grand-mères donnaient la vie: la maternité en France dans l'entre-deux-guerres*, Lyon: Presses Universitaires de Lyon.

Tilly, Louise and Scott, Joan (1978) *Women, Work and Family*, New York: Rinehart & Winston.

Tomlinson, Richard (1986) 'The Politics of Dénatalité during the French Third Republic 1890–1940', unpublished Ph.D. thesis, University of Cambridge.

CHILDHOOD, YOUTH (CHAPTER 2)

Aubert, Jeanne (1991) *JOCF qu'as-tu fait de nos vies?: la Jeunesse Ouvrière Chrétienne Féminine 1928–1945*, Editions Ouvrières.

Barrot, Olivier and Ory, Pascal (eds) (1990) *Entre-deux-guerres: la création française 1919–1939*, François Bourin.

Baudelot, Christian and Establet, Roger (1992) *Allez les filles!*, Seuil.

Baudoux, Claudine and Zaidmann, Claude (eds) (1992) *Egalité entre les sexes: mixité et démocratie*, L'Harmattan.

Beauvoir, Simone de (1980, originally published 1958) *Mémoires d'une jeune fille rangée*, Folio.

Bonheur, Gaston (1963) *Qui a cassé le Vase de Soissons?*, Laffont.

Bourdieu, Pierre (1988) *Homo Academicus*, translated by P. Collier, Cambridge: Polity.

Cacérès, Benigno (1981) *Allons au-devant de la vie: la naissance du temps des loisirs en 1936*, Maspéro.

Cavanna, François (1978) *Les Ritals*, Livre de poche edition.

Charle, Christophe (1994) *La République des universitaires*, Seuil.

Charrière, Edmé (1931) *L'évolution intellectuelle féminine*, Albert Meckelinck.

Chartier, Roger and Martin, Henri-Jean (eds) (1991) *Histoire de l'édition française*, vol. 4, *Le livre concurrencé*, Fayard.

Cheroutre, M. Th. and Cholvy, Gérard (eds) (1990) *Scoutisme féminin et promotion féminine*, Eds des Guides de France.

Cholvy, Gérard (ed.) (1985) *Mouvements de jeunesse chrétiens et juifs: sociabilité juvénile dans un cadre européen 1799–1968*, Le Cerf.

—— and Hilaire, Y. M. (1986) *Histoire religieuse de la France contemporaine*, 3 vols: vol. 2, *1880–1930*; vol. 3 *1930–1988*, Privat.

——, Conte, Bernard and Feroldi, Vincent (1991) *Jeunesses chrétiennes*, Editions Ouvrières.

Christophe, Paul (1986) *1936: les Catholiques et le Front Populaire*, Editions Ouvrières.

Clark, Linda L. (1982) 'The socialization of girls in the primary schools of the Third Republic', *Journal of Social History* 15: 685–97.
—— (1984) *Schooling the Daughters of Marianne: textbooks and the socialization of girls in modern French primary schools*, Albany: SUNY Press.
Cohen, Yolande (1989) *Les jeunes, les socialistes, la guerre: histoire des mouvements de jeunesse en France*, L'Harmattan.
Coutrot, Aline (1985) 'Le mouvement de jeunesse: un phénomène au singulier?' in G. Cholvy (ed.) *Mouvements de jeunesse chrétiens et juifs: sociabilité juvénile dans un cadre européen 1799–1968*, Le Cerf.
Crubellier, Maurice (1979) *L'Enfance et la jeunesse dans la société française 1800–1958*, Armand Colin.
Davis, Natalie Zemon (1992) 'Women and the World of the "Annales"', *History Workshop Journal* 33: 121–37.
Debes, J. and Poulat, Emile (1986) *L'Appel de la JOC 1926–1928*, Editions Ouvrières.
Decroux-Masson, Annie (1979) *Papa lit, maman coud: les manuels scolaires en bleu et rose*, Denoel-Gauthier.
Dufrasne, Claude (1991) *Le Mouvement ajiste*, University of Paris-VII.
Effenterre, H. van (1947) *Histoire du scoutisme*, PUF.
Fourment, Alain (1987) *Histoire de la presse des jeunes et des journaux pour enfants*, Eole.
Furet, François and Ozouf, Jacques (1982) *Reading and Writing: literacy in France from Calvin to Jules Ferry*, Cambridge: Cambridge University Press.
Gruny, Marguerite (1986) 'L'époque des pionniers', *Revue des livres pour enfants* no. 110: 46–59.
Heller-Goldenberg, Lucette (1984) 'Histoire des auberges de jeunesse', doctorat d'état, Nice.
Heywood, Colin (1988) *Childhood in Nineteenth-century France: work, health and education among the classes populaires*, Cambridge: Cambridge University Press.
Jackson, Julian (1986) 'Popular tourism and leisure in the vision of the Front Populaire' in M. Alexander and H. Graham, *French and Spanish Popular Fronts*, Cambridge: Cambridge University Press.
—— (1988) *The Popular Front in France: defending democracy 1934–38*, Cambridge: Cambridge University Press.
Jeunesse et ses mouvements : influence sur l'évolution des sociétés aux XIXe et XXe siècles (1992), CNRS.
JECF (1987) *Témoignages pour une histoire de la JECF 1930–1965*, Amis de la JECF, copy in BDIC.
Kergoat, Jacques (1986) *La France du Front Populaire*, La Découverte.
Kriegel, Annie (1991) *Ce que j'ai cru comprendre*, Laffont.
Lagrave, Rose-Marie (1992) 'Une émancipation sous tutelle' in F. Thébaud (ed.) *Histoire de femmes en Occident*, vol. 5, *Le XXe siècle*, Plon.
Le Doeuff, Michelle (1989) *L'Etude et le rouet: des femmes, de la philosophie etc.*, Seuil.
Lelièvre, Françoise and Claude (1991) *Histoire de la scolarisation des filles*, Nathan.
Leriche, Mathilde (1979) *Cinquante ans de littérature de jeunesse: 4 conférences sur la littérature pour enfants en France en 1939*, Magnard Ecole.
Luc, Jean-Noel (1994) 'L'invention du jeune enfant au 19e siècle, de la salle d'asile à la maternelle 1826–87', doctorat 3e cycle, University of Paris-I.
McMillan, James F. (1992) *Twentieth-century France*, London: E. Arnold.
Mayeur, Françoise (1977) *L'Enseignement secondaire des jeunes filles sous la IIIe République*, FNSP.
Mémoire de Paris, La (1993) exhibition catalogue, Mairie de Paris.
Moi, Toril (1994) *Simone de Beauvoir: the making of an intellectual woman*, Oxford: Blackwell.
Nora, Pierre (ed.) (1984–92) *Lieux de mémoire*, 7 vols, Gallimard.
Offen, Karen (1983) 'The second sex and the baccalauréat in republican France 1880–1924', *French Historical Studies* 13, 2: 252–88.
Ory, Pascal (1990) 'La politique culturelle du Front Populaire', doctorat d'état, Paris-X Nanterre.
—— (1994) *La belle illusion, culture et politique sous le signe du Front populaire*, Plon.
Ozouf, Jacques and Ozouf, Mona (1992) *La République des instituteurs*, Gallimard.
Pierrard, Pierre, Launay, Michel and Trempé, Rolande (1984) *La JOC, regards d'historiens*, Editions ouvrières.

Pierre, Michel (1990) 'Illustrés' in O. Barrot and Pascal Ory, *Entre-deux-guerres: la création française 1919–1939*, François Bourin.

Prost, Antoine (1967) *Histoire de l'enseignement en France 1800–1967*, Armand Colin.

—— (1987a) 'Jeunesse et société dans la France de l'entre-deux-guerres', *Vingtième siècle* 13: 35–43.

—— and Vincent, Gérard (1987b) *Histoire de la vie privée*, vol. 5, *De la Première Guerre mondiale à nos jours*, Seuil.

Réau, Elisabeth du (1993) *Edouard Daladier 1884–1970*, Fayard.

Renonciat, Annie (ed.) (1991) *Livre mon ami: lectures enfantines 1914–1954*, exhibition catalogue, Mairie du Ve arrondissement, Paris.

Rousseau, Renée (1983) *Les Femmes rouges: chronique des années Vermeersch*, Albin Michel.

Sartre, Jean-Paul (1964) *Les Mots*, Gallimard.

Sirinelli, Jean-François (1988) *Génération intellectuelle: khagneux et normaliens de l'entre-deux-guerres*, Fayard.

Sullerot, Evelyne (1981) 'La démographie en France' in G. Santoni (ed.) *Culture and Society in France*, Albany: SUNY Press.

Talbott, John E. (1969) *The Politics of Educational Reform in France 1918–1940*, Princeton: Princeton University Press.

Varin, Jacques (1975) *Jeunes comme JC*, Editions sociales.

Zeldin, Theodore (1973 and 1977) *France 1848–1945*, Oxford: Clarendon Press.

AVIATION (CHAPTER 3)

Bart, Guy (1980–1) 'Maryse Bastie', *Revue d'histoire du XIVe arrondissement* 25: 60–4.

Batten, Jean (1979) *Alone in the Sky*, Shrewsbury: Airlife Books.

Beauregard, Marie-Josèphe de (1992) *Femmes de l'air, chroniques d'une conquête*, France-Empire.

Berstein, Serge (1980–2) *Histoire du parti radical*, FNSP, 2 vols.

—— (1992) 'La ligue' in J.-F. Sirinelli (ed.) *Histoire des droites en France*, Gallimard, vol. 2: 61–111.

Boff, Charles (1937) *The Boys' Book of Flying*, London: Routledge.

Chadeau, Emile (1987) *De Blériot à Dassault, l'industrie aéronautique en France, 1900–1930*, Fayard.

—— (1988) 'Schumpeter, l'Etat et les capitalistes: entreprendre dans l'aviation en France (1900–1980)', *Le Mouvement social* no. 145.

Christienne, General Charles (1977a) 'L'armée de l'air française et la crise du 7 mars 1936', Colloque franco-allemand, Comité historique de la Deuxieme Guerre Mondiale, March 1977.

—— (1977b) 'L'aéronautique militaire française entre 1919 et 1939', *Revue historique des armées* 4: 9–40.

—— (1979) 'L'industrie aéronautique française de septembre 1939 à juin 1940' in *Français et britanniques dans la drôle de guerre*, Colloque franco-britannique, CNRS: 389–410.

—— and Lissarague, General P. (1981) *Histoire de l'aviation militaire: l'armée de l'air 1928–1981*, Limoges: Charles-Lavauzelle.

Corn, Joseph C. (1983) *The Winged Gospel: America's Romance with Aviation 1900–1950*, New York: Oxford University Press.

Cot, Pierre (1939) *L'Armée de l'Air 1936–38*, Grasset.

Decure, Danielle (1982) *Vous avez vu le pilote? c'est une femme*, Laffont.

Frank, Robert (1981) 'Intervention étatique et réarmement en France 1935–1939' in *Revue Economique* 31: 743–81.

Fridenson, Patrick (1988) 'Une technologie nouvelle sans vrais capitalistes?', *Le Mouvement social* no. 145.

Grémillon, Jean *et al.* (1981) screenplay of the film 'Le Ciel est à Vous', *Avant-Scène du Cinéma*, no. 276 (15 November 1981).

Heimermann, Benoit and Margaud, Olivier (1994) *L'Aéropostale*, Arthaud.

Kirkland, F. R. (1982) 'The French Officer Corps and the Fall of France 1928–1940', Ph.D. diss., University of Pennsylvania.

Lauwick, Hervé (1958) *Conquérantes du ciel*, Presses de la Cité.

Marck, Bernard (1990) 'Aérodrome du Bourget' in Olivier Barrot and Pascal Ory (eds) *Entre-deux-guerres: la création française 1919–1939*, François Bourin.

Meheust, Claire (1986) 'La merveilleuse femme volante', *Marie-Claire* April 1986.

Ory, Pascal (1990) 'La politique culturelle du Front Populaire', doctorat d'état, Paris X-Nanterre-IEP.

—— (1994) *La belle illusion : culture et politique sous le signe du Front Populaire 1935–1938*, Plon.

Petit, Edmond (1977) *La Vie quotidienne dans l'aviation en France au début du XXe siècle*, Hachette.

—— (1981) *Histoire de l'aviation*, PUF; *Que Sais-Je?*, 3rd edn.

Reynolds, Siân (1989) ' "High Flyers": Women Aviators in Pre-War France' in *History Today* 39, 4: 36–41.

Richard, Marthe (1974) *Mon Destin de femme*, Opera Mundi.

Roberts, Mary Louise (1994) *A Civilization without Sexes: reconstructing gender in postwar France 1917–1927*, Chicago: University of Chicago Press.

Semple, Jeannie (1985) 'Ambiguities in the film Le Ciel est à Vous' in H. R. Kedward and R. Austin (eds) *Vichy France and Resistance: Culture and Ideology*, London: Croom Helm.

Sirinelli, Jean-François (1992) *Histoire des droites en France*, Gallimard, 2 vols.

—— (ed.) (1995) *Dictionnaire historique de la vie politique française au XXe siècle*, PUF.

Vincent, Stéphane (1993) 'L'aviation populaire, de l'éclosion à la disparition', mémoire de maîtrise, University of Paris-I.

Webster, Paul (1993) *Antoine de Saint-Exupéry: the Life and Death of the Little Prince*, London: Macmillan.

Weiss, Louise (1980) *Combats pour les Femmes*, vol. 3 of *Mémoires d'une Européenne*, Albin Michel.

Wohl, Robert (1988) 'Par la voie des airs: l'entrée de l'aviation dans le monde des lettres françaises, 1909–1939', *Le Mouvement social* no. 145.

Young, Robert J. (1974) 'The Strategic Dream: French air doctrine and the inter-war period, 1919–39', *Journal of Contemporary History* 9: 57–76.

—— (1978) *In Command of France: French policy and military planning*, Harvard: Harvard University Press.

Zeldin, Theodore (1977) *France 1848–1945*, vol. 2, Oxford: Clarendon Press.

WORK, UNEMPLOYMENT, STRIKES (CHAPTERS 4 AND 5)

Bachrach, Susan (1987) 'La féminisation des PTT au tournant du siècle', *Le Mouvement social* no. 140: 69–88.

Bard, Christine (1993) 'La non-mixité dans le mouvement syndical chrétien en France de 1900 à 1939' in C. Baudoux and C. Zaidman (eds) *Egalité entre les sexes: mixité et démocratie*, L'Harmattan.

—— (1995) *Les Filles de Marianne: histoire des féminismes 1914–1940*, Fayard.

Becker, J. J. and Berstein, Serge (1990) *Victoire et frustrations 1914–1929*, Seuil.

Beechey, Veronica (1990) 'Rethinking the definition of work: gender and work' in J. Jenson *et al.* (eds) *Feminization of the Labour Force*, Cambridge: Polity.

Bidault (née Borel), Suzanne (1972) *Par une porte entre-baillée: comment les femmes entrent dans la carrière*, Table Ronde.

Birgi, Paulette (1969) 'Femmes salariées, syndicalisme et grèves de mai-juin 1936', Mémoire, ISST, Paris, copy in Centre Malher.

Bonnet, Charles (1939) *Les Droits pratiques des chômeurs, guide pratique du droit ouvrier*, Bureau des études de l'union des syndicats de la région parisienne.

Borne, Dominique and Dubief, Henri (1989) *La Crise des années trente 1929–1938*, Seuil.

Brown, R. 'Work, past, present and future' in K. Thompson (ed.) *Work, Employment and Unemployment*, Milton Keynes: Open University Press.

Cacouault, Marlaine (1987) 'Prof, c'est bien ... pour une femme', *Le Mouvement Social* no. 140: 107–120.

Cavanna, François (1984) *Les Ritals*, Livre de poche edition.

Chenut, Helen Harden (1987) *La Construction sociale des métiers masculins et féminins dans la bonneterie troyenne 1900–1939*, IRESCO/CNRS.

Colin, Madeleine (1975) *Ce n'est pas d'aujourd'hui: femmes, syndicats, luttes de classe*, Editions sociales.

Couteaux, Monique (1975) 'Les femmes et les grèves de 1936, l'exemple des grands magasins', maîtrise, University of Paris-VII.

Daric, Jean (1947) *L'Activité professionnelle des femmes*, Cahier no. 5, INED.

Delphy, Christine (1984) *Close to Home: a materialist analysis of women's oppression*, translated by D. Leonard, London: Hutchinson.

—— (1988), interview in *Le Féminisme et ses enjeux: 27 femmes parlent*, Edilig.

Del Re, Alisa (1994) *Les Femmes et l'Etat Providence: les politiques sociales en France dans les années 30*, L'Harmattan.

Downs, Laura Lee (1993) 'Les marraines élues de la paix sociale, les surintendantes d'usine et la rationalisation du travail en France 1917–1935', *Le Mouvement social* no. 164: 53–76.

Dubesset, Mathilde and Zancarini-Fournier, Michelle (1993) *Parcours de femmes. Réalités et représentations Saint-Etienne 1880–1950*, Lyon: PUL.

Dupâquier, Jacques (ed.) (1988) *Histoire de la population française*, vol. 4, *De 1914 à nos jours*, PUF.

Dupeux, Georges (1976) *French Society 1789–1970*, translated by P. Wait, London: Methuen.

Duval, René (1990) 'Radio Paris' in O. Barrot and P. Ory (eds) *Entre-deux-guerres: la création française 1919–1939*, F. Bourin.

Farge, Arlette and Klapisch-Zuber, Christiane (1984) *Madame ou Mademoiselle? Itinéraires de la solitude féminine 18e–20e siècle*, Montalba.

Fourcaut, Annie (1982) *Femmes à l'usine en France dans l'entre-deux-guerres*, Maspéro.

Frost, Robert (1993) 'Machine liberation: inventing housewives and home appliances in inter-war France', *French Historical Studies* 18, 1: 109–30.

Furlough, Ellen (1993) 'Selling the American way in inter-war France: Prix Unique and the Salons des Arts Ménagers', *Journal of Social History* 26: 491–519.

Germain, Christiane and de Panafieu, Christine (eds) (1982) *La Mémoire des femmes: sept témoignages de femmes nées avec le siècle*, Messinger.

Glover, Judith (1994) 'Concepts of employment and unemployment in labour force data' in Linda Hantrais and M. Th. Letablier (eds) *The Family–Employment Relationship*, European Research Centre, Loughborough University.

Glucksmann, Miriam (1990) *Women Assemble: women workers and the new industries in inter-war Britain*, London: Routledge.

Gordon, Felicia, *The Integral Feminist: Madeleine Pelletier*, Cambridge: Polity.

Guelaud-Léridon, Françoise (1964) *Le Travail des femmes en France*, PUF: Travaux et documents de l'INED no. 42.

Guilbert, Madeleine (1947) 'L'évolution des effectifs du travail féminin en France depuis 1866', *Revue française du travail*: 754–72.

—— (1966) *Les Fonctions des femmes dans l'industrie*, Mouton.

—— and Isambert-Jamati, Viviane (1956) *Travail féminin et travail à domicile*, CNRS.

Guillaume-Grimaud, Geneviève (1986) *Le Cinéma du Front Populaire*, Lherminier.

Hilden, Pátricia (1986) *Working Women and Socialist Politics in France 1880–1914*, Oxford: Clarendon Press.

Jackson, Julian (1985) *The Politics of Depression in France 1932–36*, Cambridge: Cambridge University Press.

—— (1988) *The Popular Front in France: defending democracy 1934–38*, Cambridge: Cambridge University Press.

Jenson, Jane, Hagen, Elisabeth and Reddy, Ceallaigh (eds) (1990) *Feminization of the Labour Force*, Cambridge: Polity.

Kergoat, Jacques (1986) *La France du Front Populaire*, La Découverte.

Lagrave, Rose-Marie (1992) 'Une émancipation sous tutelle' in F. Thébaud (ed.) *Histoire de femmes en Occident*, vol. 5, *Le XXe siècle*, Plon.

Largillière, Arlette (1981) 'Madeleine Pelletier, femme, médecin, féministe' in *Pénélope* no. 5: 'La femme soignante'.

Larkin, Maurice (1995) *Religion, Politics and Preferment in France since 1891*, Cambridge: Cambridge University Press.

Launay, Michel (1981) 'Le syndicalisme chrétien en France, 1885–1940, origines et développement', doctorat d'état, University of Paris-I, Sorbonne.

Lefranc, Georges (1965) *Histoire du Front populaire*, Payot.

Léon Blum, chef de gouvernement 1936–7, actes du colloque (1967).

Letellier, Gabrielle (1934) address to 5th International congress of Soroptimists, Proceedings, Paris, July 1934, 57–61, copy in BMD.

—— with Perret, J. and Zuber, H. (1938) *Enquête sur le chômage*, Sirey, 3 vols.

Lewis, Jane (1984) *Women in England 1870–1950: sexual divisions and social change*, Brighton: Wheatsheaf.

McMillan, James (1981) *Housewife or Harlot: the condition of women in France 1870–1940*, Brighton: Harvester.

Magraw, Roger (1990) 'France' in Stephen Salter and John Stevenson (eds) *The Working Class and Politics in Europe and America*, London: Longman.

—— (1992) *A History of the French Working Class*, Oxford: Blackwell, 2 vols.

Marchand, Olivier and Thélot, Claude (1991) *Deux siècles de travail en France*, INSEE.

Margadant, Jo Burr (1990) *Madame le Professeur: women educators in the Third Republic*, Princeton: Princeton University Press.

Marseille, Jacques (1980) 'Les origines "inopportunes" de la crise de 1929 en France', *Revue économique* 31: 648–84.

Martin, Martine (1987) 'Ménagère une profession? Les dilemmes de l'entre-deux-guerres', *Le Mouvement social* no. 140: 89–106.

Mayeur, Françoise (1977) *L'Enseignement secondaire des jeunes filles sous la IIIe République*, FNSP.

Mémoire de Paris (La) 1919–1938 (1993) exhibition catalogue, Mairie de Paris.

Milza, Pierre (1986) *Les Italiens en France de 1914 à 1940*, Rome: Ecole française de Rome.

Moi, Toril (1994) *Simone de Beauvoir, the making of an intellectual woman*, Oxford: Blackwell.

Montmoullin, M. de and Pastré, P. (1984) *Le Taylorisme*, La Découverte.

Navel, Georges (1945) *Travaux*, Stock, translated by G. Reavey (1947) as *Man at Work*, London: Denis Dobson.

Noiriel, Gérard (1986) *Les Ouvriers dans la société française XIXe–XXe siècle*, Seuil.

—— (1988) *Le Creuset français: histoire de l'immigration XIXe–XXe siècles*, Seuil.

Oakley, Ann (1981) *Subject Women*, London: Fontana.

Omnès, Catherine (1991) 'La politique d'emploi de la Compagnie Française des Téléphones Thomson-Houston, face à la crise des années 1930', *Le Mouvement social* no. 154: 41–61.

Ozouf, Jacques and Ozouf, Mona (1992) *La République des instituteurs*, Gallimard.

Paulin, V. (1938) 'Le travail à domicile en France, ses origines, son évolution, son avenir', *Revue internationale du travail*.

Pember-Reeves, M. S. (1979) *Round About a Pound a Week*, London: Virago.

Pénélope (1981) no. 5, 'La femme soignante'.

Petrément, Simone (1976) *Simone Weil, A Life*, translated by R. Rosenthal, Oxford: Mowbrays.

Pézérat, Pierrette and Poublan, Danielle (1984) 'Femmes sans maris: les employées des postes' in A. Farge *et al.* (eds) *Madame ou Mademoiselle*, Montalba.

Prost, Antoine (1964) *La CGT à l'époque du Front Populaire 1934–39*, Armand Colin.

—— (1967) 'Les grèves de juin 1936, essai d'interprétation' in *Léon Blum chef de gouvernement*, colloque, FNSP.

Rebérioux, Madeleine (1988) 'Les femmes et la révolution industrielle' in *Le Féminisme et ses enjeux*, Edilig.

Reynolds, Siân (1989) 'Women, men and the 1936 strikes in France' in Martin Alexander and Helen Graham (eds) *The French and Spanish Popular Fronts, comparative perspectives*, Cambridge: Cambridge University Press.

—— (1992) 'Camera culture and gender in Paris in the 1930s, stills and movies' in *Nottingham French Studies* 31: 39–51.

—— (1993a) 'Love on the dole, gender and the 1930s depression in France', *Journal of the Institute of Romance Studies* 2: 351–66.

—— (1993b) 'Simone Weil and women workers in the 1930s: *condition ouvrière* and *condition féminine*' in D. Berry and A. Hargreaves (eds) *Women in 20th Century French History and Culture, papers in memory of Andrea Cady*, Loughborough: European Research Centre.

Rhein, Catherine (1977) 'Jeunes femmes au travail dans le Paris de l'entre-deux-guerres', thesis, University of Paris-VII.

Robert, Jean-Louis (1989) 'Ouvriers et mouvement ouvrier parisiens pendant la grande guerre et l'immédiat après-guerre', doctorat d'état, University of Paris-I.

Saint-Martin, Monique de (1990) 'Les "femmes-écrivains" et le champ littéraire', *Actes de recherche en sciences sociales* no. 83: 52–6.

Salais, Robert, Baverez, Nicolas and Reynaud, Benedicte (1986) *L'Invention du chômage*, PUF.

Sauvy, Alfred (ed.) (1984) *Histoire économique de la France entre les deux guerres*, Economica, 3 vols.

Schweitzer, Sylvie (1982) *Des engrenages à la chaîne, les usines Citroën 1915–1935*, Lyon: Presses Universitaires de Lyon.

Scot, J.-P. (1988) 'La crise sociale des années trente en France', *Le Mouvement social* no. 142: 75–101.

Scott, Joan W. (1988) *Gender and the Politics of History*, New York: Columbia University Press.

Smith, Bonnie (1981) *Ladies of the Leisure Class: the bourgeoises of northern France in the nineteenth century*, Princeton: Princeton University Press.

Sohn, Anne-Marie (1992) 'Entre-deux guerres: les rôles féminins en France et en Angleterre' in F. Thébaud (ed.) *Le XXe siècle*, vol. 5 of *Histoire des femmes en Occident*.

Sornaga, Annie (1984) 'Autour des débuts de la dactylographie: les femmes et la machine à écrire', *Pénélope* no. 10: 'Femmes au bureau'.

Sowerwine, Charles and Maignien, Claude (1992) *Madeleine Pelletier, une femme dans l'arène politique*, Editions Ouvrières.

Spring Rice, M. (1981) *Working Class Wives*, London: Virago.

Sullerot, Evelyne (1984) 'Condition de la femme', chap. 6 in A. Sauvy (ed.) *Histoire économique de la France*, vol. III: 418–34.

Thébaud, Françoise (1984) *La Femme au temps de la guerre de quatorze*, Stock.

—— (ed.) (1992) *Le XXe siècle*, vol. 5 of *Histoire des femmes en Occident*.

Thibert, Marguerite (1933) 'Crise économique et travail feminin' in *Revue Internationale du Travail* 27: 465–93 and 647–57.

Thompson, K. (ed.) (1984) *Work, Employment and Unemployment*, Milton Keynes: Open University Press.

Thuillier, Guy (1988) *Les Femmes dans l'administration française depuis 1900*, PUF.

Tilly, Charles (1986) *The Contentious French*, Cambridge: Harvard University Press.

Trouillard-Riolle, Y. (1935) *Les Activitiés féminines en agriculture*, Spes.

Trouvé-Finding, Susan (1987) 'French State Primary Teachers during the First World War and the 1920s', DPhil thesis, University of Sussex.

Weil, Simone (1951) *La Condition ouvrière*, Gallimard, quotations from 'Idées' edn.

—— (1991) *Oeuvres complètes*, Gallimard, vol. 2, *Ecrits historiques et politiques*, edited by G. Leroy and Anne Roche.

Windebank, Jan (1991) *The Informal Economy in France*, Aldershot: Avebury.

Zeldin, Theodore (1973, 1977) *France 1848–1945*, Oxford: Clarendon Press, 2 vols.

Zerner, Sylvie (1985) 'Travail domestique et force de travail: ouvrières et employées entre la Première Guerre mondiale et la grande crise', doctoral thesis, University of Paris-X.

—— (1987) 'De la couture aux presses: l'emploi féminin entre les deux guerres', *Le Mouvement social* no. 140: 9–26.

Zylberberg-Hocquart, Marie-Hélène (1978) *Féminisme et syndicalisme en France*, Anthropos.

—— (1981) *Femmes et féminisme dans le mouvement ouvrier français*, Edns Ouvrières.

SOCIAL INTERVENTION (CHAPTER 6)

Albrecht, Mireille (1986) *La grande figure féminine de la Résistance, Berty,* Laffont.

Bard, Christine (1995) *Les Filles de Marianne: histoire des féminismes 1914–1940,* Fayard.

Blum, Françoise, Chambelland, Colette and Dreyfus, Michel (1984) 'Mouvements de femmes 1919–1940', special number of *Vie sociale* no. 11/12: 507–653.

Boulonnois, Louis (1938) *La Municipalité en service social; l'oeuvre municipale de M. Henri Sellier à Suresnes,* Berger-Lévrault.

Burlen, Katherine (ed.) (1987) *La Banlieue-oasis: Henri Sellier et les cités-jardins 1900–1940,* Presses Universitaires de Vincennes.

Cholvy, Gérard (1991) *La Religion en France de la fin du XVIIIe siècle à nos jours,* Hachette.

Corbin, Alain (1978) *Les Filles de noce, misère sexuelle et prostitution aux XIXe et XX siècles,* Aubier.

Crapuchet, Simone (1987) 'Qui étaient-elles et qui sont-elles? (Les élèves des écoles de service social 1905–1976)', *Vie sociale* no. 8–9: 417–42.

—— (1988) 'Les Français à la Conférence internationale', *Vie sociale* no. 5–6: 183–193.

Del Re, Alisa (1994) *Les Femmes et l'Etat-providence: les politiques sociales en France dans les années trente,* L'Harmattan.

Donzelot, Jacques (1980) *The Policing of Families,* London: Hutchinson.

Downs, Laura Lee (1993) 'Les marraines élues de la paix sociale? Les surintendantes d'usine et la rationalisation du travail en France', *Le Mouvement social* no. 164: 53–76.

Eck, Hélène (1992) 'Les Françaises sous Vichy' in F. Thébaud (ed.) *Histoire des femmes en Occident,* vol. 5, *Le XXe siècle,* Plon.

Fayet-Scribe, Sylvie (1990) *Associations féminines et catholicisme: de la charité à l'action sociale, 19e–20e siècles,* Editions ouvrières.

Fourcaut, Annie (1982) *Femmes à l'usine, ouvrières et surintendantes dans les entreprises françaises de l'entre-deux-guerres,* Maspéro.

—— (ed.) (1992) *Banlieue rouge 1920–1960,* Autrement.

Gourlet, Apolline de (1947) *Cinquante ans de service social,* Eds Sociales françaises.

Gradvohl, Paul (1986) 'Les premières années de l'association des surintendantes (1917–1939)', *Vie sociale* no. 8–9: 377–453.

—— (1987) 'Questions d'approche, de méthode et de sources autour de l'histoire des surintendantes entre les deux guerres', *Vie sociale* no. 8–9: 447–61.

Guerrand, Roger-Henri and Rupp, Marie-Antoinette (1978) *Brève histoire du service social en France 1896–1976,* Privat.

Hazemann, R. H. (1928) *Le Service social municipal et ses relations avec les oeuvres privées,* Eds du Mouvement Sanitaire.

Hurtado, Ysabel de (1966) 'Le service social, tel que je l'ai connu', *Informations sociales* no. 4–5: 9–42.

Knibielher, Yvonne (1980) *Nous les assistantes sociales, naissance d'une profession: trente ans de souvenirs 1930–1960,* Aubier Montaigne.

Lhemanne, J. L. (1977) 'Henri Sellier, la cité-jardin de Suresnes, un exemple du socialisme municipal entre les deux guerres', mémoire de maîtrise, University of Paris-X, Nanterre.

Murard, Lion and Zylberman, Patrick (1987a) 'L'idée de service social dans la pensée hygiéniste (1928–1936)', *Vie sociale* no. 8–9: 463–84.

—— (1987b) 'Robert-Henri Hazemann, urbaniste social', in *URBI* X: LIX–XCI.

Pedersen, Susan (1993) *Family, Dependence and the Origins of the Welfare State, Britain and France 1914–1945,* Cambridge: Cambridge University Press.

Pennetier, Claude and Viet-Depaule, Nathalie (1992) 'Biographies croisées des maires de banlieue' in Annie Fourcaut (ed.) *Banlieue rouge 1920–1960,* Autrement.

'Quelques figures féminines' (1993): 'Aux origines du service social professionnel: quelques figures féminines', *Vie sociale,* special number, no. 3–4.

Rabinow, Paul (1989) *French Modern: norms and forms of the social environment,* Cambridge, Mass: MIT Press.

Reynolds, S. (1994) 'Women and the Popular Front: the case of the three women ministers', *French History,* 8: 196–224.

Rollet, Henri (1948) *Sur le chantier social: l'action sociale des catholiques en France 1870–1940*, Lyon: Eds de la chronique sociale.

Rollet-Echalier, Catherine (1990) *La Politique de la petite enfance sous la Troisième République*, INED.

Reverdy, Ch. J. (n. d. but 1972) *Mme Edmond Gillet et son temps 1884–1965*, n.p., copy in Musée Social.

Sowerwine, Charles (1982) *Sisters or Citizens? Women and socialism in France since 1876*, Cambridge: Cambridge University Press.

Tardieu, Cécile (1984) 'Les fléaux sociaux' in A. Sauvy, *Histoire économique de la France de l'entre-deux-guerres*, Economica, vol. 2.

Verdès-Leroux, Janine (1977) *Le Travail social*, Minuit.

Zeldin, Theodore (1973) *France 1848–1945*, vol. 1, Oxford: Clarendon Press.

POLITICS, PEACE, SUFFRAGISM (CHAPTERS 7, 8 AND 9)

Adler, Laure (1993) *Les Femmes politiques*, Seuil.

Albistur, Maité and Armogathe, Daniel (1977) *Histoire du féminisme français*, Editions des femmes.

Andrieu, Claire (1984) *Le Programme commun de la Résistance: des idées dans la guerre*, Editions de l'Erudit.

Ardagh, John (1982 edn) *France in the 80s*, Harmondsworth: Penguin.

Aubrun, Juliette (1992) 'Cécile Brunschvicg 1877–1946, itinéraire d'une femme politique', unpublished DEA, Histoire, Institut d'Etudes Politiques, Paris.

Auzias, Claire (1993) *Mémoires libertaires, Lyon 1919–1939*, L'Harmattan.

Bard, Christine (1993) 'Les féminismes en France: vers l'intégration des femmes dans la cité', doctoral thesis, University of Paris-VII.

—— (1995) *Les Filles de Marianne: histoire des féminismes 1914–1940*, Fayard.

Basch, Françoise (1994) *Victor Basch: de l'affaire Dreyfus au crime de la Milice*, Plon.

Becker, Jean-Jacques (1988) *Histoire politique de la France depuis 1945*, Armand Colin.

—— and Berstein, S. (1990) *Victoire et frustrations 1914–1929*, Seuil.

Berstein, Serge (1982) *Histoire du parti radical*, FNSP, 2 vols.

—— (1992), 'La IVe République: république nouvelle ou restauration du modèle de la IIIe République?' in S. Berstein and Odile Rudelle (eds) *Le Modèle républicain*, PUF.

—— and Milza, Pierre (1983) *Histoire: Terminale, De 1939 à nos jours*, Hatier.

Bertin, Celia (1993) *Femmes sous l'Occupation*, Stock.

Bloch, Marc (1990 edn) *L'Etrange Défaite*, Gallimard/Folio.

Blum, Françoise, Chambelland, Colette and Dreyfus, Michel (1984) 'Mouvements de femmes 1919–1940', special number of *Vie sociale* no. 11/12.

—— and Horne, Janet (1988) 'Féminisme et Musée Social', special number of *Vie sociale* no. 8–9.

Borne, Dominique and Dubief, Henri (1989) *La Crise des années trente*, Seuil.

Braudel, Fernand and Labrousse, Ernest (eds) (1982) *Histoire économique et sociale de la France*, vol. 4, *1880–1980*, PUF.

Brossat, Alain (1992) *Les Tondues: un carnaval moche*, Manya.

Bruley, Sue (1986) 'Women against war and fascism: communism, feminism and the People's Front' in J. Fyrth (ed.) *Britain, Fascism and the Popular Front*, London: Lawrence and Wishart.

Bussey, Gertrude and Tims, Margaret (1965) *The Women's International League for Peace and Freedom, 1915–1965: a record of fifty years' work*, London: Allen & Unwin.

Caedel, Martin (1980) *Pacifism in Britain 1914–1945*, Oxford: Oxford University Press.

—— (1987) *Thinking about Peace and War, the defining of a faith*, Oxford: Clarendon Press.

Carroll, Beatrice (1987) 'Feminism and pacifism, historical and theoretical connections' in R. Pierson (ed.) *Women and Peace: theoretical, historical and practical perspectives*, New York/London: Croom Helm.

Challener, R. D. (1955) *The French Theory of the Nation in Arms 1866–1939*, New York: Columbia University Press.

Corcos, Fernand (1929) *La Paix? oui si les femmes voulaient*, n.p.

Dab, Sandra (1980) 'La politique du Parti communiste français en direction des femmes entre les deux guerres', mémoire de maîtrise, University of Paris-VII.

Defrasne, J. (1983) *Le Pacifisme*, PUF.

de Gaulle, Charles (1954) *Mémoires de guerre*, Plon, 3 vols.

Diamond, Hanna (1992) 'Women's experience during and after World War Two in the Toulouse area 1939–1948, choices and constraints', unpublished Ph.D. thesis, University of Sussex.

—— (1995) 'Gaining the vote – a liberating experience?', *Modern and Contemporary France*, NS3: 129–40.

Dreyfus, Michel (1982) 'La Ligue internationale des femmes pour la paix et la liberté' in *Cahiers du féminisme* no. 18.

—— (1988) 'Pacifistes socialistes et humanistes des années trente, *Revue d'histoire moderne et contemporaine* 35, 3: 452–69.

—— (1993) 'Des femmes pacifistes durant les années 30' in *Matériaux*: 32–4.

Dubief, H. (1976) *Le Déclin de la Troisième République 1929–1938*, Seuil.

Duchen, Claire (1986) *Feminism in France from May 1968 to Mitterrand*, London: Routledge.

—— (1994) *Women's Rights, Women's Lives in France 1944–1968*, London: Routledge.

Duroselle, J.-B. (1966) *Histoire diplomatique de 1919 à nos jours*, Dalloz.

Du Roy, see Roy, du.

Elshtain, Jean Bethke (1987) *Women and War*, Brighton: Harvester.

Enloe, Cynthia (1989) *Bananas, Beaches and Bases: making feminist sense of international politics*, London: Pandora.

Footitt, Hilary (1995) 'The first women deputies: les 33 glorieuses' in H. R. Kedward and Nancy Wood (eds) *Liberation: Image and Event*, Oxford: Berg.

Frank, Robert (1982) *Le Prix du réarmament français 1935–1939*, Publications de la Sorbonne.

Gaspard, Françoise, Servan-Schreiber, Claude and Le Gall, Anne (1992) *Au pouvoir citoyennes!*, Seuil.

Grant, Rebecca (1989) 'The sources of gender bias in international relations theory' in R. Grant and Kathleen Newland (eds) *Gender and International Relations*, Milton Keynes: Open University Press.

Grenier, Fernand (1977) 'La Résistance et le droit de vote aux femmes' in Union des Femmes Françaises, *Les Femmes dans la Résistance* (conference proceedings), Editions du Rocher.

Guichard, Marie-Thérèse (1991) *Les Egéries de la République*, Payot.

Guidez, Guylaine (1989) *Femmes dans la guerre 1939–1945*, Perrin.

Hause, Steven with Kenney, Anne (1984) *Women's Suffrage and Social Politics in the French Third Republic*, Princeton: Princeton University Press.

Hilden, Patricia (1986) *Working Women and Socialist Politics in France 1880–1914, a regional study*, Oxford: Clarendon Press.

Ingram, Norman (1991) *The Politics of Dissent, Pacifism in France 1919–1935*, Oxford: Clarendon Press.

Jackson, Julian (1988) *The Popular Front in France: defending democracy 1934–38*, Cambridge: Cambridge University Press.

Jenson, Jane (1987) 'The Liberation and new rights for French women' in M. Higonnet *et al.*, *Behind the Lines: gender and the two world wars*, London/New York: Yale University Press.

Jones, Kathleen B. (1990) 'Citizenship in a woman-friendly polity', *Signs* 15, 4: 848–59.

Jouvenel, Bertrand de (1979) *Un Voyageur dans le siècle*, Laffont.

Kergoat, Jacques (1986) *La France du Front populaire*, La Découverte.

Klejman, Laurence and Rochefort, Florence (1989) *L'Egalité en marche: le féminisme sous la Troisième République*, des femmes.

Kraemer-Bach, Marcelle (1988) *La longue route*, Pensée Universelle.

Lacouture, Jean (1977) *Léon Blum*, Seuil.

Landes, Joan B. (1988) *Women and the Public Sphere in the Age of the French Revolution*, Ithaca: Cornell University Press.

Larkin, Maurice (1988) *France since the Popular Front 1936–1986*, Oxford: Clarendon Press.

Liddington, Jill (1985) *The Long Road to Greenham, feminism and antimilitarism in Britain since 1820*, London: Virago.

Louis, Marie-Victoire (1994) 'Le nouveau code pénal français' in *Projets féministes* no. 3: 40–69.

McMillan, James F. (1981) *Housewife or Harlot: the condition of women in France 1870–1940*, Brighton: Harvester.

—— (1988) 'Women, religion and politics, the case of the Ligue Patriotique des Françaises' in *Proceedings of the Annual Meeting of the Western Society for French History* 15: 355–64.

Matériaux (1993): 'S'engager pour la paix dans la France de l'entre-deux-guerres', special issue of *Matériaux pour l'histoire de notre temps* no. 30, Nanterre: BDIC.

Mayeur, Jean-Marie (1984) *La Vie politique sous la Troisième République*, Seuil.

Mazuy, Rachel (1993) 'Le Rassemblement Universel pour la Paix 1935–9: une organisation de masse?' in *Matériaux*: 40–4.

Miller, Carol (1989) 'Women in international relations? The debate in inter-war Britain' in R. Grant and K. Newland (eds) *Gender in International Relations*, Milton Keynes: Open University Press.

—— (1994) ' "Geneva – the Key to Equality": inter-war feminists and the League of Nations', *Women's History Review* 3: 221.

Milza, Pierre (1988) 'Politique intérieure et politique étrangère' in René Rémond (ed.) *Pour une histoire politique*, Seuil.

Moses, Claire Goldberg (1984) *French Feminism in the 19th Century*, New York: SUNY Press.

Offenstadt, Nicolas (1993a) 'Le pacifisme extrême à la conquête des masses: la LICP (1931–1939) et la propagande' in *Matériaux*, q.v.

—— and Olivera, Ph. (1993b) 'Pour une histoire de l'engagement pacifiste en France 1919–1939, sources et bibliographie', *Bulletin de l'Institut d'Histoire du Temps Présent* no. 51.

Oudin, Bernard (1987) *Aristide Briand: la paix une idée neuve en Europe*, Laffont.

Pascal, Jean (1990) *Les premières femmes députés*, chez l'auteur.

Pierson, Ruth R. (ed.) (1987) *Women and Peace: theoretical, historical and practical perspectives*, New York/London: Croom Helm.

Price, Roger (1993) *A Concise History of France*, Cambridge: Cambridge University Press.

Prost, Antoine (1977) *Les anciens combattants*, FNSP, 3 vols.

Réau, Elisabeth du (1993) *Edouard Daladier 1884–1970*, Fayard.

Reynolds, Siân (1986) 'Marianne's citizens? Women, universal suffrage and the republic in France' in S. Reynolds (ed.) *Women, State and Revolution: gender and politics in Europe since 1789*, Brighton: Harvester.

—— (1990) ' "The Sorrow and the Pity" revisited' in *French Cultural Studies* 1, 2: 149–59.

—— (1993) 'Alternative politics: women and public life in France between the wars', *Stirling French Publications* no. 1.

—— (1994) 'Women and the Popular Front: the case of the three women ministers', *French History* 8, 2: 196–224.

Rioux, Jean-Pierre (1980) *La France de la Quatrième République*, vol. 1, Seuil.

Robert, Jean-Louis (1989) 'Ouvriers et mouvement ouvrier parisiens pendant la grande guerre et l'immédiat après-guerre', doctorat d'état, University of Paris-I.

Roberts, Mary Louise (1994) *A Civilization Without Sexes: reconstructing gender in postwar France 1917–1927*, Chicago: Chicago University Press.

Robrieux, Philippe (1975) *Maurice Thorez, vie secrète et vie publique*, Fayard.

Rosanvallon, Pierre (1992) *Le Sacre du citoyen: histoire du suffrage universel en France*, Gallimard.

Rossiter, Margaret (1986) *Women in the Resistance*, New York: Praeger.

Rousseau, Renée (1983) *Les Femmes rouges: chroniques des années Vermeersch*, Albin Michel.

Roy, Albert du and Roy, Nicole du (1994) *Citoyennes! Il y a cinquante ans le vote des femmes*, Flammarion.

Rupp, Leila (1994) 'Constructing internationalism: the case of transnational women's organizations 1888–1945', *American Historical Review* 99, 5: 1,571–1,600.

Rustenholz, Alain and Treiner, Sandrine (1993) *La Saga Servan-Schreiber: une famille dans le siècle*, Seuil.

Sauvy, Alfred (1984) *Histoire économique de la France de l'entre-deux-guerres*, Economica, 3 vols.

Schwarz, Paula (1987) 'Redefining Resistance: women's activism in wartime France' in M. Higonnet *et al.* (eds) *Behind the Lines, gender and two World Wars*, London: Yale University Press.

Scott, Joan W. (1987) 'Rethinking history' in M. Higonnet *et al.* (eds) *Behind the Lines: gender and two World Wars*, London: Yale University Press.

—— (1988) *Gender and the Politics of History*, New York: Columbia University Press.

Shennan, Andrew (1989) *Rethinking France: Plans for Renewal 1940–46*, Oxford: Oxford University Press.

Sirinelli, Jean-François (1992) *Histoire des droites en France*, Gallimard, 2 vols.

—— (ed.) (1995) *Dictionnaire historique de la vie politique française au XXe siècle*, PUF.

—— *et al.* (1993) *La France de 1914 à nos jours*, PUF.

Smith, Paul (1991) 'Women's political and civil rights in the French Third Republic', unpublished DPhil thesis, Oxford University.

Sohn, Anne-Marie (1975) 'Féminisme et syndicalisme: les institutrices de la Fédération unitaire de l'enseignement de 1918 à 1935', doctorat 3e cycle, University of Paris-X.

—— (1984) 'Les femmes catholiques et la vie publique: l'exemple de la Ligue Patriotique des Françaises' in *Stratégies de femmes*, Tierce.

Soucy, Robert (1986) *French Fascism: the first wave*, New Haven: Yale University Press.

Sowerwine, Charles (1983) *Sisters or Citizens? Women and Socialism in France since 1876*, Cambridge: Cambridge University Press.

Spears, Edward (1954) *Assignment to Catastrophe*, vol. I, *Prelude to Dunkirk*, London: Heinemann.

Spencer, Samia (1984) 'Women cabinet ministers: ornament of government?', *Proceedings of the Annual Meeting of the Western Society for French History* 12: 243–56.

Steel, James (1993) 'Une certaine image de la France (1940–44)' in William Craw (ed.) *France Free and Unfree*, Glasgow: University of Glasgow Press.

Tabouis, Geneviève (1938) *Le Chantage ou la guerre*, translated as *Blackmail or War?*, London: Penguin Special.

—— (1942) *They Called Me Cassandra*, New York: Scribners.

—— (1953) *Vingt ans de suspense diplomatique*, Albin Michel.

Thébaud, Françoise (1984) *La Femme au temps de la guerre de '14*, Stock.

Touchard, Jean (1977) *La gauche en France depuis 1900*, Seuil.

Vaisse, Maurice (1995) 'Pacifisme' in J.-F. Sirinelli (ed.) *Dictionnaire historique de la vie politique française au XXe siècle*, PUF.

Vellacott, Jo (1993) 'A place for pacifism and transnationalism in feminist theory: the early work of the Women's International League for Peace and Freedom' in *Women's History Review* 2, 1: 23–56.

Wall, Irwin (1991) *The United States and the Making of Post-war France 1945–54*, Cambridge: Cambridge University Press.

Walters, F. P. (1965 edn) *A History of the League of Nations*, Oxford: Oxford University Press.

Warner, Marina (1985) *Monuments and Maidens: the allegory of the female form*, London: Picador.

Watson, David R. (1984) 'France between Germany and Great Britain 1870–1945, a survey of the historiography of the immediate post-war years' in M. Kohler (ed.) *Deutschland und der Westen, Colloquium in honour of Gordon Craig*, Berlin: Colloquium Verlag.

Watt, Donald Cameron (1992) 'La storia internazionale al femminile' (in English and Italian) in *Passepartout* December 1992.

Weiss, Louise (1980) *Mémoires d'une Européenne*, vol. 2, *Combats pour l'Europe*; vol. 3, *Combats pour les femmes*, Albin Michel.

Williams, Philip (1972 edn) *Crisis and Compromise: Politics in the Fourth Republic*, London: Longman.

Wiltsher, Anne (1985) *Most Dangerous Women: feminist peace campaigners of the Great War*, London: Pandora.

Woolf, Virginia (1938) *Three Guineas*, London: Hogarth (quoted from Penguin edition, 1982).

Zay, Jean (1987) *Souvenirs et solitude*, Le Roeulx: Ed. Talus de l'Approche.

Zeldin, Theodore (1973, 1977) *France 1848–1945*, Oxford: Clarendon Press.

CHRONOLOGY

1919

18 January	Opening of Paris Peace conference
10 February	Opening of inter-allied women's suffrage conference, Paris
12–20 May	WILPF conference, Zurich
20 May	Chamber of Deputies votes to enfranchise women (c344–c97)
28 June	Treaty of Versailles signed
7 July	French electoral law modified after long debate (system, not electorate)
14 July	Victory parade
15 July	Pope Benedict XV approves women's suffrage
16 November	Elections to Assembly: bloc national wins: 'Chambre bleu horizon'
During year	Adrienne Bolland flies Andes
	Henri Sellier becomes mayor of Suresnes

1920

During year	Founding of UNVF, and Union des Femmes pour la SDN
10 January	League of Nations created
16 January	Clemenceau defeated for presidency
20 January	Millerand Prime Minister
March–May	Strike wave in railways, mines, etc.
31 July	Law on abortion and contraception: propaganda made illegal
end December	Congress of Tours, SFIO splits, foundation of Communist party
	CGT also splits, formation of CGTU
	Astier law on apprenticeship

1921

16 January	Briand Prime Minister
10 May	M. Vernet founds Ligue des Femmes contre la guerre
April–May	Reparations: amounts decided
	Eugene and Jeanne Humbert sentenced for birth control propaganda
	Mme de Witt-Schlumberger appointed to League of Nations commission

1922

12 January	Poincaré Prime Minister
10 April	Genoa conference
12 July	Publication of *La Garçonne* by V. Margueritte
12 December	Senate rejects votes for women 156–134

1923

11 January	French occupation of Ruhr
27 March	Law referring abortion to magistrates court (second 'loi scélérate')
	First Salon des arts ménagers
May	First Bérard decree on reform of secondary education (through to 1924)
6 December	Chamber discusses Roulleau-Degage bill on family vote

1924

January–April	Dawes Plan talks
4–11 May	Elections to Assembly: victory of Cartel des gauches
14 June	Herriot Prime Minister
	Run on franc
	Radical party admits women members
26 June	Cachin proposes voting rights for women
	Bérard decree on syllabus for girls' lycées
1 September	France agrees to evacuate Ruhr
1 October	Geneva Protocol on collective security signed (eventually unsuccessful)
16 December	Louis Marin proposes municipal vote for women and sets up Senate group for women's rights
	L'Heure Joyeuse library opens

1925

25 January	Proposal for municipal women's vote, backed by SFIO
7 April	Chamber adopts local vote 390–183
10 April	Painlevé Prime Minister, Briand at Foreign Office (until 1931)
5–16 October	Locarno conference
19 October–	
21 July 1926	Series of short-lived ministries
6 December	Marthe Bray creates Ligue d'action féminine
During year	Andrée Butillard founds Union féminine civique et sociale UFCS
	First JOC branch founded in Clichy

1926

23 July	Poincaré heads Union national government; stabilization of franc begins
	Marcelle Legrand-Falco founds Union temporaire contre la prostitution réglementée

	Women allowed by law to have different nationality from husband
	Germany enters League of Nations
17 September	Briand–Stresemann meeting at Thoiry
During year	Renoult commission set up to discuss *Civil Code* provisions for married women
	Rockefeller mission leaves France

1927

March	French evacuate Saar
	Paul-Boncour bill in Assembly
May	Mobilization of feminists against bill
17 May	Creation of Union fraternelle des femmes contre la guerre
June	Electoral law changes back to scrutin d'arrondissement
7 July	Chamber asks Senate to move to debate on women's vote
	Lindbergh solo flight of Atlantic
10 December	Trial and acquittal of Henriette Alquier and Marie Guillot

1928

16 March	Compulsory social insurance for wage-earners in industry and commerce
	Feminist demonstration in Senate
22–9 April	Elections to Assembly. Centre and right win; Poincaré stays
May	Odette Laguerre founds Ligue Internationale des Mères et Educatrices pour la Paix LIMEP
	First International Conference of the Comité Français de Service Social
27 August	Briand–Kellogg Pact 'outlaws war'
	First branch of JOCF in France

1929

14 February	Estates-general of Feminism meets in Paris
31 May	Young Plan
June	Founding congress of Open Door International (against discriminatory rules on women's labour)
July	Briand Prime Minister
October	Wall Street crash
November	Tardieu Prime Minister

1930

All year	Ministerial instability, financial crisis
	Marc Sangnier introduces youth hostels movement to France
	Secondary school fees end

1931

January	Laval Prime Minister
7 May	Jeanne Melin founds Cercle Pax-Orient-Occident
13 May	Briand defeated for presidency
13 July	Germany suspends international payments
	Jane Addams, president of WILPF, receives Nobel peace prize
Summer	Colonial Exhibition in Paris
5 November	Charles Richet article in *Le Matin* against women's employment during crisis
During year	Andrée Butillard founds Ligue de la Mère au foyer
	Marguerite Durand gifts her library to the Ville de Paris (BMD)
	V. Meric founds Ligue Internationale des Combattants de la Paix, with M. Capy and others
	Suzanne Borel admitted to Foreign Office
	OPMI/OPMES set up in Seine dept

1932

20 February	Tardieu Prime Minister
11 March	Law on family allowances for wage-earners
2 February	Disarmament conference
	Chamber again votes for full voting rights for women
6 February	International feminist organizations take disarmament petition to League of Nations (8 million signatures)
May	Elections to Assembly: left-wing gains; some feminist candidates stand
10 May	Lebrun President (until 1940)
June	Lausanne conference: reparations abandoned
	Ministerial instability: Herriot Prime Minister June–December
July	Senate postpones discussion of women's vote

1933

	Ministerial instability continues
	Air-France created
30 January	Hitler becomes Chancellor of Germany
	Extreme right-wing leagues demonstrate in France
	Amsterdam–Pleyel committee against war and fascism set up, linked to Communist party

1934

January	Stavisky affair breaks; Daladier becomes Prime Minister
6 February	Violent demonstration outside Assembly by (mostly) right-wing leagues
	Daladier resigns, Doumergue Prime Minister
12 February	General strike against fascism; beginning of Popular Front
August	Rassemblement mondial des femmes contre la guerre et le fascisme holds meeting in France

271

	Hélène Boucher killed on test flight
September	USSR enters League of Nations
8 November	Flandin Prime Minister
During year	Trial of Violette Nozière
	Louise Weiss sets up Femme Nouvelle suffragist group

1935

13 January	Saar plebiscite
14 April	Stresa three-way talks confirm Locarno
1 March	Chamber adopts proposal for women's vote
	Feminist campaign unseats fierce misogynist senator Duplantier at election
2 May	Franco–Soviet mutual assistance agreement
12 May	Spectacular feminist demonstrations by Femme nouvelle (Louise Weiss)
	Women municipal councillors appointed in some cities after local elections
7 June	Laval Prime Minister: decree-laws start
14 July	First big Popular Front procession
July	Discriminatory decrees against women civil servants
	Irène and Frédéric Joliot-Curie receive Nobel prize for chemistry
October	First users' club of Centre Laïque des Auberges de Jeunesse
27 December	First congress of French section of Comité Mondial de Femmes contre la Guerre et le Fascisme, presided over by G. Duchêne

1936

January	Sarraut Prime Minister
7 March	Hitler enters Rhineland
	CGT–CGTU reunite
26 April–	
3 May	Elections to Assembly: Popular Front victory
May–June	Strike wave
4 June	Blum Prime Minister: three women junior ministers, Lacore, Brunschvicg, Joliot-Curie; Sellier at Health Ministry, Zay at Education, Léo Lagrange at Sport and Leisure, Cot at Air
7 June	Matignon agreements: wage rises, union recognition, followed by forty-hour week, two weeks' paid holiday
18 June	Leagues banned
	More spectacular demonstrations by Femme Nouvelle over summer
30 July	Chamber votes full political rights for women nem.con
1 August	Blum proposes non-intervention in Spain
	School-leaving age raised to fourteen
	Aviation populaire introduced
September	Irène Joliot-Curie leaves government
30 December	Maryse Bastié beats solo record for crossing South Atlantic
	Rassemblement Universel pour la Paix created
During year	Duvivier's film *La Belle Equipe*
	Split in LIFPL

1937

13 February	Blum announces 'pause' in reforms
May	International Paris Exhibition
21 June	Blum resigns, Chautemps Prime Minister. Neither women ministers nor Sellier reappointed

1938

10 April	Daladier Prime Minister (until March 1940): decree-laws
15 February	Law ending civil incapacity of married women
May	International women's peace conference at Marseille, organized by G. Malaterre-Sellier
August 29–30	Reservists recalled
September	Munich agreement
11 November	Lebrun inaugurates monument to 'sublime mothers' in Paris: feminist demonstration
12 November	Allowance introduced for 'mère au foyer' Andrée Dupeyron record for 'longest solo flight in straight line by woman' causes criticism over danger Geneviève Tabouis: *Le Chantage à la guerre*

1939

15 March	German army enters Prague
29 July	Code de la Famille for implementation 1 January 1940
23 August	Molotov–Ribbentrop pact
3 September	War declared Saint-Exupéry: *La Terre des Hommes* Jean Renoir: *La Règle du Jeu*

All chronologies are selective, incongruous and, I suppose, ideological, since they are confined to 'events'. This has been compiled from dates suggested in the *Nouvelle Histoire de la France Contemporaine*, from *Les grandes dates de l'histoire de France* (Paris: Larousse, 1986), and from Christine Bard, *Les Filles de Marianne* (Paris: Fayard, 1995), and has included some dates referred to in the text.

INDEX

Index references to other historians have been kept to a minimum and mostly concern debates: see Notes and Bibliography

Verne, Jules 41–3, 45, 61
Vernet, Madeleine 192, 198, 248n, 268
Vérone, Maria 126, 187, 188, 216, 240n
Versailles, Treaty of 3, 15, 18, 184–6, 193–4, 225, 268
Vichy, government during World War II 7, 15, 22, 79, 134, 182–3, 212, 214–15, 224, 227n
Viollis, Andrée 165, 244n
Viviani, René 210

Weil, Simone 103, 110, 114, 129–31, 238n, 240n
Weiss, Louise 80, 165–6, 178, 187, 189, 244n, 249n, 272
white-collar employment 92–4
Wilson, Woodrow 185

Winckler, Paul 44
Windebank, Jan 84–6, 88, 237n
Witt-Schlumberger, Marguerite de 157, 187, 193, 242n
Women's International League for Peace and Freedom (WILPF) 184, 188, 192–4, 196, 200, 202
World War I 8, 21, 25, 39, 43, 49, 66, 75, 83, 99–101, 137, 190–1, 210
World War II 21, 90, 213–17

youth movements 50–61

Zay, Jean 160, 243n, 244n, 272
Zeldin, Theodore 6–7, 227n, 232n
Zerner, Sylvie 102–4
Zurich peace conference 193–4, 268